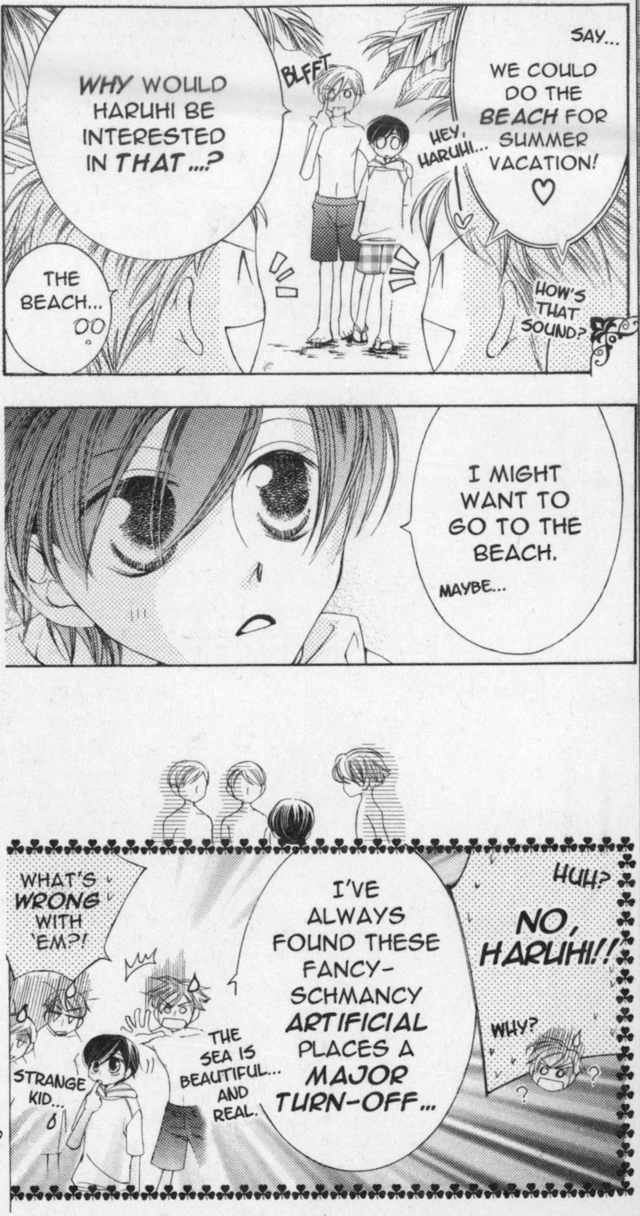
SAY...
WE COULD DO THE BEACH FOR SUMMER VACATION! ♡
HOW'S THAT SOUND?
HEY, HARUHI...
BLFFT
WHY WOULD HARUHI BE INTERESTED IN THAT...?
THE BEACH...
I MIGHT WANT TO GO TO THE BEACH.
MAYBE...
HUH?
NO, HARUHI!!
WHY?
I'VE ALWAYS FOUND THESE FANCY-SCHMANCY ARTIFICIAL PLACES A MAJOR TURN-OFF...
THE SEA IS BEAUTIFUL... AND REAL.
WHAT'S WRONG WITH 'EM?!
STRANGE KID...

FROM VOL. TWO:

WITH SUMMER VACATION COMING UP, THE MEMBERS OF THE HOST CLUB ARE VISITING "OHTORI AQUA GARDEN," A POOLSIDE RESORT MANAGED BY THE OHTORI FAMILY. BEING THE UNPLAYFUL TYPE SHE IS, OUR HARUHI HAS SHOWN ZERO INTEREST. THE TWINS JOKE ABOUT HARUHI'S PREDICTABLE ATTITUDE, BUT SHE SHOCKS EVERYONE BY ADMITTING THAT SHE'D LIKE TO VISIT THE BEACH. ONCE THE GUYS GET OVER THEIR SURPRISE, WILL HARUHI ACTUALLY GET TO ENJOY SAND AND SURF? WILL SHE WEAR A BATHING SUIT? READ ON AND FIND OUT!

Ouran High School

Host Club

Vol.3

CONTENTS

OURAN HIGH SCHOOL HOST CLUB
EPISODE 8

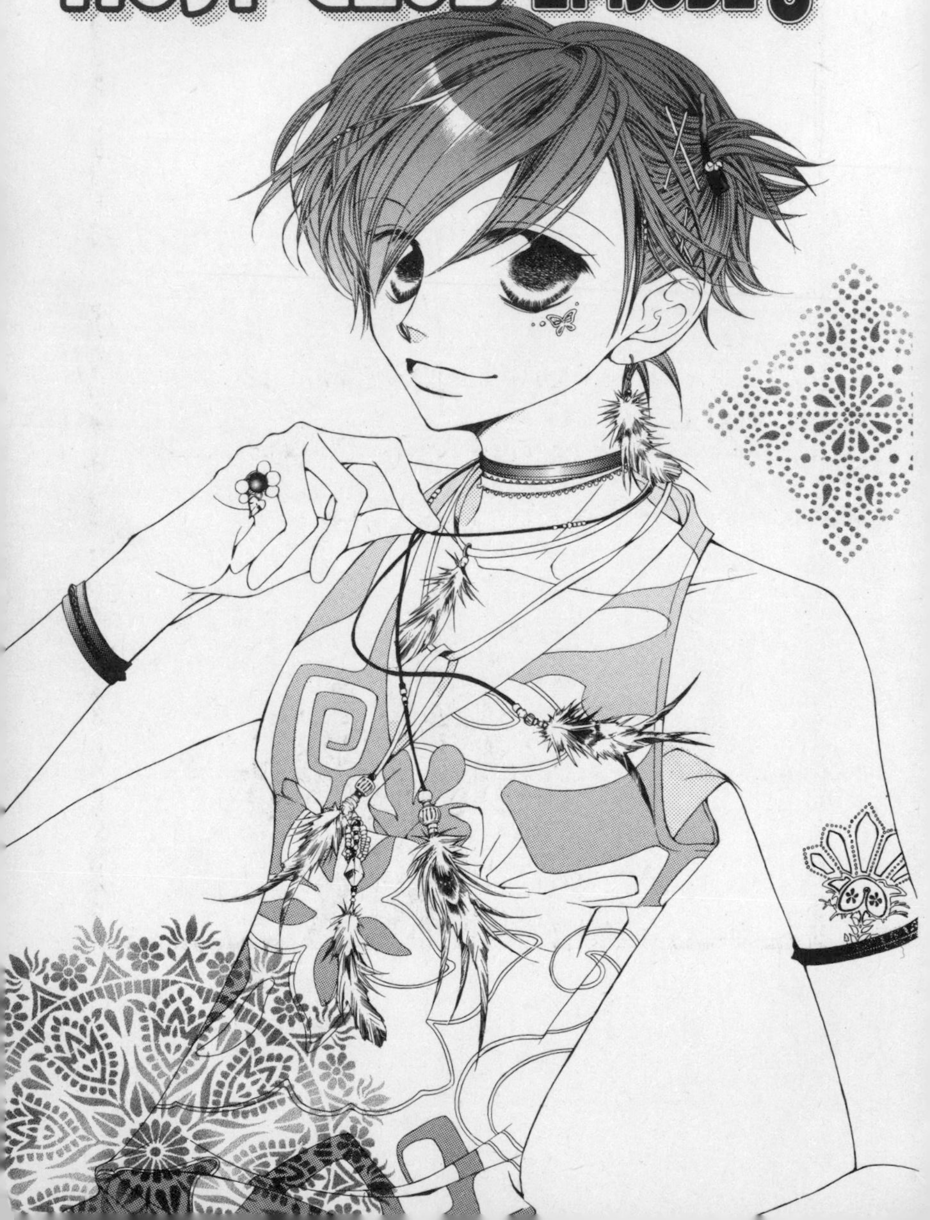

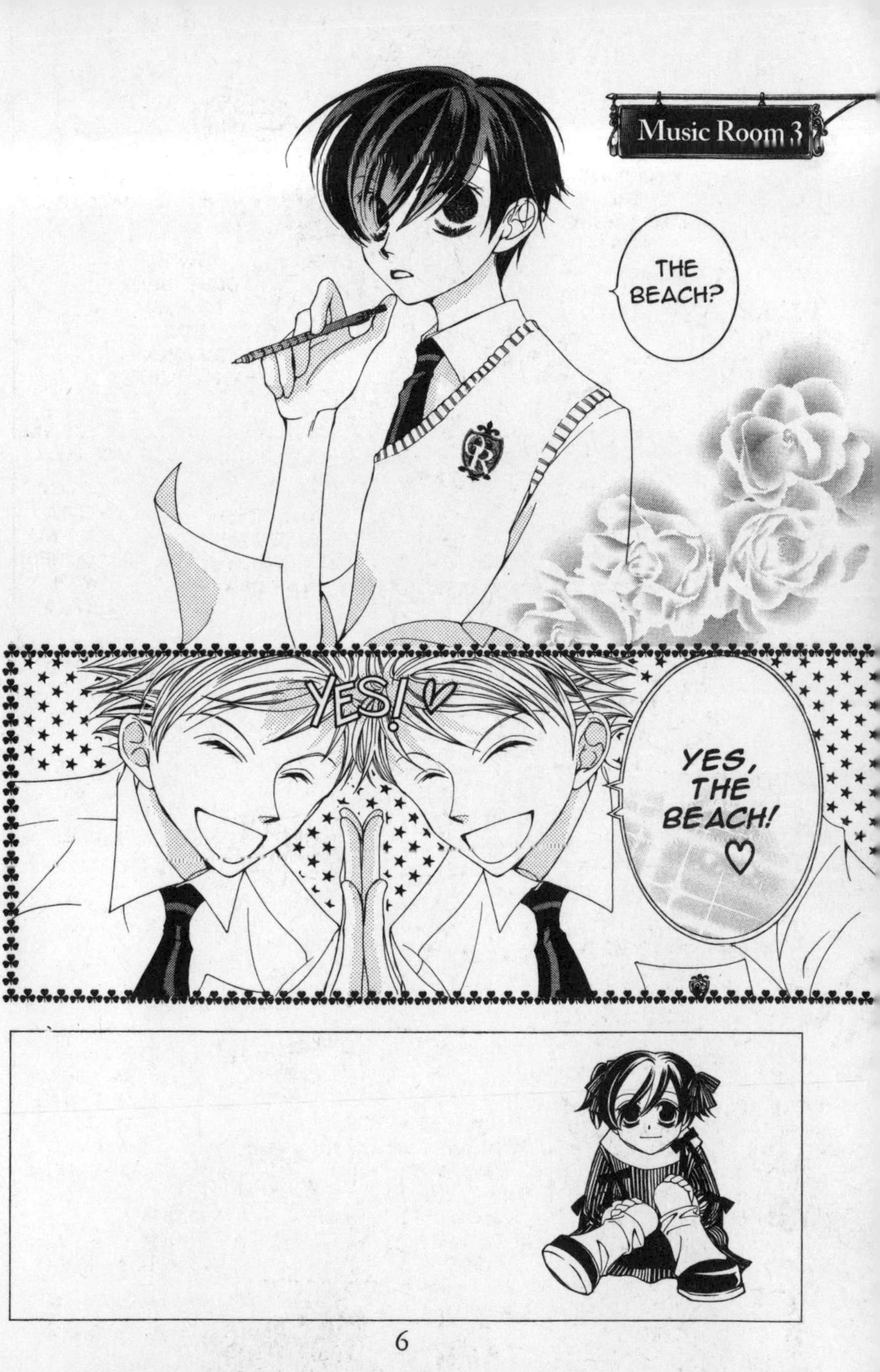
Music Room 3
THE BEACH?
YES, THE BEACH! ♡
YES! ♡

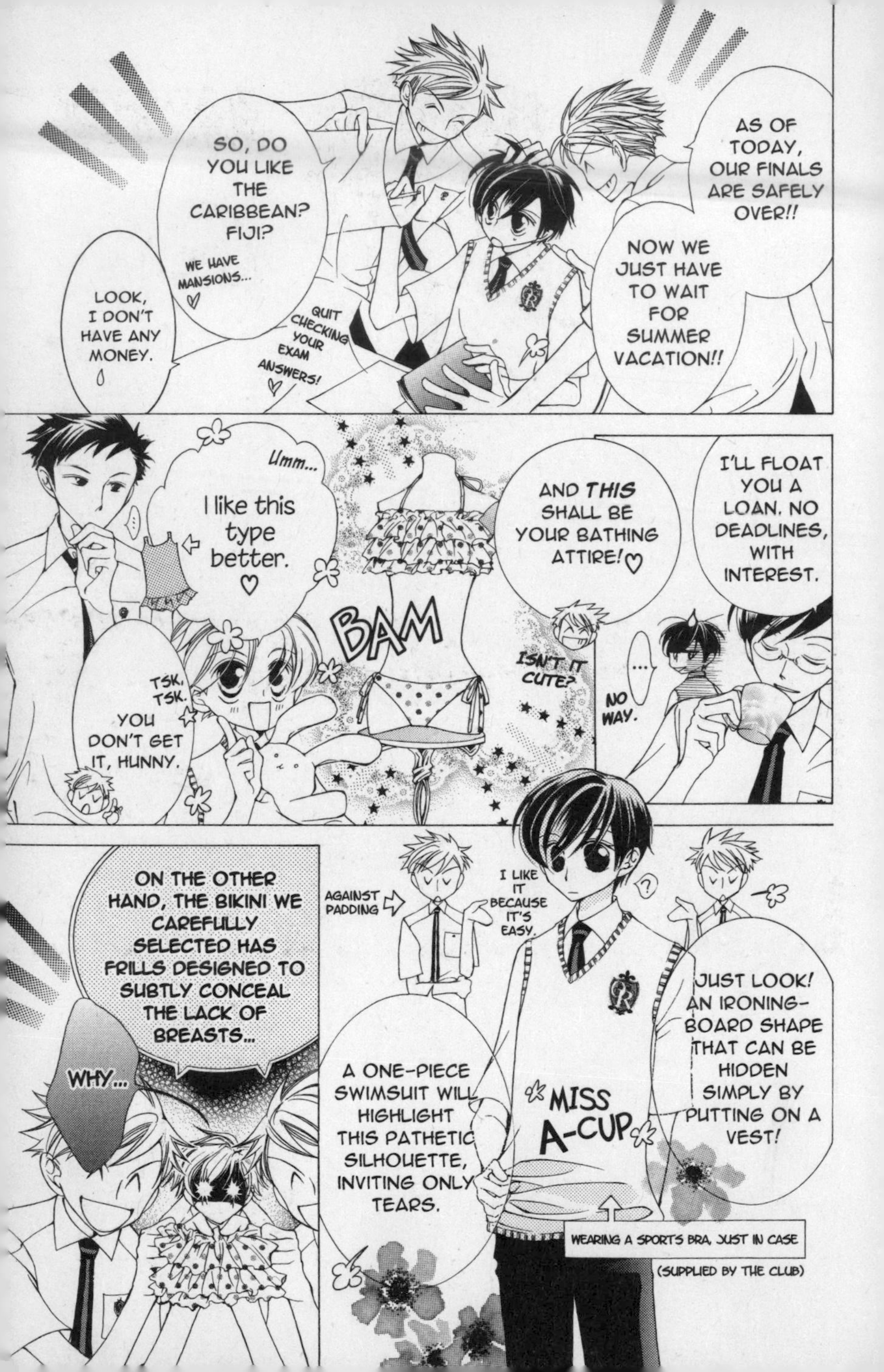
AS OF TODAY, OUR FINALS ARE SAFELY OVER!!
NOW WE JUST HAVE TO WAIT FOR SUMMER VACATION!!
SO, DO YOU LIKE THE CARIBBEAN? FIJI?
WE HAVE MANSIONS...
QUIT CHECKING YOUR EXAM ANSWERS!
LOOK, I DON'T HAVE ANY MONEY.
I'LL FLOAT YOU A LOAN. NO DEADLINES, WITH INTEREST.
...
NO WAY.
AND THIS SHALL BE YOUR BATHING ATTIRE!
ISN'T IT CUTE?
BAM
Umm...
I like this type better.
TSK, TSK.
YOU DON'T GET IT, HUNNY.
JUST LOOK! AN IRONING-BOARD SHAPE THAT CAN BE HIDDEN SIMPLY BY PUTTING ON A VEST!
MISS A-CUP
WEARING A SPORTS BRA, JUST IN CASE
(SUPPLIED BY THE CLUB)
I LIKE IT BECAUSE IT'S EASY.
AGAINST PADDING
A ONE-PIECE SWIMSUIT WILL HIGHLIGHT THIS PATHETIC SILHOUETTE, INVITING ONLY TEARS.
ON THE OTHER HAND, THE BIKINI WE CAREFULLY SELECTED HAS FRILLS DESIGNED TO SUBTLY CONCEAL THE LACK OF BREASTS...
WHY...

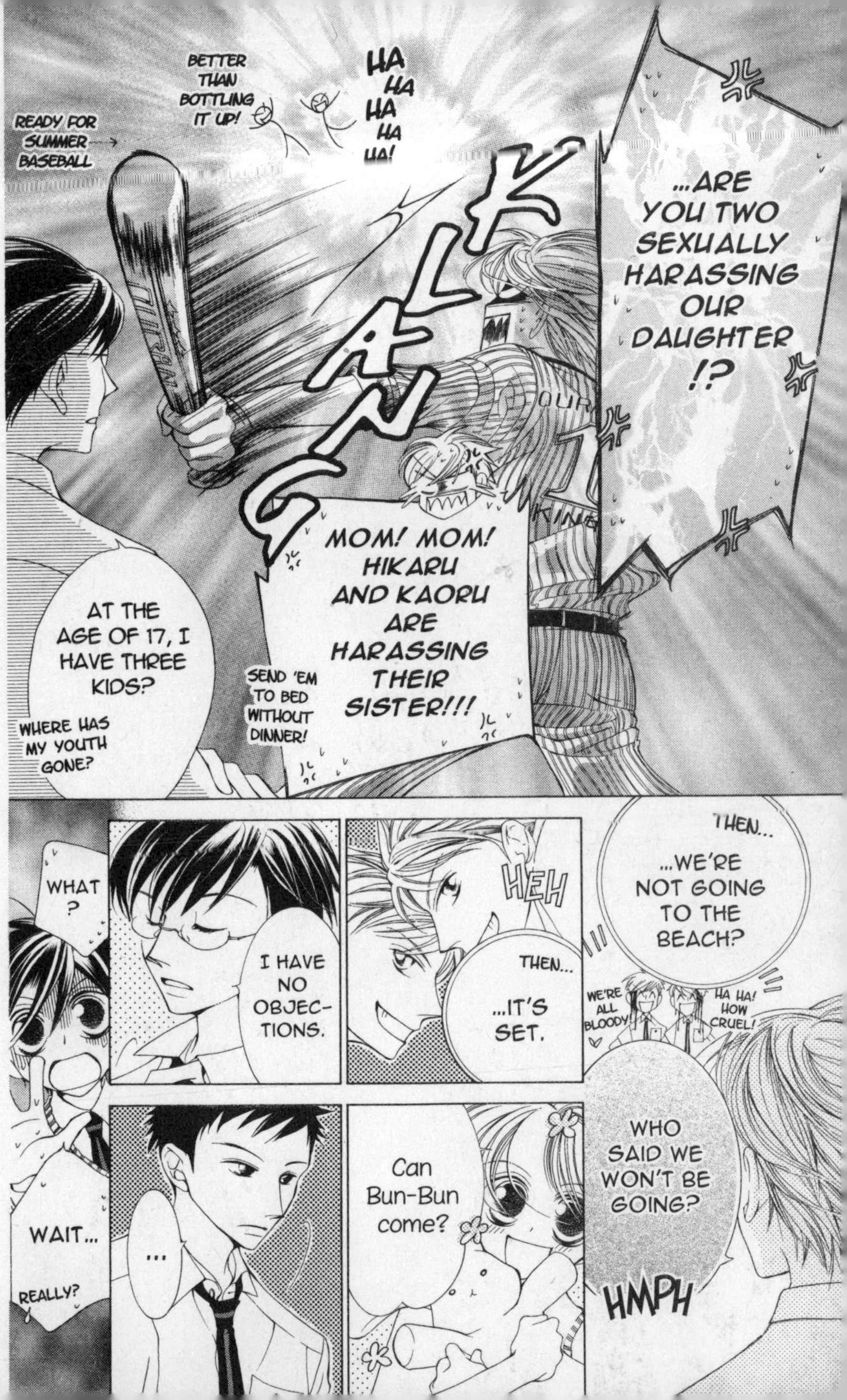
...ARE YOU TWO SEXUALLY HARASSING OUR DAUGHTER !?
KLANG
HA HA HA HA HA!
BETTER THAN BOTTLING IT UP!
READY FOR SUMMER BASEBALL
MOM! MOM! HIKARU AND KAORU ARE HARASSING THEIR SISTER!!!
SEND 'EM TO BED WITHOUT DINNER!
AT THE AGE OF 17, I HAVE THREE KIDS?
WHERE HAS MY YOUTH GONE?
THEN... ...WE'RE NOT GOING TO THE BEACH?
WE'RE ALL BLOODY
HA HA! HOW CRUEL!
WHO SAID WE WON'T BE GOING?
HMPH
HEH
THEN... ...IT'S SET.
I HAVE NO OBJEC-TIONS.
Can Bun-Bun come?
...
WHAT?
WAIT...
REALLY?

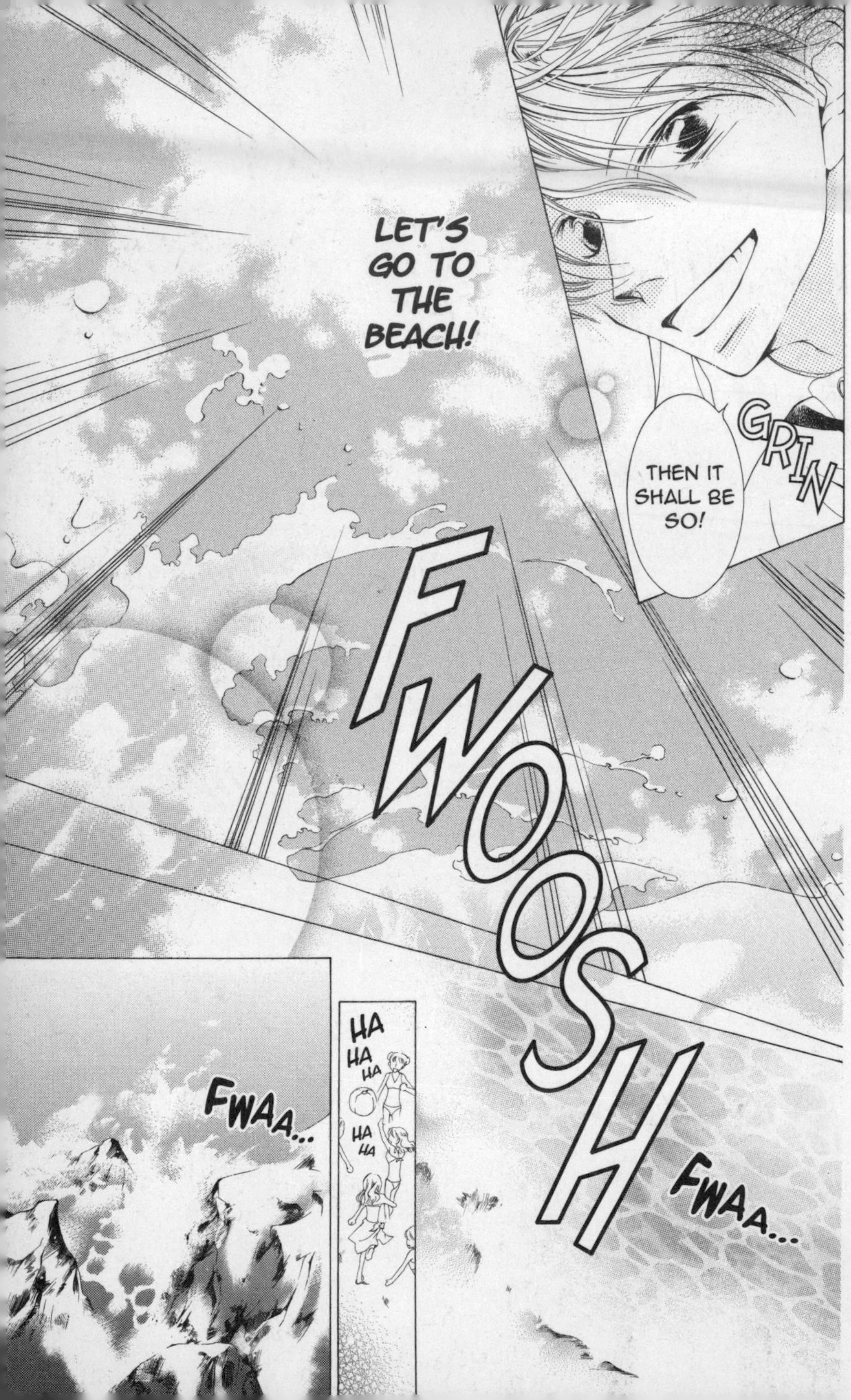
THEN IT SHALL BE SO!
GRIN
LET'S GO TO THE BEACH!
FWOOSH
FWAA...
HA HA HA
HA HA
FWAA...

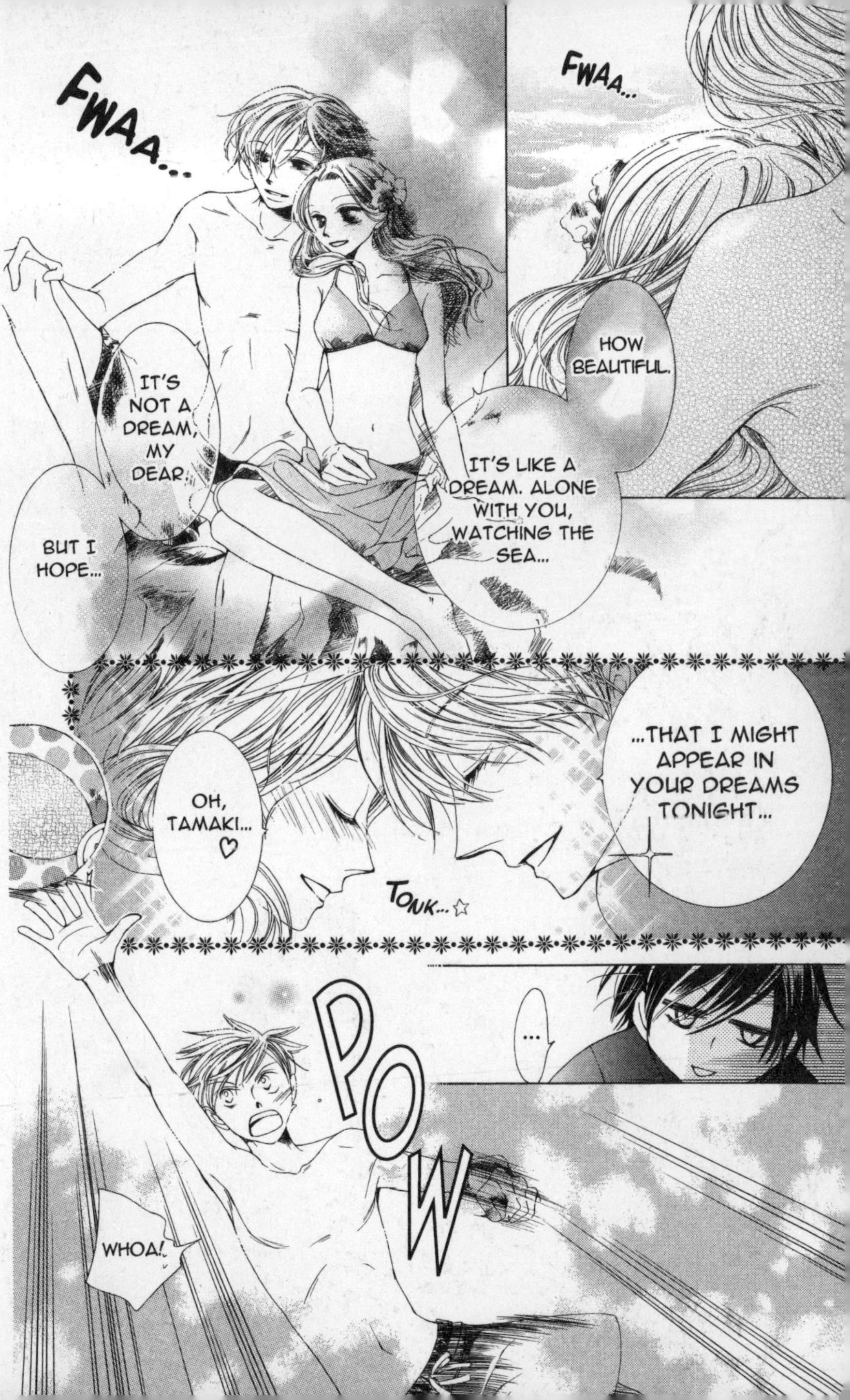
FWAA...
HOW BEAUTIFUL.
FWAA...
IT'S LIKE A DREAM. ALONE WITH YOU, WATCHING THE SEA...
IT'S NOT A DREAM, MY DEAR.
BUT I HOPE...
...THAT I MIGHT APPEAR IN YOUR DREAMS TONIGHT...
TONK...☆
OH, TAMAKI...♡
...
POW
WHOA!

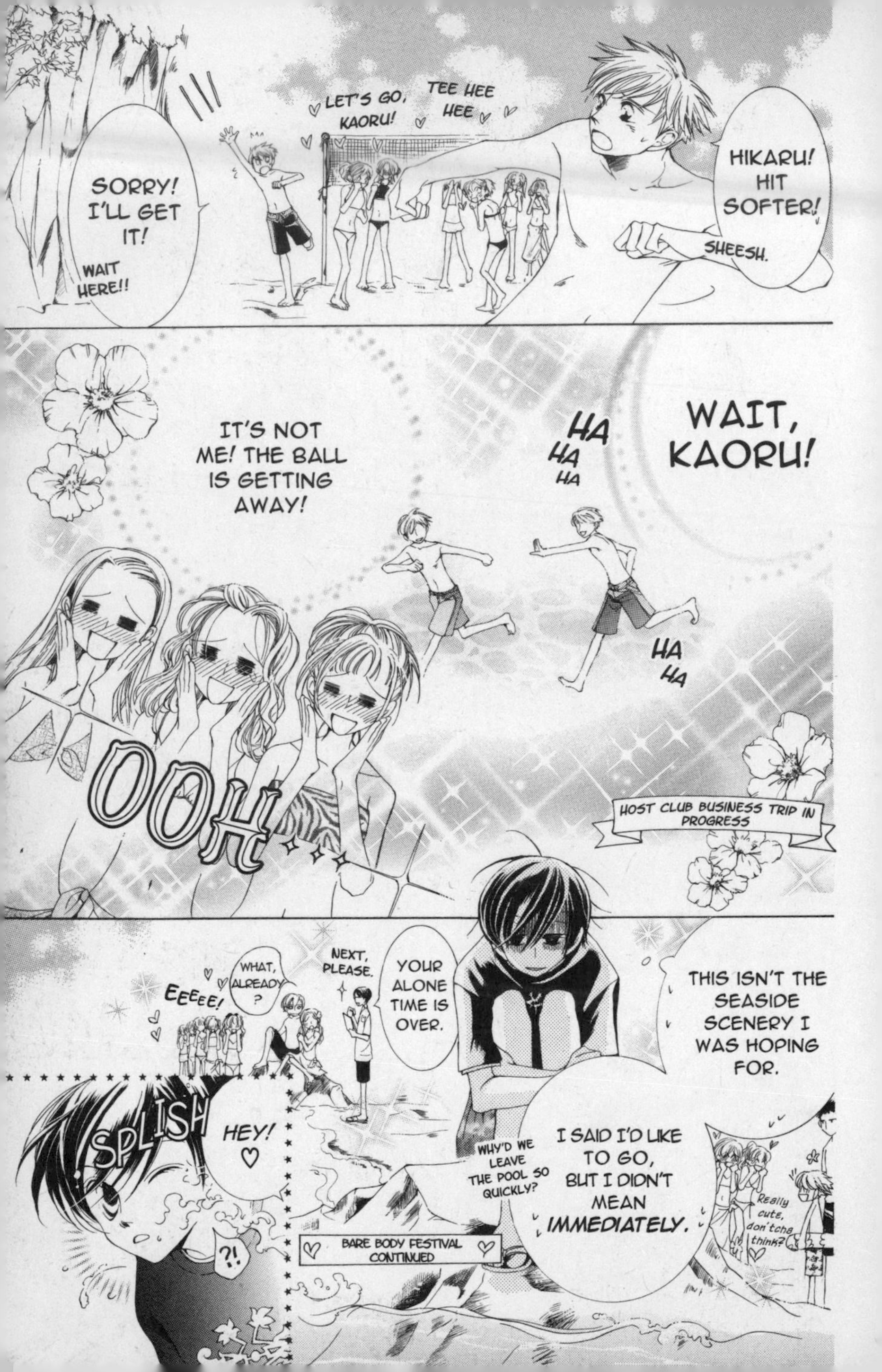
HIKARU! HIT SOFTER!
SHEESH.
TEE HEE HEE
LET'S GO, KAORU!
SORRY! I'LL GET IT!
WAIT HERE!!
WAIT, KAORU!
HA HA HA
IT'S NOT ME! THE BALL IS GETTING AWAY!
HA HA
OOH
HOST CLUB BUSINESS TRIP IN PROGRESS
THIS ISN'T THE SEASIDE SCENERY I WAS HOPING FOR.
I SAID I'D LIKE TO GO, BUT I DIDN'T MEAN IMMEDIATELY.
Really cute, don'tcha think?
WHY'D WE LEAVE THE POOL SO QUICKLY?
BARE BODY FESTIVAL CONTINUED
YOUR ALONE TIME IS OVER.
NEXT, PLEASE.
WHAT, ALREADY?
EEEEE!
HEY! ♡
SPLISH
?!

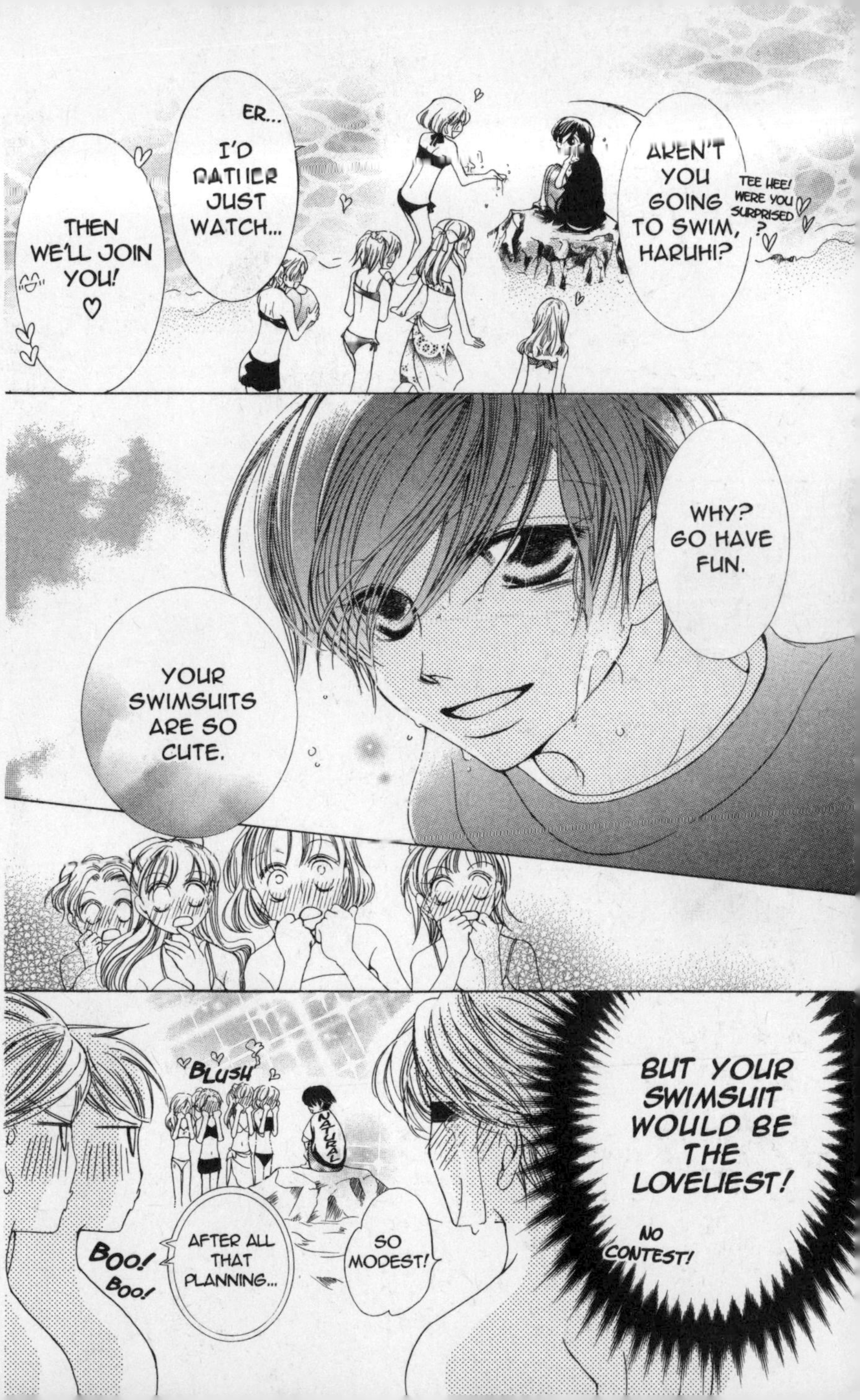
AREN'T YOU GOING TO SWIM, HARUHI?
TEE HEE! WERE YOU SURPRISED?
ER...
I'D RATHER JUST WATCH...
THEN WE'LL JOIN YOU! ♡
WHY? GO HAVE FUN.
YOUR SWIMSUITS ARE SO CUTE.
BUT YOUR SWIMSUIT WOULD BE THE LOVELIEST!
NO CONTEST!
NATURAL
BLUSH
SO MODEST!
AFTER ALL THAT PLANNING...
BOO!
BOO!

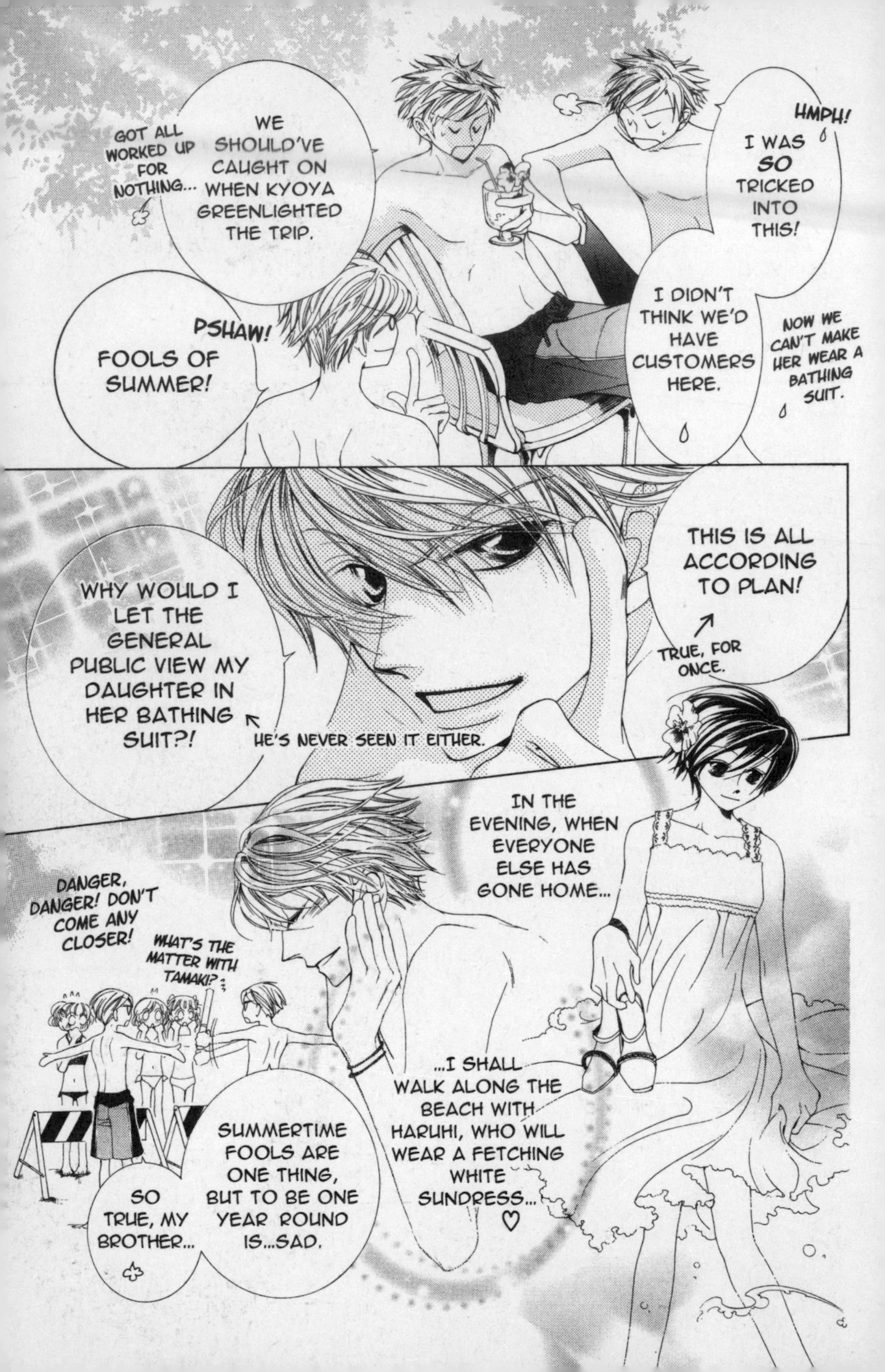
HMPH! I WAS SO TRICKED INTO THIS!
WE SHOULD'VE CAUGHT ON WHEN KYOYA GREENLIGHTED THE TRIP.
GOT ALL WORKED UP FOR NOTHING...
I DIDN'T THINK WE'D HAVE CUSTOMERS HERE.
NOW WE CAN'T MAKE HER WEAR A BATHING SUIT.
PSHAW! FOOLS OF SUMMER!
THIS IS ALL ACCORDING TO PLAN!
TRUE, FOR ONCE.
WHY WOULD I LET THE GENERAL PUBLIC VIEW MY DAUGHTER IN HER BATHING SUIT?!
HE'S NEVER SEEN IT EITHER.
IN THE EVENING, WHEN EVERYONE ELSE HAS GONE HOME...
...I SHALL WALK ALONG THE BEACH WITH HARUHI, WHO WILL WEAR A FETCHING WHITE SUNDRESS... ♡
SUMMERTIME FOOLS ARE ONE THING, BUT TO BE ONE YEAR ROUND IS...SAD.
SO TRUE, MY BROTHER...
DANGER, DANGER! DON'T COME ANY CLOSER!
WHAT'S THE MATTER WITH TAMAKI?

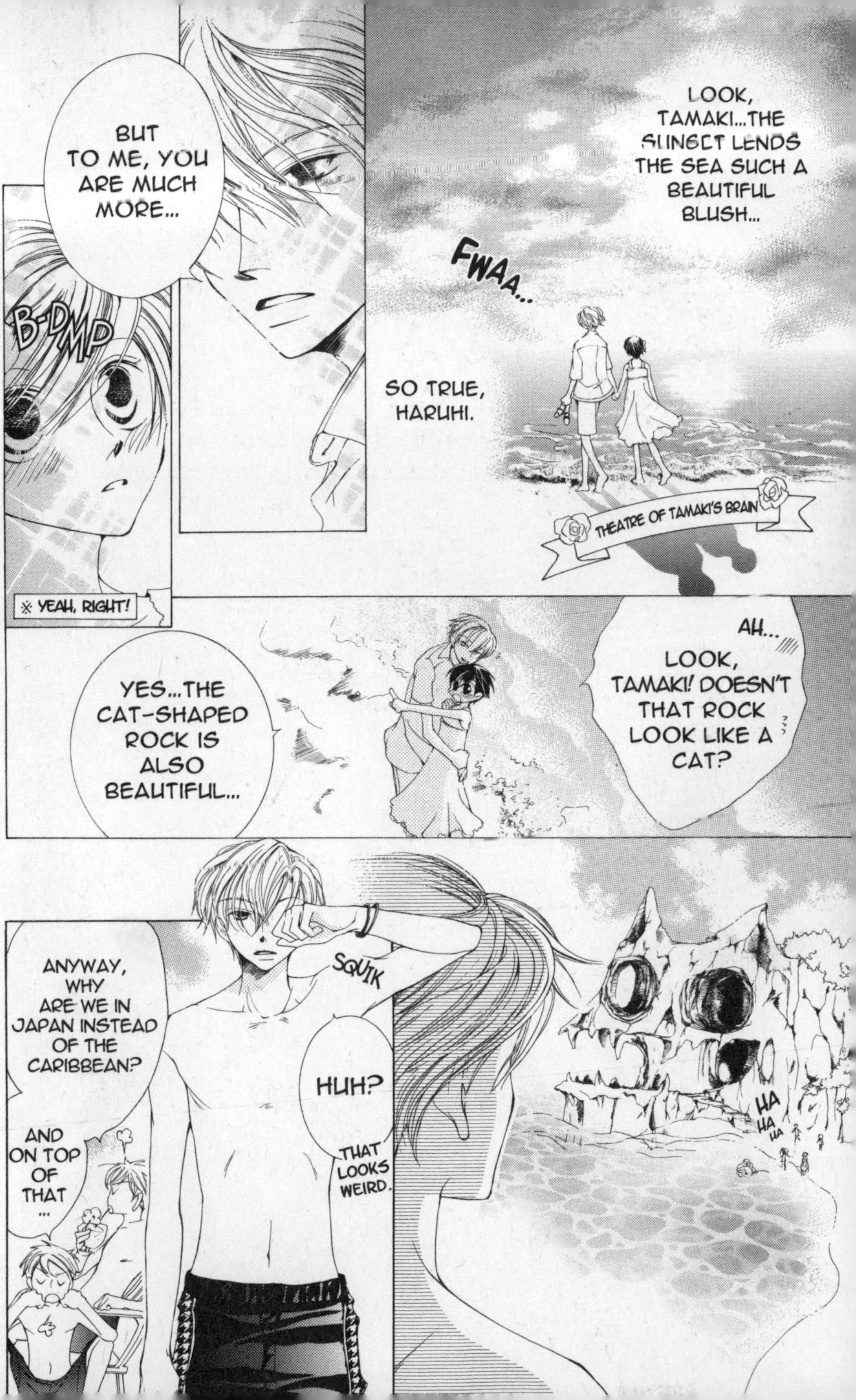
LOOK, TAMAKI...THE SUNSET LENDS THE SEA SUCH A BEAUTIFUL BLUSH...
FWAA...
SO TRUE, HARUHI.
THEATRE OF TAMAKI'S BRAIN
BUT TO ME, YOU ARE MUCH MORE...
B-DMP
※ YEAH, RIGHT!
AH...
LOOK, TAMAKI! DOESN'T THAT ROCK LOOK LIKE A CAT?
YES...THE CAT-SHAPED ROCK IS ALSO BEAUTIFUL...
HA HA HA
HUH?
THAT LOOKS WEIRD.
SQUIK
ANYWAY, WHY ARE WE IN JAPAN INSTEAD OF THE CARIBBEAN?
AND ON TOP OF THAT ...

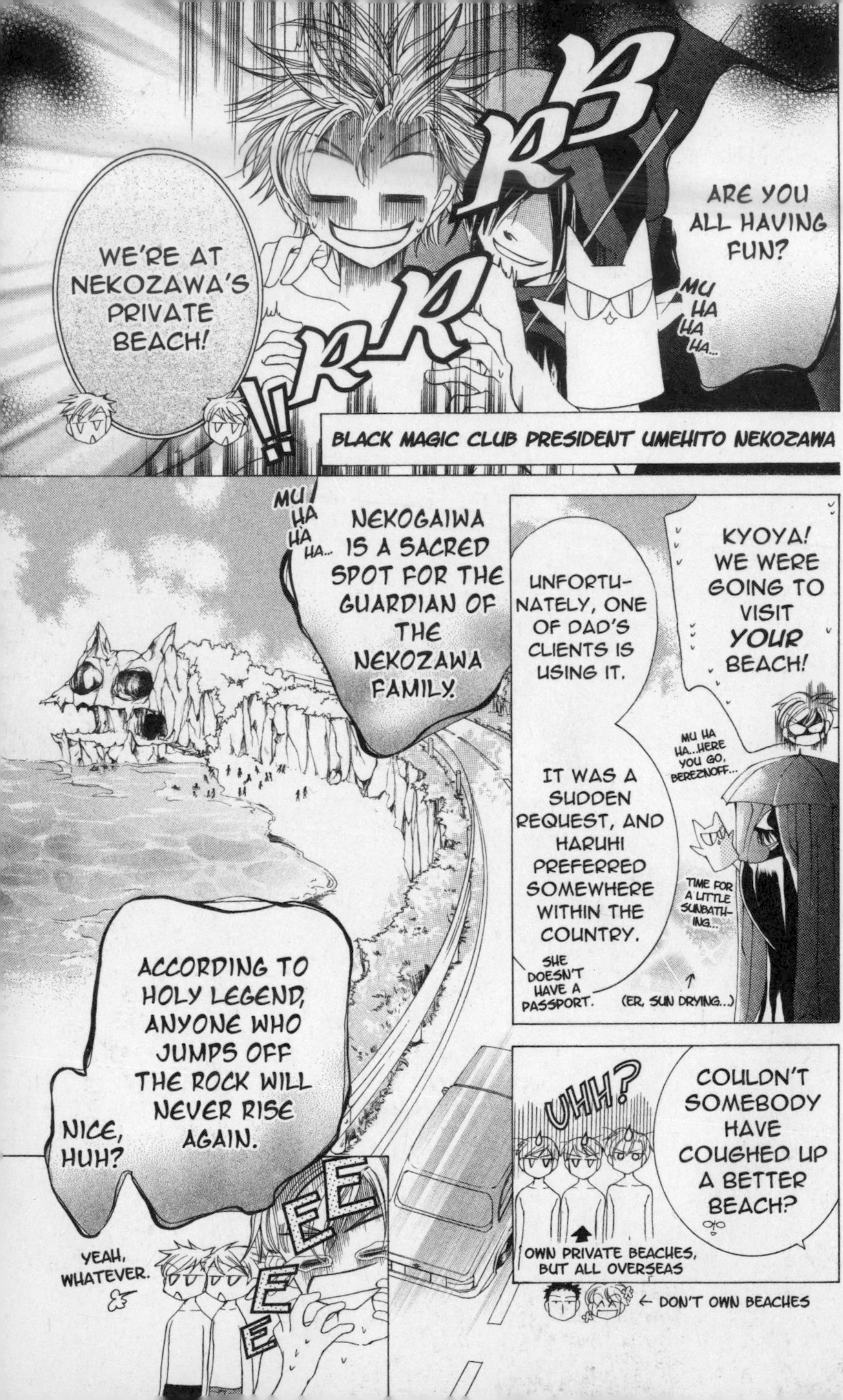
ARE YOU ALL HAVING FUN?
MU HA HA HA...
RRB
WE'RE AT NEKOZAWA'S PRIVATE BEACH!
!!
BLACK MAGIC CLUB PRESIDENT UMEHITO NEKOZAWA
KYOYA! WE WERE GOING TO VISIT YOUR BEACH!
UNFORTUNATELY, ONE OF DAD'S CLIENTS IS USING IT.
MU HA HA...HERE YOU GO, BEREZNOFF...
IT WAS A SUDDEN REQUEST, AND HARUHI PREFERRED SOMEWHERE WITHIN THE COUNTRY.
TIME FOR A LITTLE SUNBATHING...
(ER, SUN DRYING...)
SHE DOESN'T HAVE A PASSPORT.
COULDN'T SOMEBODY HAVE COUGHED UP A BETTER BEACH?
UHH?
OWN PRIVATE BEACHES, BUT ALL OVERSEAS
← DON'T OWN BEACHES
MU HA HA HA...
NEKOGAIWA IS A SACRED SPOT FOR THE GUARDIAN OF THE NEKOZAWA FAMILY.
ACCORDING TO HOLY LEGEND, ANYONE WHO JUMPS OFF THE ROCK WILL NEVER RISE AGAIN.
NICE, HUH?
EEEE
YEAH, WHATEVER.

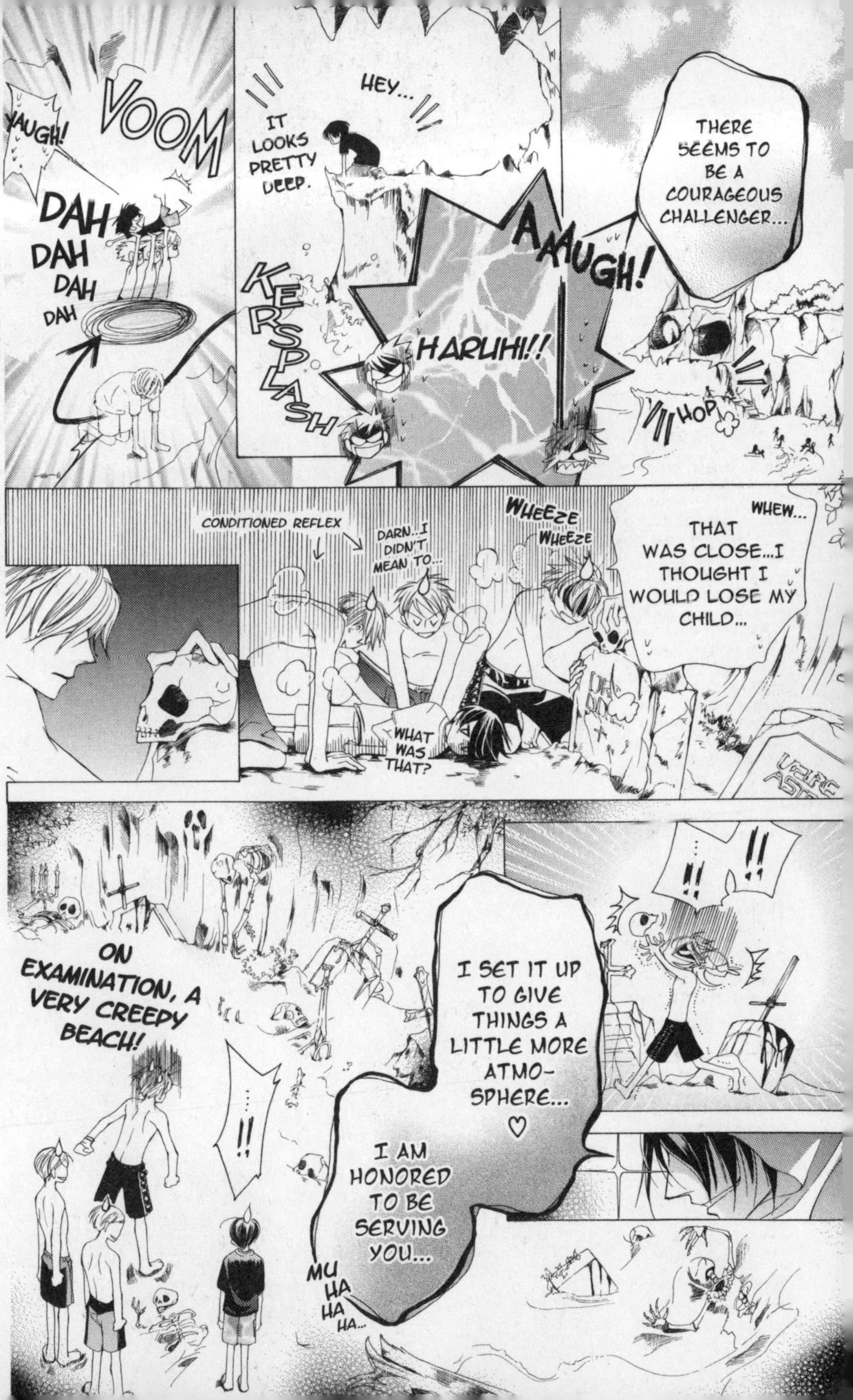
THERE SEEMS TO BE A COURAGEOUS CHALLENGER...
HOP
AAAUGH!
HARUHI!!
HEY...
IT LOOKS PRETTY DEEP.
KERSPLASH
VOOM
YAUGH!
DAH DAH DAH DAH
WHEW...
THAT WAS CLOSE...I THOUGHT I WOULD LOSE MY CHILD...
WHEEZE WHEEZE
DARN...I DIDN'T MEAN TO...
CONDITIONED REFLEX
WHAT WAS THAT?
...!!
!!
I SET IT UP TO GIVE THINGS A LITTLE MORE ATMO-SPHERE... ♡
I AM HONORED TO BE SERVING YOU...
MU HA HA HA...
ON EXAMINATION, A VERY CREEPY BEACH!
...!!

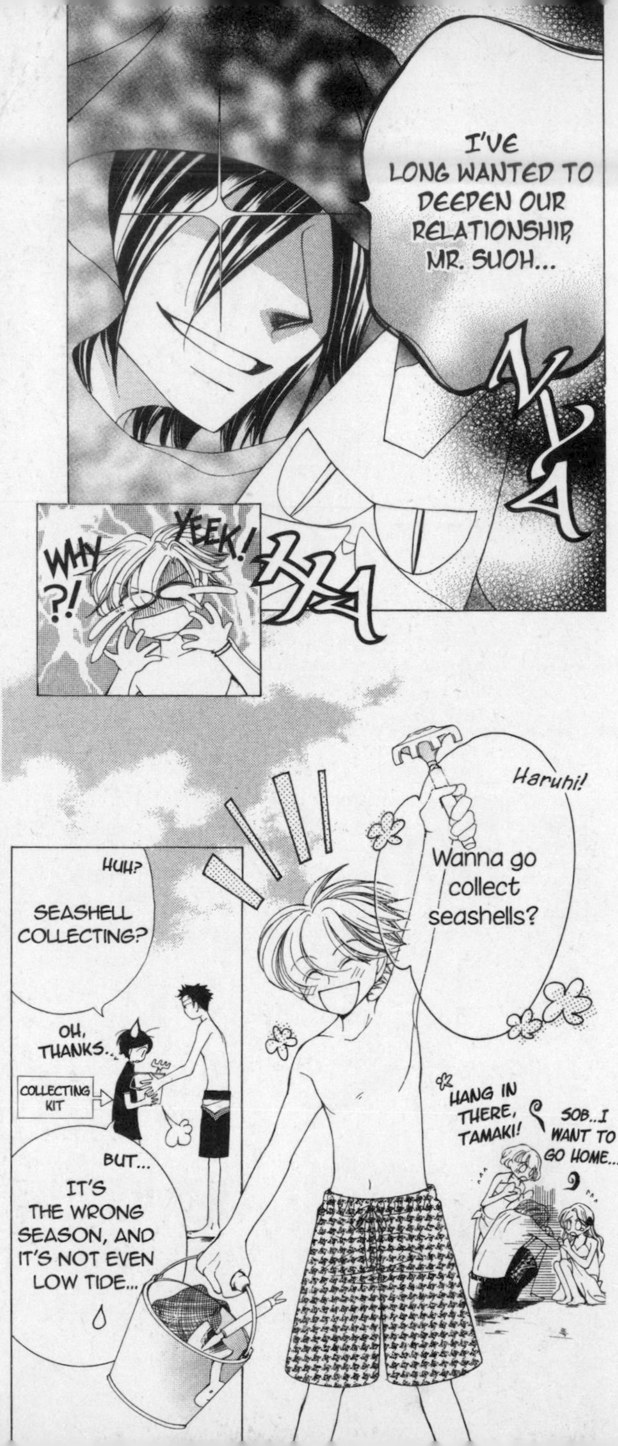
I'VE LONG WANTED TO DEEPEN OUR RELATIONSHIP, MR. SUOH...
YEEK!
WHY?!
Haruhi!
Wanna go collect seashells?
HANG IN THERE, TAMAKI!
SOB...I WANT TO GO HOME...
HUH?
SEASHELL COLLECTING?
OH, THANKS...
COLLECTING KIT
BUT...
IT'S THE WRONG SEASON, AND IT'S NOT EVEN LOW TIDE...

1

HELLO EVERYONE!!

THANKS TO YOUR SUPPORT, WE'RE ALREADY ON VOLUME 3!! WOW!! THOSE OF YOU WHO OWN THE FIRST EDITION OF VOLUME 2 MAY KNOW THIS, BUT VOLUME 3 WAS ACTUALLY PUBLISHED A MONTH EARLIER THAN WE ANNOUNCED.* AHHHH!! HOW SCARY!! SCARY BUT HAPPY!! GYAAAH!!

AS STATED IN VOLUME 2, WE'RE AT THE BEACH EVEN THOUGH THE LAST EPISODE TOOK PLACE AT A POOL. IT'S NICE TO BE YOUNG!! (LAUGH) THE BEACH EPISODE (ESPECIALLY PART 2) WAS A LOT OF FUN TO WRITE. ORIGINALLY, THERE WERE MISTAKES LIKE TAMAKI HAVING SIX FINGERS IN HIS IMPORTANT (AND RARE) SERIOUS SCENE...TWICE! I'M VERY SORRY. I FIXED IT!! THERE WILL BE NO EVIDENCE OF IT HERE!! (LAUGH)

IN THE COLUMNS IN THIS VOLUME, I WOULD LIKE TO REVEAL HOW HOST CLUB IS CREATED EACH MONTH. I WILL TAKE IT AT MY PACE, AND GO OFF ON TANGENTS! I HOPE YOU LOOK FORWARD TO IT. ♡

BY THE WAY, ONE OF THE CHAPTERS IN THIS VOLUME ORIGINALLY HAD A PANEL WITH HIKARU AND KAORU SWITCHED AROUND... I FIXED IT. THOSE OF YOU WITH COPIES OF THE MAGAZINE** CAN TRY TO FIND IT.

*JAPANESE EDITION
**LALA MAGAZINE

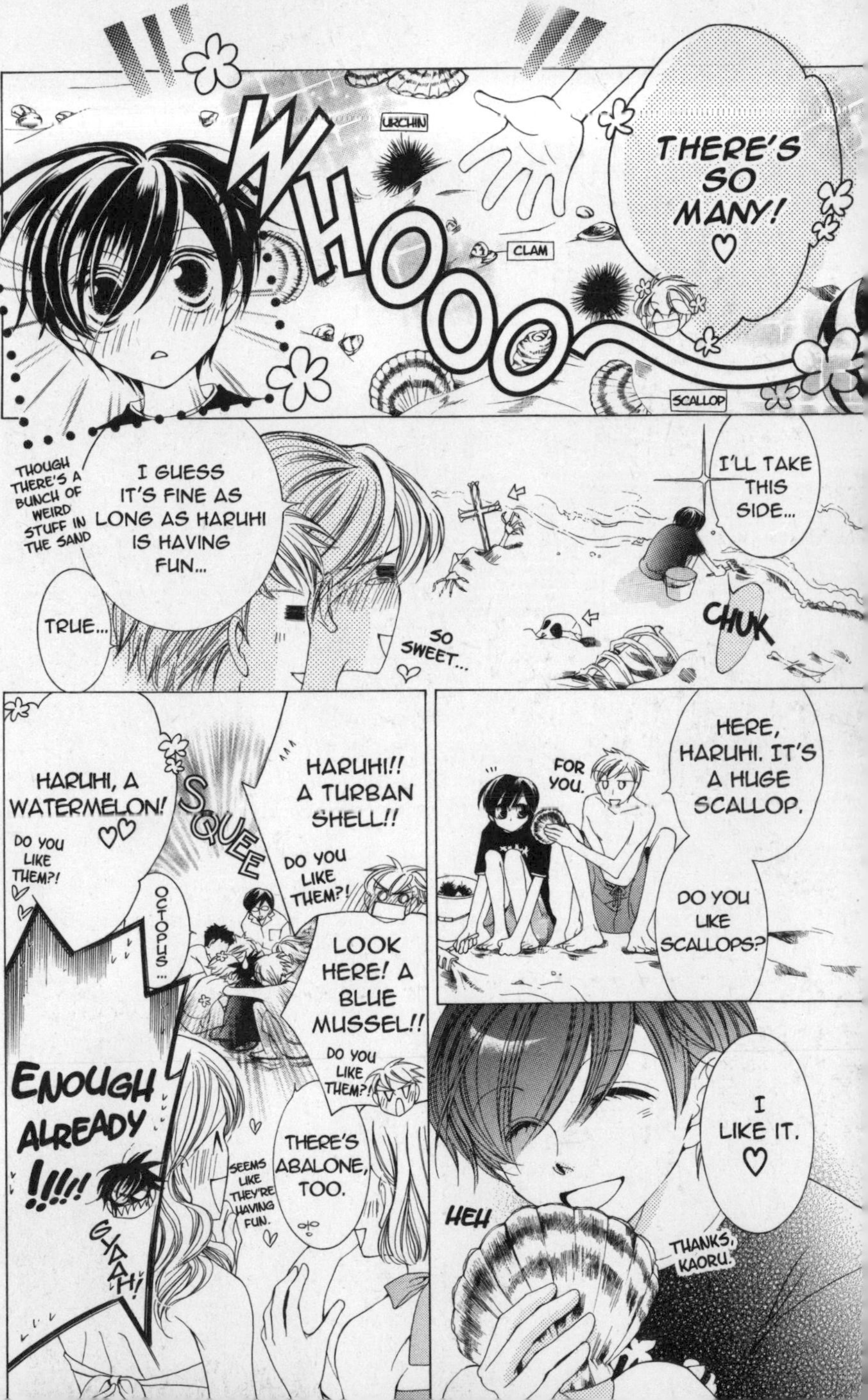
THERE'S SO MANY! ♡
WHOOOO
URCHIN
CLAM
SCALLOP
I'LL TAKE THIS SIDE...
CHUK
I GUESS IT'S FINE AS LONG AS HARUHI IS HAVING FUN...
THOUGH THERE'S A BUNCH OF WEIRD STUFF IN THE SAND
TRUE...
SO SWEET... ♡
HERE, HARUHI. IT'S A HUGE SCALLOP.
FOR YOU.
DO YOU LIKE SCALLOPS?
I LIKE IT. ♡
HEH
THANKS, KAORU.
HARUHI!! A TURBAN SHELL!!
DO YOU LIKE THEM?!
HARUHI, A WATERMELON! ♡♡
DO YOU LIKE THEM?!
SQUEE
OCTOPUS...
LOOK HERE! A BLUE MUSSEL!!
DO YOU LIKE THEM?!
THERE'S ABALONE, TOO.
SEEMS LIKE THEY'RE HAVING FUN.
ENOUGH ALREADY!!!!!
GYAAH!

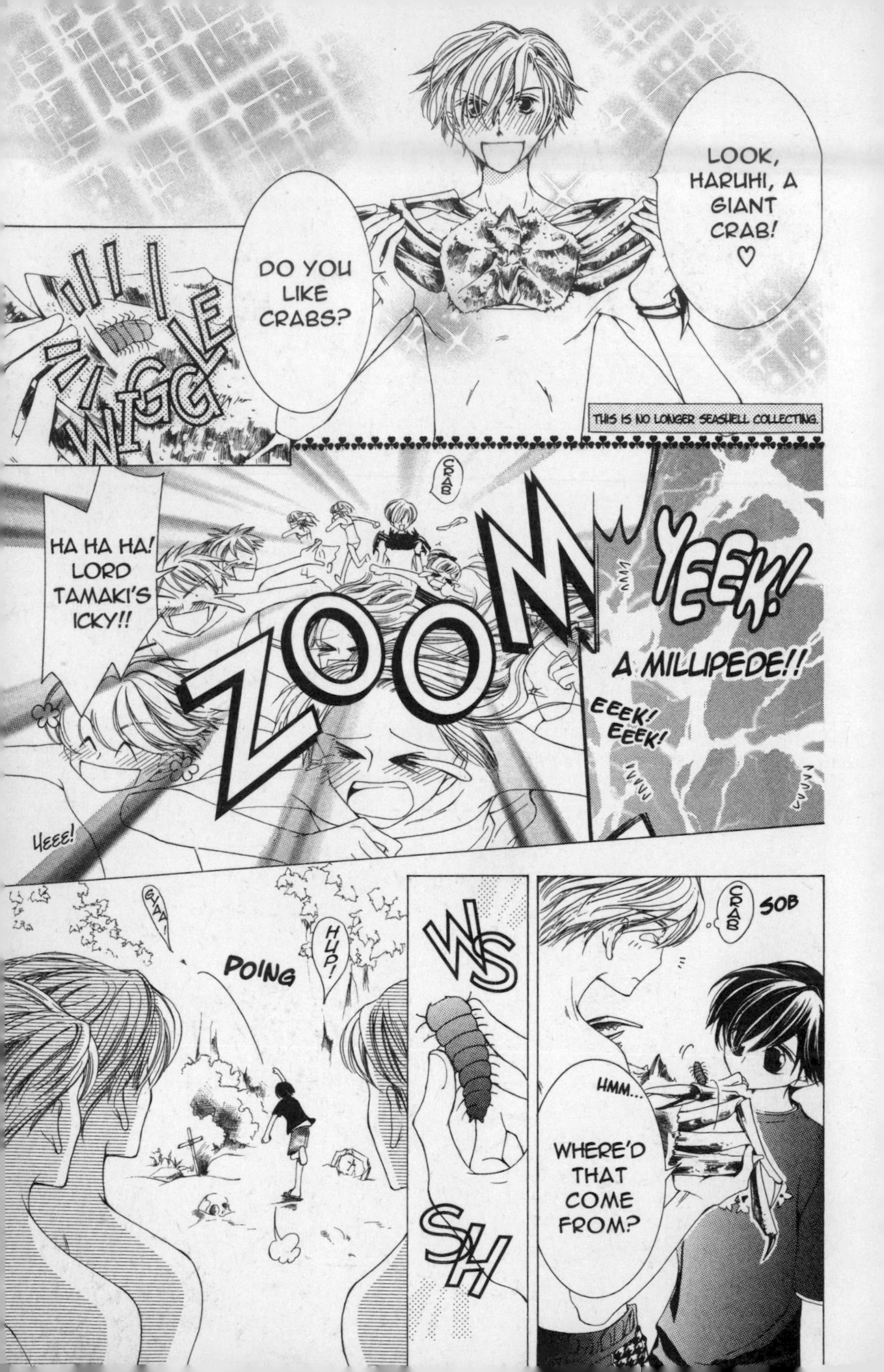
LOOK, HARUHI, A GIANT CRAB! ♡
DO YOU LIKE CRABS?
WIGGLE
THIS IS NO LONGER SEASHELL COLLECTING.
YEEK!
A MILLIPEDE!!
EEEK! EEEK!
CRAB
ZOOM
HA HA HA! LORD TAMAKI'S ICKY!!
YEEE!
CRAB
SOB
HMM...
WHERE'D THAT COME FROM?
WS
SH
HUP!
POING
GYAA!

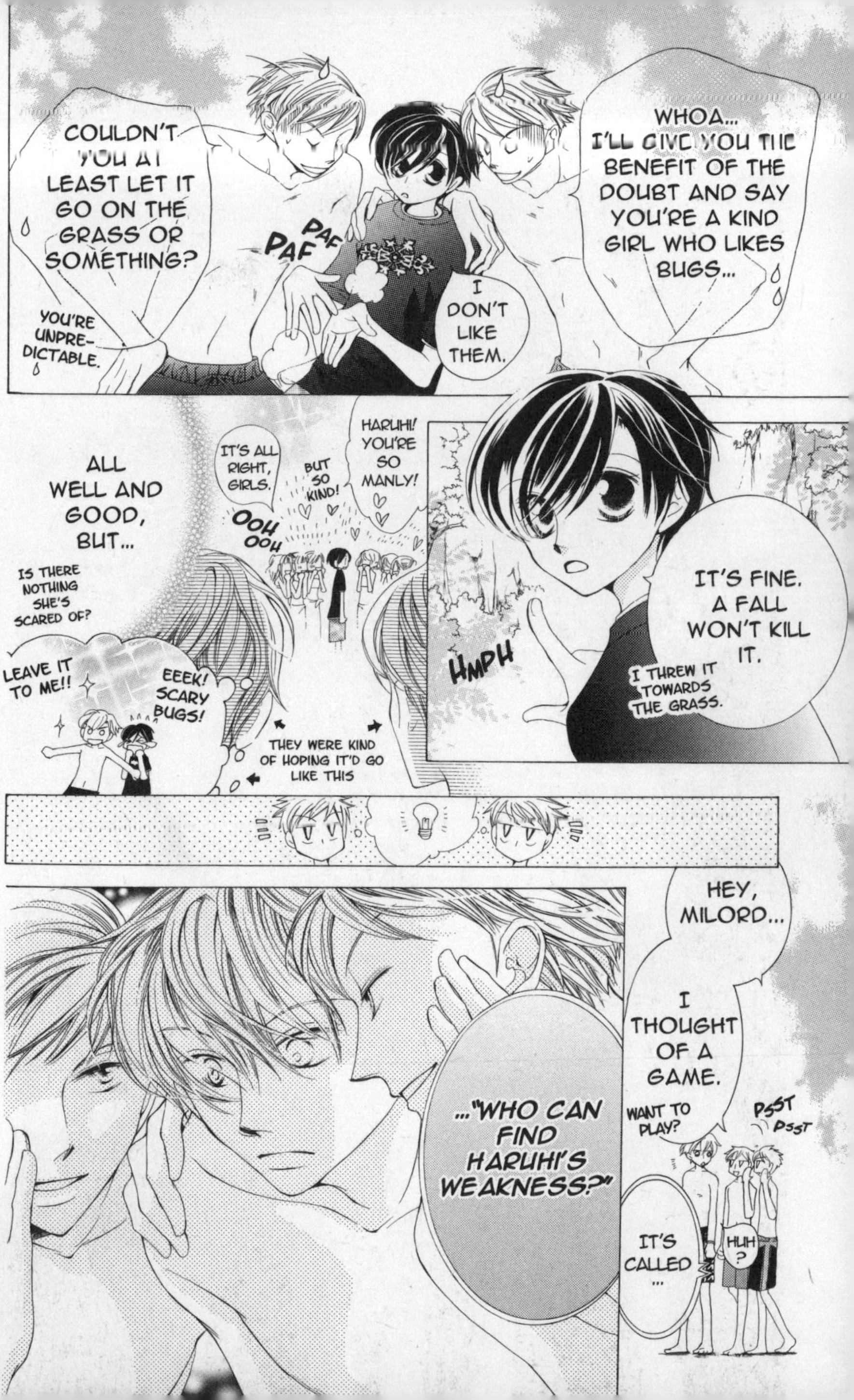
WHOA... I'LL GIVE YOU THE BENEFIT OF THE DOUBT AND SAY YOU'RE A KIND GIRL WHO LIKES BUGS...
I DON'T LIKE THEM.
PAF PAF
COULDN'T YOU AT LEAST LET IT GO ON THE GRASS OR SOMETHING?
YOU'RE UNPRE-DICTABLE.
IT'S FINE. A FALL WON'T KILL IT.
I THREW IT TOWARDS THE GRASS.
HMPH
HARUHI! YOU'RE SO MANLY!
BUT SO KIND!
IT'S ALL RIGHT, GIRLS.
OOH OOH
ALL WELL AND GOOD, BUT...
IS THERE NOTHING SHE'S SCARED OF?
EEEK! SCARY BUGS!
LEAVE IT TO ME!!
THEY WERE KIND OF HOPING IT'D GO LIKE THIS
HEY, MILORD...
I THOUGHT OF A GAME.
WANT TO PLAY?
PSST PSST
HUH?
IT'S CALLED...
..."WHO CAN FIND HARUHI'S WEAKNESS?"

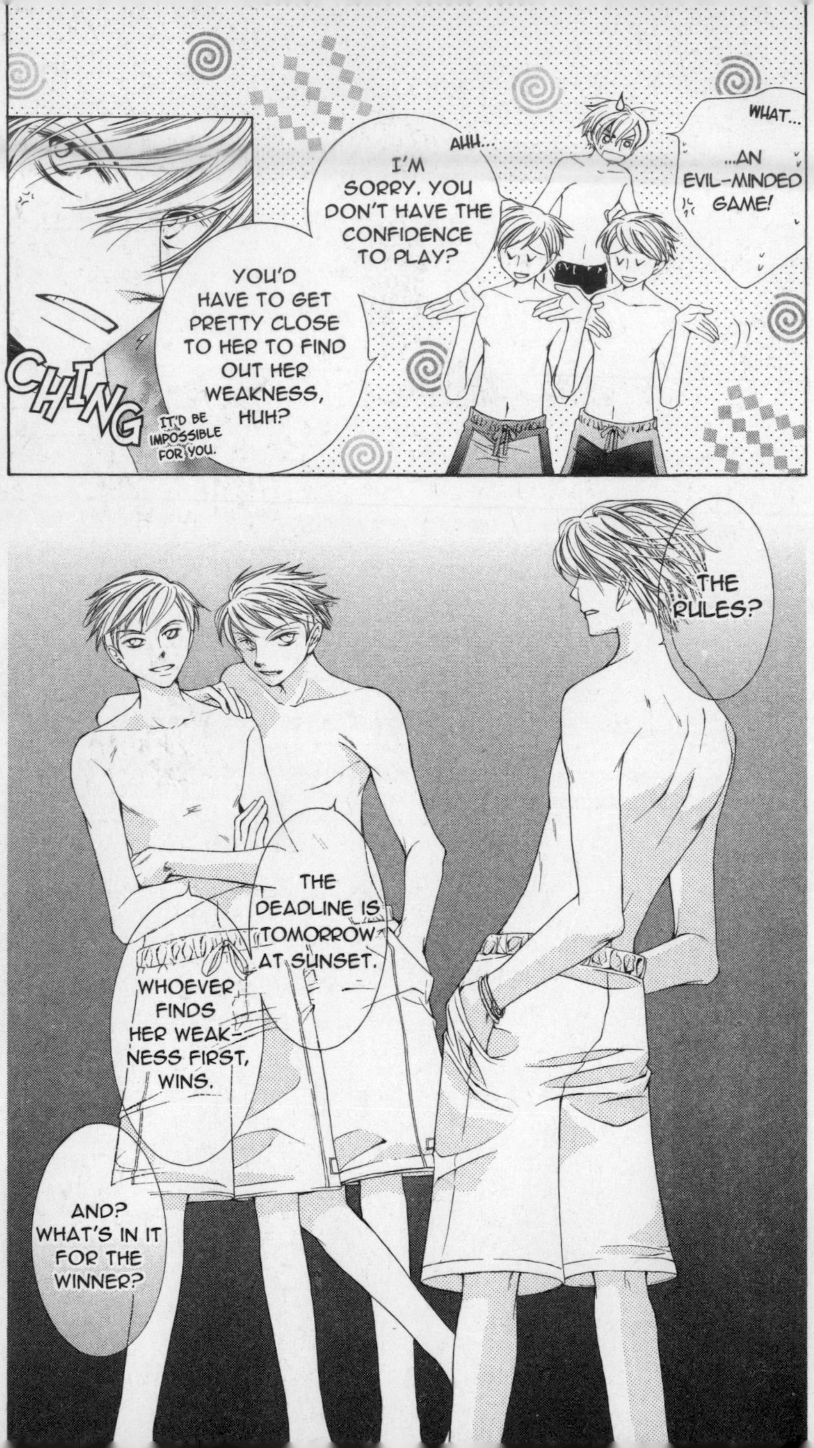
WHAT...
...AN EVIL-MINDED GAME!
AHH...
I'M SORRY. YOU DON'T HAVE THE CONFIDENCE TO PLAY?
YOU'D HAVE TO GET PRETTY CLOSE TO HER TO FIND OUT HER WEAKNESS, HUH?
CHING
IT'D BE IMPOSSIBLE FOR YOU.
THE RULES?
THE DEADLINE IS TOMORROW AT SUNSET.
WHOEVER FINDS HER WEAK-NESS FIRST, WINS.
AND? WHAT'S IN IT FOR THE WINNER?

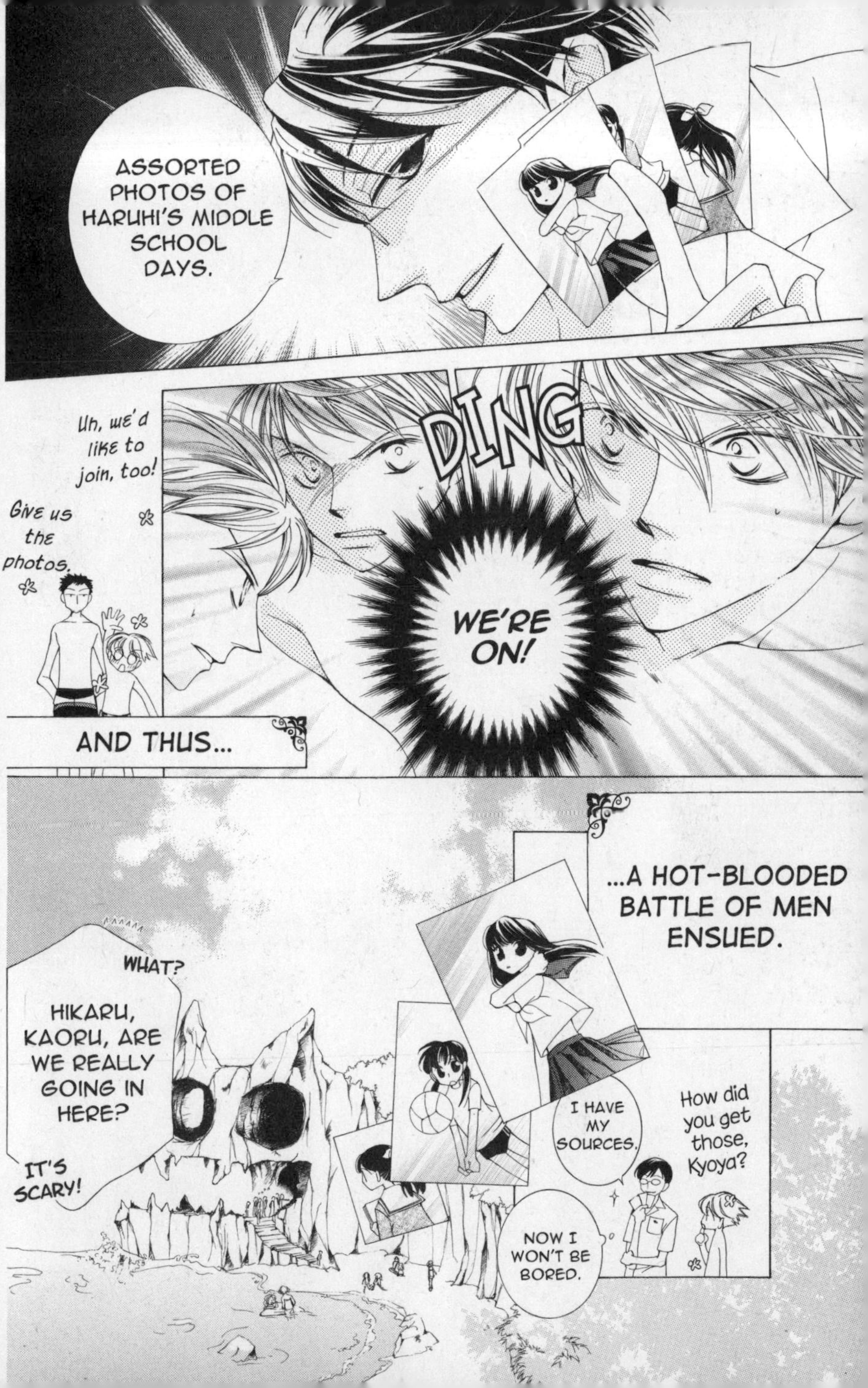
ASSORTED PHOTOS OF HARUHI'S MIDDLE SCHOOL DAYS.
DING
WE'RE ON!
Uh, we'd like to join, too!
Give us the photos.
AND THUS...
...A HOT-BLOODED BATTLE OF MEN ENSUED.
How did you get those, Kyoya?
I HAVE MY SOURCES.
NOW I WON'T BE BORED.
WHAT?
HIKARU, KAORU, ARE WE REALLY GOING IN HERE?
IT'S SCARY!

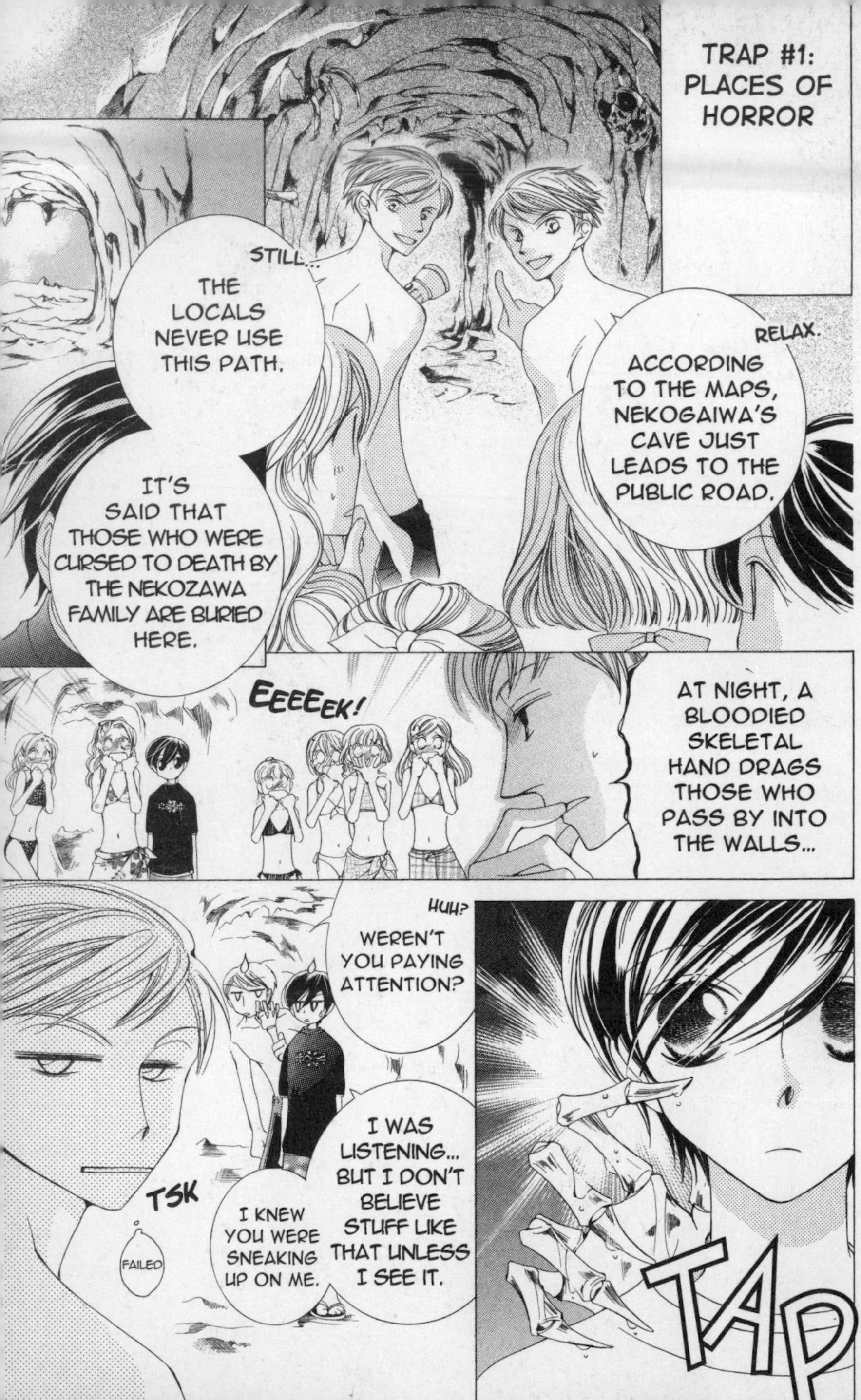
TRAP #1: PLACES OF HORROR
RELAX.
ACCORDING TO THE MAPS, NEKOGAIWA'S CAVE JUST LEADS TO THE PUBLIC ROAD.
STILL...
THE LOCALS NEVER USE THIS PATH.
IT'S SAID THAT THOSE WHO WERE CURSED TO DEATH BY THE NEKOZAWA FAMILY ARE BURIED HERE.
AT NIGHT, A BLOODIED SKELETAL HAND DRAGS THOSE WHO PASS BY INTO THE WALLS...
EEEEEK!
TAP
HUH?
WEREN'T YOU PAYING ATTENTION?
I WAS LISTENING... BUT I DON'T BELIEVE STUFF LIKE THAT UNLESS I SEE IT.
I KNEW YOU WERE SNEAKING UP ON ME.
TSK
FAILED

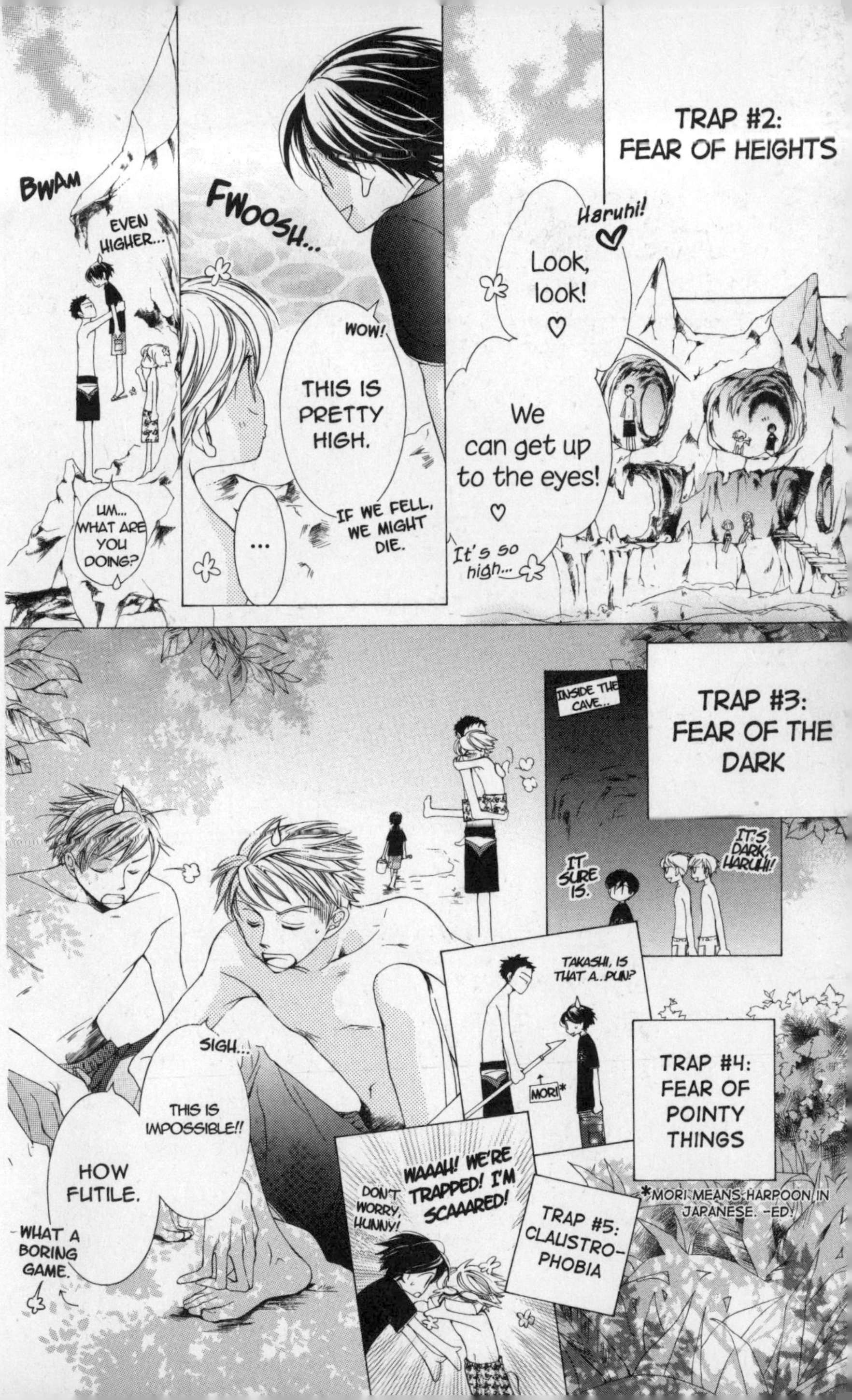
TRAP #2: FEAR OF HEIGHTS
Haruhi! ♡
Look, look! ♡
We can get up to the eyes! ♡
It's so high...
FWOOSH...
WOW!
THIS IS PRETTY HIGH.
IF WE FELL, WE MIGHT DIE.
...
BWAM
EVEN HIGHER...
UM... WHAT ARE YOU DOING?
TRAP #3: FEAR OF THE DARK
INSIDE THE CAVE...
IT'S DARK, HARUHI!
IT SURE IS.
TAKASHI, IS THAT A...PUN?
MORI*
TRAP #4: FEAR OF POINTY THINGS
*MORI MEANS HARPOON IN JAPANESE. -ED.
TRAP #5: CLAUSTROPHOBIA
WAAAH! WE'RE TRAPPED! I'M SCAAARED!
DON'T WORRY, HUNNY!
SIGH...
THIS IS IMPOSSIBLE!!
HOW FUTILE.
WHAT A BORING GAME.

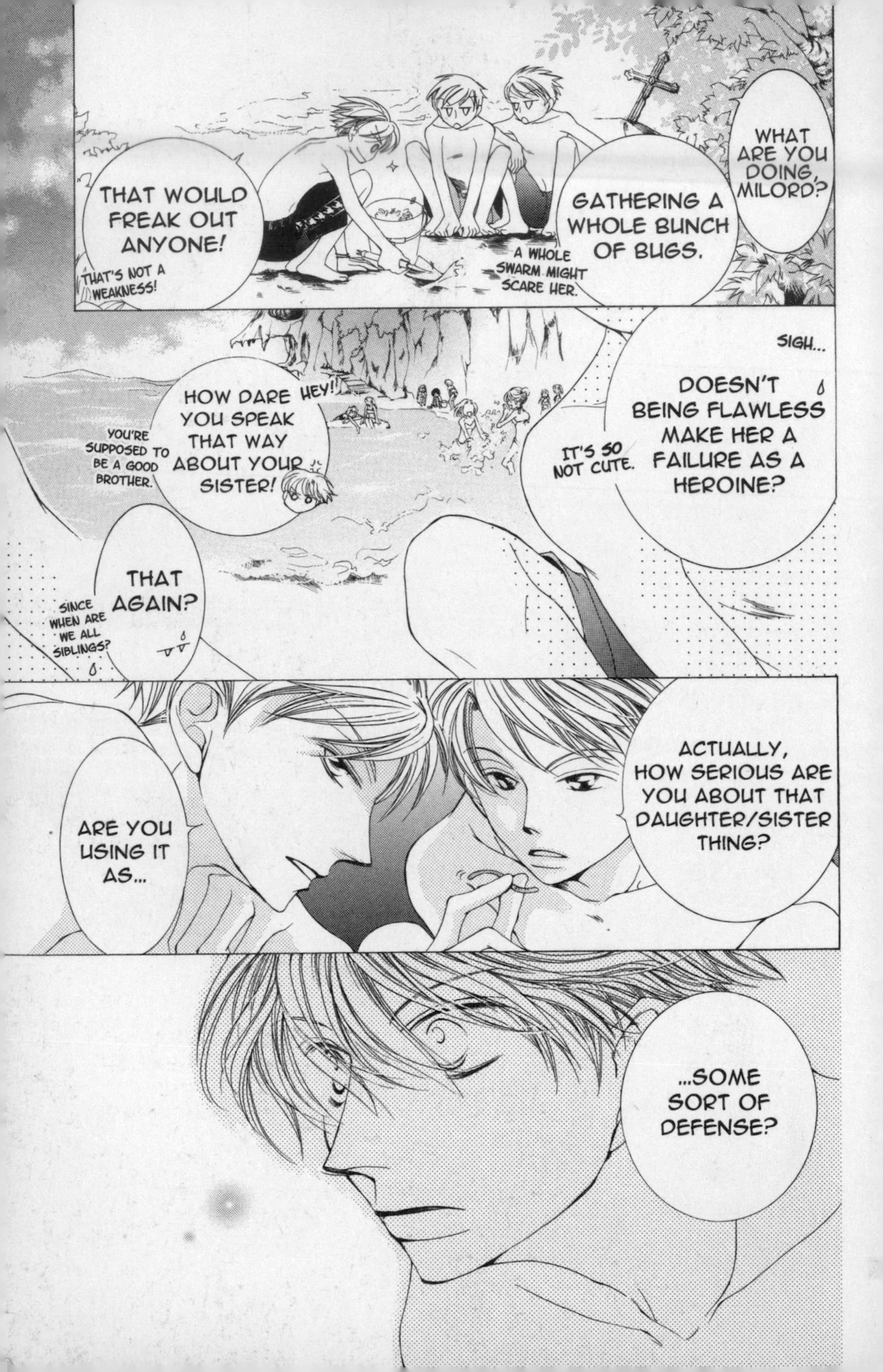
WHAT ARE YOU DOING, MILORD?
GATHERING A WHOLE BUNCH OF BUGS.
A WHOLE SWARM MIGHT SCARE HER.
THAT WOULD FREAK OUT ANYONE!
THAT'S NOT A WEAKNESS!
SIGH...
DOESN'T BEING FLAWLESS MAKE HER A FAILURE AS A HEROINE?
IT'S SO NOT CUTE.
HEY!!
HOW DARE YOU SPEAK THAT WAY ABOUT YOUR SISTER!
YOU'RE SUPPOSED TO BE A GOOD BROTHER.
THAT AGAIN?
SINCE WHEN ARE WE ALL SIBLINGS?
ACTUALLY, HOW SERIOUS ARE YOU ABOUT THAT DAUGHTER/SISTER THING?
ARE YOU USING IT AS...
...SOME SORT OF DEFENSE?

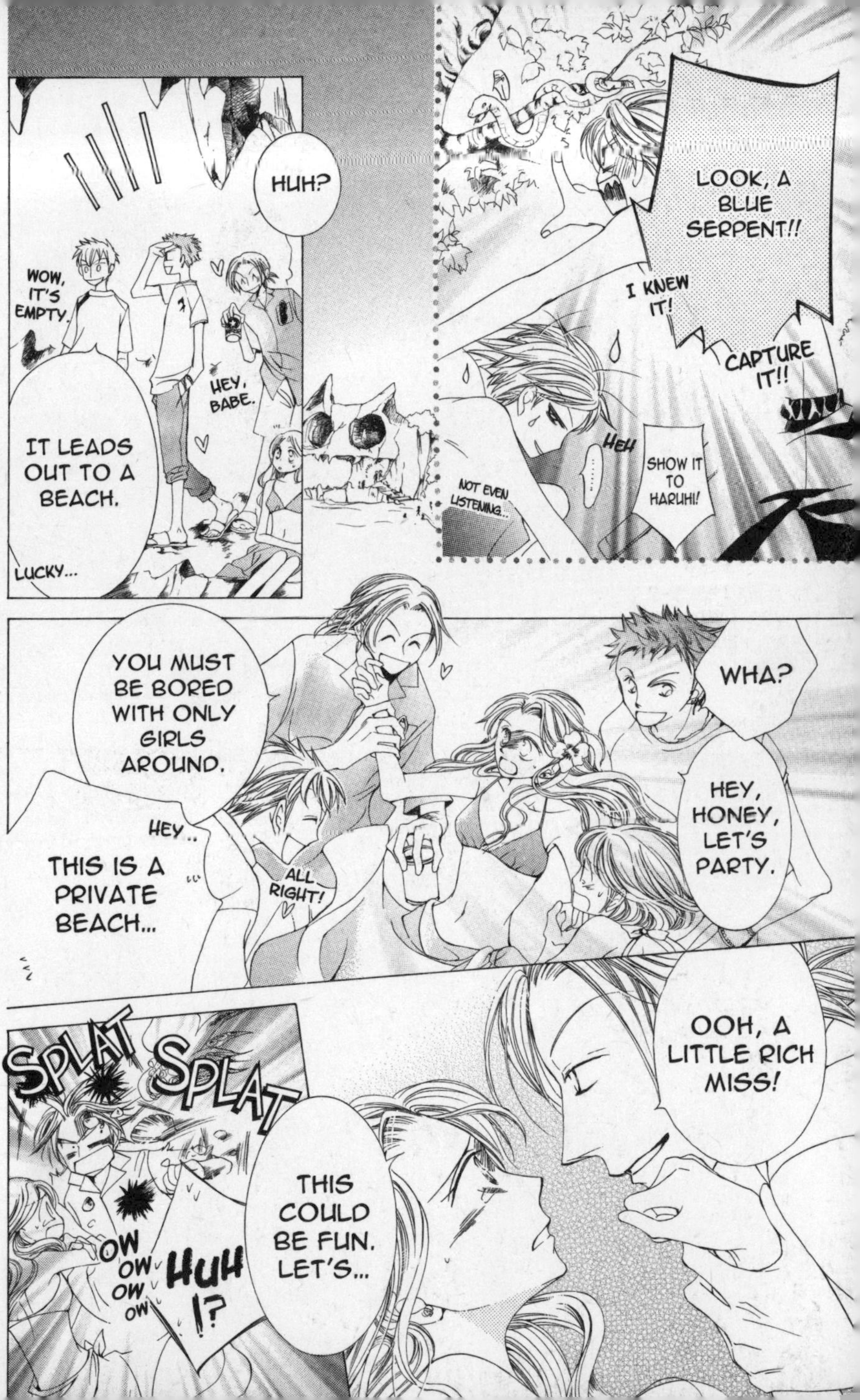
LOOK, A BLUE SERPENT!!
I KNEW IT!
CAPTURE IT!!
HEH
...
SHOW IT TO HARUHI!
NOT EVEN LISTENING...
HUH?
WOW, IT'S EMPTY.
HEY, BABE.
IT LEADS OUT TO A BEACH.
LUCKY...
WHA?
HEY, HONEY, LET'S PARTY.
ALL RIGHT!
YOU MUST BE BORED WITH ONLY GIRLS AROUND.
HEY...
THIS IS A PRIVATE BEACH...
OOH, A LITTLE RICH MISS!
THIS COULD BE FUN. LET'S...
SPLAT SPLAT
HUH!?
OW OW OW OW

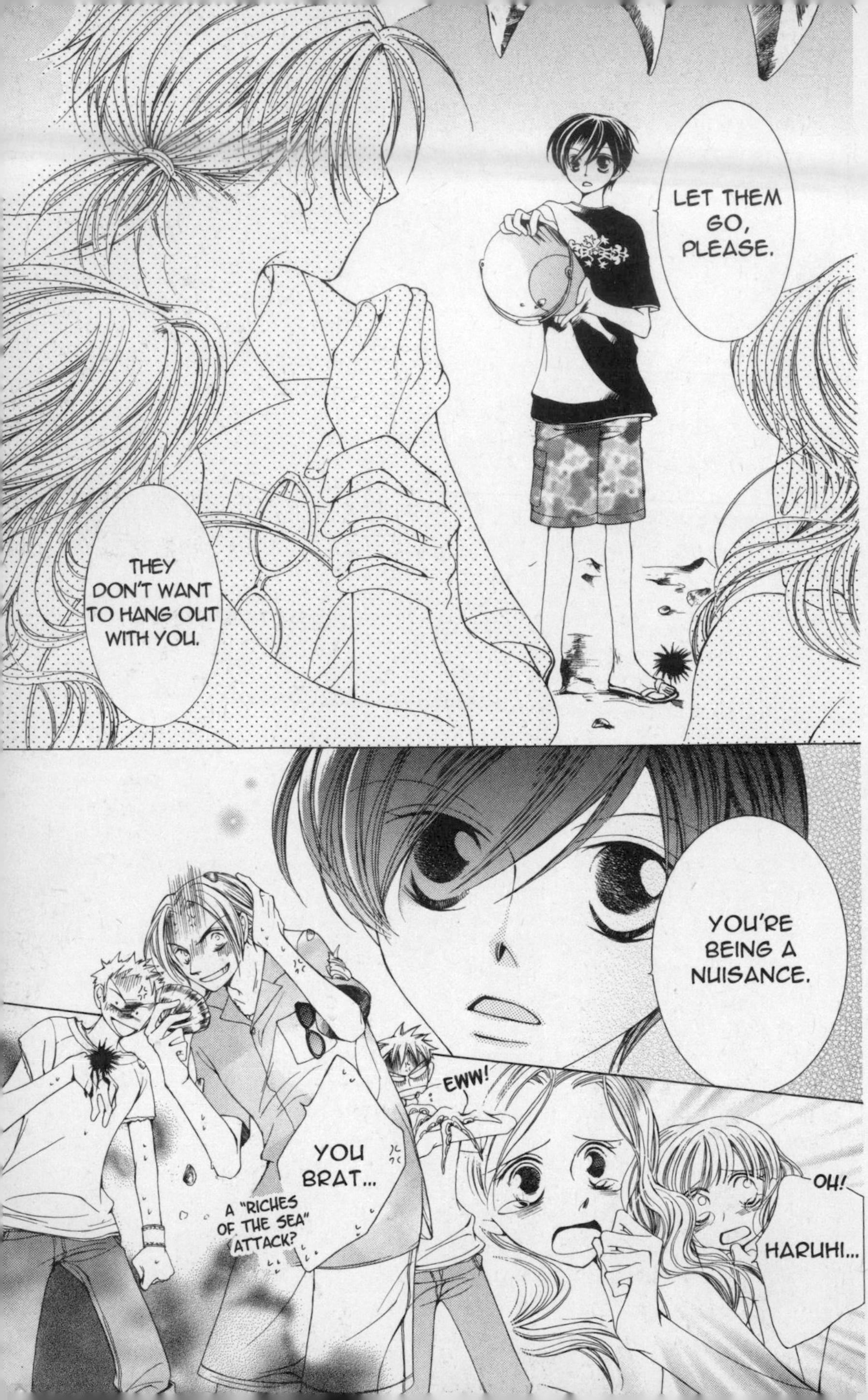
LET THEM GO, PLEASE.
THEY DON'T WANT TO HANG OUT WITH YOU.
YOU'RE BEING A NUISANCE.
OH!
HARUHI...
EWW!
YOU BRAT...
A "RICHES OF THE SEA" ATTACK?

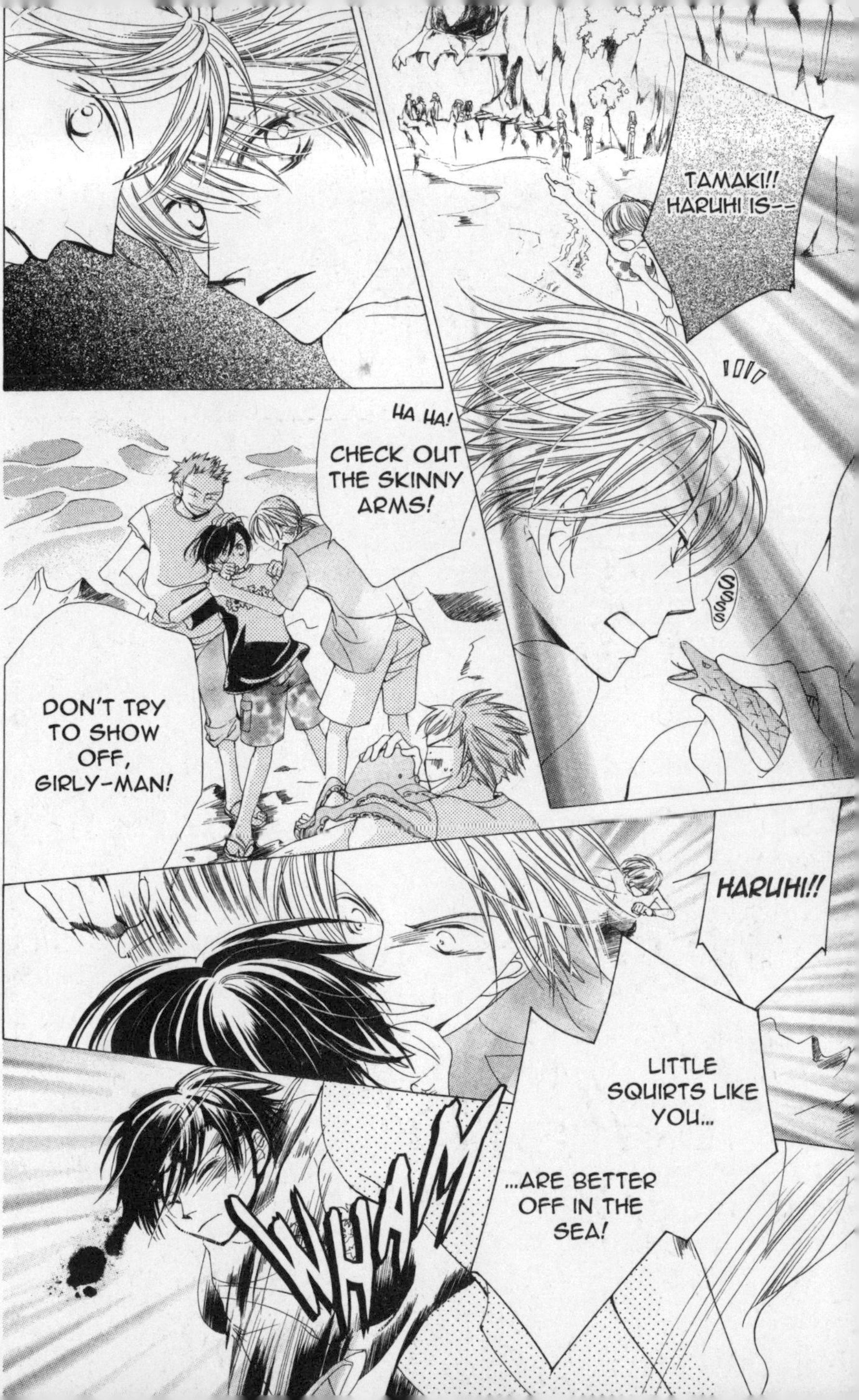
TAMAKI!! HARUHI IS--
SSS
HA HA!
CHECK OUT THE SKINNY ARMS!
DON'T TRY TO SHOW OFF, GIRLY-MAN!
HARUHI!!
LITTLE SQUIRTS LIKE YOU...
...ARE BETTER OFF IN THE SEA!
WHAM

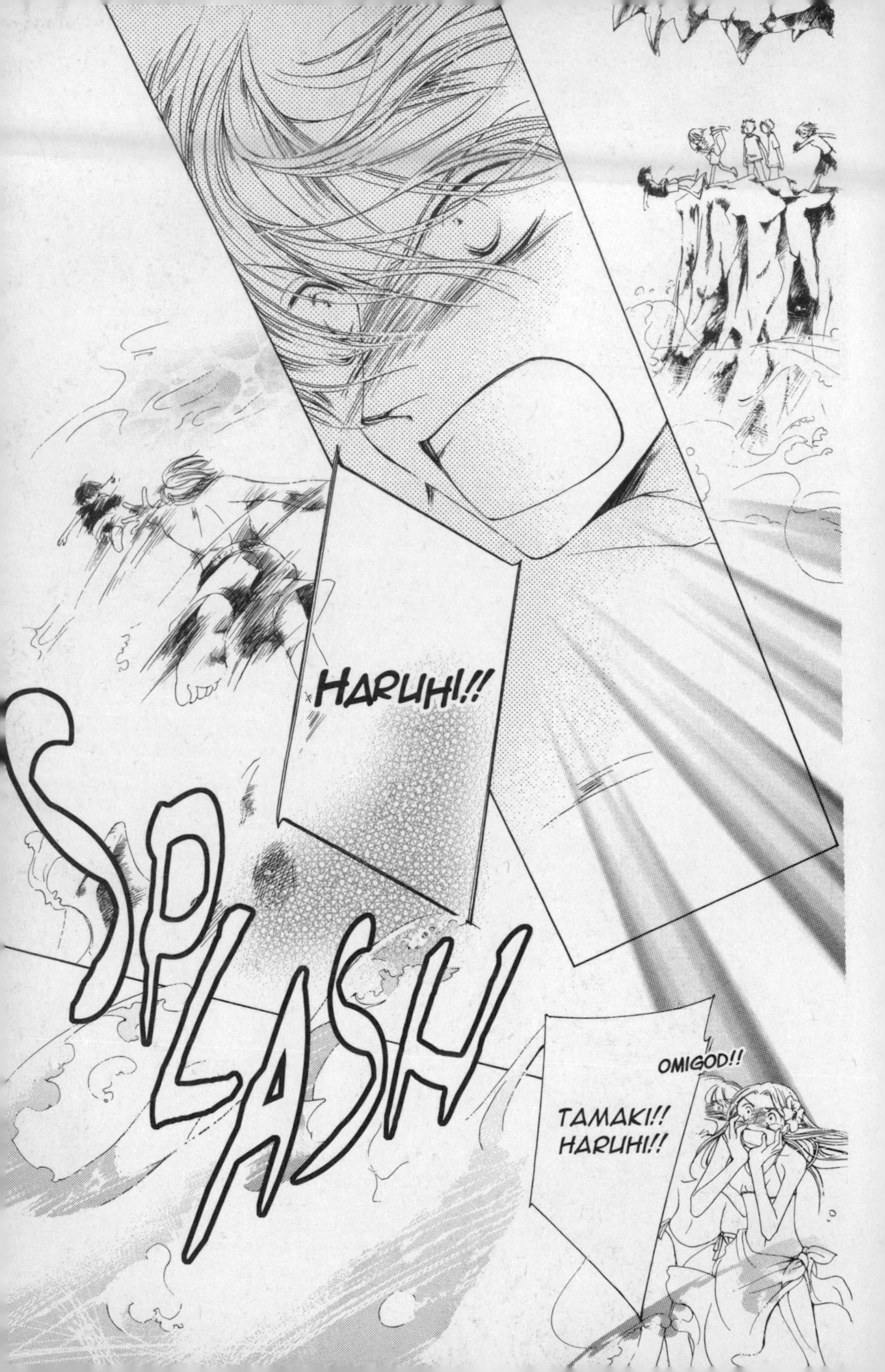
HARUHI!!
SPLASH
OMIGOD!!
TAMAKI!! HARUHI!!

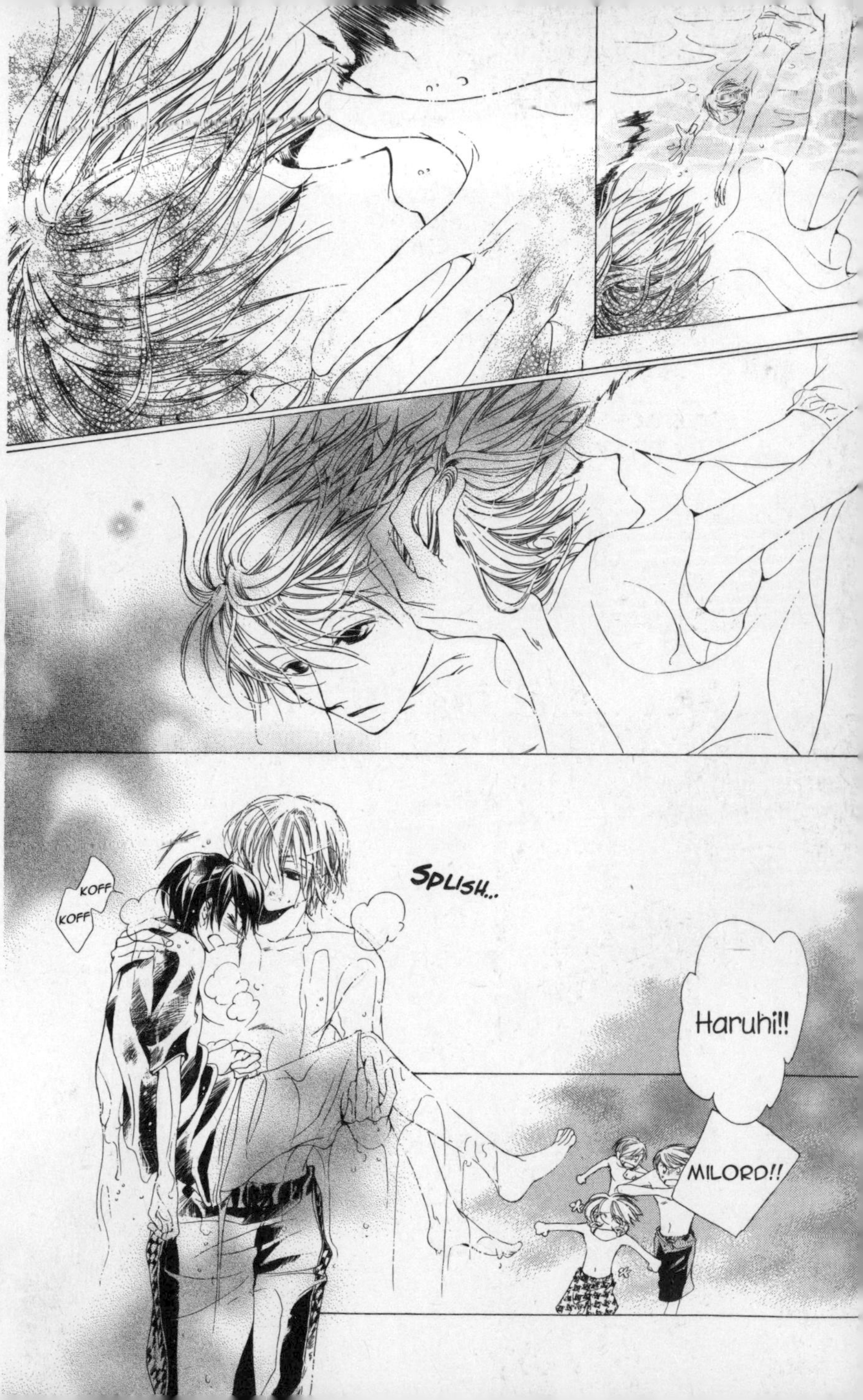
SPLISH...
KOFF
KOFF
Haruhi!!
MILORD!!

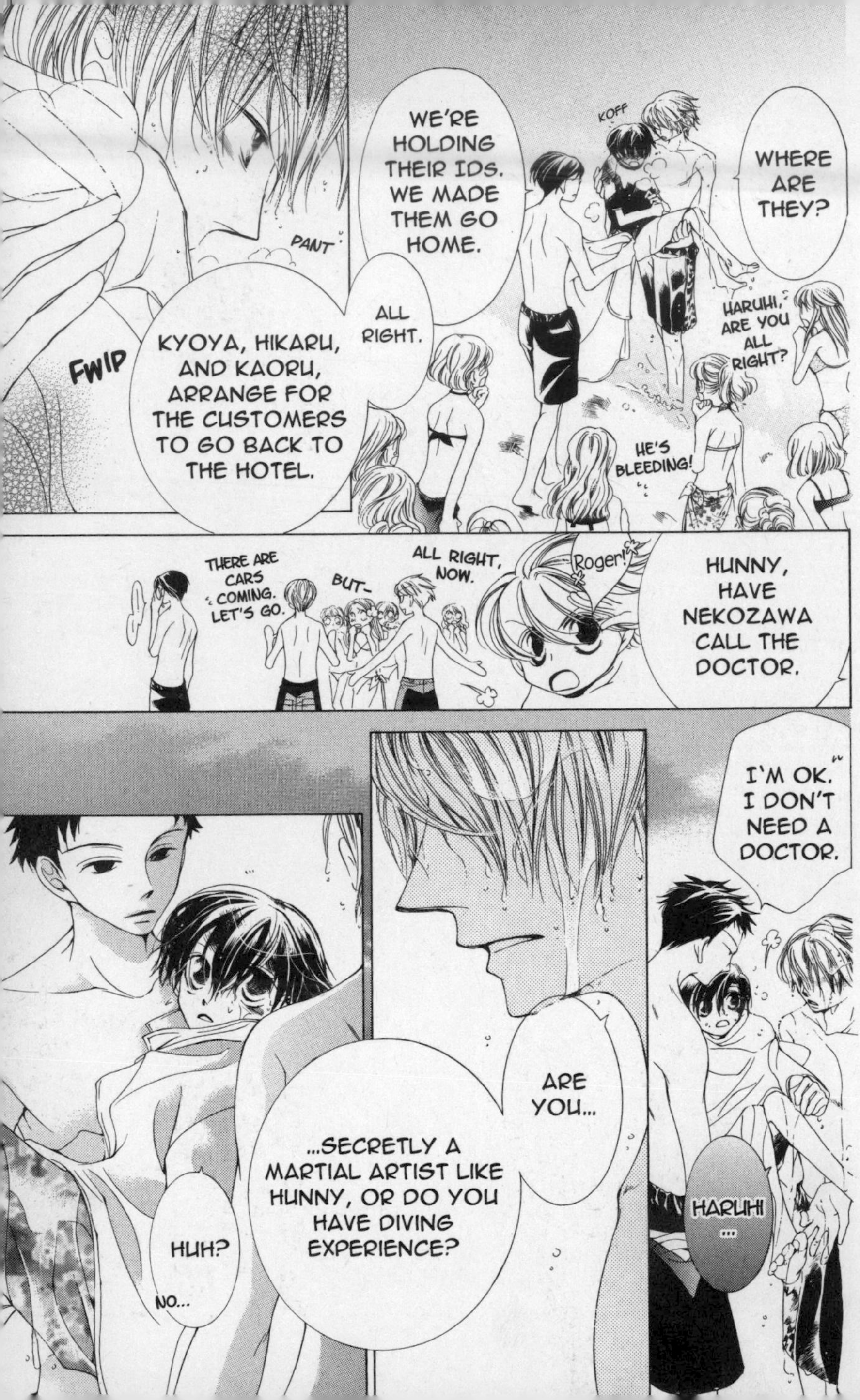
WHERE ARE THEY?
KOFF
WE'RE HOLDING THEIR IDS. WE MADE THEM GO HOME.
HARUHI, ARE YOU ALL RIGHT?
HE'S BLEEDING!
PANT
KYOYA, HIKARU, AND KAORU, ARRANGE FOR THE CUSTOMERS TO GO BACK TO THE HOTEL.
ALL RIGHT.
FWIP
HUNNY, HAVE NEKOZAWA CALL THE DOCTOR.
Roger!
ALL RIGHT, NOW.
BUT–
THERE ARE CARS COMING. LET'S GO.
I'M OK. I DON'T NEED A DOCTOR.
HARUHI ...
ARE YOU...
...SECRETLY A MARTIAL ARTIST LIKE HUNNY, OR DO YOU HAVE DIVING EXPERIENCE?
HUH?
NO...

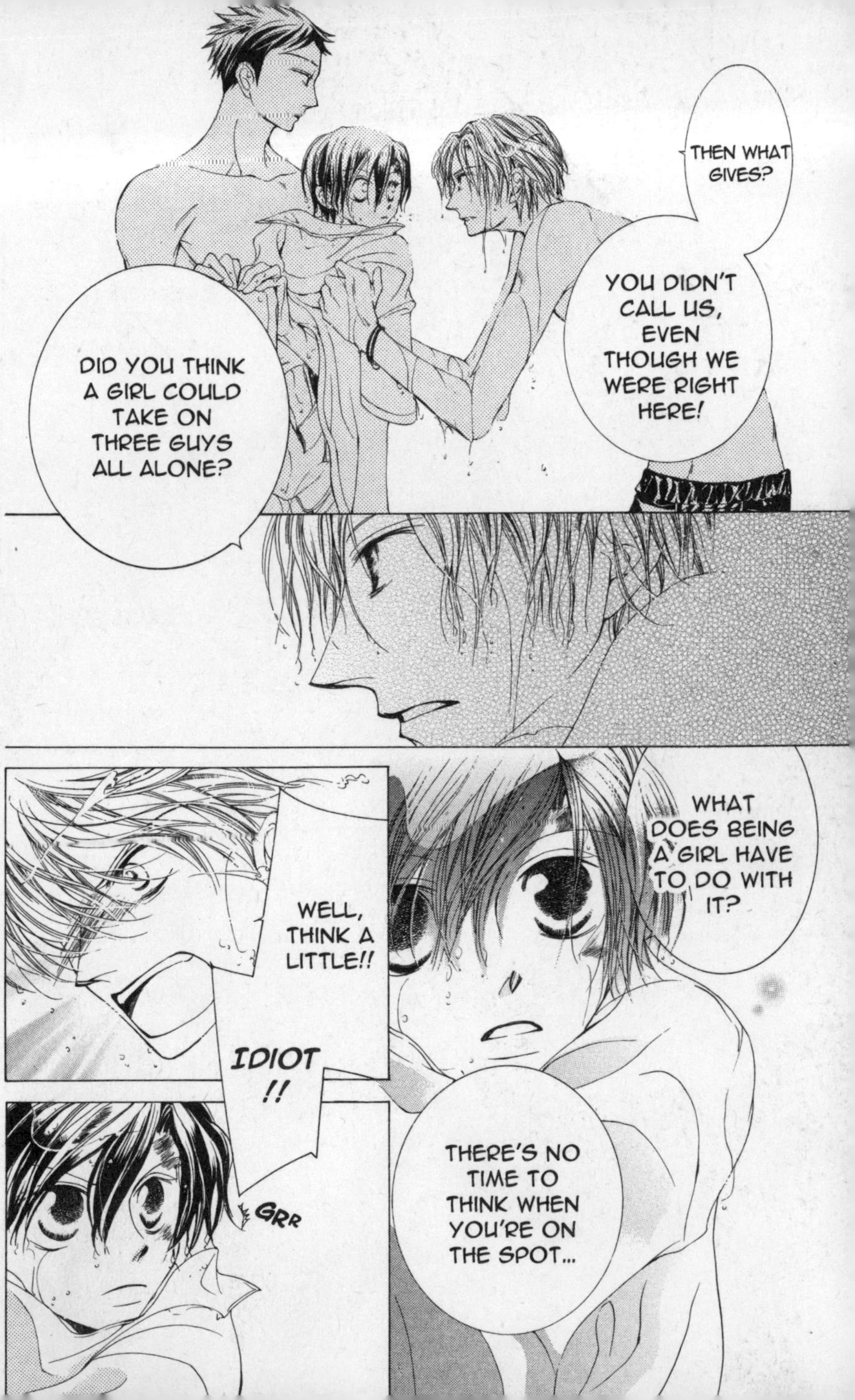
THEN WHAT GIVES?
YOU DIDN'T CALL US, EVEN THOUGH WE WERE RIGHT HERE!
DID YOU THINK A GIRL COULD TAKE ON THREE GUYS ALL ALONE?
WHAT DOES BEING A GIRL HAVE TO DO WITH IT?
THERE'S NO TIME TO THINK WHEN YOU'RE ON THE SPOT...
WELL, THINK A LITTLE!!
IDIOT !!
GRR

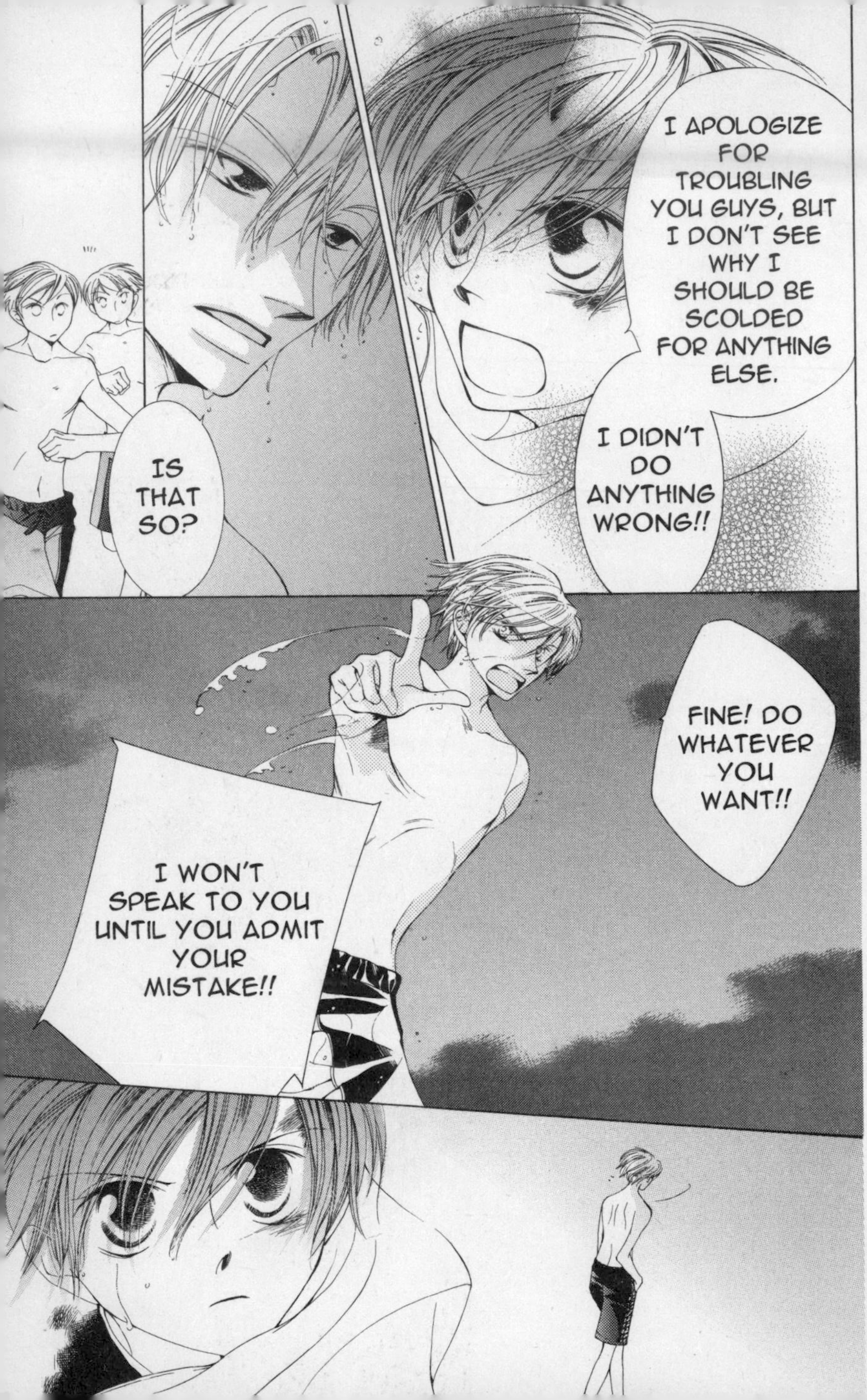
I APOLOGIZE FOR TROUBLING YOU GUYS, BUT I DON'T SEE WHY I SHOULD BE SCOLDED FOR ANYTHING ELSE.
I DIDN'T DO ANYTHING WRONG!!
IS THAT SO?
FINE! DO WHATEVER YOU WANT!!
I WON'T SPEAK TO YOU UNTIL YOU ADMIT YOUR MISTAKE!!

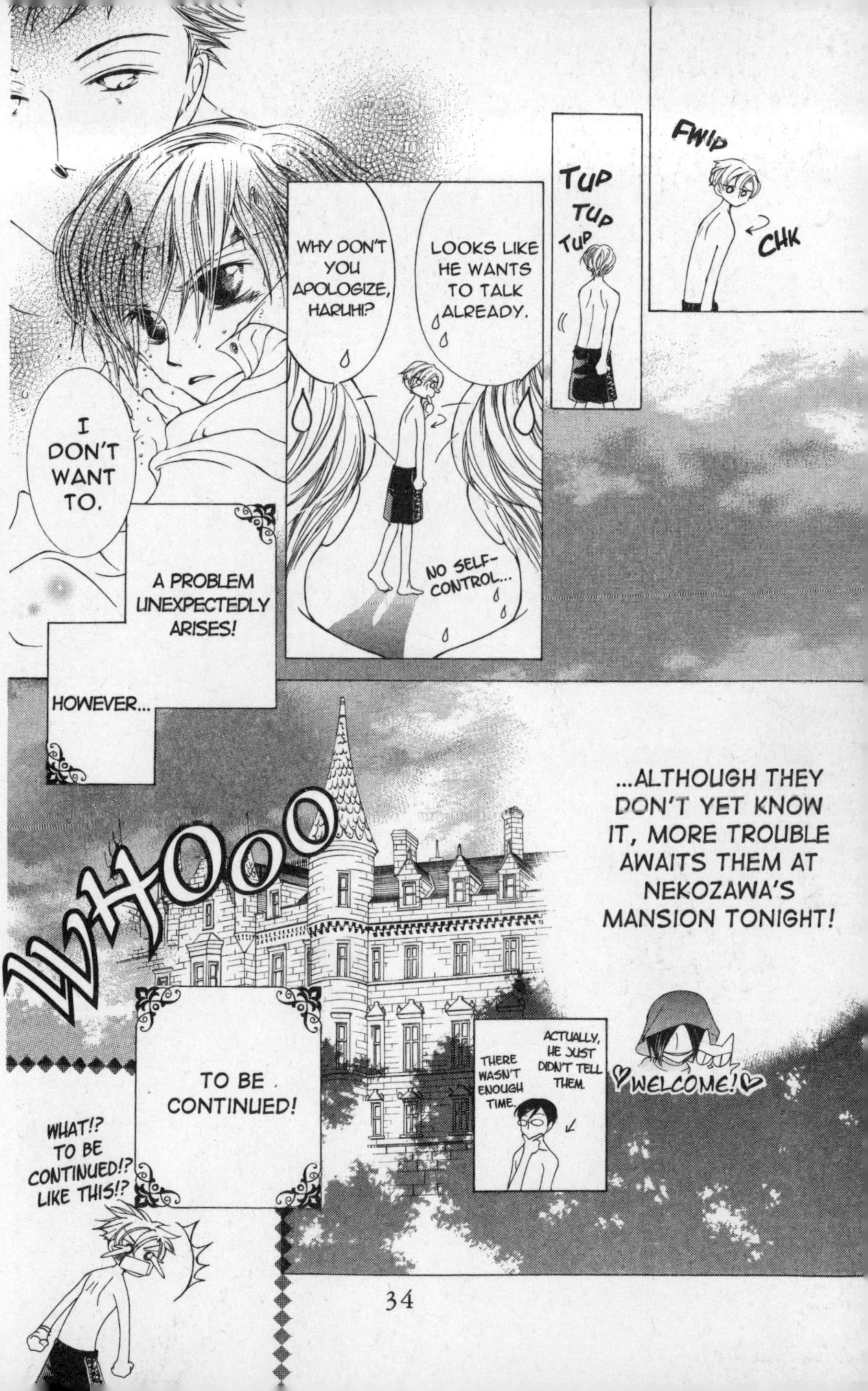
FWIP
CHK
TUP TUP TUP
LOOKS LIKE HE WANTS TO TALK ALREADY.
WHY DON'T YOU APOLOGIZE, HARUHI?
NO SELF-CONTROL...
I DON'T WANT TO.
A PROBLEM UNEXPECTEDLY ARISES!
HOWEVER...
...ALTHOUGH THEY DON'T YET KNOW IT, MORE TROUBLE AWAITS THEM AT NEKOZAWA'S MANSION TONIGHT!
WELCOME!
ACTUALLY, HE JUST DIDN'T TELL THEM.
THERE WASN'T ENOUGH TIME.
WHOOO
TO BE CONTINUED!
WHAT!? TO BE CONTINUED!? LIKE THIS!?

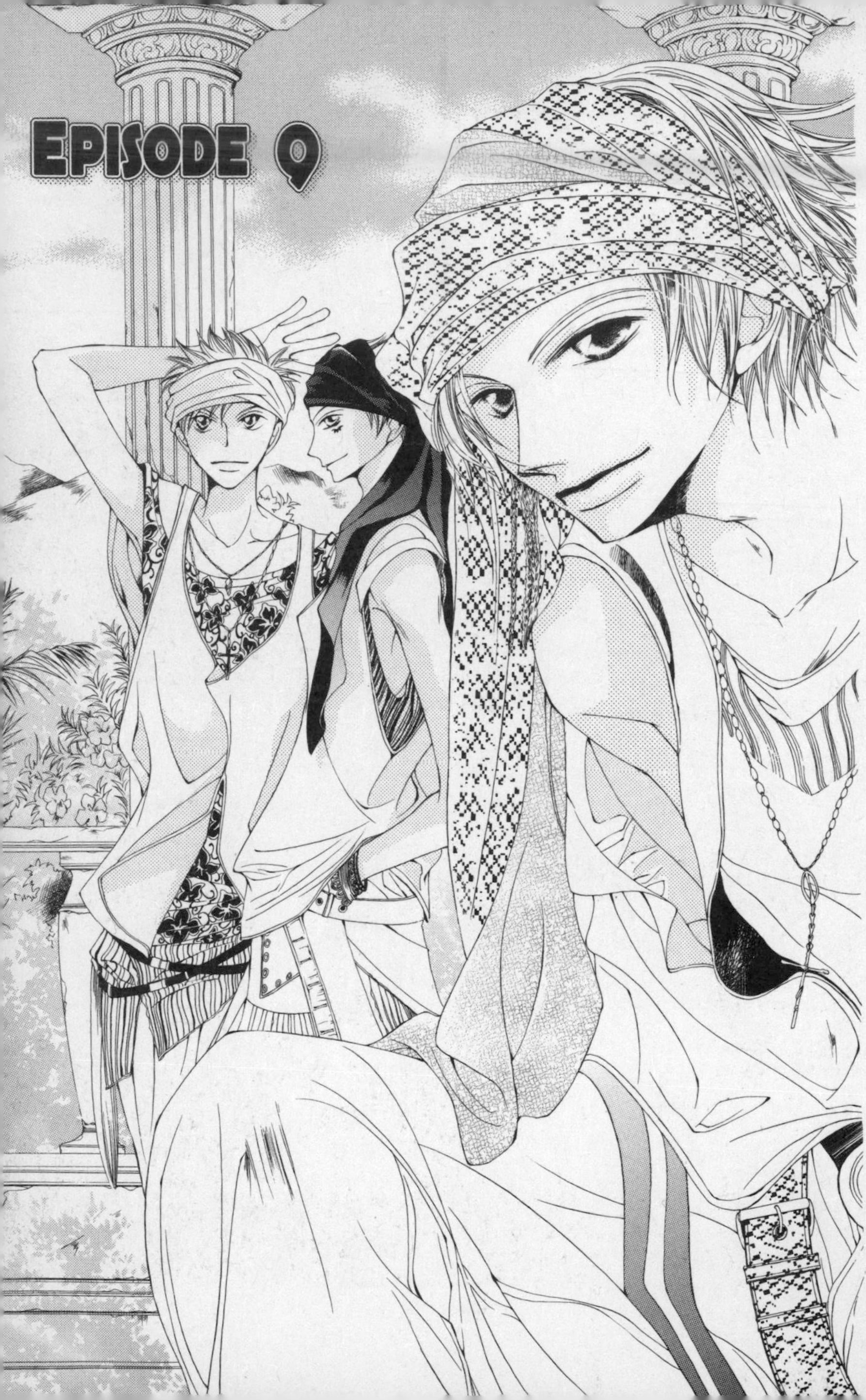
EPISODE 9

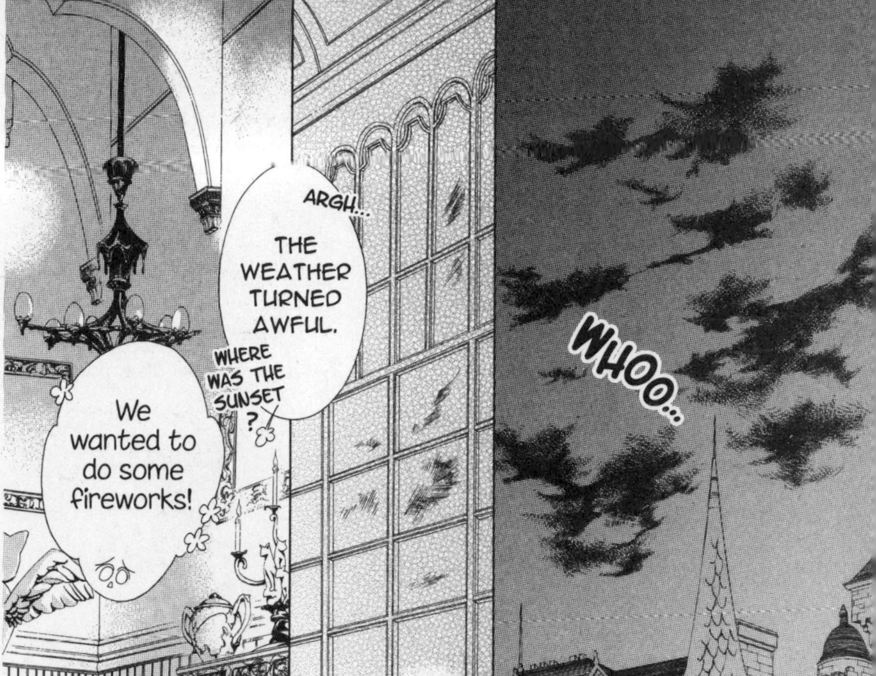
WHOO...
ARGH...
THE WEATHER TURNED AWFUL.
WHERE WAS THE SUNSET?
We wanted to do some fireworks!
I KNOW... OH, IT'S YOUR TURN, HIKARU.

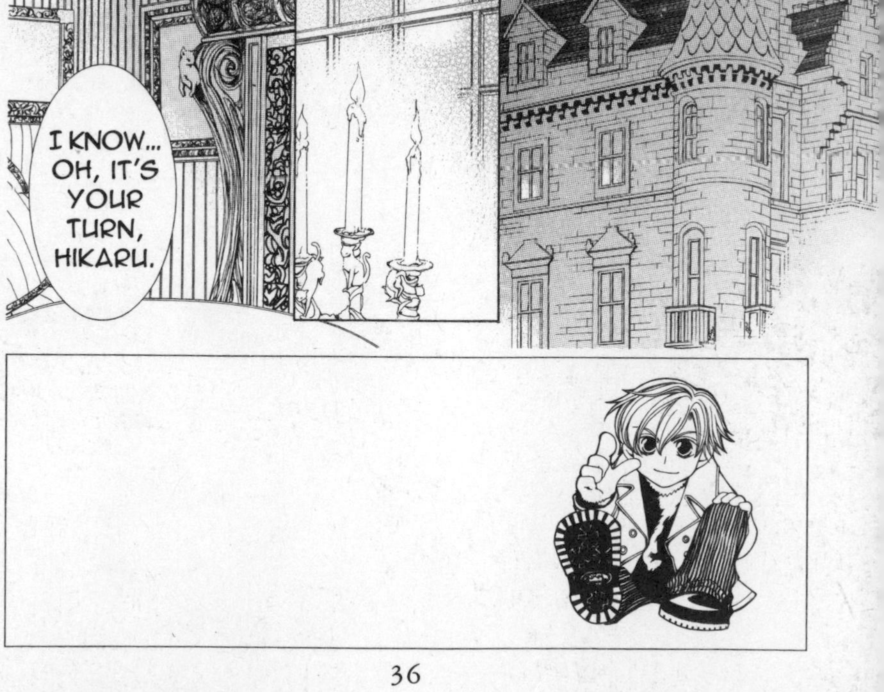

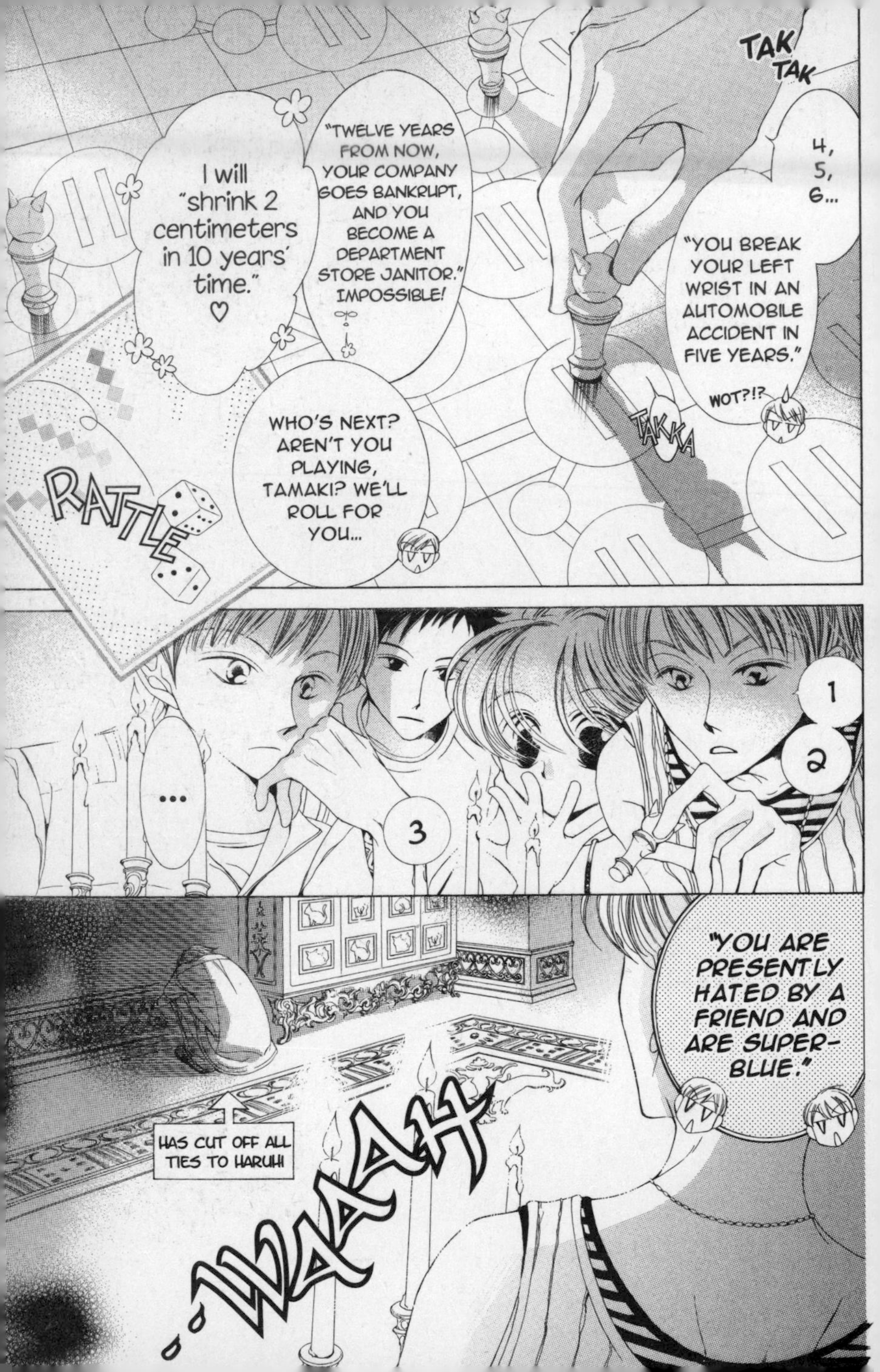
TAK TAK
4, 5, 6...
"YOU BREAK YOUR LEFT WRIST IN AN AUTOMOBILE ACCIDENT IN FIVE YEARS."
WOT?!?
TAKKA
"TWELVE YEARS FROM NOW, YOUR COMPANY GOES BANKRUPT, AND YOU BECOME A DEPARTMENT STORE JANITOR." IMPOSSIBLE!
I will "shrink 2 centimeters in 10 years' time." ♡
WHO'S NEXT? AREN'T YOU PLAYING, TAMAKI? WE'LL ROLL FOR YOU...
RATTLE
1
2
3
...
"YOU ARE PRESENTLY HATED BY A FRIEND AND ARE SUPER-BLUE."
WAAAH
HAS CUT OFF ALL TIES TO HARUHI

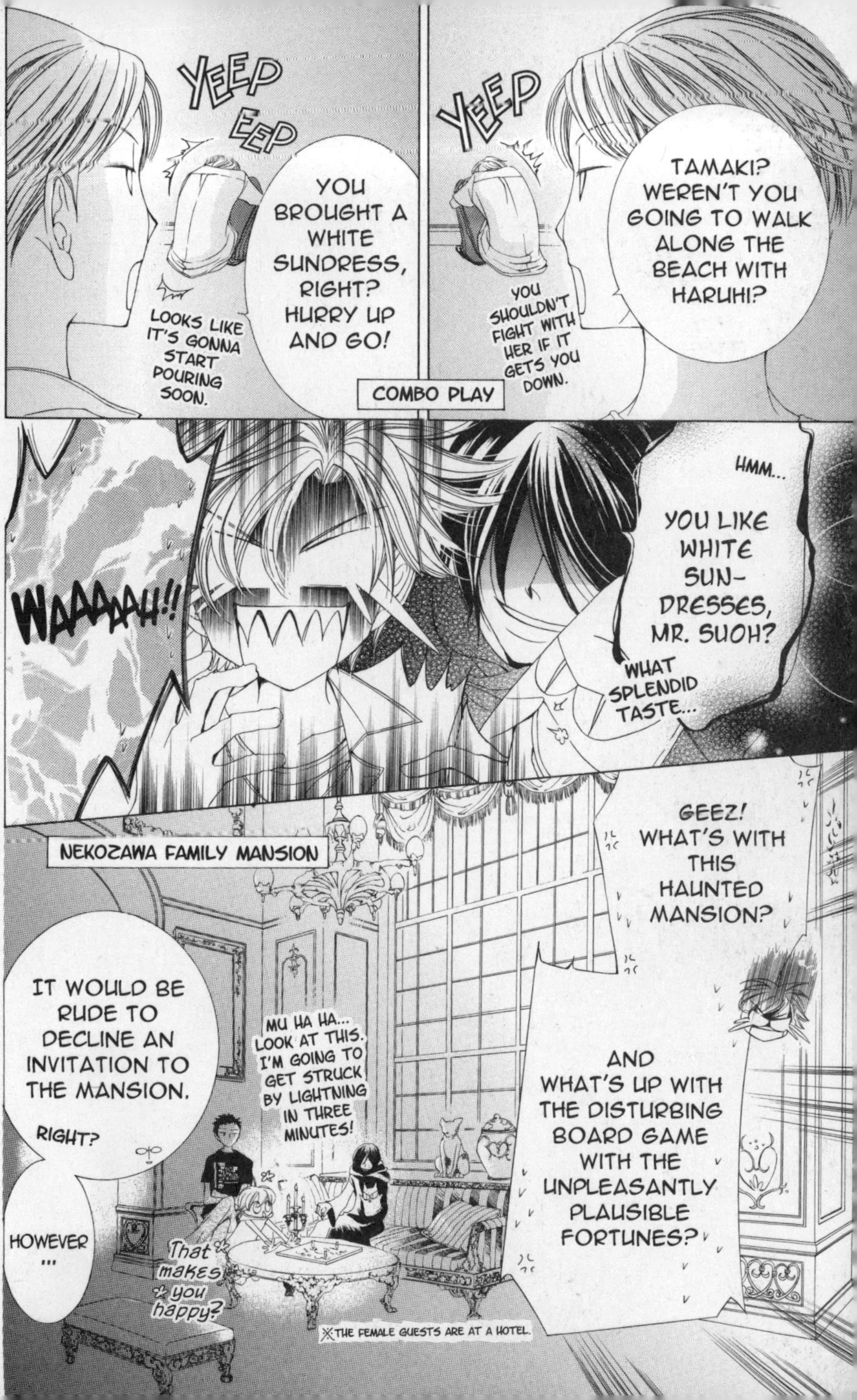
YEEP
TAMAKI? WEREN'T YOU GOING TO WALK ALONG THE BEACH WITH HARUHI?
YOU SHOULDN'T FIGHT WITH HER IF IT GETS YOU DOWN.
COMBO PLAY
YEEP EEP
YOU BROUGHT A WHITE SUNDRESS, RIGHT? HURRY UP AND GO!
LOOKS LIKE IT'S GONNA START POURING SOON.
HMM...
YOU LIKE WHITE SUN-DRESSES, MR. SUOH?
WHAT SPLENDID TASTE...
WAAAAAH!!
NEKOZAWA FAMILY MANSION
GEEZ! WHAT'S WITH THIS HAUNTED MANSION?
AND WHAT'S UP WITH THE DISTURBING BOARD GAME WITH THE UNPLEASANTLY PLAUSIBLE FORTUNES?
MU HA HA... LOOK AT THIS. I'M GOING TO GET STRUCK BY LIGHTNING IN THREE MINUTES!
That makes you happy?
IT WOULD BE RUDE TO DECLINE AN INVITATION TO THE MANSION.
RIGHT?
HOWEVER...
※THE FEMALE GUESTS ARE AT A HOTEL.

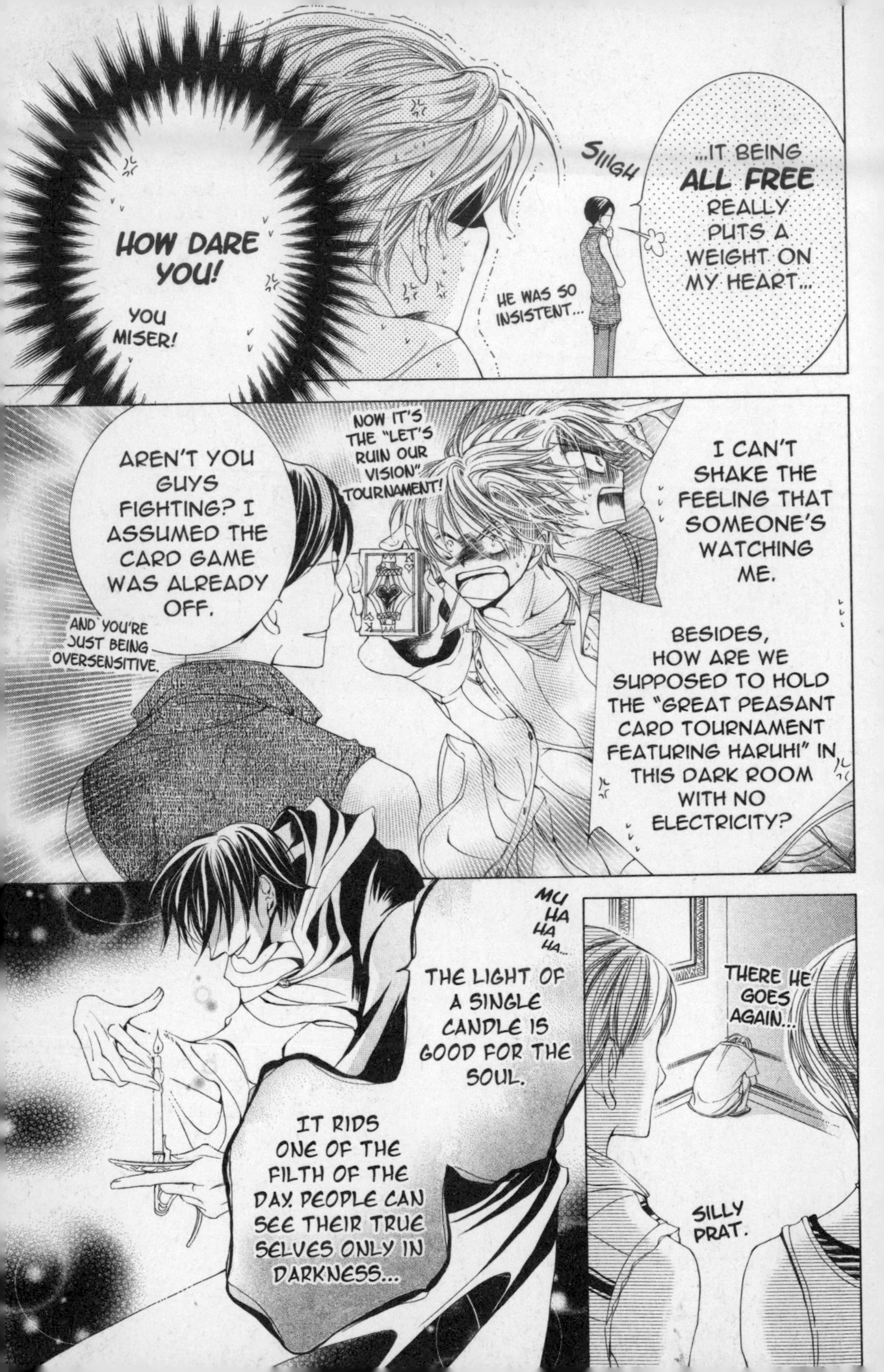
SIIGH
...IT BEING **ALL FREE** REALLY PUTS A WEIGHT ON MY HEART...
HE WAS SO INSISTENT...
HOW DARE YOU!
YOU MISER!
I CAN'T SHAKE THE FEELING THAT SOMEONE'S WATCHING ME.
BESIDES, HOW ARE WE SUPPOSED TO HOLD THE "GREAT PEASANT CARD TOURNAMENT FEATURING HARUHI" IN THIS DARK ROOM WITH NO ELECTRICITY?
NOW IT'S THE "LET'S RUIN OUR VISION" TOURNAMENT!
AREN'T YOU GUYS FIGHTING? I ASSUMED THE CARD GAME WAS ALREADY OFF.
AND YOU'RE JUST BEING OVERSENSITIVE.
THERE HE GOES AGAIN...
SILLY PRAT.
MU HA HA HA...
THE LIGHT OF A SINGLE CANDLE IS GOOD FOR THE SOUL.
IT RIDS ONE OF THE FILTH OF THE DAY. PEOPLE CAN SEE THEIR TRUE SELVES ONLY IN DARKNESS...

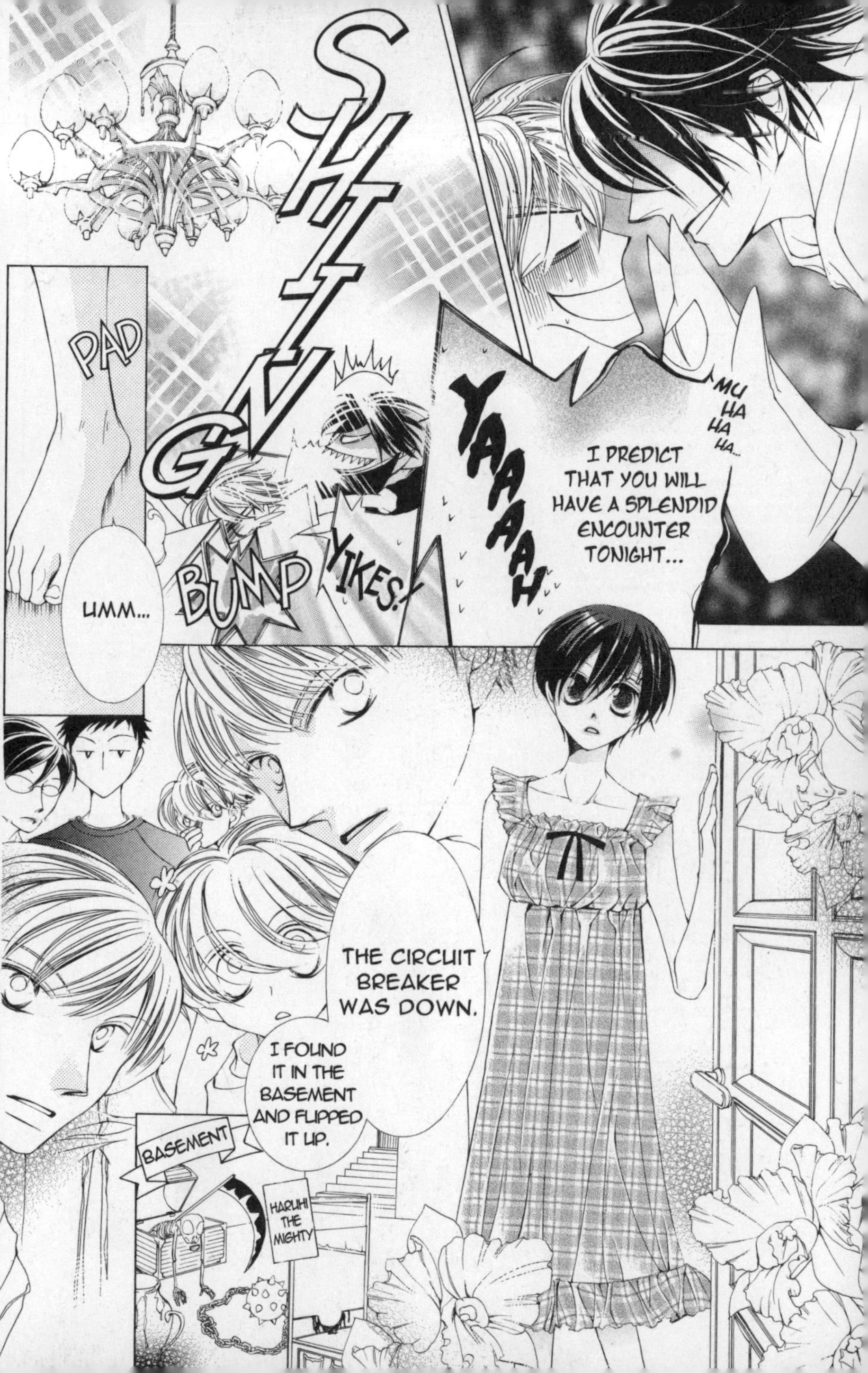
MU HA HA HA...
I PREDICT THAT YOU WILL HAVE A SPLENDID ENCOUNTER TONIGHT...
YAAAAAH
SHIIING
YIKES!
BUMP
PAD
UMM...
THE CIRCUIT BREAKER WAS DOWN.
I FOUND IT IN THE BASEMENT AND FLIPPED IT UP.
BASEMENT
HARUHI THE MIGHTY

HARUHI... ARE THOSE CLOTHES... YOURS?

IT'S NOT VERY PRACTICAL!

UH...

YEAH. DAD MUST'VE REPACKED MY LUGGAGE.

HE WANTS TO MAKE ME WEAR THINGS LIKE THIS. WE'RE ALWAYS BROKE.

BRAND NAME

OH...

GOOD JOB, HARUHI'S DAD!!

LEAVE IT TO ME!

HO HO HO!

WOO

2

✿ HOW HOST CLUB IS CREATED (SUBTITLE: A MONTH FOR HATORI) ✿

① I MEET WITH THE EDITORS TO PLAN WHAT THE CONTENT WILL BE. SOMETIMES I GO TO AN EDITOR'S APARTMENT ✚ AND GET TREATED TO DINNER, AND SOMETIMES IT'S ALL DONE OVER THE PHONE.

YAMASHI-!!

SOUNDS GREAT. LET'S GO WITH THAT!!

HOW ABOUT THIS FOR THE NEXT STORY?

LATELY, WE USUALLY TRY TO DECIDE ON THE NEXT STORYLINE WHILE DRAWING OUT THE CURRENT ONE.

② CREATING THE PLOT

MAC

TAK TAK

I OFTEN TYPE OUT THE STORYLINE ON THE COMPUTER. COMPUTERS ARE MYSTERIOUS. EVEN IF MY MIND IS A BLANK, MY HANDS MOVE ON THEIR OWN TO COME UP WITH A STORY. THE COMPUTER PERFORMED WELL WHEN I HAD TO COME UP WITH MATERIAL FOR THE DRAMA CD, ESPECIALLY THE GOOD-NIGHT MESSAGES.

TO BE CONTINUED...

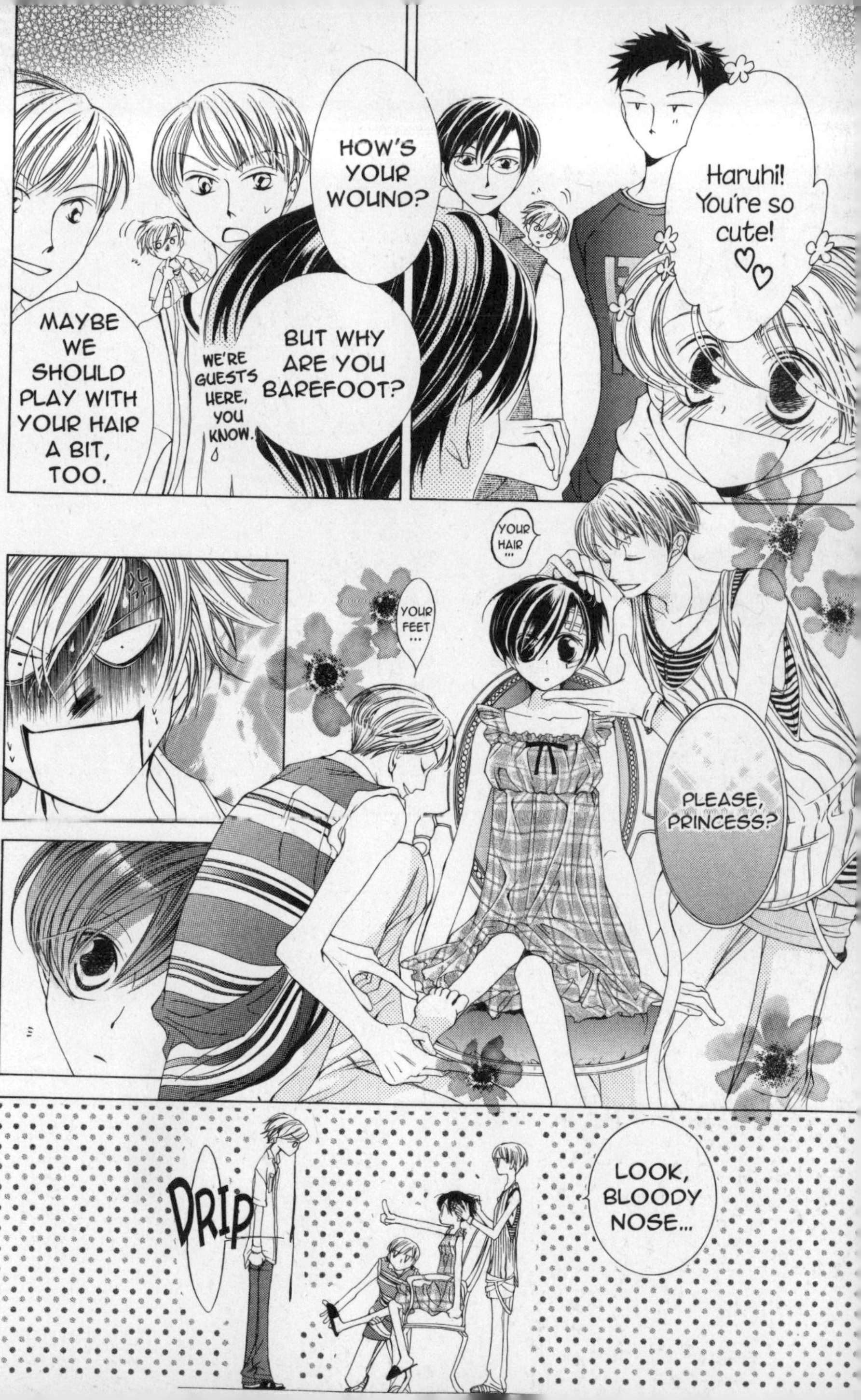
Haruhi! You're so cute! ♡♡
HOW'S YOUR WOUND?
BUT WHY ARE YOU BAREFOOT?
WE'RE GUESTS HERE, YOU KNOW.
MAYBE WE SHOULD PLAY WITH YOUR HAIR A BIT, TOO.
YOUR HAIR...
YOUR FEET...
PLEASE, PRINCESS?
LOOK, BLOODY NOSE...
DRIP

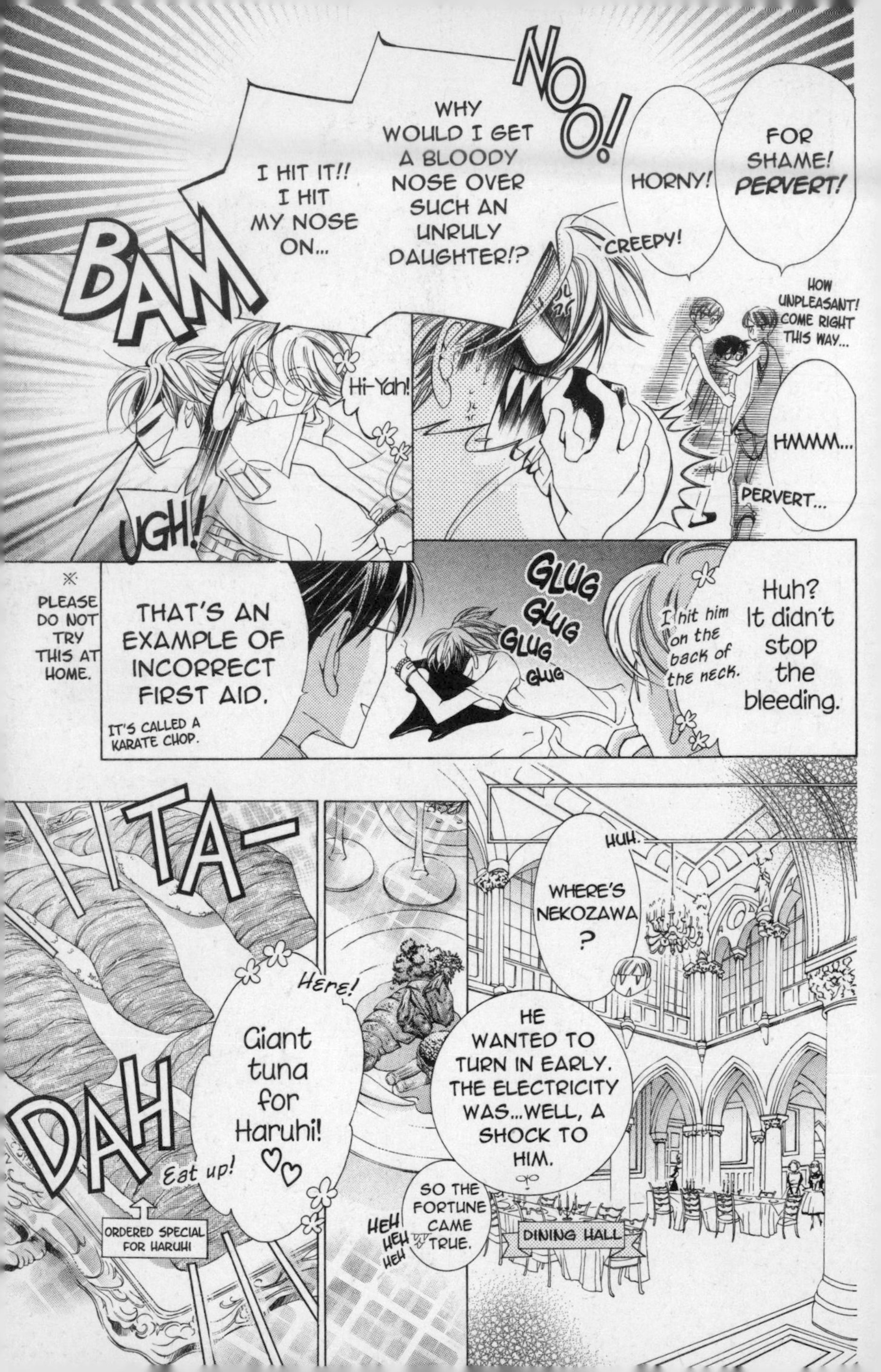
FOR SHAME! PERVERT!
HORNY!
CREEPY!
NOO!
WHY WOULD I GET A BLOODY NOSE OVER SUCH AN UNRULY DAUGHTER!?
I HIT IT!! I HIT MY NOSE ON...
HOW UNPLEASANT! COME RIGHT THIS WAY...
HMMM...
PERVERT...
BAM
Hi-Yah!
UGH!
Huh? It didn't stop the bleeding.
I hit him on the back of the neck.
GLUG GLUG GLUG GLUG
THAT'S AN EXAMPLE OF INCORRECT FIRST AID.
IT'S CALLED A KARATE CHOP.
※ PLEASE DO NOT TRY THIS AT HOME.
HUH.
WHERE'S NEKOZAWA?
HE WANTED TO TURN IN EARLY. THE ELECTRICITY WAS...WELL, A SHOCK TO HIM.
SO THE FORTUNE CAME TRUE.
HEH HEH HEH
DINING HALL
Here!
Giant tuna for Haruhi! ♡♡
Eat up!
TA-DAH
ORDERED SPECIAL FOR HARUHI

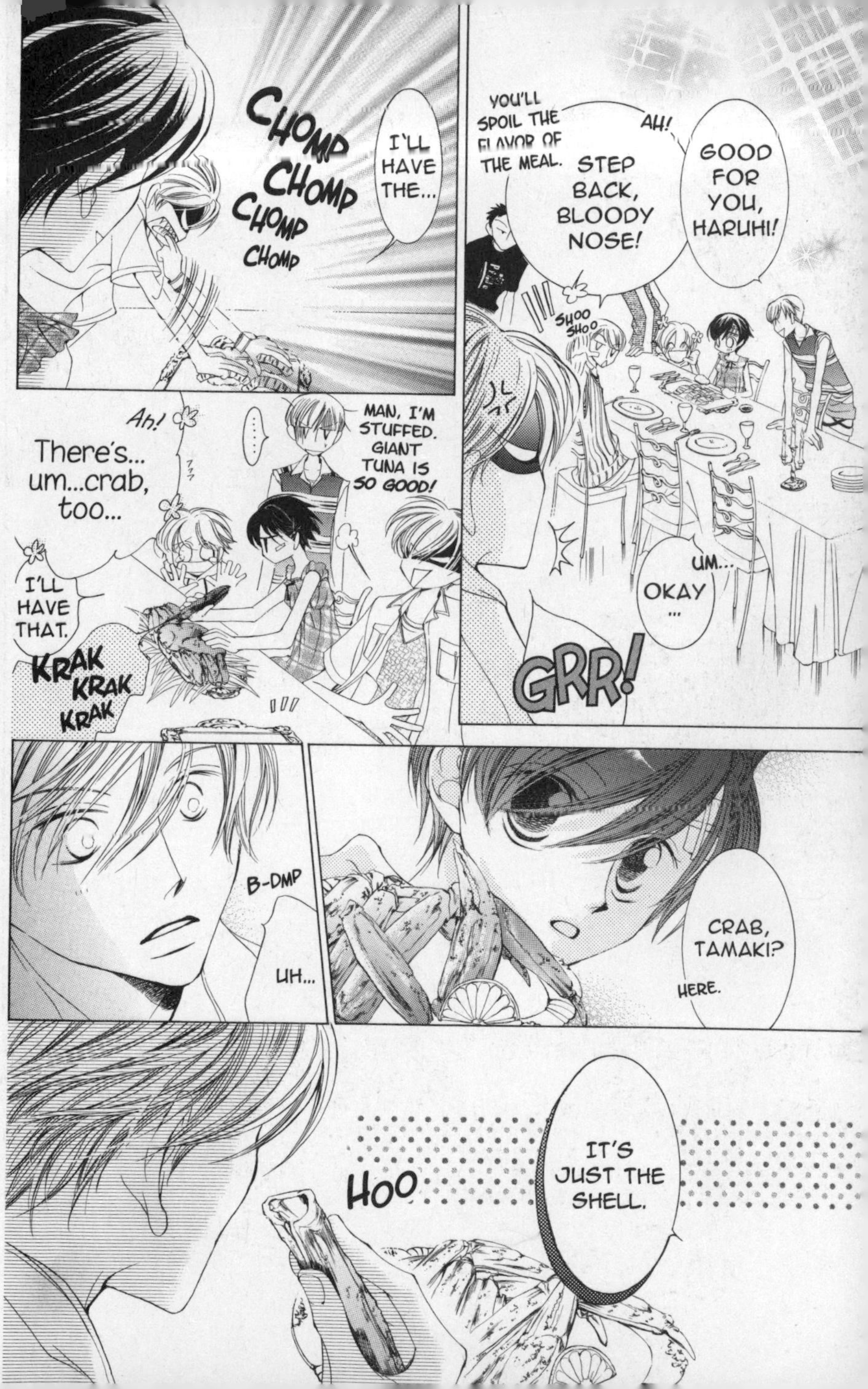
GOOD FOR YOU, HARUHI!
AH!
STEP BACK, BLOODY NOSE!
YOU'LL SPOIL THE FLAVOR OF THE MEAL.
SHOO SHOO
UM... OKAY...
GRR!
I'LL HAVE THE...
CHOMP CHOMP CHOMP CHOMP
MAN, I'M STUFFED. GIANT TUNA IS SO GOOD!
...
Ah!
There's... um...crab, too...
I'LL HAVE THAT.
KRAK KRAK KRAK
CRAB, TAMAKI?
HERE.
B-DMP
UH...
IT'S JUST THE SHELL.
HOO

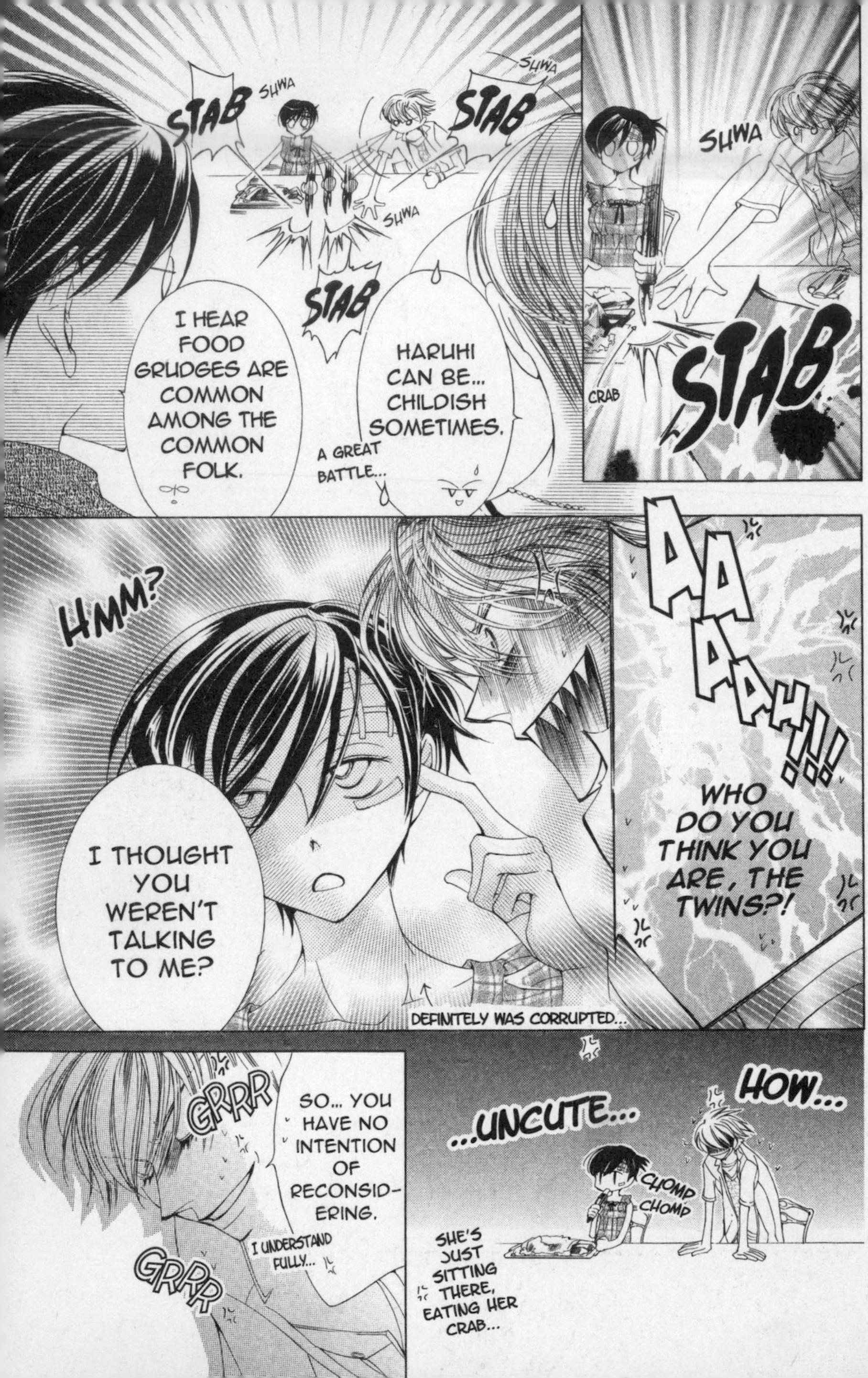
SHWA
STAB
CRAB
SHWA
STAB
STAB
SHWA
SHWA
STAB
HARUHI CAN BE... CHILDISH SOMETIMES.
I HEAR FOOD GRUDGES ARE COMMON AMONG THE COMMON FOLK.
A GREAT BATTLE...
AAAAH!!!
WHO DO YOU THINK YOU ARE, THE TWINS?!
HMM?
I THOUGHT YOU WEREN'T TALKING TO ME?
DEFINITELY WAS CORRUPTED...
HOW...
...UNCUTE...
CHOMP CHOMP
SHE'S JUST SITTING THERE, EATING HER CRAB...
GRRR
SO... YOU HAVE NO INTENTION OF RECONSID-ERING.
I UNDERSTAND FULLY...
GRRR

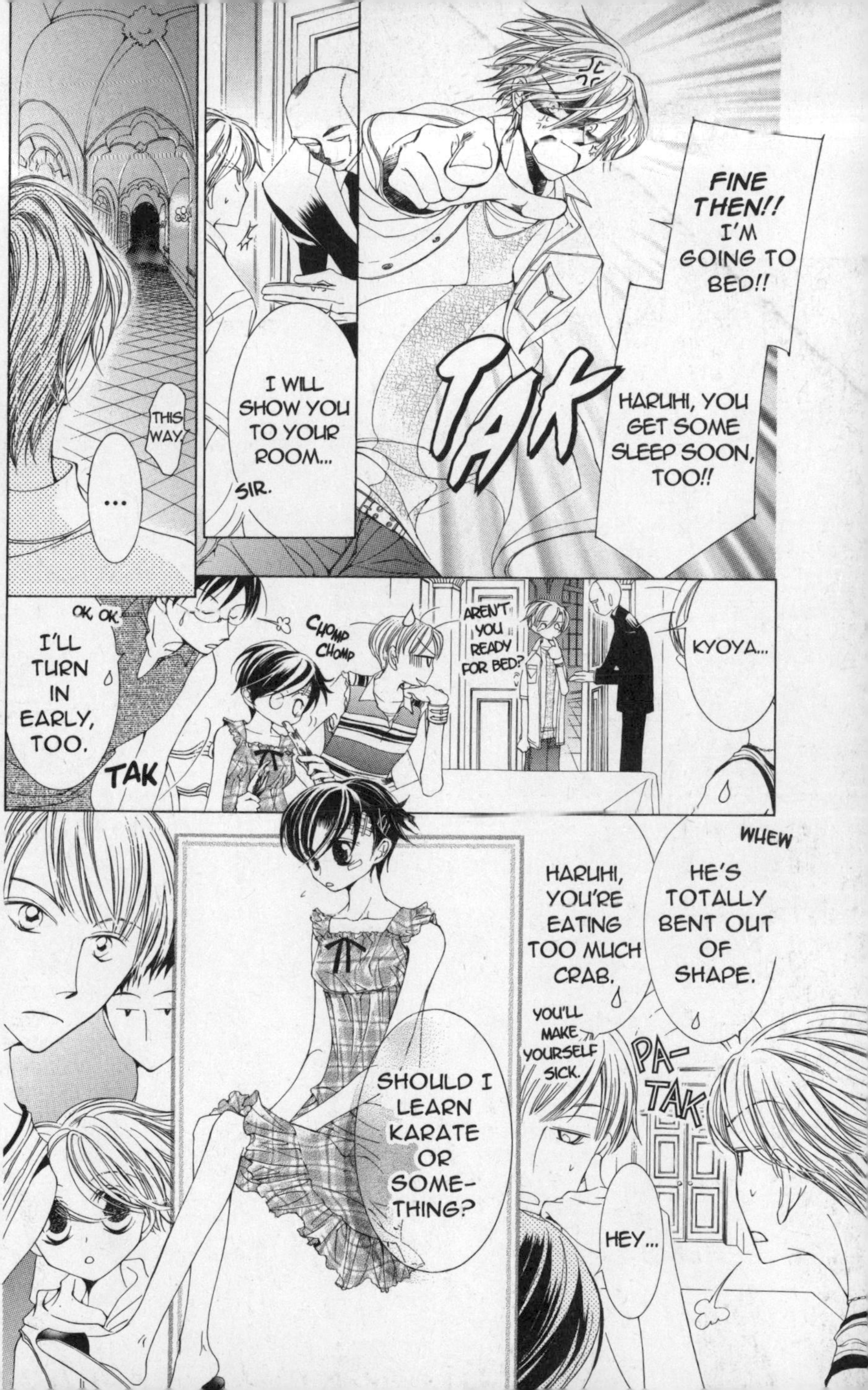
FINE THEN!! I'M GOING TO BED!!
TAK
HARUHI, YOU GET SOME SLEEP SOON, TOO!!
I WILL SHOW YOU TO YOUR ROOM...
SIR.
THIS WAY.
...
KYOYA...
AREN'T YOU READY FOR BED?
CHOMP CHOMP
OK, OK
I'LL TURN IN EARLY, TOO.
TAK
WHEW
HE'S TOTALLY BENT OUT OF SHAPE.
HARUHI, YOU'RE EATING TOO MUCH CRAB.
YOU'LL MAKE YOURSELF SICK.
PA-TAK
HEY...
SHOULD I LEARN KARATE OR SOME-THING?

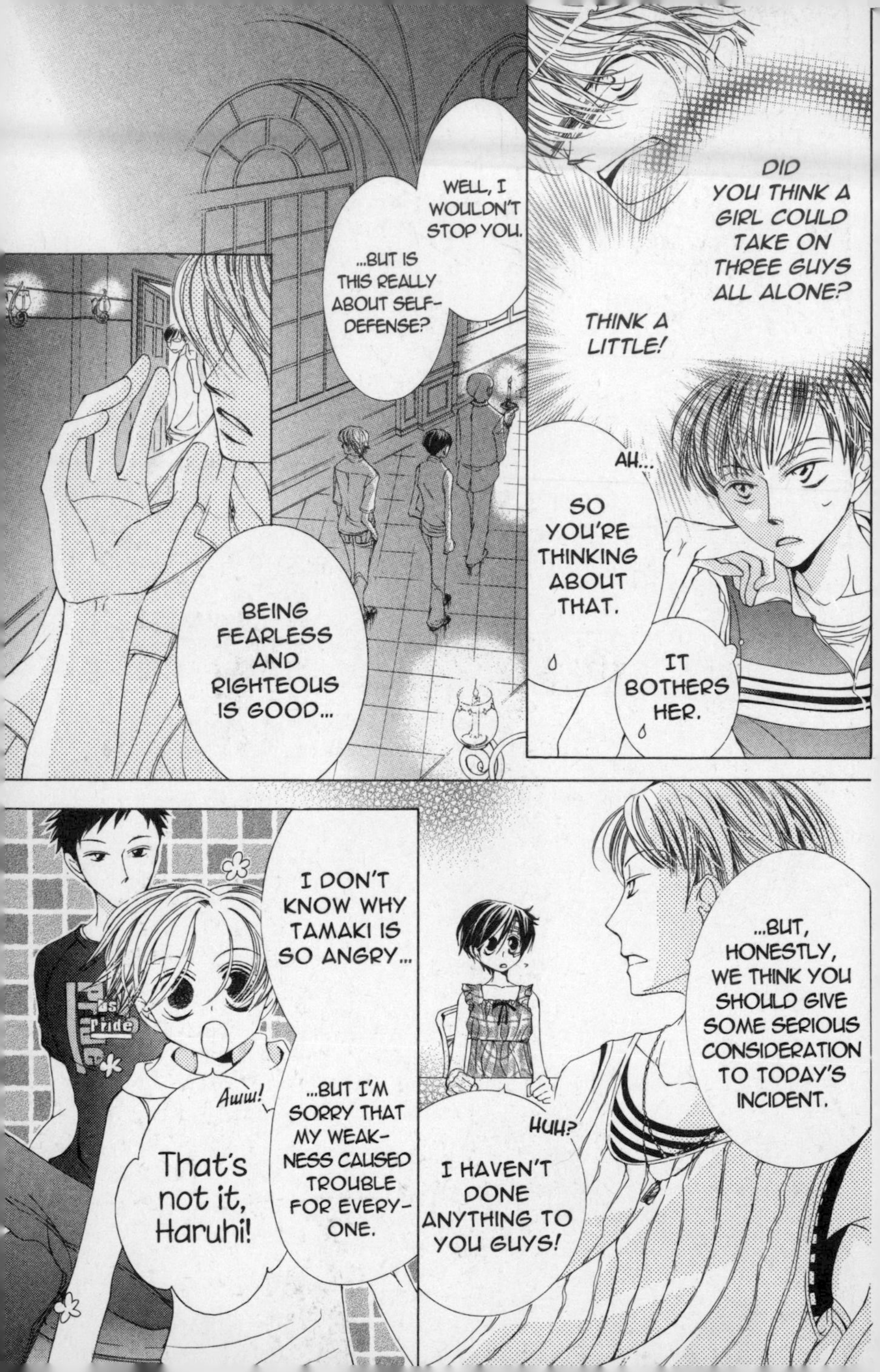
DID YOU THINK A GIRL COULD TAKE ON THREE GUYS ALL ALONE?
THINK A LITTLE!
AH...
SO YOU'RE THINKING ABOUT THAT.
IT BOTHERS HER.
WELL, I WOULDN'T STOP YOU.
...BUT IS THIS REALLY ABOUT SELF-DEFENSE?
BEING FEARLESS AND RIGHTEOUS IS GOOD...
...BUT, HONESTLY, WE THINK YOU SHOULD GIVE SOME SERIOUS CONSIDERATION TO TODAY'S INCIDENT.
HUH?
I HAVEN'T DONE ANYTHING TO YOU GUYS!
I DON'T KNOW WHY TAMAKI IS SO ANGRY...
...BUT I'M SORRY THAT MY WEAK-NESS CAUSED TROUBLE FOR EVERY-ONE.
Awww!
That's not it, Haruhi!

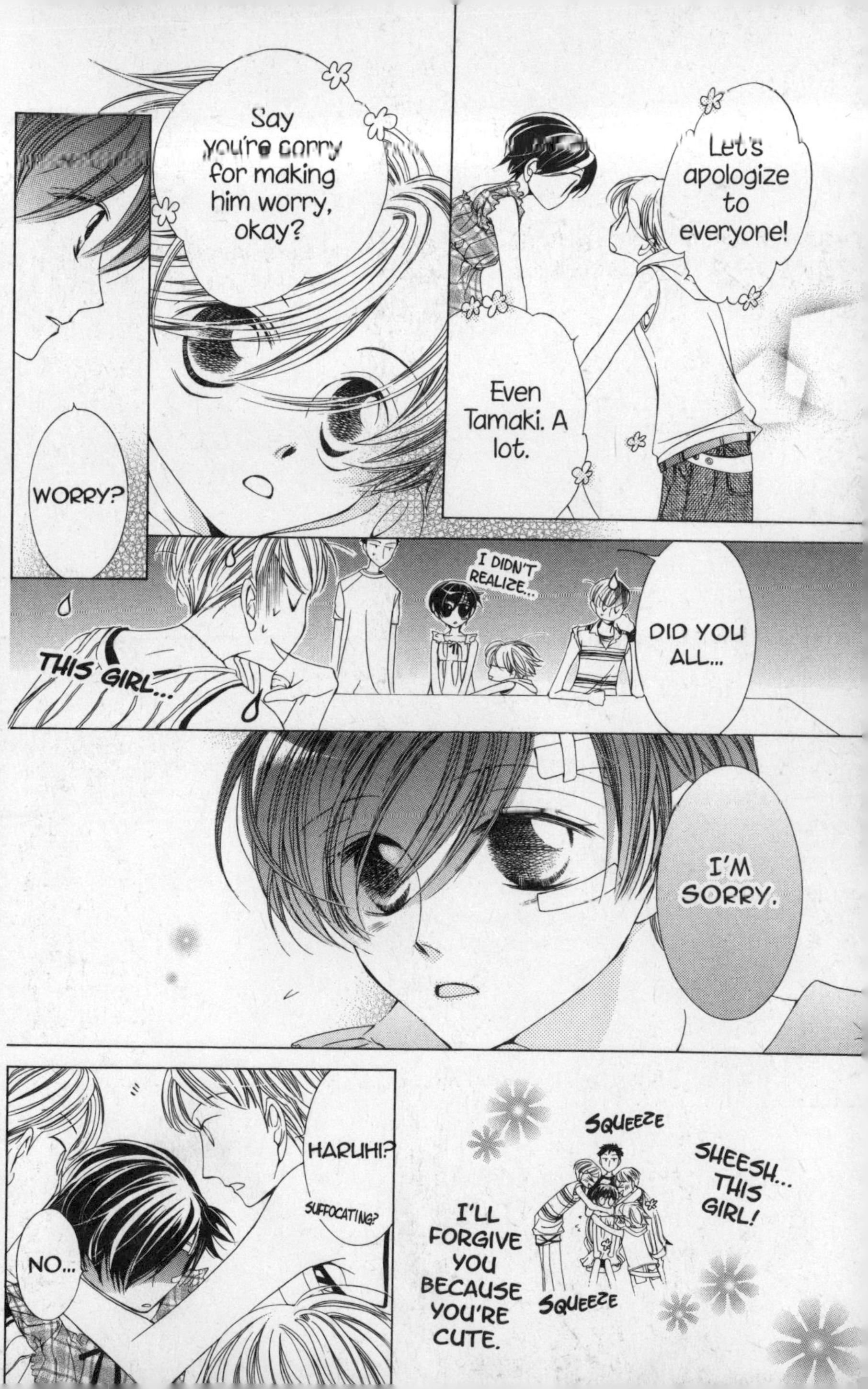
Let's apologize to everyone!
Even Tamaki. A lot.
Say you're sorry for making him worry, okay?
WORRY?
DID YOU ALL...
I DIDN'T REALIZE...
THIS GIRL...
I'M SORRY.
SHEESH... THIS GIRL!
SQUEEZE
I'LL FORGIVE YOU BECAUSE YOU'RE CUTE.
SQUEEZE
HARUHI?
SUFFOCATING?
NO...

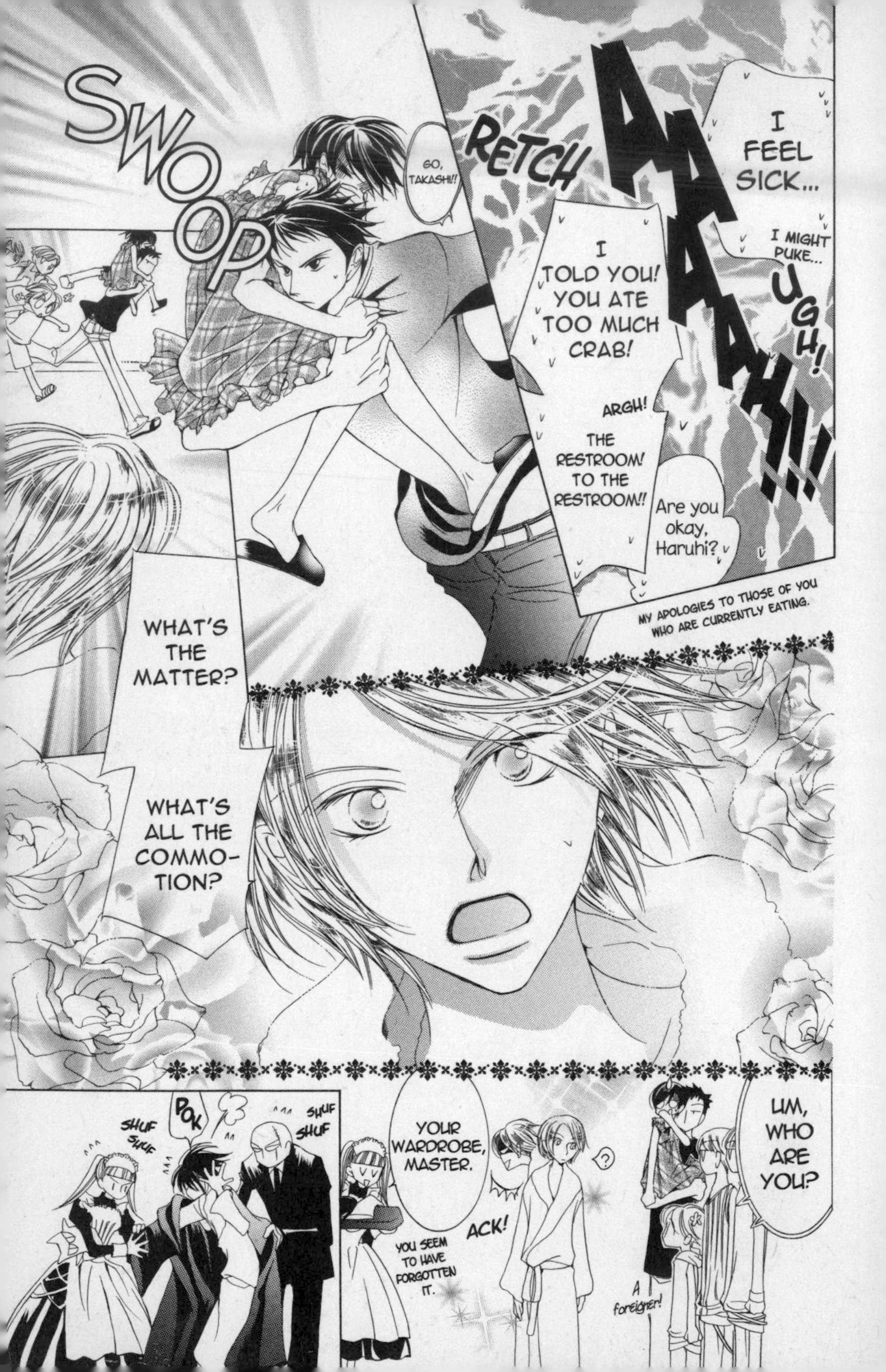
I FEEL SICK...
I MIGHT PUKE...
UGH!
AAAAAH!!!
RETCH
I TOLD YOU! YOU ATE TOO MUCH CRAB!
ARGH!
THE RESTROOM! TO THE RESTROOM!!
Are you okay, Haruhi?
MY APOLOGIES TO THOSE OF YOU WHO ARE CURRENTLY EATING.
GO, TAKASHI!!
SWOOP
WHAT'S THE MATTER?
WHAT'S ALL THE COMMOTION?
UM, WHO ARE YOU?
A foreigner!
ACK!
YOUR WARDROBE, MASTER.
YOU SEEM TO HAVE FORGOTTEN IT.
SHUF SHUF
POK
SHUF SHUF

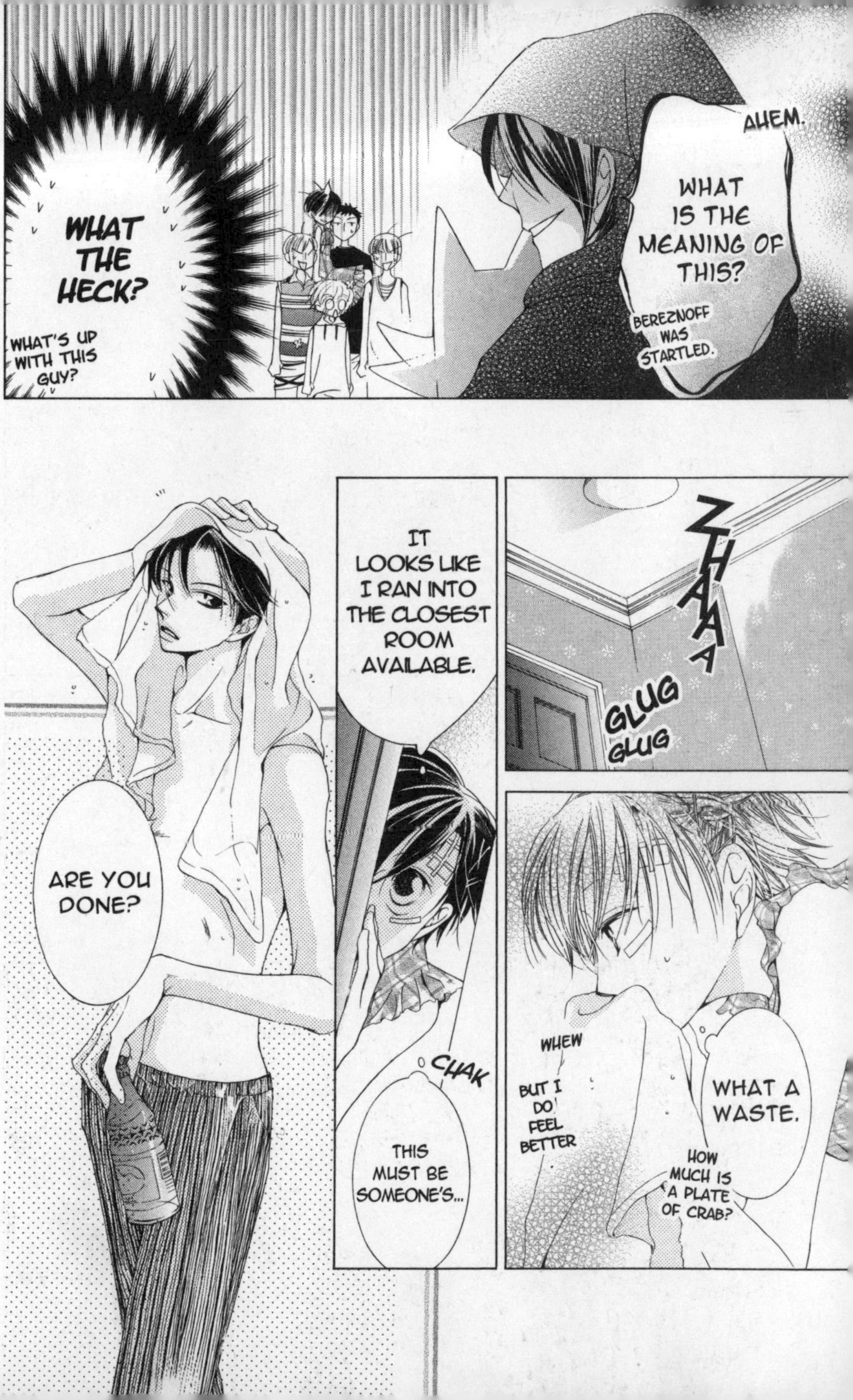
AHEM.
WHAT IS THE MEANING OF THIS?
BEREZNOFF WAS STARTLED.
WHAT THE HECK?
WHAT'S UP WITH THIS GUY?
ZHAAAA
GLUG GLUG
WHAT A WASTE.
HOW MUCH IS A PLATE OF CRAB?
WHEW
BUT I DO FEEL BETTER
IT LOOKS LIKE I RAN INTO THE CLOSEST ROOM AVAILABLE.
CHAK
THIS MUST BE SOMEONE'S...
ARE YOU DONE?

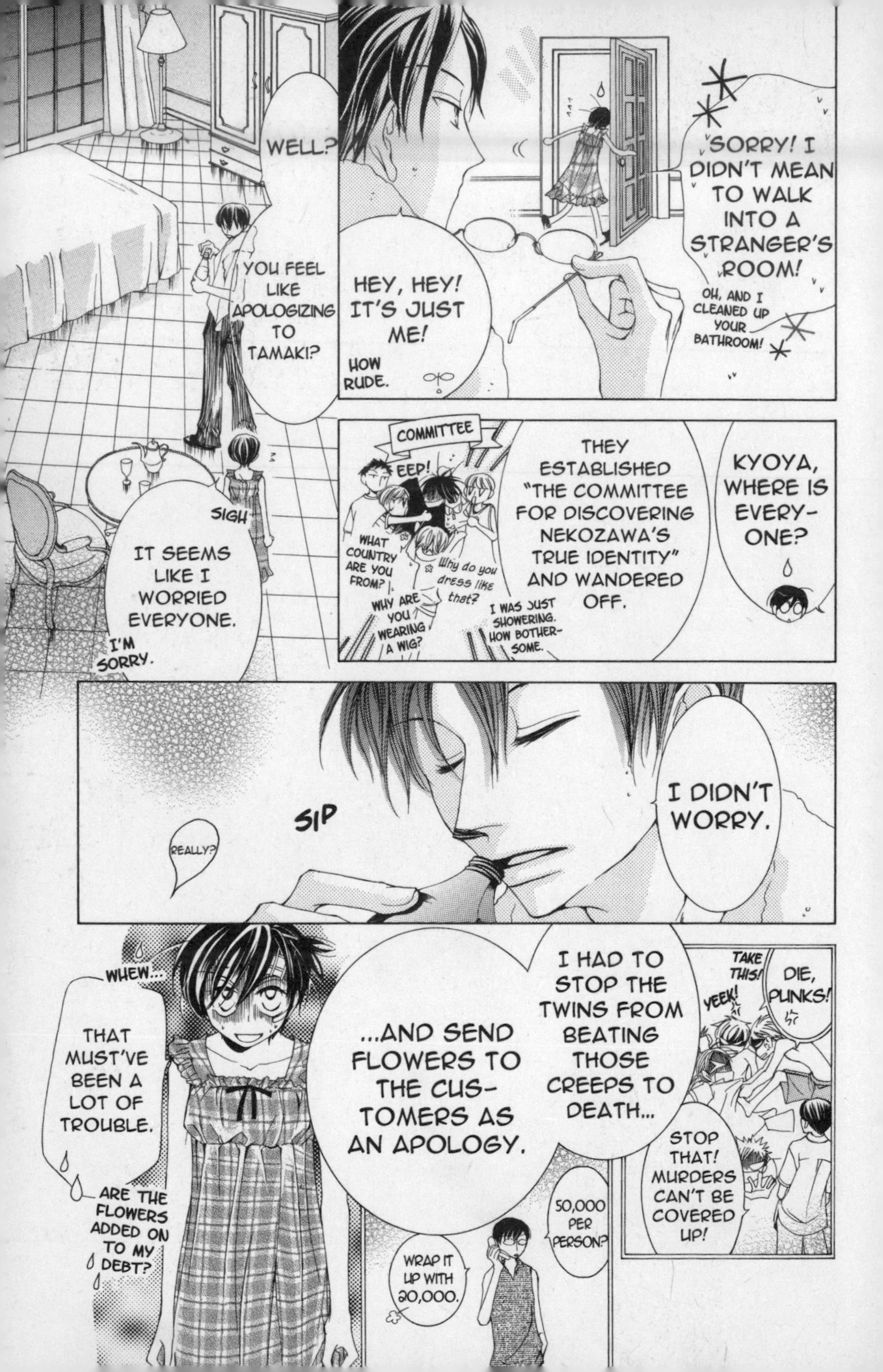
SORRY! I DIDN'T MEAN TO WALK INTO A STRANGER'S ROOM!
OH, AND I CLEANED UP YOUR BATHROOM!
HEY, HEY! IT'S JUST ME!
HOW RUDE.
KYOYA, WHERE IS EVERY-ONE?
THEY ESTABLISHED "THE COMMITTEE FOR DISCOVERING NEKOZAWA'S TRUE IDENTITY" AND WANDERED OFF.
COMMITTEE
EEP!
WHAT COUNTRY ARE YOU FROM?
Why do you dress like that?
WHY ARE YOU WEARING A WIG?
I WAS JUST SHOWERING. HOW BOTHER-SOME.
WELL?
YOU FEEL LIKE APOLOGIZING TO TAMAKI?
SIGH
IT SEEMS LIKE I WORRIED EVERYONE.
I'M SORRY.
I DIDN'T WORRY.
SIP
REALLY?
I HAD TO STOP THE TWINS FROM BEATING THOSE CREEPS TO DEATH...
TAKE THIS!
DIE, PUNKS!
YEEK!
STOP THAT! MURDERS CAN'T BE COVERED UP!
...AND SEND FLOWERS TO THE CUS-TOMERS AS AN APOLOGY.
50,000 PER PERSON?
WRAP IT UP WITH 20,000.
WHEW...
THAT MUST'VE BEEN A LOT OF TROUBLE.
ARE THE FLOWERS ADDED ON TO MY DEBT?

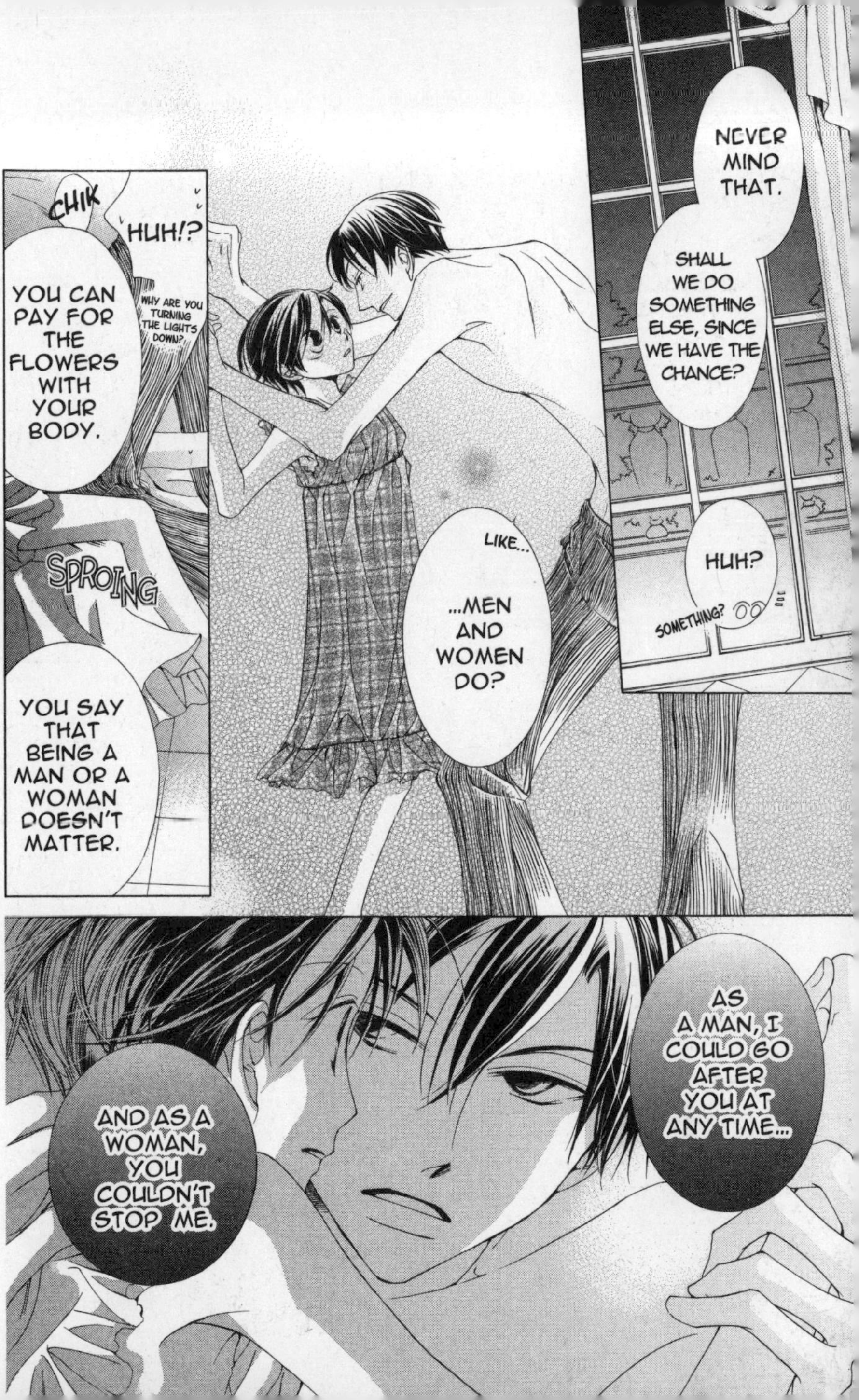
NEVER MIND THAT.
SHALL WE DO SOMETHING ELSE, SINCE WE HAVE THE CHANCE?
HUH?
SOMETHING?
LIKE...
...MEN AND WOMEN DO?
CHIK
HUH!?
WHY ARE YOU TURNING THE LIGHTS DOWN?
YOU CAN PAY FOR THE FLOWERS WITH YOUR BODY.
SPROING
YOU SAY THAT BEING A MAN OR A WOMAN DOESN'T MATTER.
AS A MAN, I COULD GO AFTER YOU AT ANY TIME...
AND AS A WOMAN, YOU COULDN'T STOP ME.

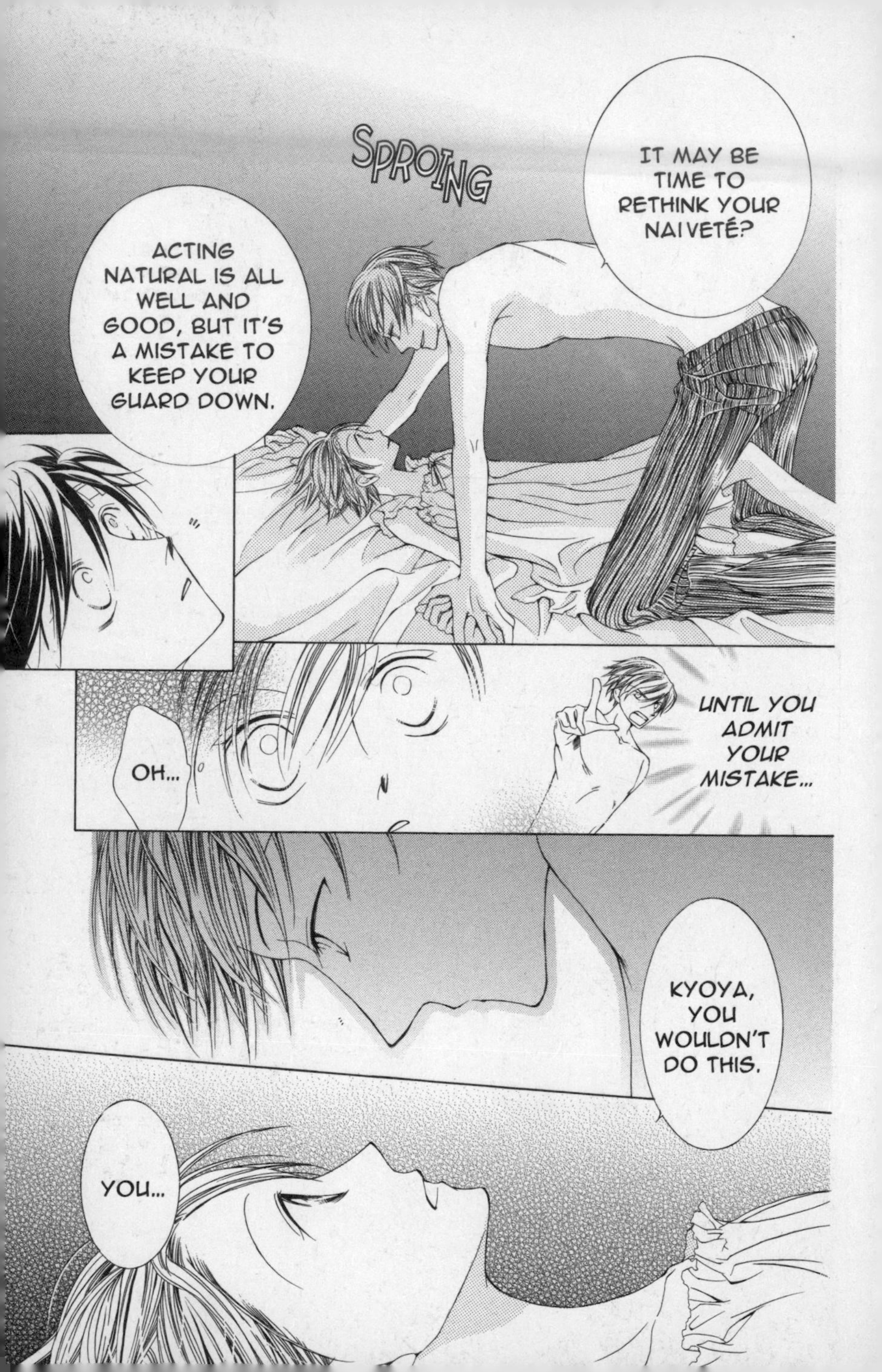
IT MAY BE TIME TO RETHINK YOUR NAIVETÉ?
SPROING
ACTING NATURAL IS ALL WELL AND GOOD, BUT IT'S A MISTAKE TO KEEP YOUR GUARD DOWN.
UNTIL YOU ADMIT YOUR MISTAKE...
OH...
KYOYA, YOU WOULDN'T DO THIS.
YOU...

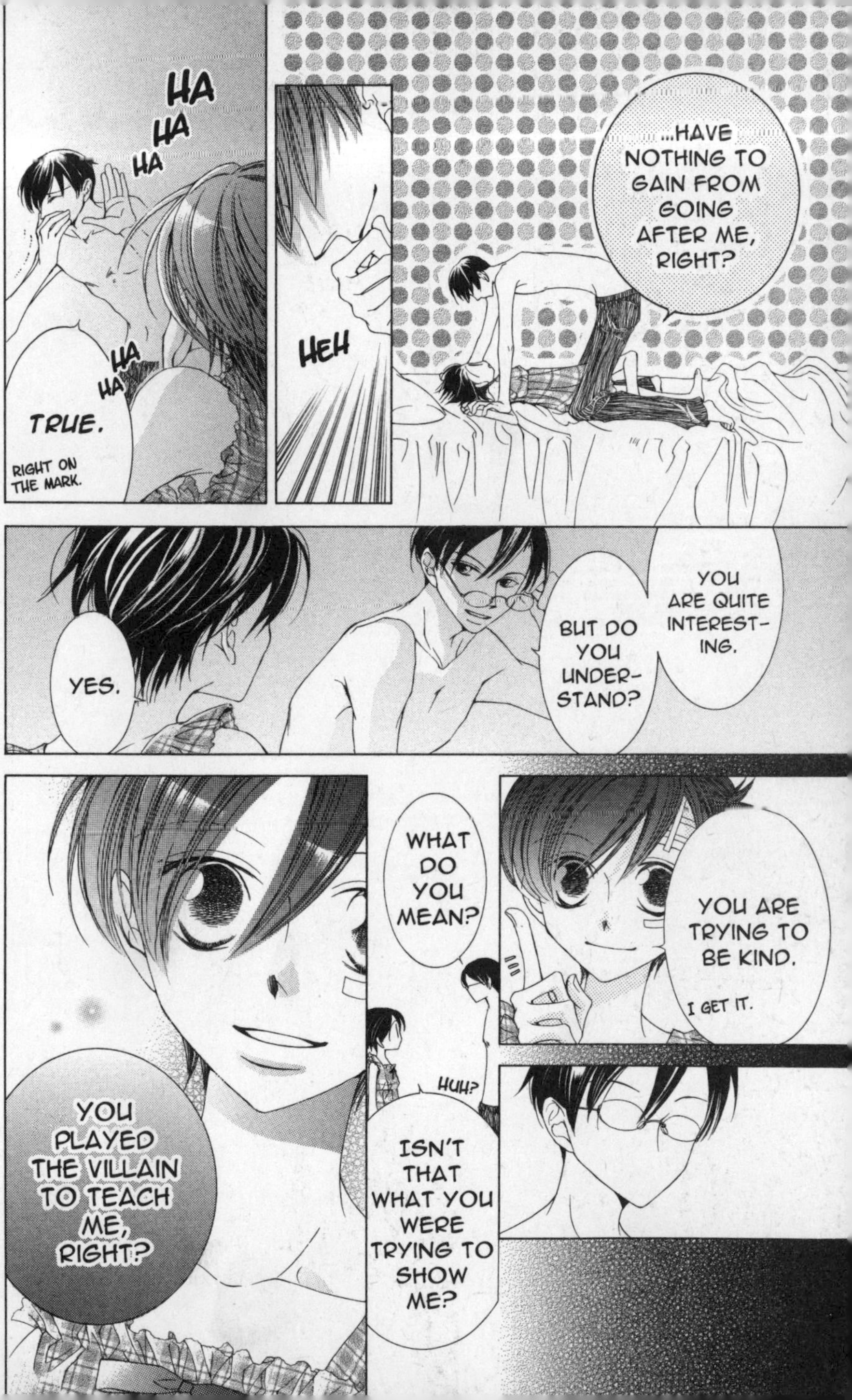
...HAVE NOTHING TO GAIN FROM GOING AFTER ME, RIGHT?
HEH
HA
HA
HA
HA
HA
TRUE.
RIGHT ON THE MARK.
YOU ARE QUITE INTEREST-ING.
BUT DO YOU UNDER-STAND?
YES.
YOU ARE TRYING TO BE KIND.
I GET IT.
WHAT DO YOU MEAN?
HUH?
ISN'T THAT WHAT YOU WERE TRYING TO SHOW ME?
YOU PLAYED THE VILLAIN TO TEACH ME, RIGHT?

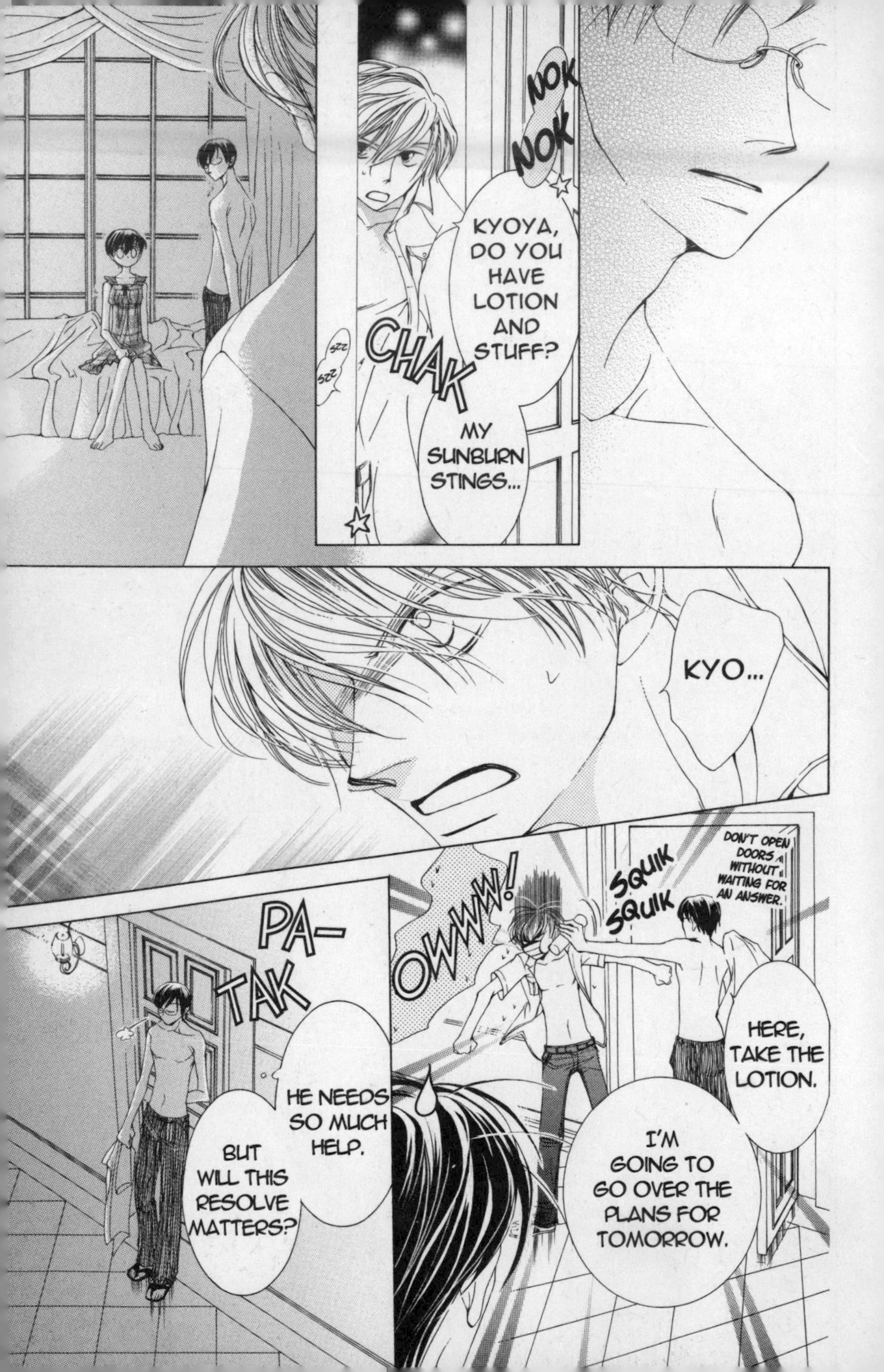
NOK NOK
KYOYA, DO YOU HAVE LOTION AND STUFF?
CHAK
MY SUNBURN STINGS...
SZZ SZZ
KYO...
DON'T OPEN DOORS WITHOUT WAITING FOR AN ANSWER.
SQUIK SQUIK
OWWW!
HERE, TAKE THE LOTION.
I'M GOING TO GO OVER THE PLANS FOR TOMORROW.
PA-TAK
HE NEEDS SO MUCH HELP.
BUT WILL THIS RESOLVE MATTERS?

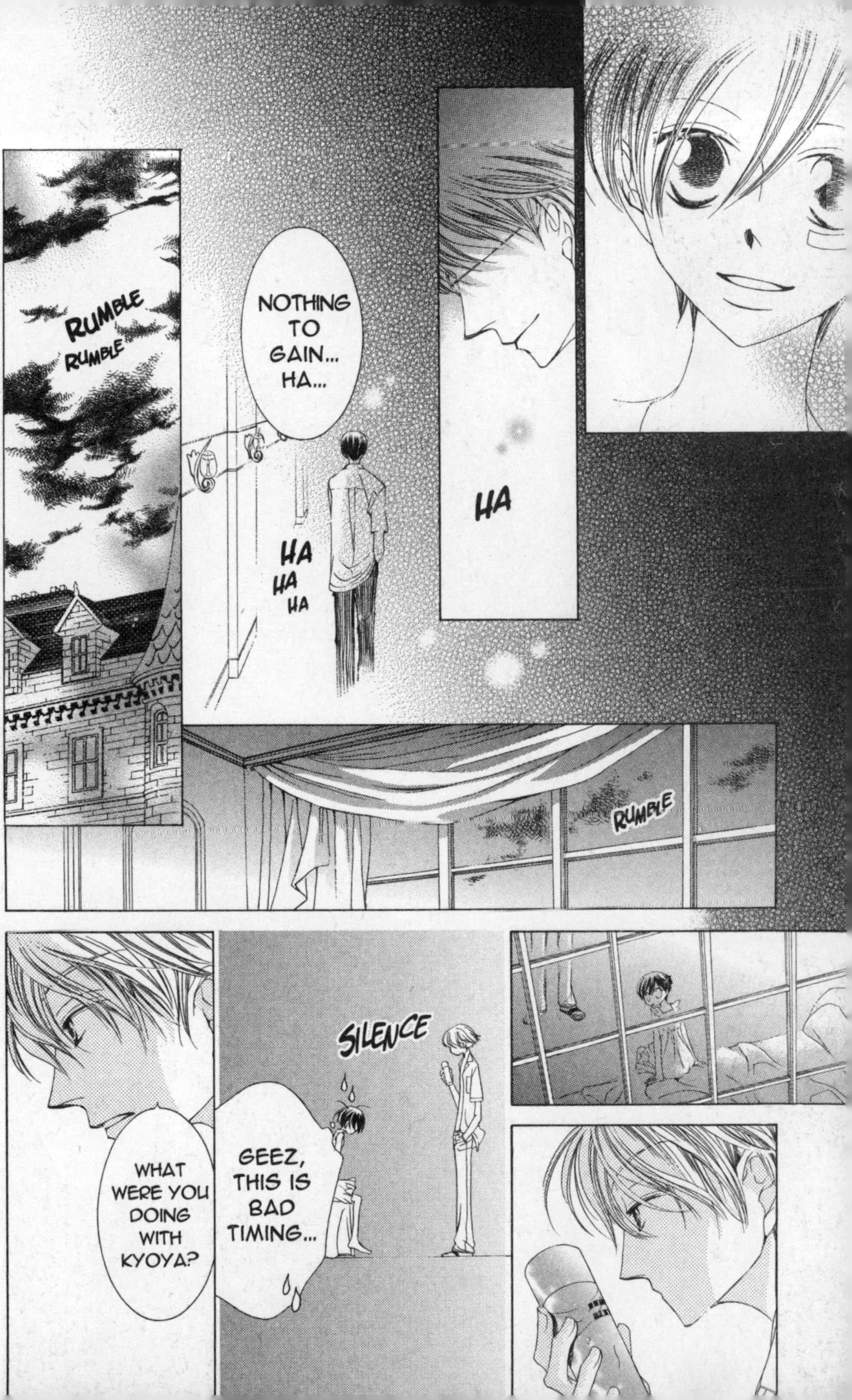
HA
NOTHING TO GAIN... HA...
HA HA HA
RUMBLE RUMBLE
RUMBLE
SILENCE
GEEZ, THIS IS BAD TIMING...
WHAT WERE YOU DOING WITH KYOYA?

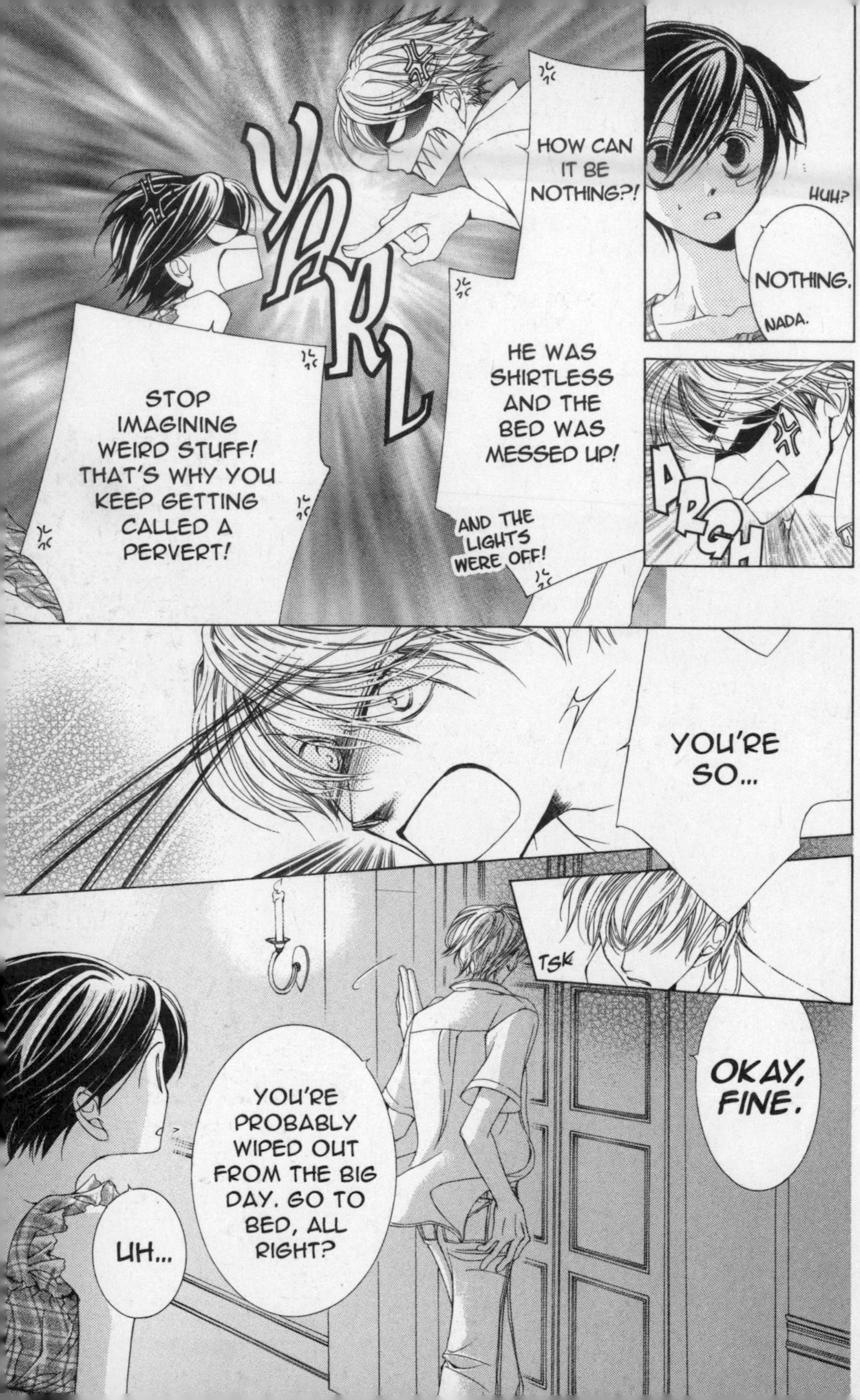
HUH?
NOTHING.
NADA.
ARGH
HOW CAN IT BE NOTHING?!
HE WAS SHIRTLESS AND THE BED WAS MESSED UP!
AND THE LIGHTS WERE OFF!
STOP IMAGINING WEIRD STUFF! THAT'S WHY YOU KEEP GETTING CALLED A PERVERT!
YOU'RE SO...
TSK
OKAY, FINE.
YOU'RE PROBABLY WIPED OUT FROM THE BIG DAY. GO TO BED, ALL RIGHT?
UH...

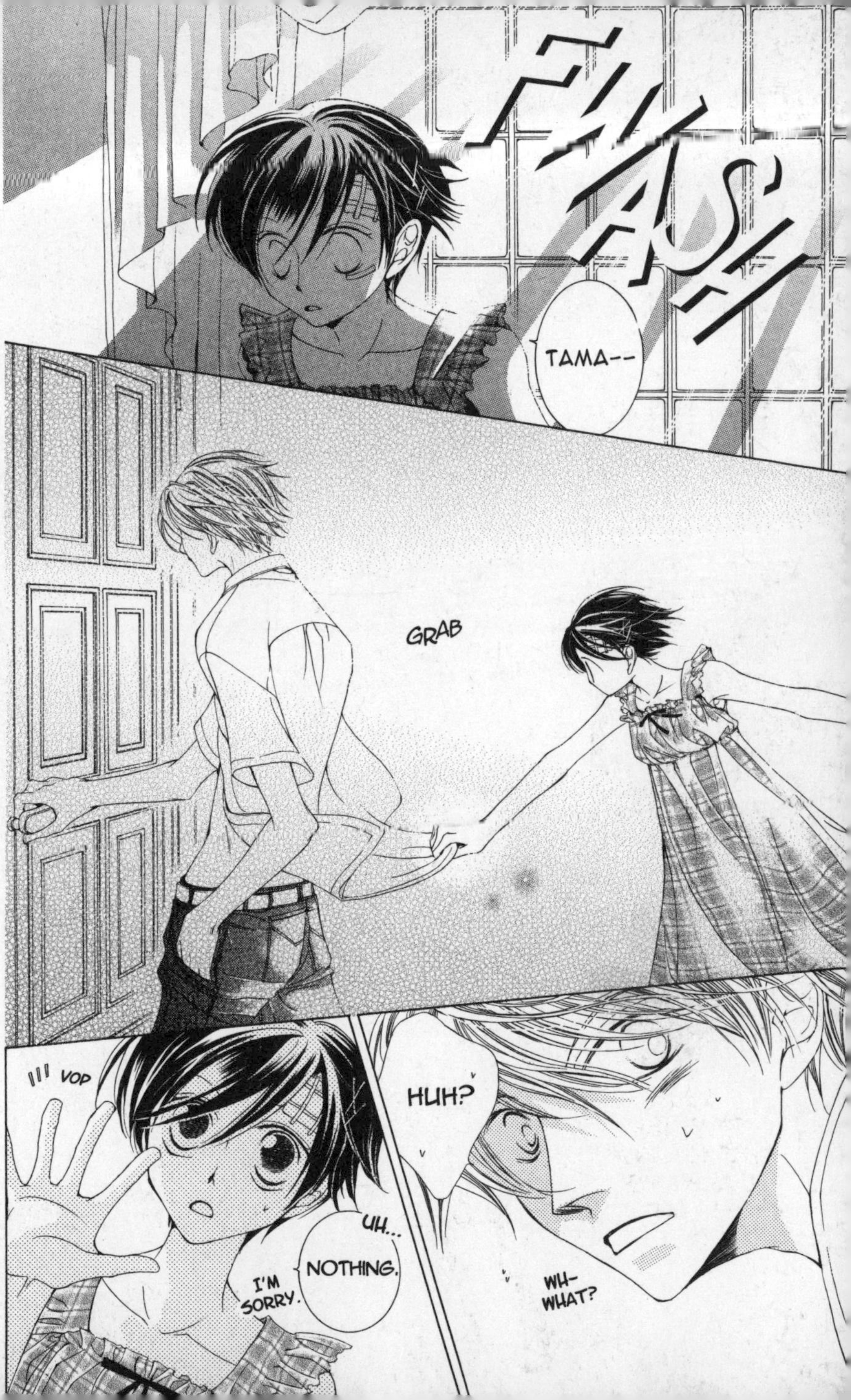
FLASH
TAMA--
GRAB
HUH?
WH-WHAT?
VOP
UH... NOTHING.
I'M SORRY.

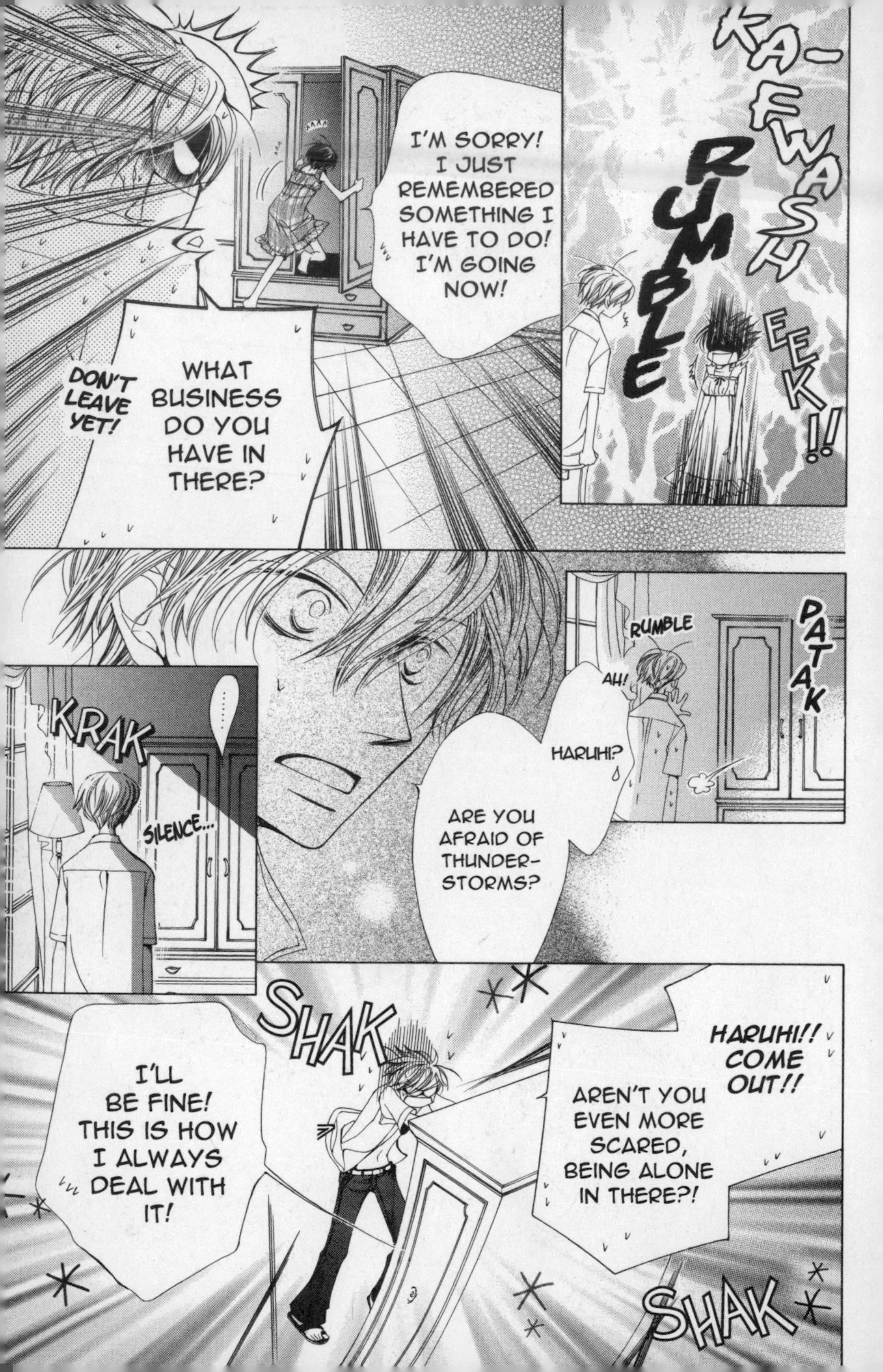
KA-FWASH
RUMBLE
EEK!!
I'M SORRY! I JUST REMEMBERED SOMETHING I HAVE TO DO! I'M GOING NOW!
WHAT BUSINESS DO YOU HAVE IN THERE?
DON'T LEAVE YET!
RUMBLE
PATAK
AH!
HARUHI?
ARE YOU AFRAID OF THUNDER-STORMS?
KRAK
......
SILENCE...
HARUHI!! COME OUT!!
AREN'T YOU EVEN MORE SCARED, BEING ALONE IN THERE?!
SHAK
SHAK
I'LL BE FINE! THIS IS HOW I ALWAYS DEAL WITH IT!

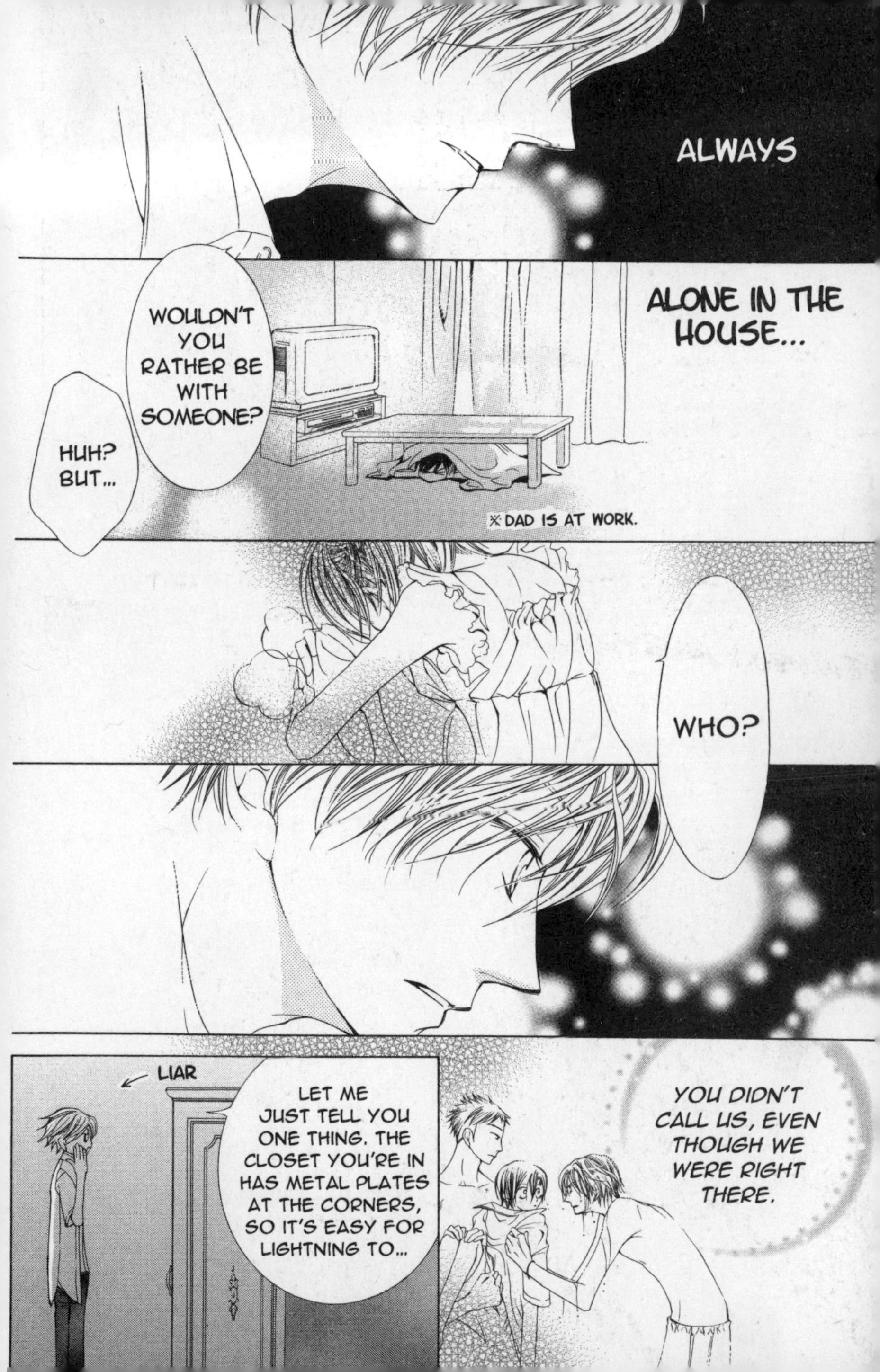
ALWAYS
ALONE IN THE HOUSE...
WOULDN'T YOU RATHER BE WITH SOMEONE?
HUH? BUT...
※DAD IS AT WORK.
WHO?
YOU DIDN'T CALL US, EVEN THOUGH WE WERE RIGHT THERE.
LET ME JUST TELL YOU ONE THING. THE CLOSET YOU'RE IN HAS METAL PLATES AT THE CORNERS, SO IT'S EASY FOR LIGHTNING TO...
LIAR

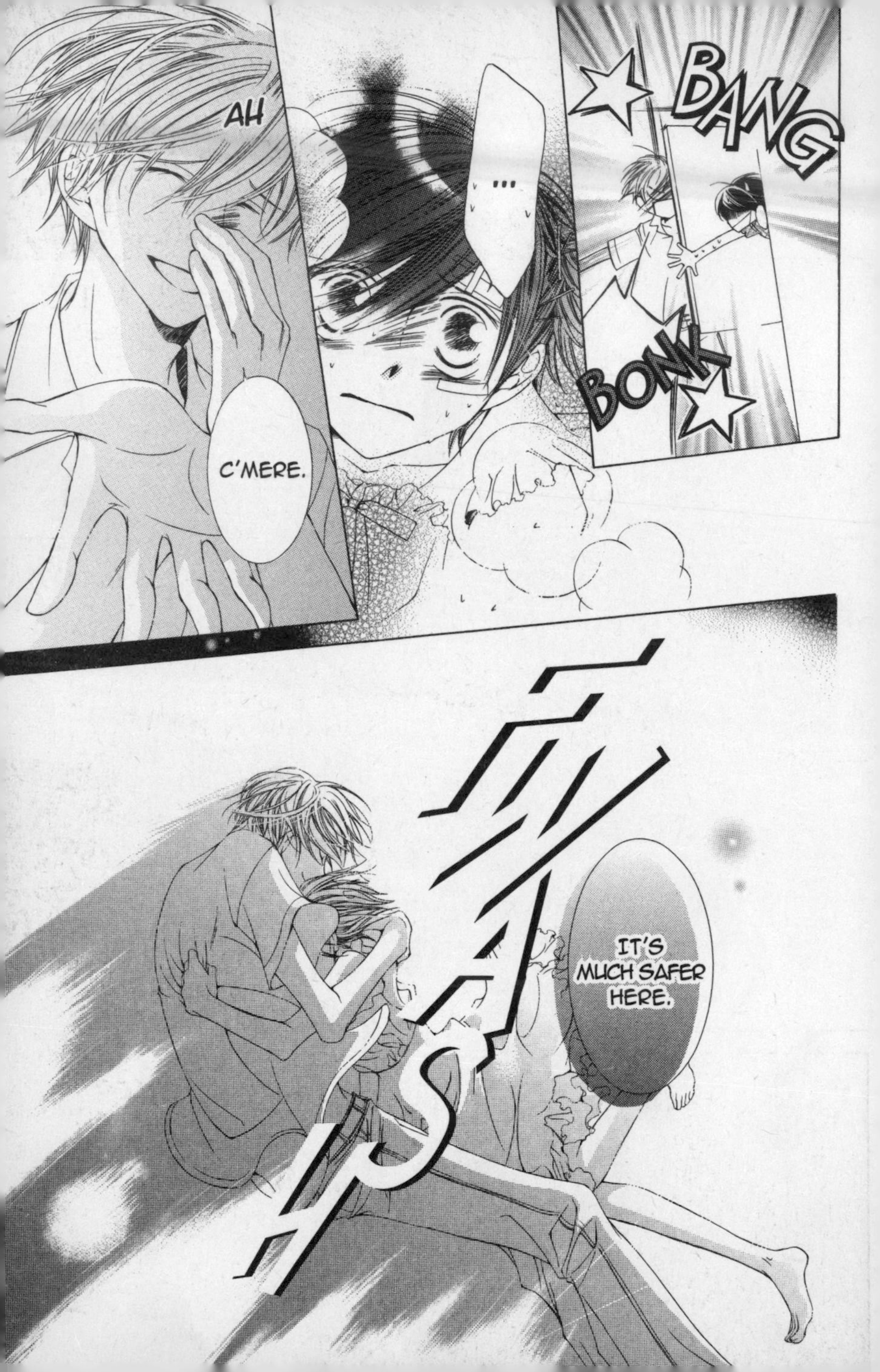
BANG
BONK
...
AH
C'MERE.
IT'S MUCH SAFER HERE.

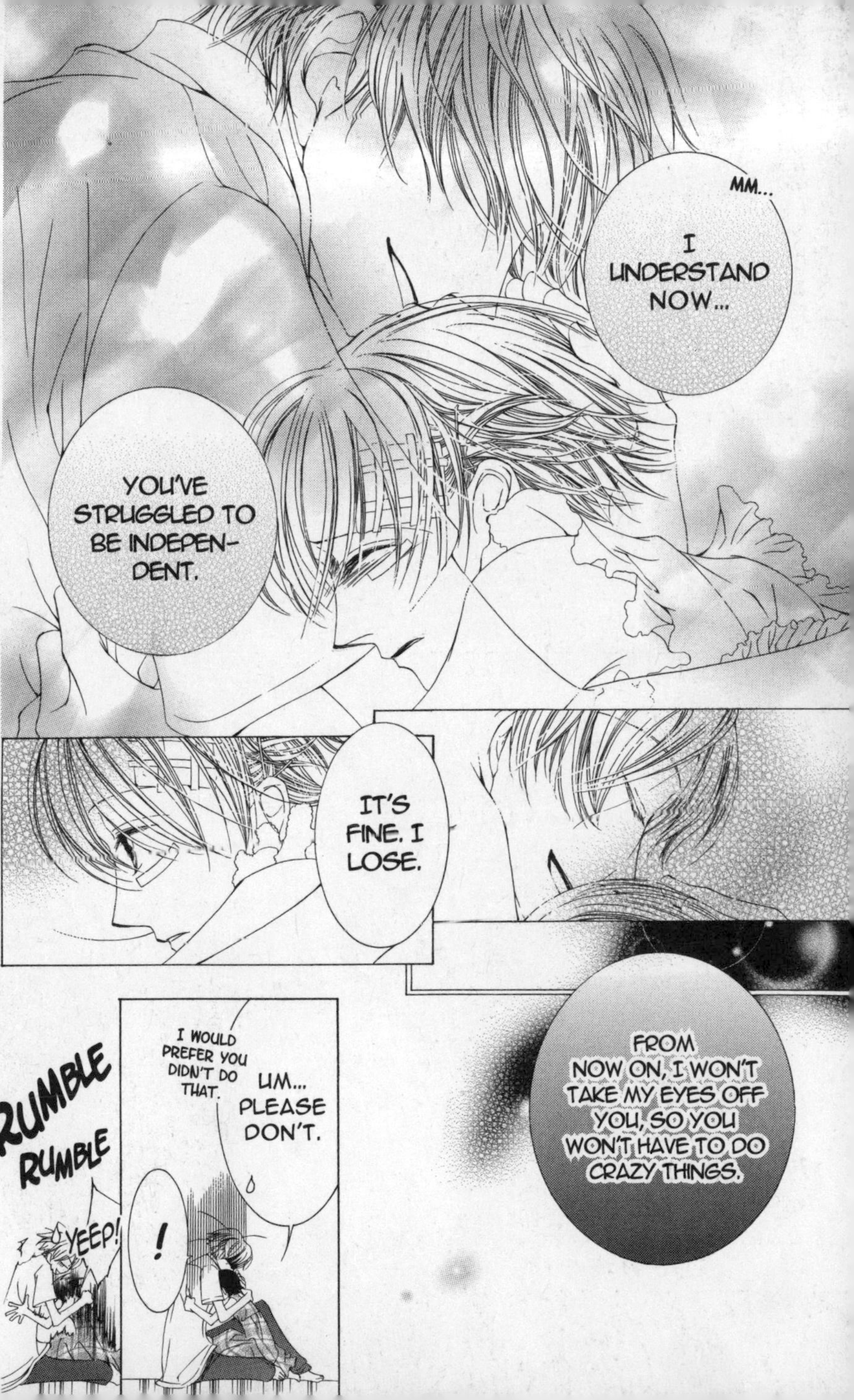
MM...
I UNDERSTAND NOW...
YOU'VE STRUGGLED TO BE INDEPEN-DENT.
IT'S FINE. I LOSE.
FROM NOW ON, I WON'T TAKE MY EYES OFF YOU, SO YOU WON'T HAVE TO DO CRAZY THINGS.
UM... PLEASE DON'T.
I WOULD PREFER YOU DIDN'T DO THAT.
!
YEEP!
RUMBLE
RUMBLE

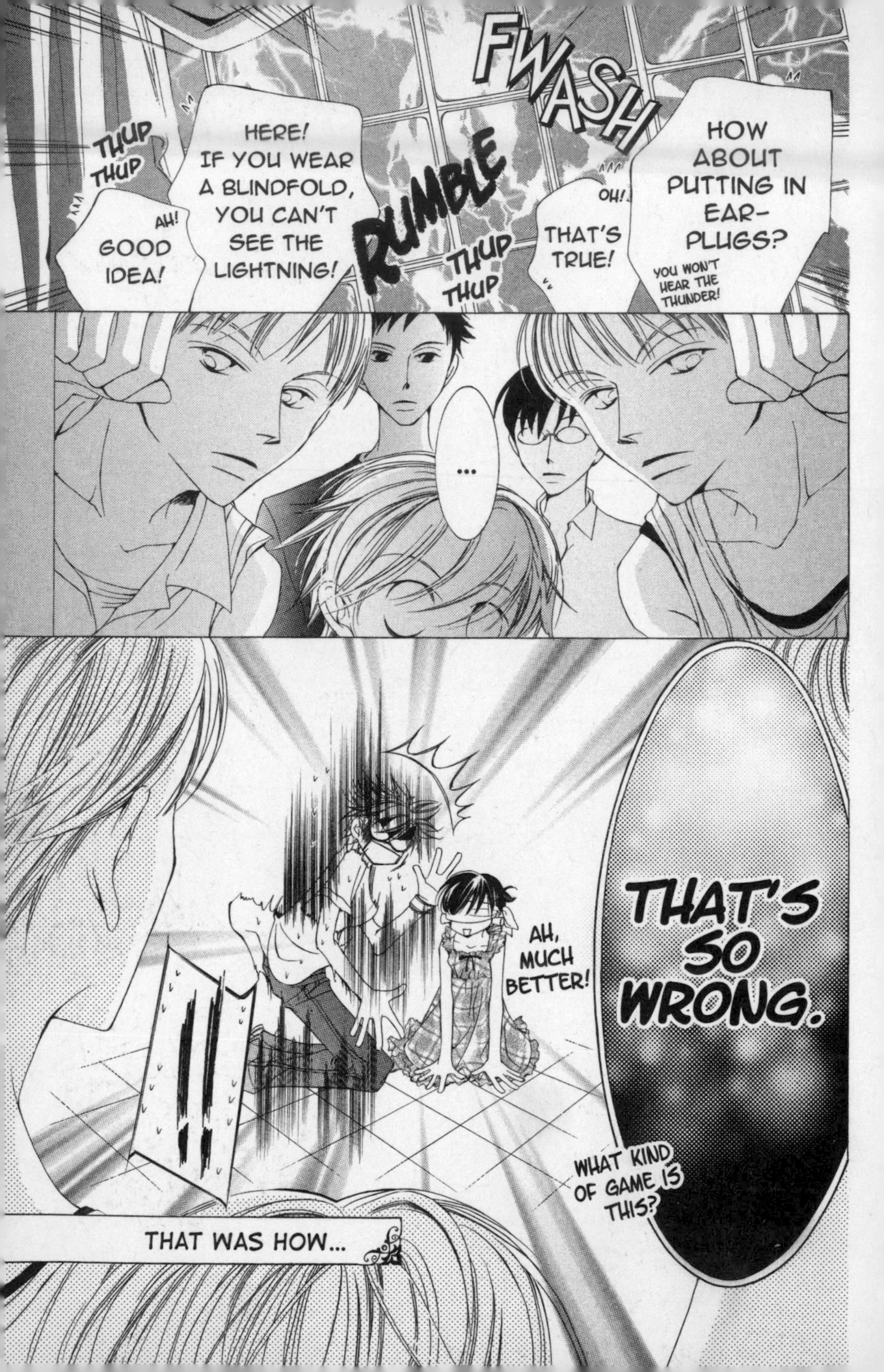
FWASH
HOW ABOUT PUTTING IN EAR-PLUGS?
YOU WON'T HEAR THE THUNDER!
OH! THAT'S TRUE!
THUP THUP
RUMBLE
HERE! IF YOU WEAR A BLINDFOLD, YOU CAN'T SEE THE LIGHTNING!
THUP THUP
AH! GOOD IDEA!
...
THAT'S SO WRONG.
WHAT KIND OF GAME IS THIS?
AH, MUCH BETTER!
THAT WAS HOW...

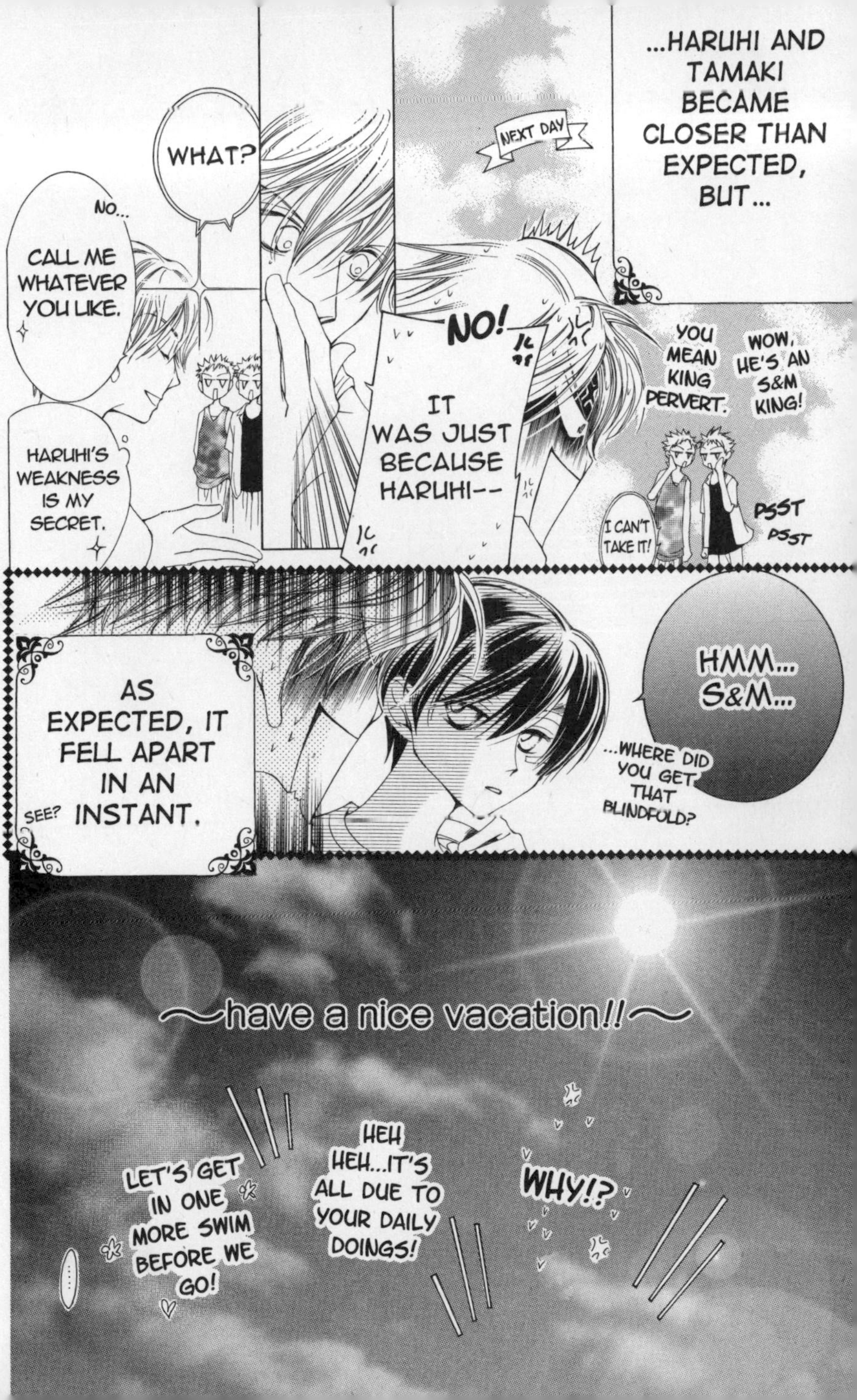
...HARUHI AND TAMAKI BECAME CLOSER THAN EXPECTED, BUT...
NEXT DAY
WOW, HE'S AN S&M KING!
YOU MEAN KING PERVERT.
PSST PSST
I CAN'T TAKE IT!
NO!
IT WAS JUST BECAUSE HARUHI--
WHAT?
NO...
CALL ME WHATEVER YOU LIKE.
HARUHI'S WEAKNESS IS MY SECRET.
HMM... S&M...
...WHERE DID YOU GET THAT BLINDFOLD?
AS EXPECTED, IT FELL APART IN AN INSTANT.
SEE?
~have a nice vacation!!~
WHY!?
HEH HEH...IT'S ALL DUE TO YOUR DAILY DOINGS!
LET'S GET IN ONE MORE SWIM BEFORE WE GO!
......

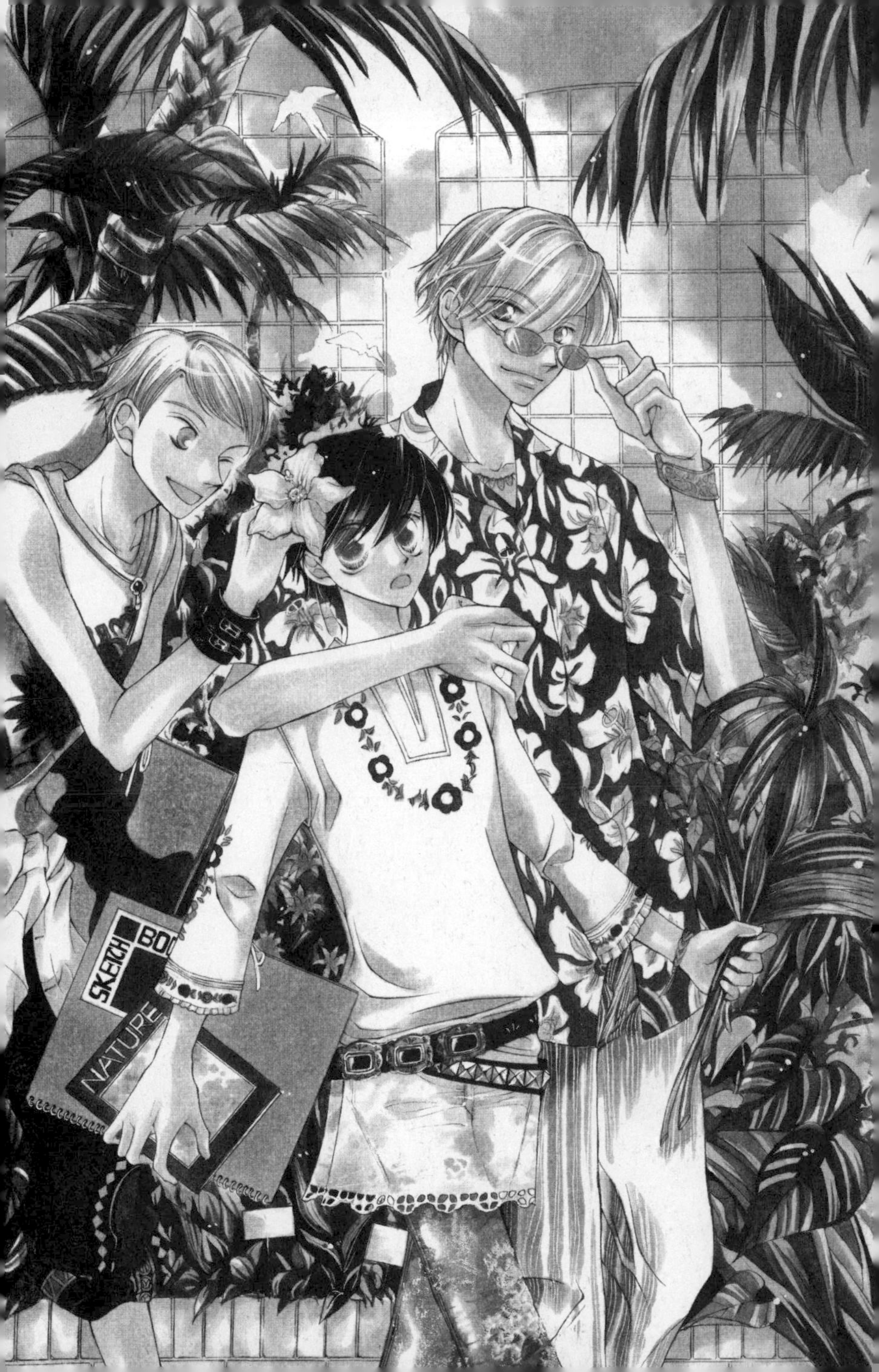
SKETCH BOO
NATURE

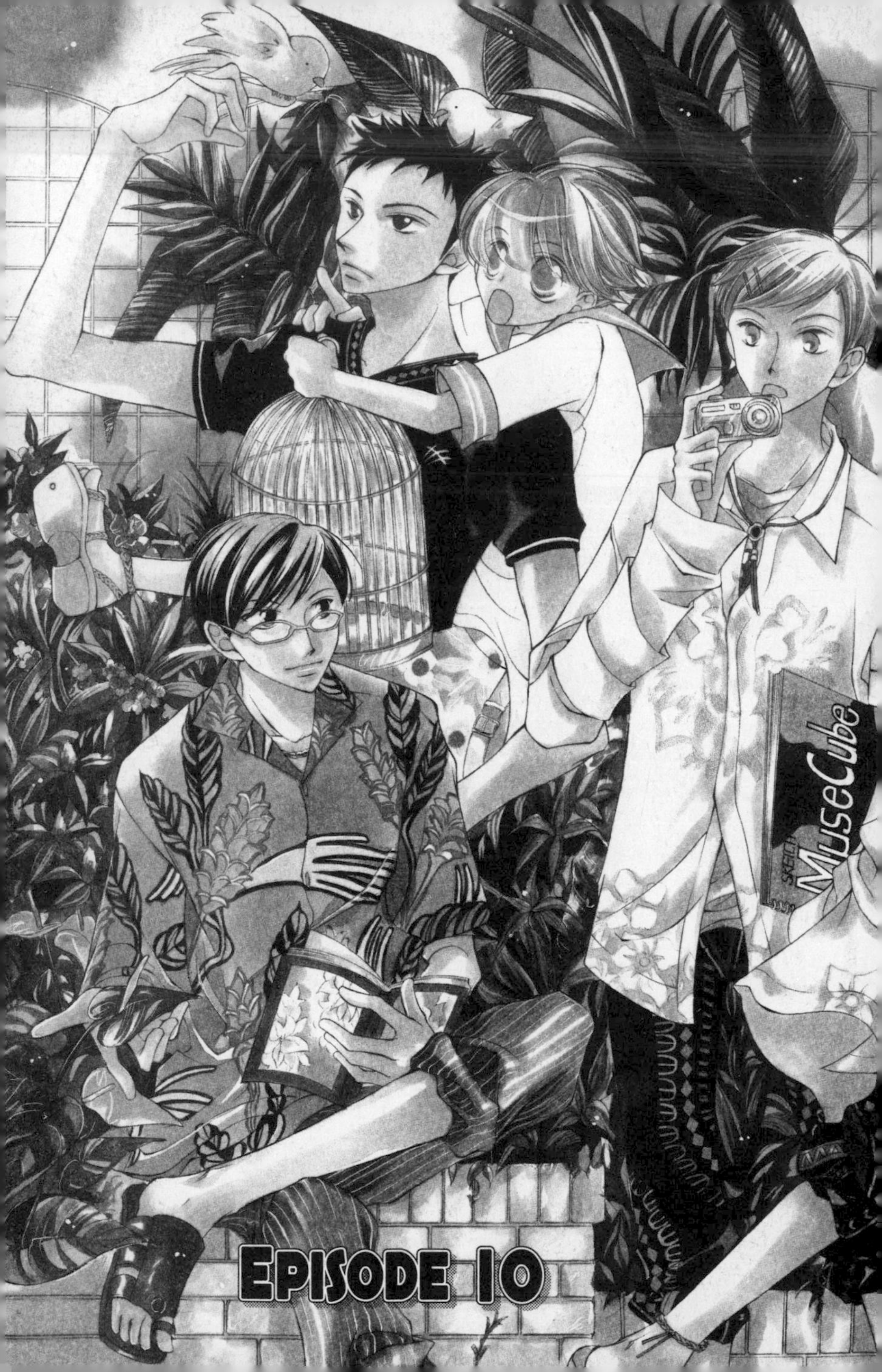
MuseCube
Episode 10

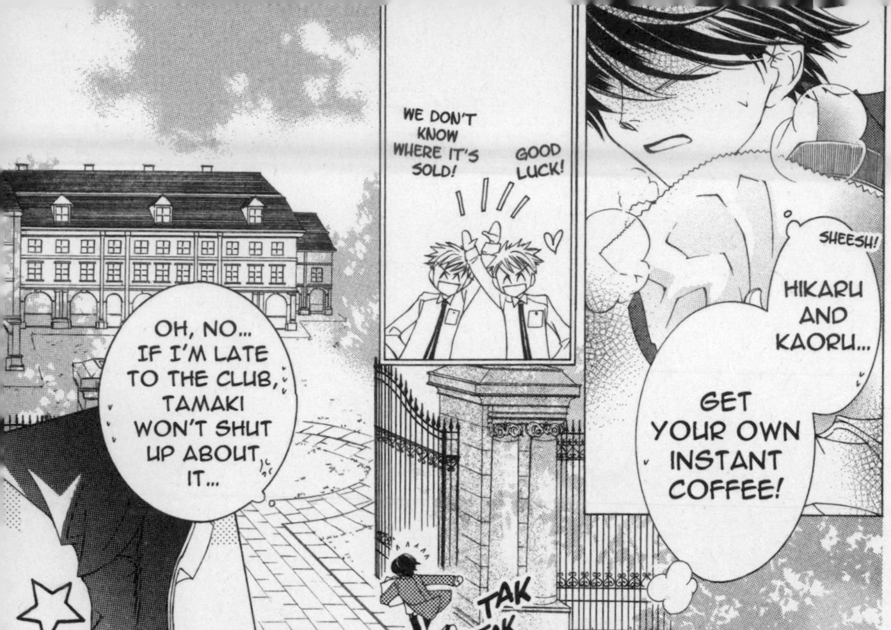
SHEESH!
HIKARU AND KAORU...
GET YOUR OWN INSTANT COFFEE!
WE DON'T KNOW WHERE IT'S SOLD!
GOOD LUCK!
OH, NO... IF I'M LATE TO THE CLUB, TAMAKI WON'T SHUT UP ABOUT IT...
TAK TAK
TUP
WAH!

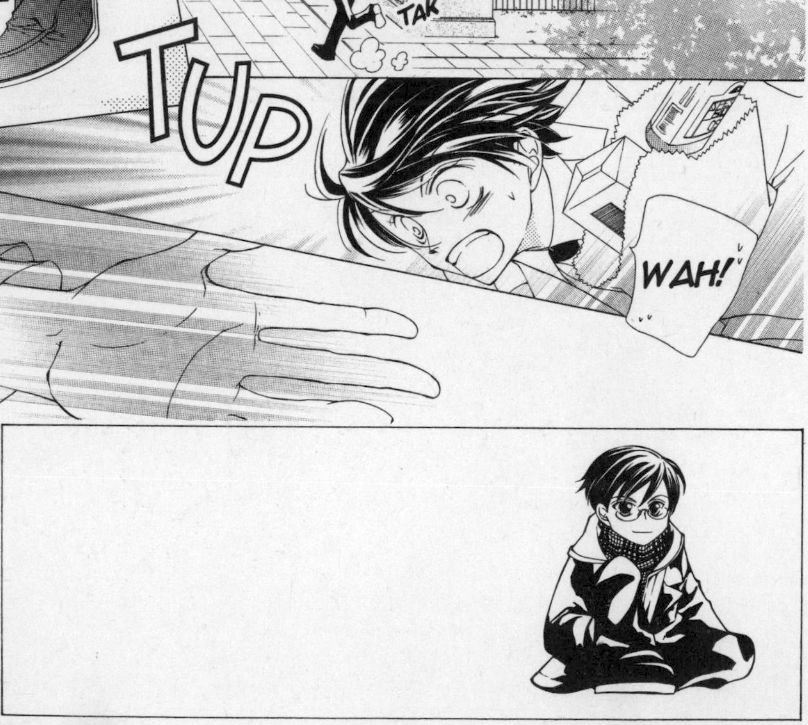

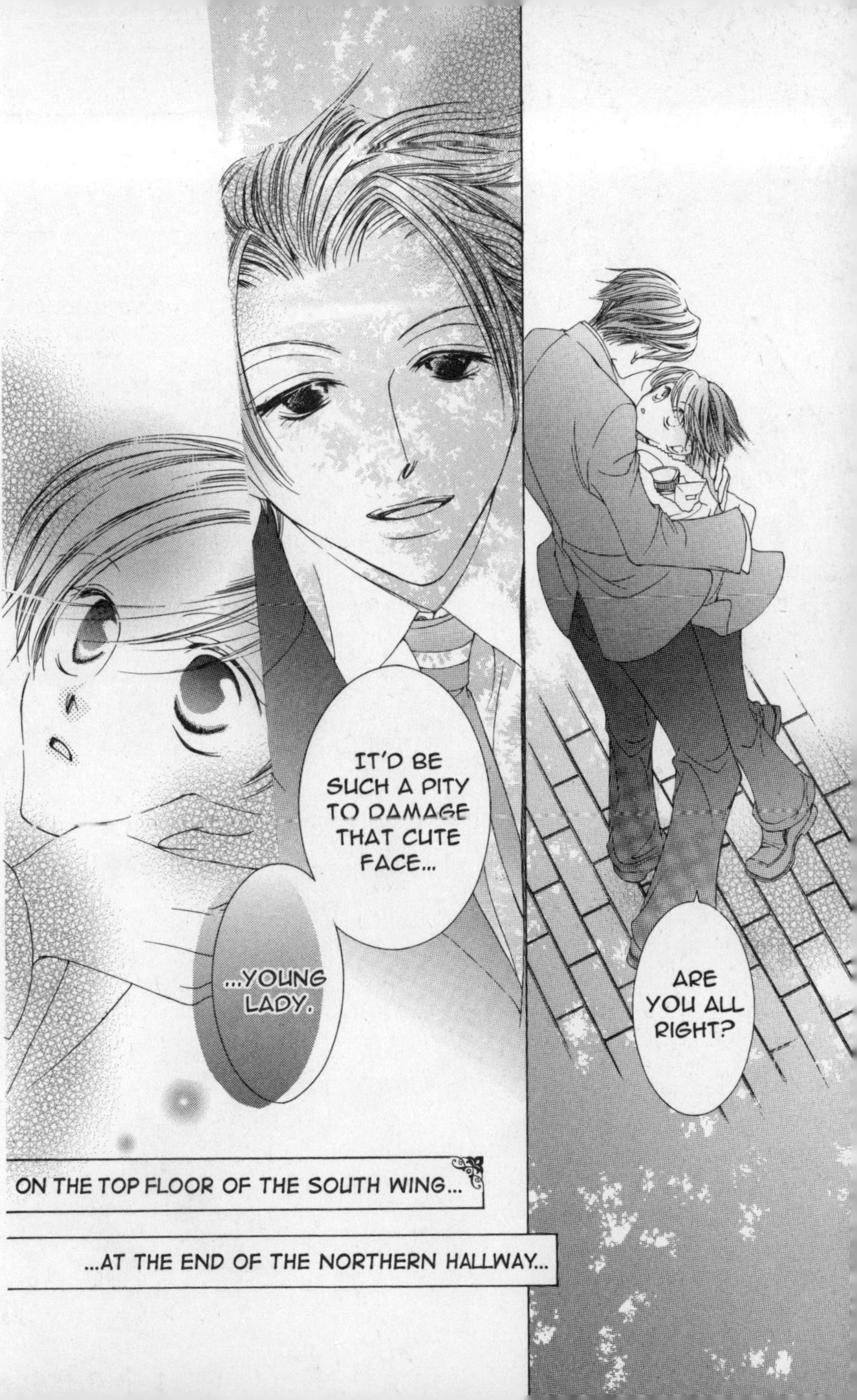
ARE YOU ALL RIGHT?
IT'D BE SUCH A PITY TO DAMAGE THAT CUTE FACE...
...YOUNG LADY.
ON THE TOP FLOOR OF THE SOUTH WING...
...AT THE END OF THE NORTHERN HALLWAY...

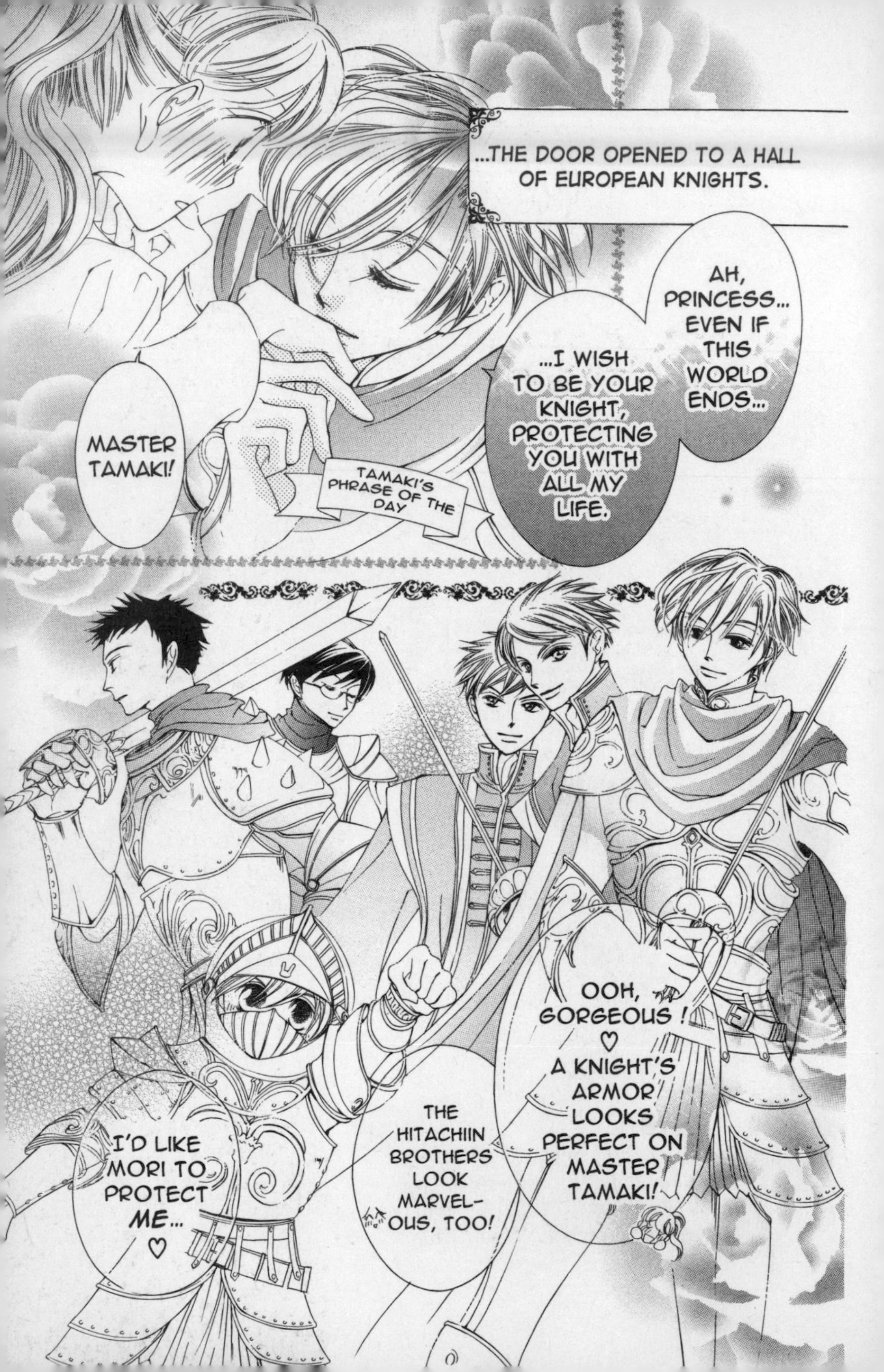
...THE DOOR OPENED TO A HALL OF EUROPEAN KNIGHTS.
AH, PRINCESS... EVEN IF THIS WORLD ENDS...
...I WISH TO BE YOUR KNIGHT, PROTECTING YOU WITH ALL MY LIFE.
TAMAKI'S PHRASE OF THE DAY
MASTER TAMAKI!
OOH, GORGEOUS! ♡ A KNIGHT'S ARMOR LOOKS PERFECT ON MASTER TAMAKI!
THE HITACHIIN BROTHERS LOOK MARVEL-OUS, TOO!
I'D LIKE MORI TO PROTECT ME... ♡

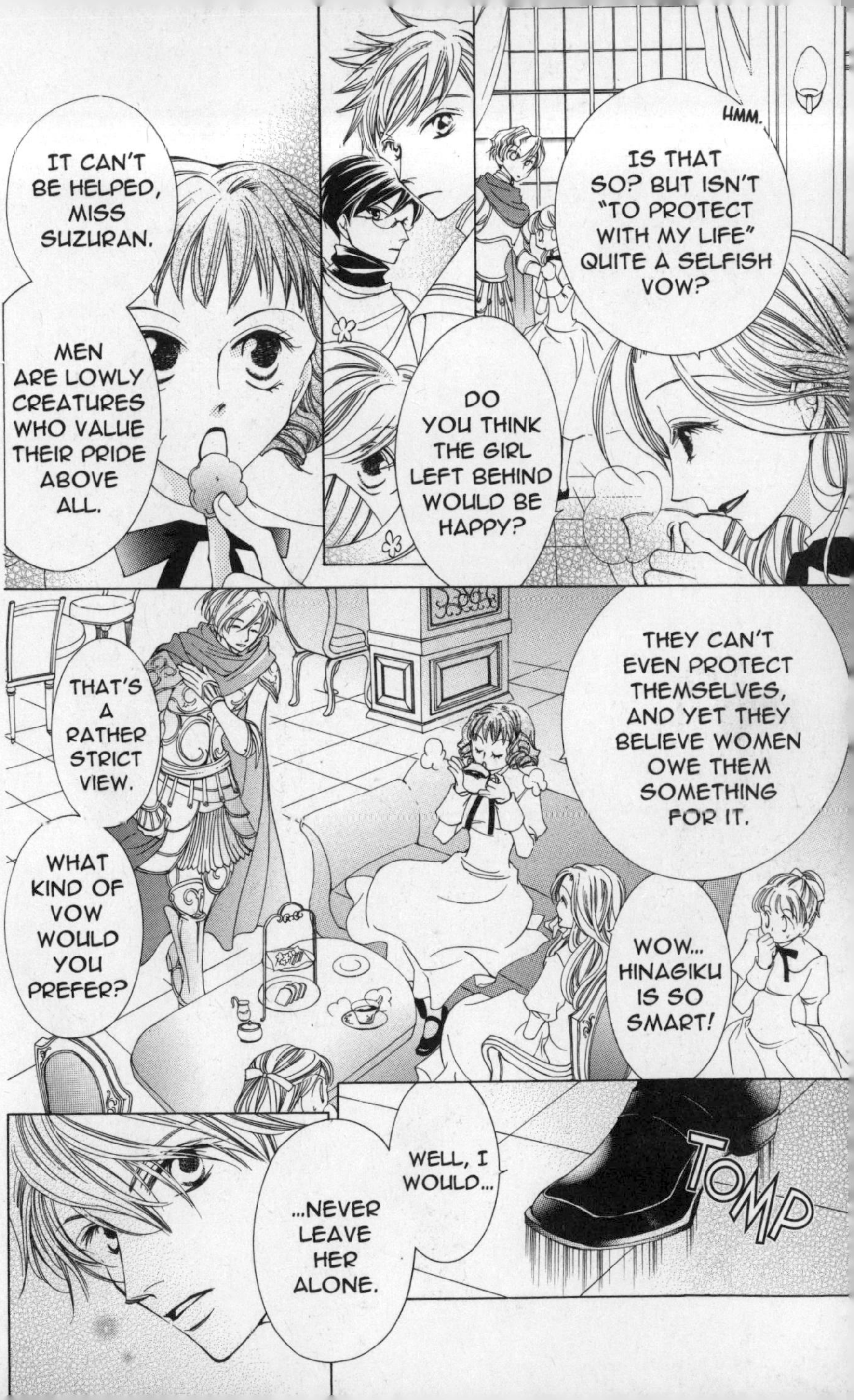
HMM.
IS THAT SO? BUT ISN'T "TO PROTECT WITH MY LIFE" QUITE A SELFISH VOW?
DO YOU THINK THE GIRL LEFT BEHIND WOULD BE HAPPY?
IT CAN'T BE HELPED, MISS SUZURAN.
MEN ARE LOWLY CREATURES WHO VALUE THEIR PRIDE ABOVE ALL.
THEY CAN'T EVEN PROTECT THEMSELVES, AND YET THEY BELIEVE WOMEN OWE THEM SOMETHING FOR IT.
WOW... HINAGIKU IS SO SMART!
THAT'S A RATHER STRICT VIEW.
WHAT KIND OF VOW WOULD YOU PREFER?
TOMP
WELL, I WOULD...
...NEVER LEAVE HER ALONE.

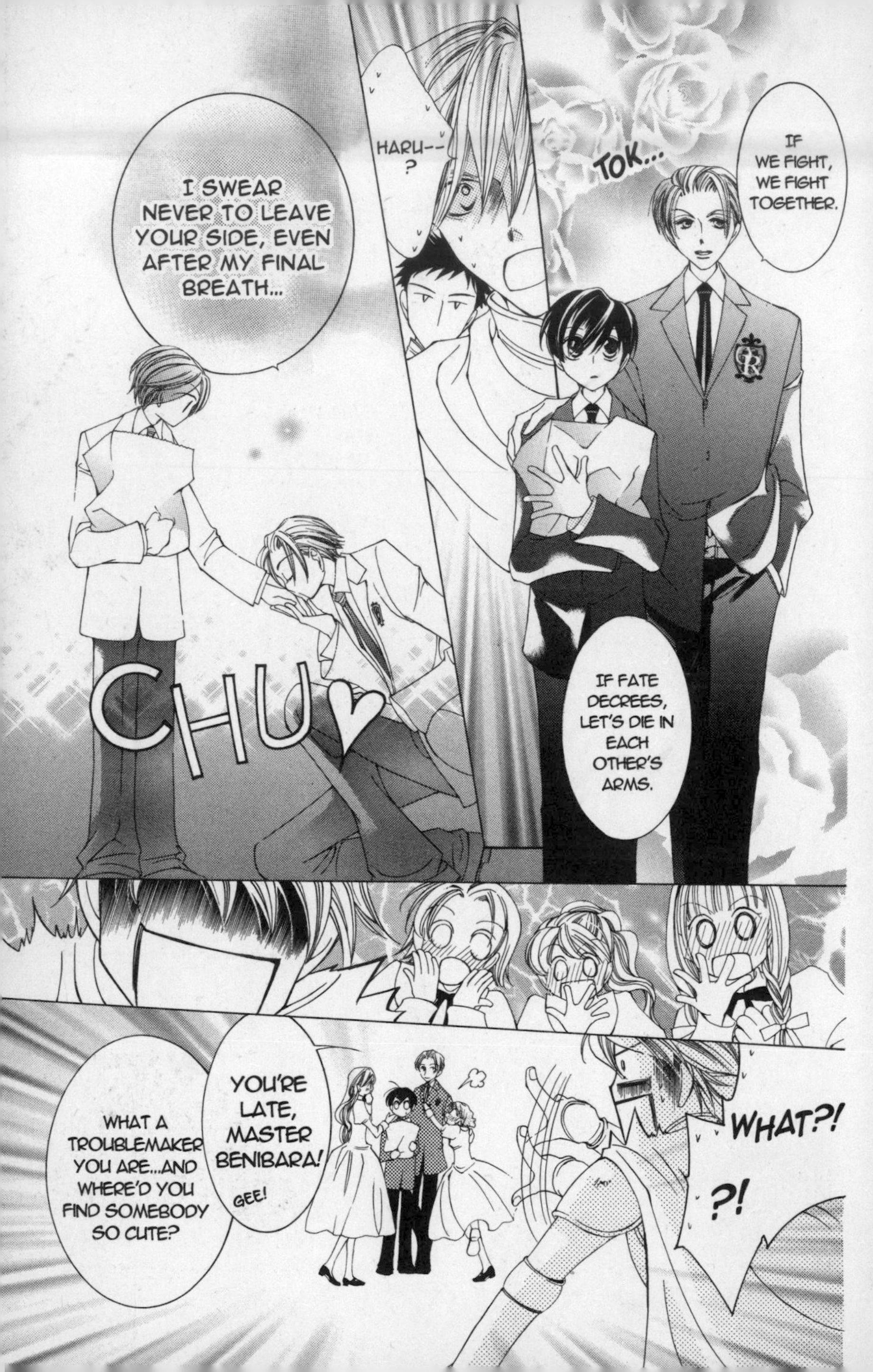
TOK...
IF WE FIGHT, WE FIGHT TOGETHER.
IF FATE DECREES, LET'S DIE IN EACH OTHER'S ARMS.
HARU-- ?
I SWEAR NEVER TO LEAVE YOUR SIDE, EVEN AFTER MY FINAL BREATH...
CHU♥
WHAT?!
?!
YOU'RE LATE, MASTER BENIBARA!
GEE!
WHAT A TROUBLEMAKER YOU ARE...AND WHERE'D YOU FIND SOMEBODY SO CUTE?

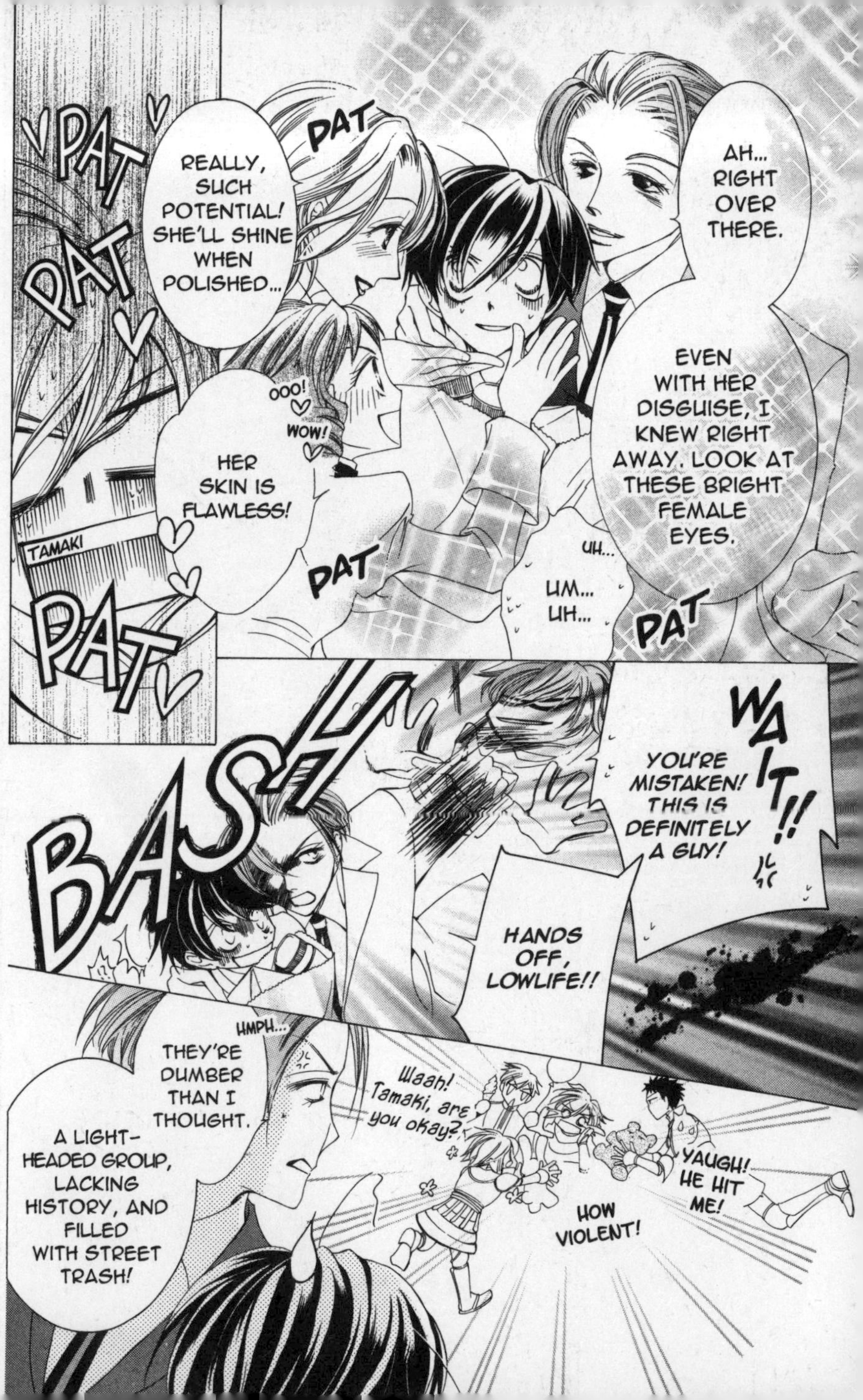
AH... RIGHT OVER THERE.
EVEN WITH HER DISGUISE, I KNEW RIGHT AWAY. LOOK AT THESE BRIGHT FEMALE EYES.
PAT
UH...
UM... UH...
PAT
REALLY, SUCH POTENTIAL! SHE'LL SHINE WHEN POLISHED...
OOO! WOW!
HER SKIN IS FLAWLESS!
PAT
PAT PAT
TAMAKI
PAT PAT
WAIT!!
YOU'RE MISTAKEN! THIS IS DEFINITELY A GUY!
BASH
HANDS OFF, LOWLIFE!!
YAUGH! HE HIT ME!
HOW VIOLENT!
Waah! Tamaki, are you okay?
HMPH...
THEY'RE DUMBER THAN I THOUGHT.
A LIGHT-HEADED GROUP, LACKING HISTORY, AND FILLED WITH STREET TRASH!

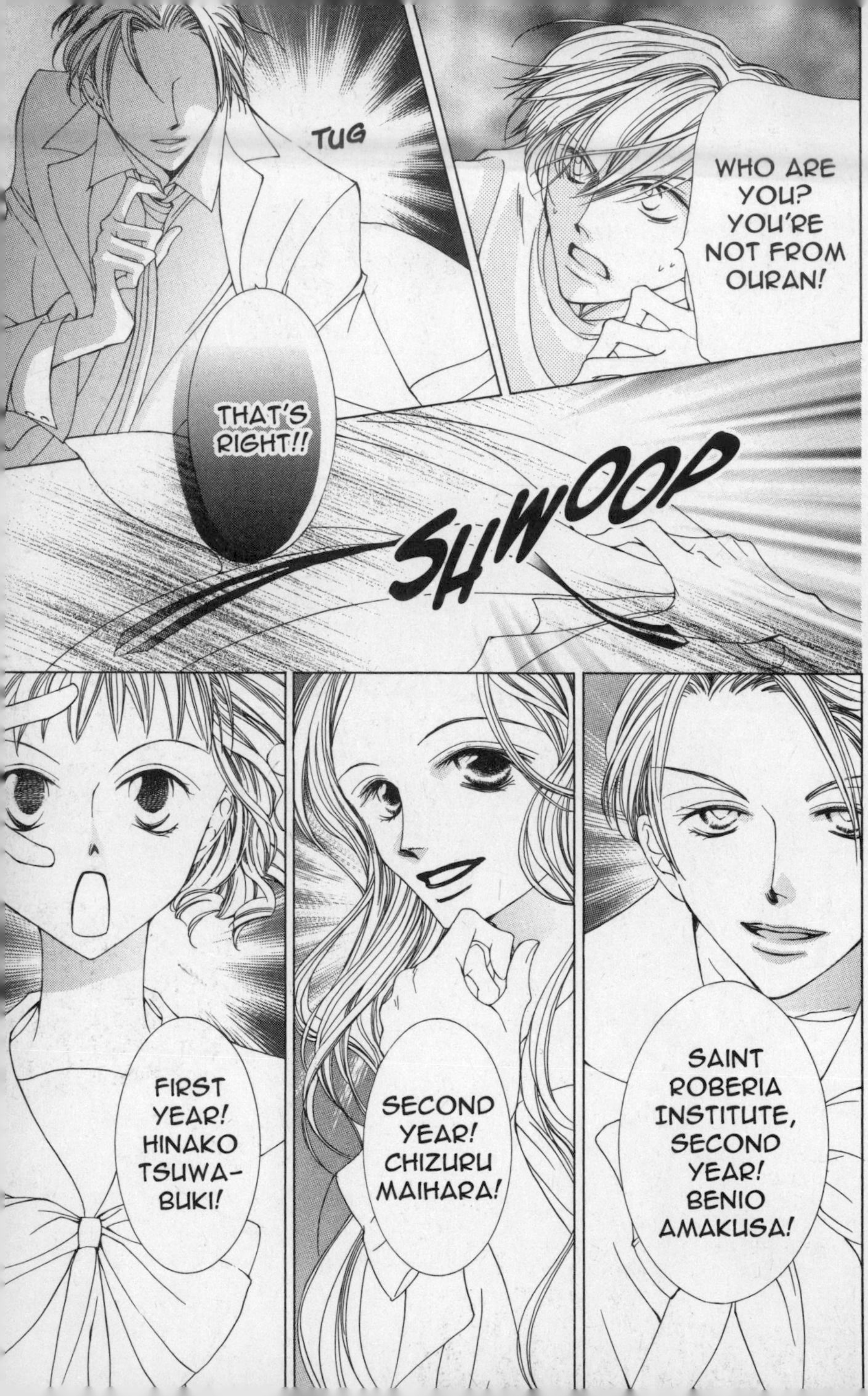
WHO ARE YOU? YOU'RE NOT FROM OURAN!
TUG
THAT'S RIGHT!!
SHWOOP
SAINT ROBERIA INSTITUTE, SECOND YEAR! BENIO AMAKUSA!
SECOND YEAR! CHIZURU MAIHARA!
FIRST YEAR! HINAKO TSUWA-BUKI!

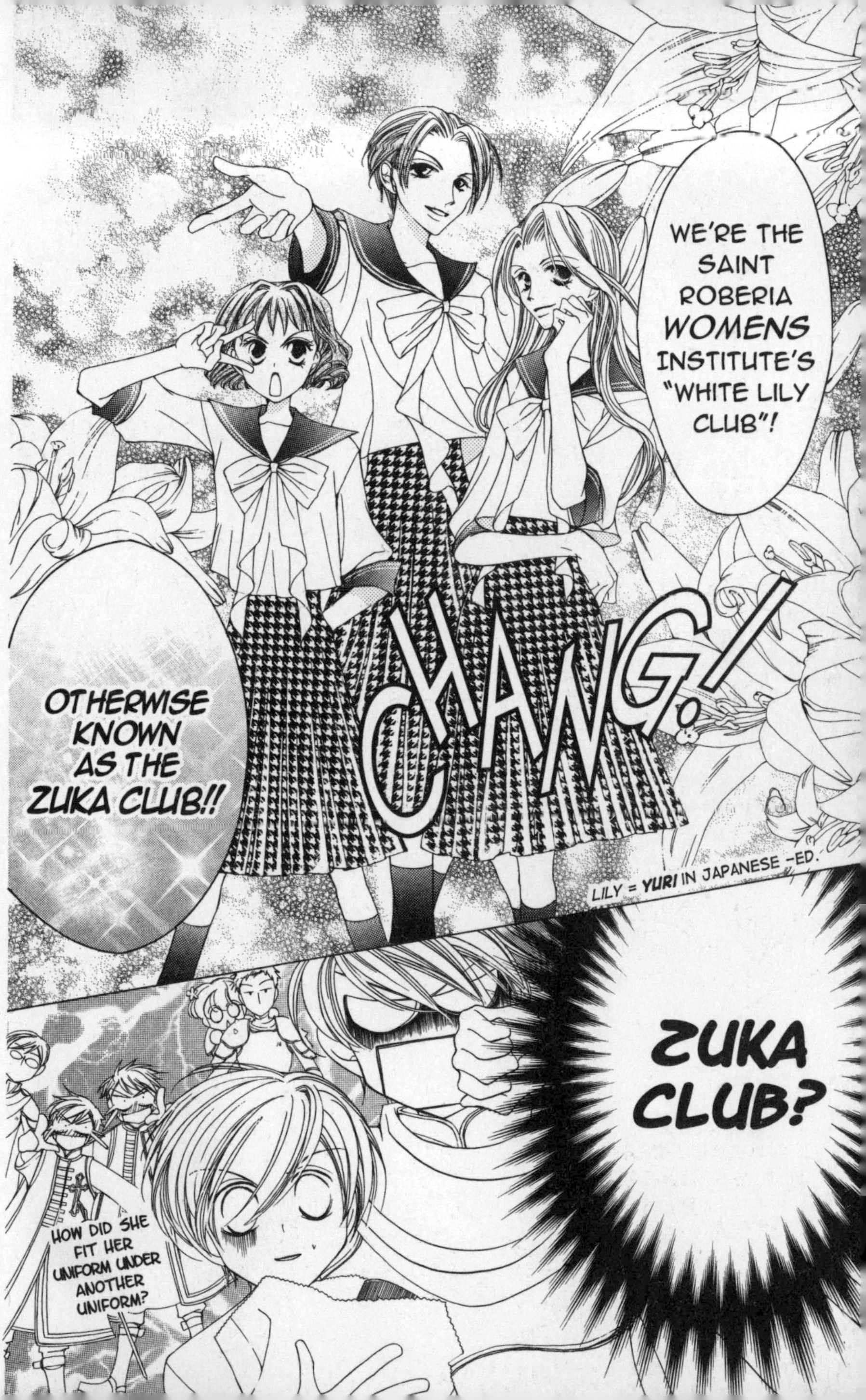
WE'RE THE SAINT ROBERIA *WOMENS* INSTITUTE'S "WHITE LILY CLUB"!
CHANG!
OTHERWISE KNOWN AS THE ZUKA CLUB!!
LILY = *YURI* IN JAPANESE –ED.
ZUKA CLUB?
HOW DID SHE FIT HER UNIFORM UNDER ANOTHER UNIFORM?

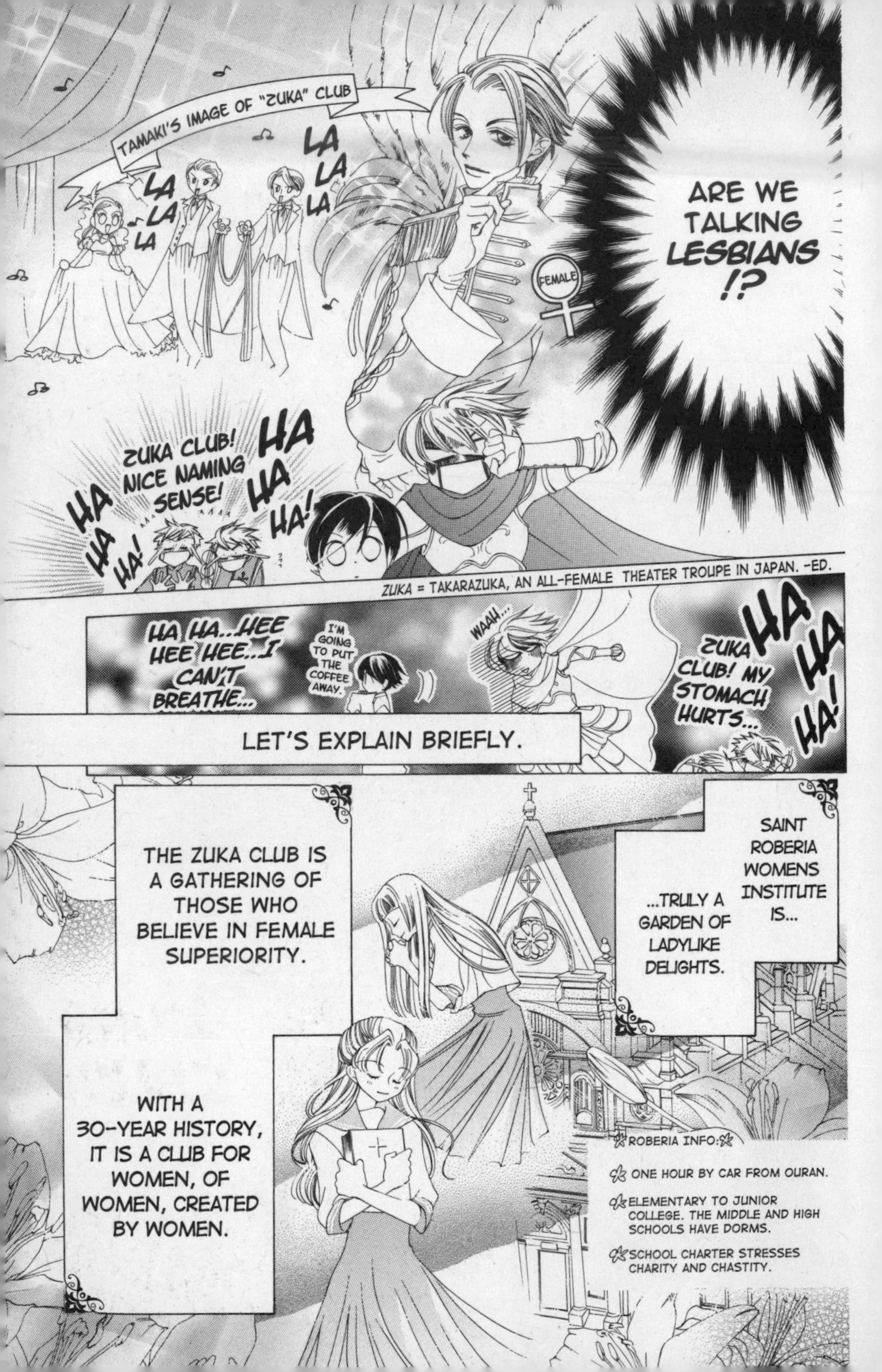
ARE WE TALKING LESBIANS !?
TAMAKI'S IMAGE OF "ZUKA" CLUB
LA LA LA
LA LA LA
LA LA LA
FEMALE
HA HA HA!
ZUKA CLUB! NICE NAMING SENSE!
HA HA HA!
ZUKA = TAKARAZUKA, AN ALL-FEMALE THEATER TROUPE IN JAPAN. -ED.
HA HA HA!
ZUKA CLUB! MY STOMACH HURTS...
WAAH...
I'M GOING TO PUT THE COFFEE AWAY.
HA HA... HEE HEE HEE... I CAN'T BREATHE...
LET'S EXPLAIN BRIEFLY.
SAINT ROBERIA WOMENS INSTITUTE IS...
...TRULY A GARDEN OF LADYLIKE DELIGHTS.
THE ZUKA CLUB IS A GATHERING OF THOSE WHO BELIEVE IN FEMALE SUPERIORITY.
WITH A 30-YEAR HISTORY, IT IS A CLUB FOR WOMEN, OF WOMEN, CREATED BY WOMEN.
ROBERIA INFO:
ONE HOUR BY CAR FROM OURAN.
ELEMENTARY TO JUNIOR COLLEGE. THE MIDDLE AND HIGH SCHOOLS HAVE DORMS.
SCHOOL CHARTER STRESSES CHARITY AND CHASTITY.

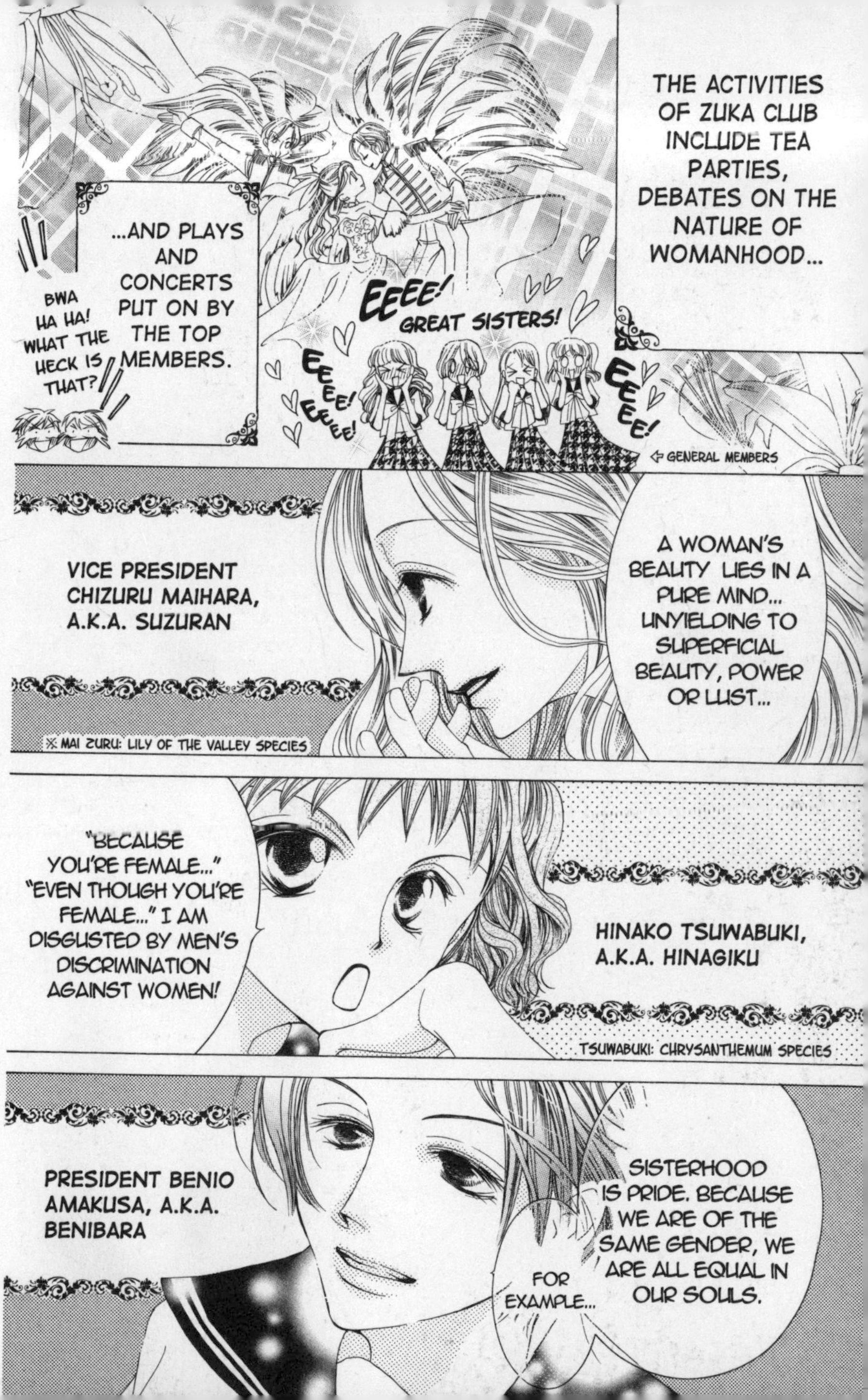
THE ACTIVITIES OF ZUKA CLUB INCLUDE TEA PARTIES, DEBATES ON THE NATURE OF WOMANHOOD...
EEEE!
EEEE!
GREAT SISTERS!
EEEE!
EEEE!
GENERAL MEMBERS
...AND PLAYS AND CONCERTS PUT ON BY THE TOP MEMBERS.
BWA HA HA! WHAT THE HECK IS THAT?
A WOMAN'S BEAUTY LIES IN A PURE MIND... UNYIELDING TO SUPERFICIAL BEAUTY, POWER OR LUST...
VICE PRESIDENT CHIZURU MAIHARA, A.K.A. SUZURAN
※ MAI ZURU: LILY OF THE VALLEY SPECIES
HINAKO TSUWABUKI, A.K.A. HINAGIKU
TSUWABUKI: CHRYSANTHEMUM SPECIES
"BECAUSE YOU'RE FEMALE..." "EVEN THOUGH YOU'RE FEMALE..." I AM DISGUSTED BY MEN'S DISCRIMINATION AGAINST WOMEN!
SISTERHOOD IS PRIDE. BECAUSE WE ARE OF THE SAME GENDER, WE ARE ALL EQUAL IN OUR SOULS.
FOR EXAMPLE...
PRESIDENT BENIO AMAKUSA, A.K.A. BENIBARA

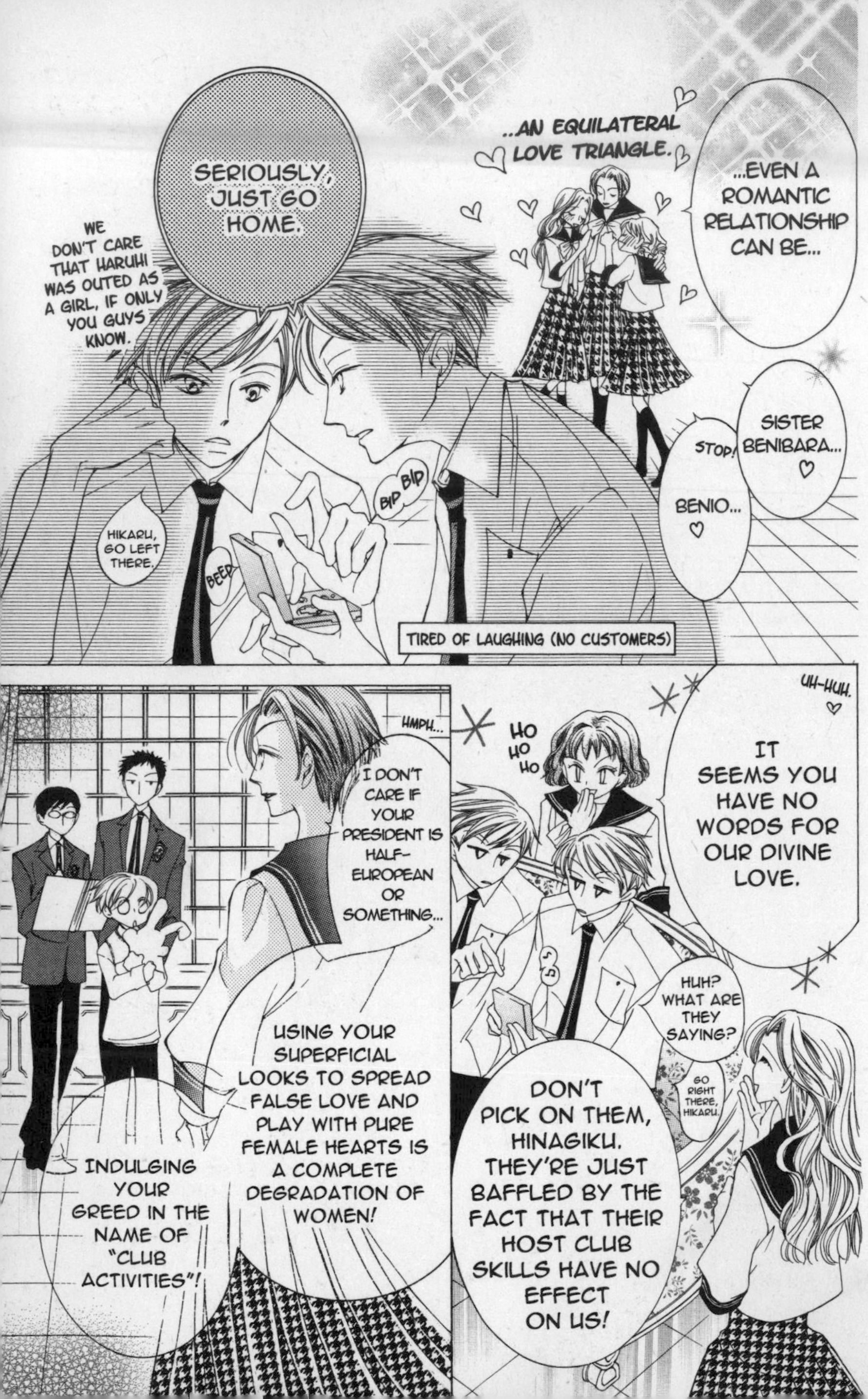
...EVEN A ROMANTIC RELATIONSHIP CAN BE...
...AN EQUILATERAL LOVE TRIANGLE.
SISTER BENIBARA...
STOP!
BENIO...
SERIOUSLY, JUST GO HOME.
WE DON'T CARE THAT HARUHI WAS OUTED AS A GIRL, IF ONLY YOU GUYS KNOW.
BIP BIP
HIKARU, GO LEFT THERE.
BEEP
TIRED OF LAUGHING (NO CUSTOMERS)
UH-HUH.
IT SEEMS YOU HAVE NO WORDS FOR OUR DIVINE LOVE.
HO HO HO
HUH? WHAT ARE THEY SAYING?
GO RIGHT THERE, HIKARU.
DON'T PICK ON THEM, HINAGIKU. THEY'RE JUST BAFFLED BY THE FACT THAT THEIR HOST CLUB SKILLS HAVE NO EFFECT ON US!
HMPH...
I DON'T CARE IF YOUR PRESIDENT IS HALF-EUROPEAN OR SOMETHING...
USING YOUR SUPERFICIAL LOOKS TO SPREAD FALSE LOVE AND PLAY WITH PURE FEMALE HEARTS IS A COMPLETE DEGRADATION OF WOMEN!
INDULGING YOUR GREED IN THE NAME OF "CLUB ACTIVITIES"!

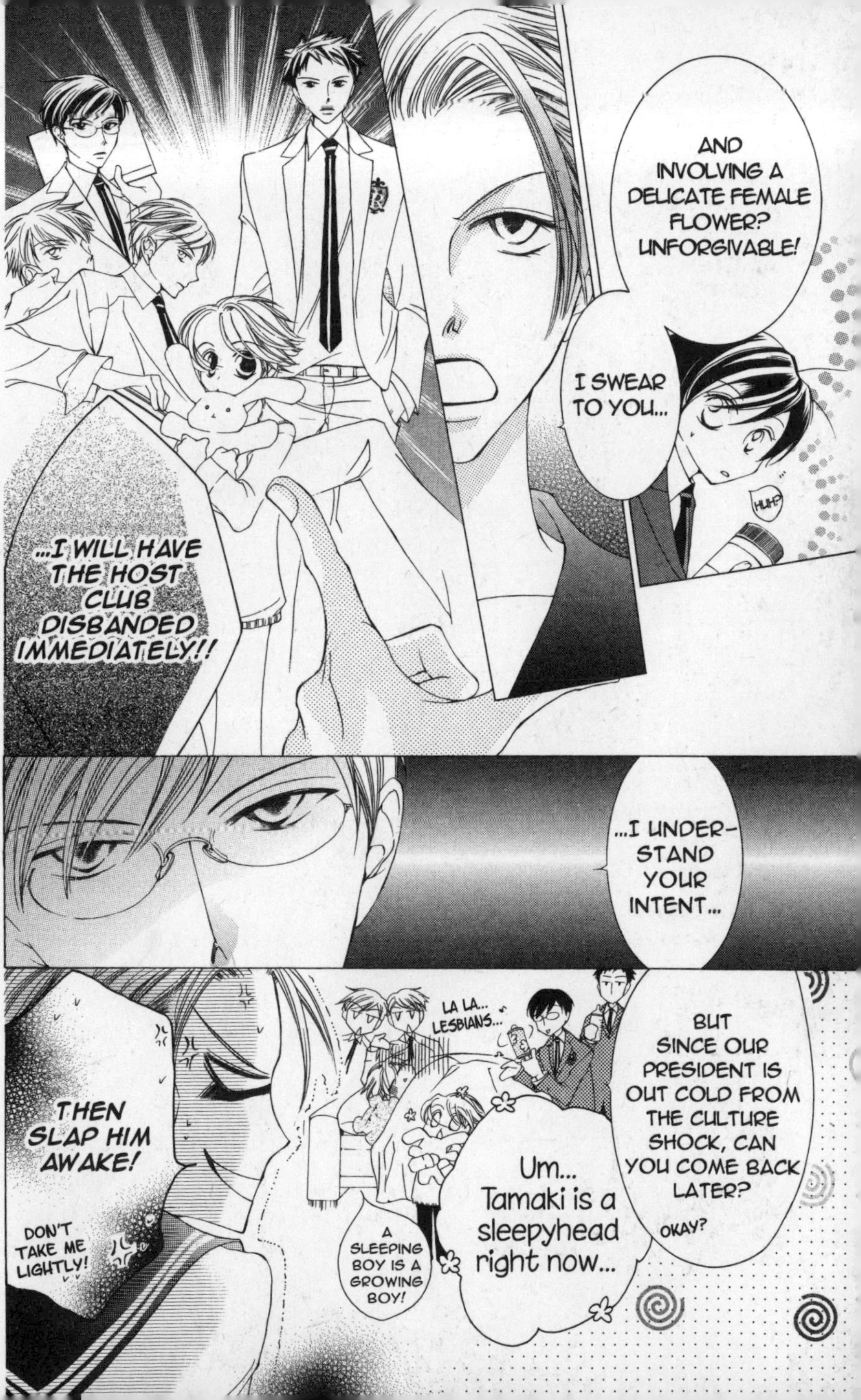
AND INVOLVING A DELICATE FEMALE FLOWER? UNFORGIVABLE!
I SWEAR TO YOU...
HUH?
...I WILL HAVE THE HOST CLUB DISBANDED IMMEDIATELY!!
...I UNDER-STAND YOUR INTENT...
BUT SINCE OUR PRESIDENT IS OUT COLD FROM THE CULTURE SHOCK, CAN YOU COME BACK LATER?
OKAY?
LA LA... LESBIANS...
Um... Tamaki is a sleepyhead right now...
A SLEEPING BOY IS A GROWING BOY!
THEN SLAP HIM AWAKE!
DON'T TAKE ME LIGHTLY!

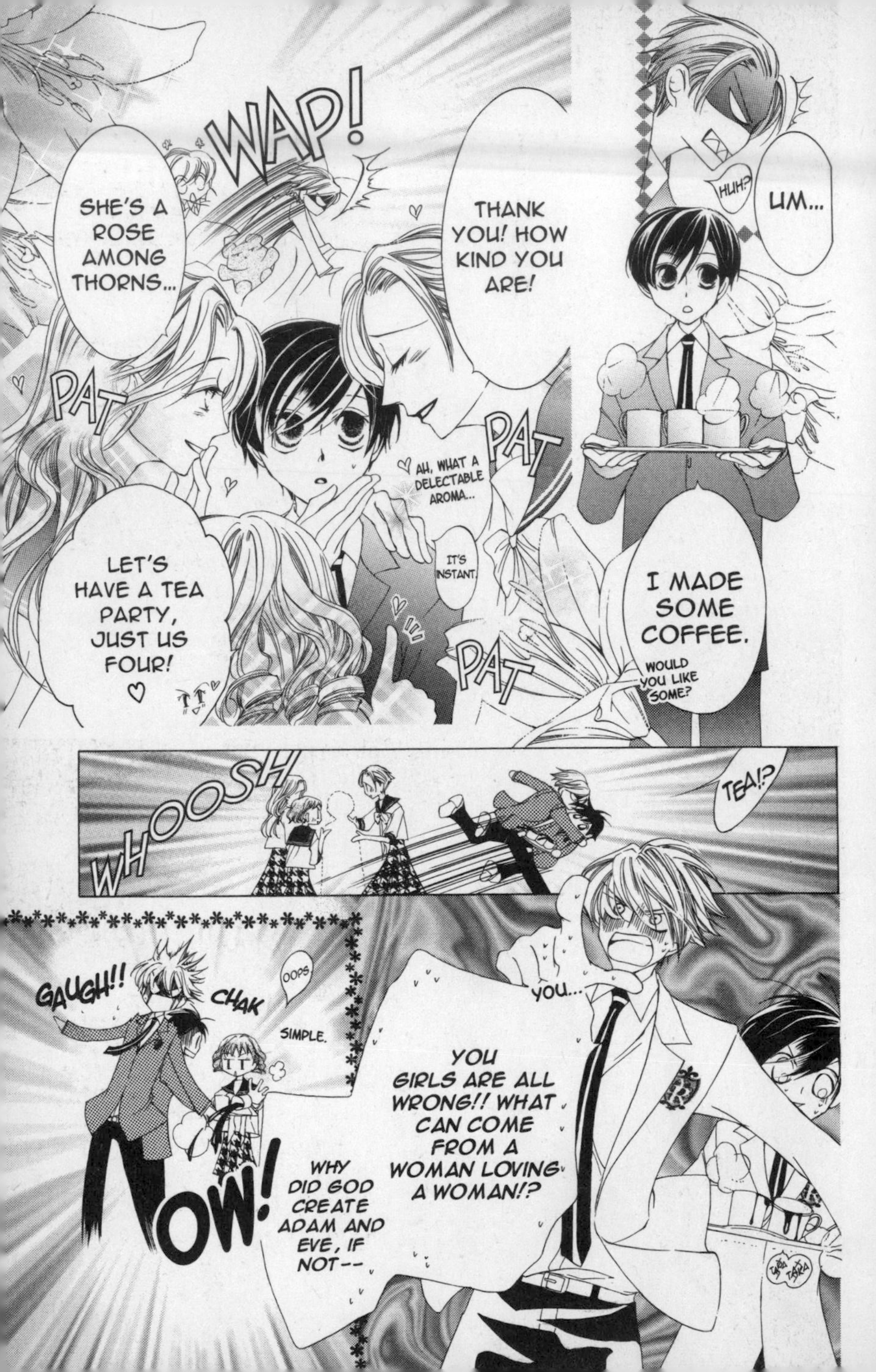
HUH?
UM...
I MADE SOME COFFEE.
WOULD YOU LIKE SOME?
THANK YOU! HOW KIND YOU ARE!
WAP!
SHE'S A ROSE AMONG THORNS...
PAT
PAT
AH, WHAT A DELECTABLE AROMA...
IT'S INSTANT.
PAT
LET'S HAVE A TEA PARTY, JUST US FOUR!
TEA!?
WHOOSH
YOU...
YOU GIRLS ARE ALL WRONG!! WHAT CAN COME FROM A WOMAN LOVING A WOMAN!?
WHY DID GOD CREATE ADAM AND EVE, IF NOT--
OOPS.
CHAK
GAUGH!!
SIMPLE.
OW!

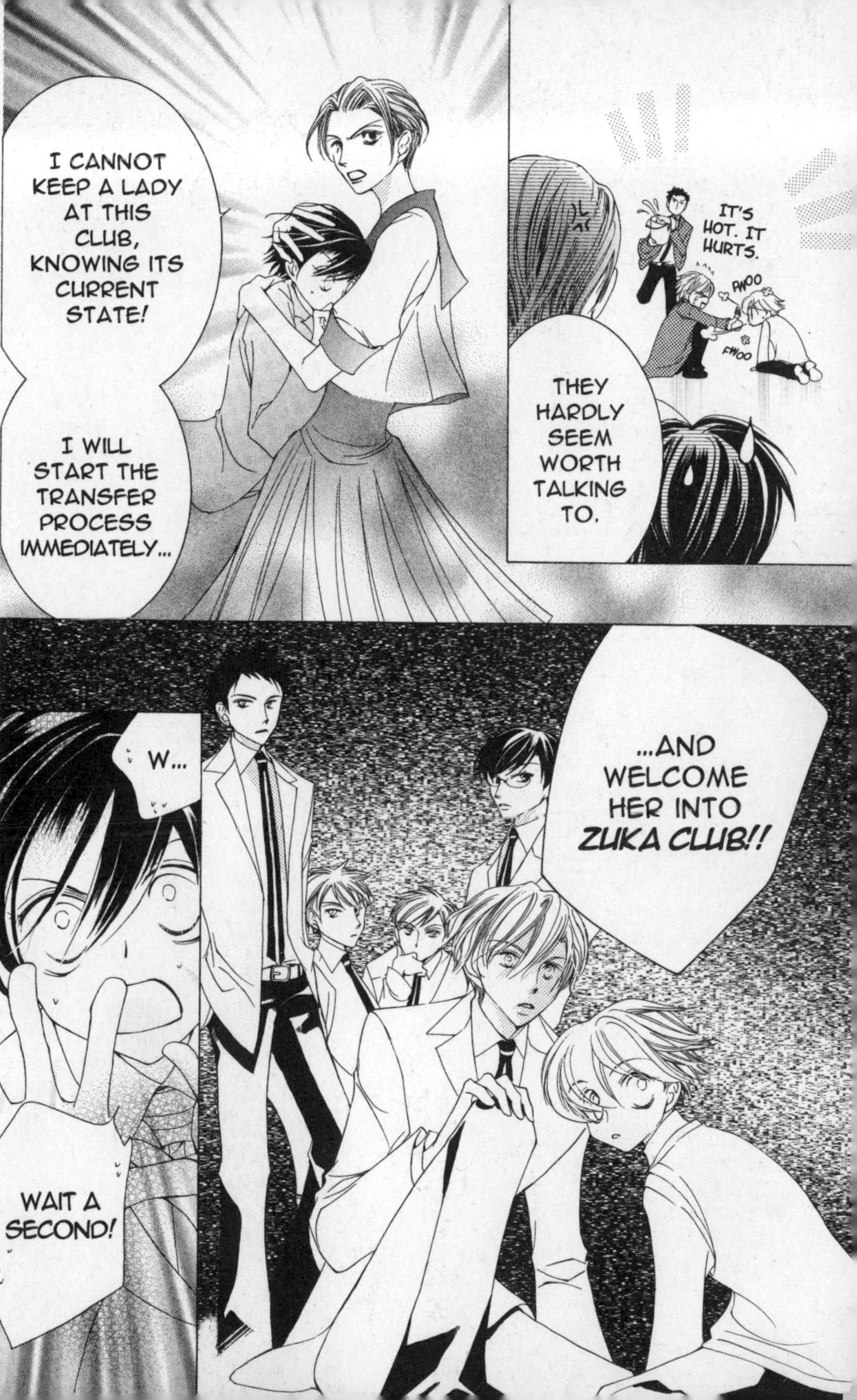
IT'S HOT. IT HURTS.
FWOO
FWOO
THEY HARDLY SEEM WORTH TALKING TO.
I CANNOT KEEP A LADY AT THIS CLUB, KNOWING ITS CURRENT STATE!
I WILL START THE TRANSFER PROCESS IMMEDIATELY...
...AND WELCOME HER INTO ZUKA CLUB!!
W...
WAIT A SECOND!

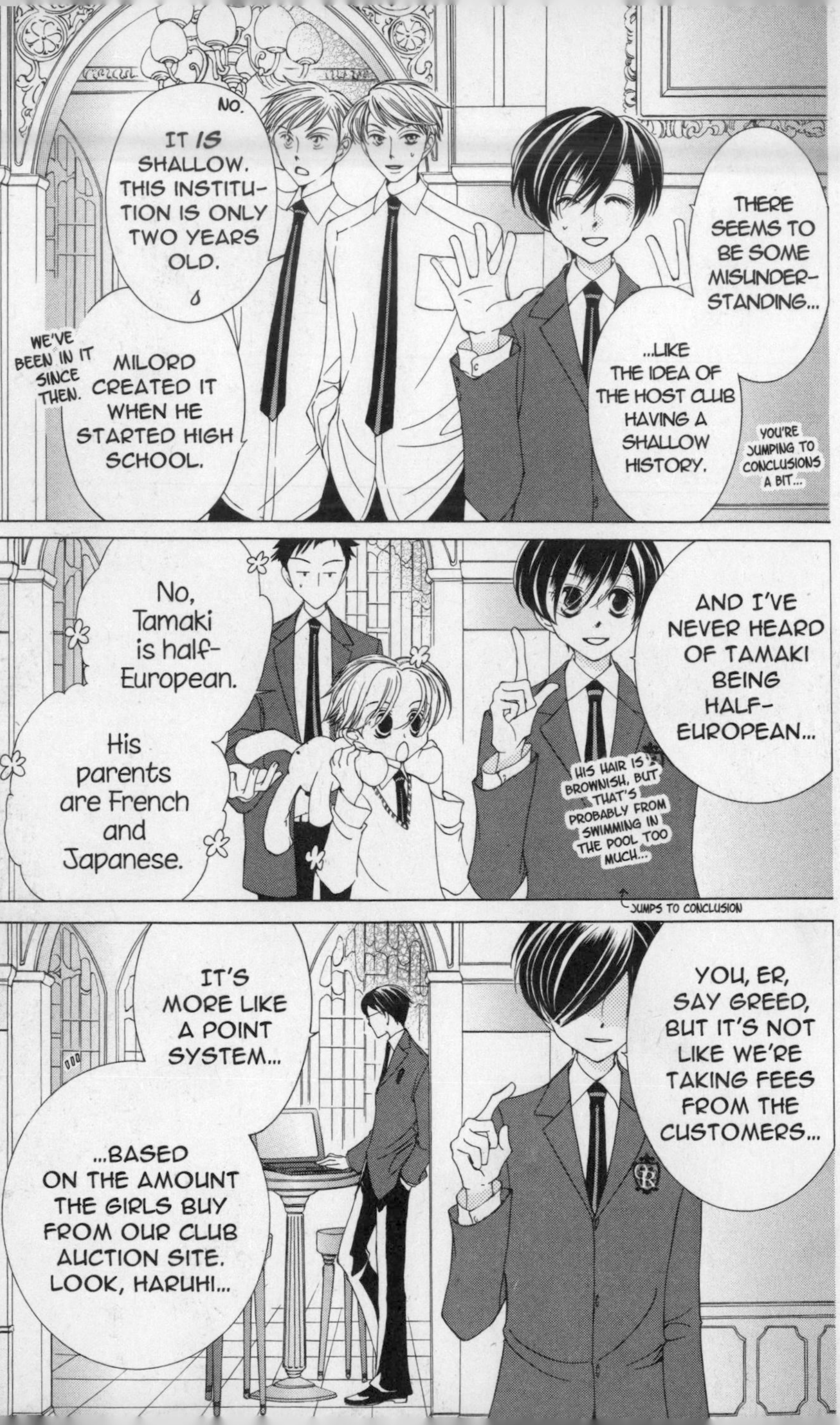
THERE SEEMS TO BE SOME MISUNDERSTANDING...
...LIKE THE IDEA OF THE HOST CLUB HAVING A SHALLOW HISTORY.
YOU'RE JUMPING TO CONCLUSIONS A BIT...
NO.
IT *IS* SHALLOW. THIS INSTITUTION IS ONLY TWO YEARS OLD.
MILORD CREATED IT WHEN HE STARTED HIGH SCHOOL.
WE'VE BEEN IN IT SINCE THEN.
AND I'VE NEVER HEARD OF TAMAKI BEING HALF-EUROPEAN...
HIS HAIR IS BROWNISH, BUT THAT'S PROBABLY FROM SWIMMING IN THE POOL TOO MUCH...
JUMPS TO CONCLUSION
No, Tamaki is half-European.
His parents are French and Japanese.
YOU, ER, SAY GREED, BUT IT'S NOT LIKE WE'RE TAKING FEES FROM THE CUSTOMERS...
IT'S MORE LIKE A POINT SYSTEM...
...BASED ON THE AMOUNT THE GIRLS BUY FROM OUR CLUB AUCTION SITE. LOOK, HARUHI...

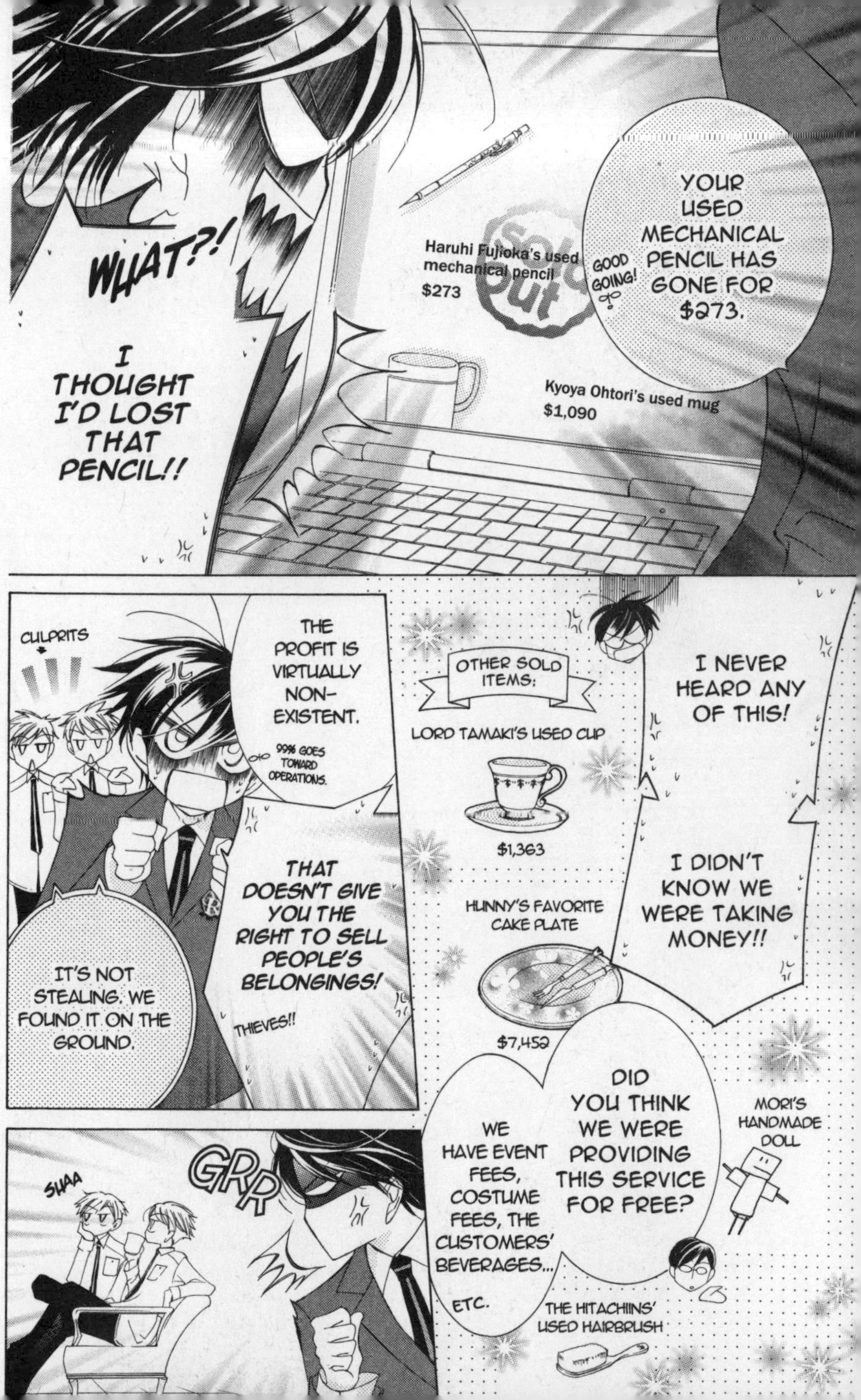
YOUR USED MECHANICAL PENCIL HAS GONE FOR $273.
GOOD GOING!
Sold Out
Haruhi Fujioka's used mechanical pencil
$273
Kyoya Ohtori's used mug
$1,090
WHAT?!
I THOUGHT I'D LOST THAT PENCIL!!
I NEVER HEARD ANY OF THIS!
I DIDN'T KNOW WE WERE TAKING MONEY!!
OTHER SOLD ITEMS:
LORD TAMAKI'S USED CUP
$1,363
HUNNY'S FAVORITE CAKE PLATE
$7,452
MORI'S HANDMADE DOLL
THE HITACHIINS' USED HAIRBRUSH
DID YOU THINK WE WERE PROVIDING THIS SERVICE FOR FREE?
WE HAVE EVENT FEES, COSTUME FEES, THE CUSTOMERS' BEVERAGES...
ETC.
THE PROFIT IS VIRTUALLY NON-EXISTENT.
99% GOES TOWARD OPERATIONS.
THAT DOESN'T GIVE YOU THE RIGHT TO SELL PEOPLE'S BELONGINGS!
THIEVES!!
IT'S NOT STEALING. WE FOUND IT ON THE GROUND.
CULPRITS
GRR
SHAA

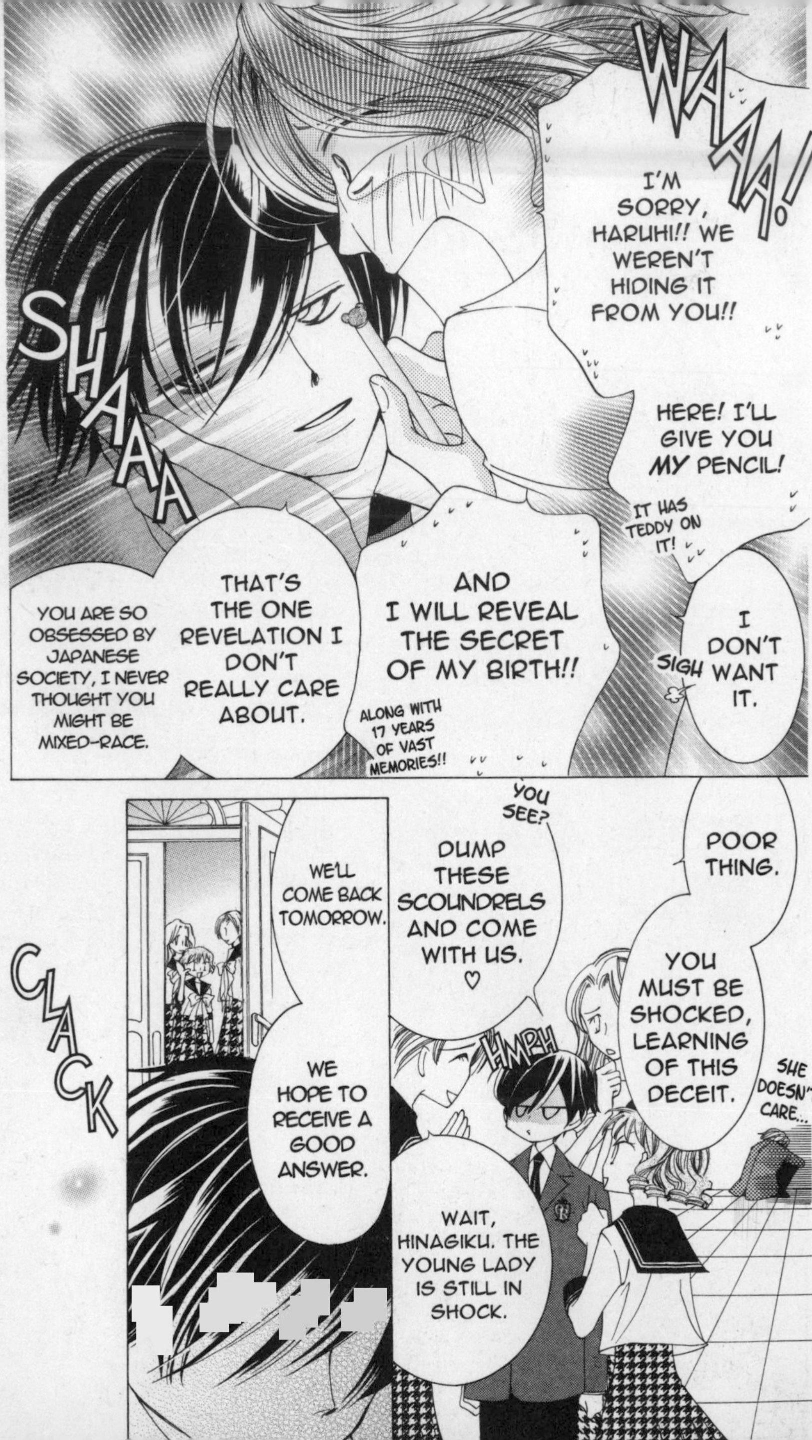
WAAAA!
I'M SORRY, HARUHI!! WE WEREN'T HIDING IT FROM YOU!!
HERE! I'LL GIVE YOU MY PENCIL!
IT HAS TEDDY ON IT!
SHAAAA
I DON'T WANT IT.
SIGH
AND I WILL REVEAL THE SECRET OF MY BIRTH!!
ALONG WITH 17 YEARS OF VAST MEMORIES!!
THAT'S THE ONE REVELATION I DON'T REALLY CARE ABOUT.
YOU ARE SO OBSESSED BY JAPANESE SOCIETY, I NEVER THOUGHT YOU MIGHT BE MIXED-RACE.
POOR THING.
YOU MUST BE SHOCKED, LEARNING OF THIS DECEIT.
SHE DOESN'T CARE...
YOU SEE?
DUMP THESE SCOUNDRELS AND COME WITH US. ♡
HMPH
WAIT, HINAGIKU. THE YOUNG LADY IS STILL IN SHOCK.
WE'LL COME BACK TOMORROW.
WE HOPE TO RECEIVE A GOOD ANSWER.
CLACK

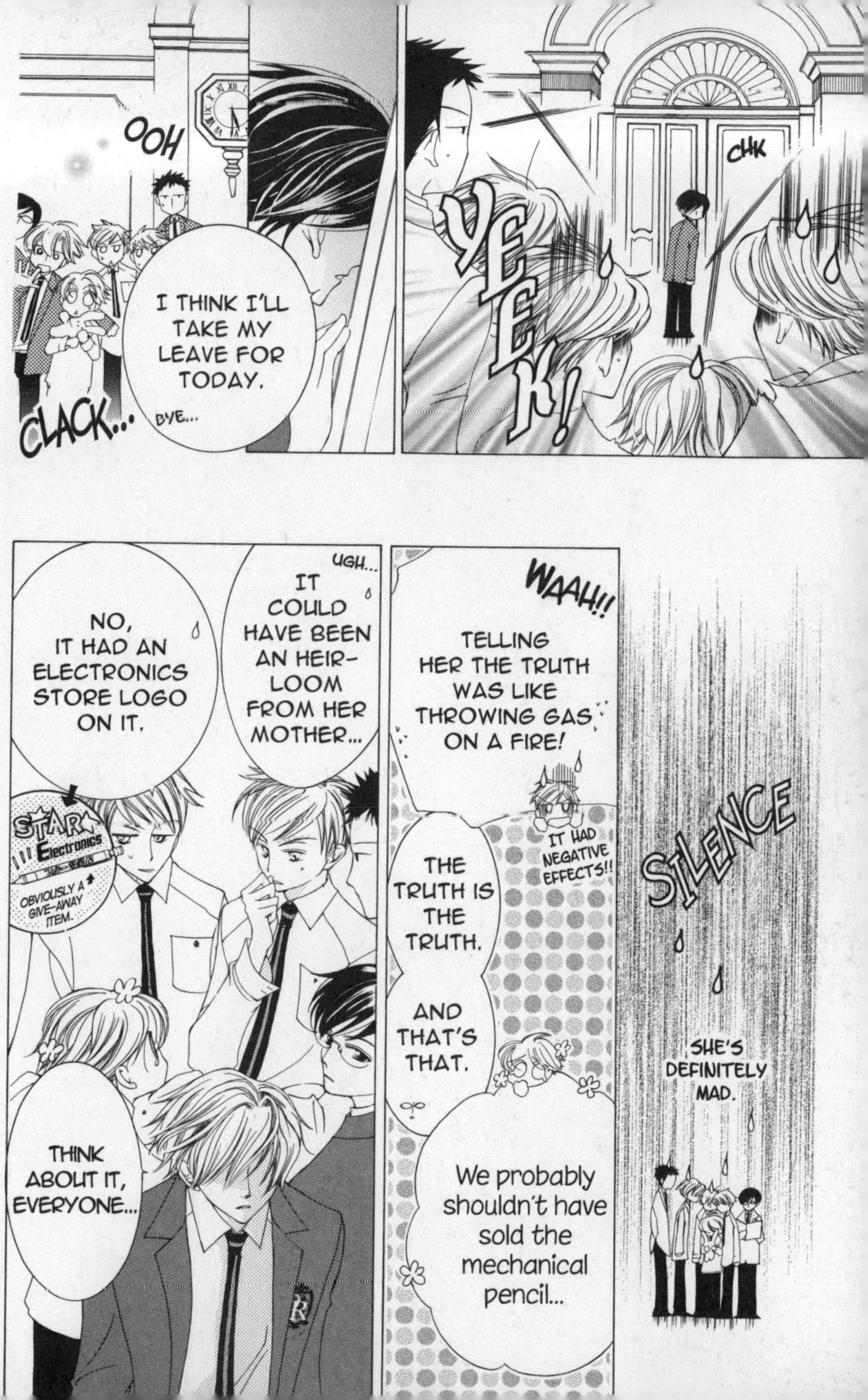
CHK
YEEK!
I THINK I'LL TAKE MY LEAVE FOR TODAY.
OOH
CLACK...
BYE...
SILENCE
SHE'S DEFINITELY MAD.
WAAH!!
TELLING HER THE TRUTH WAS LIKE THROWING GAS ON A FIRE!
IT HAD NEGATIVE EFFECTS!!
THE TRUTH IS THE TRUTH.
AND THAT'S THAT.
We probably shouldn't have sold the mechanical pencil...
UGH...
IT COULD HAVE BEEN AN HEIR-LOOM FROM HER MOTHER...
NO, IT HAD AN ELECTRONICS STORE LOGO ON IT.
STAR Electronics
OBVIOUSLY A GIVE-AWAY ITEM.
THINK ABOUT IT, EVERYONE...

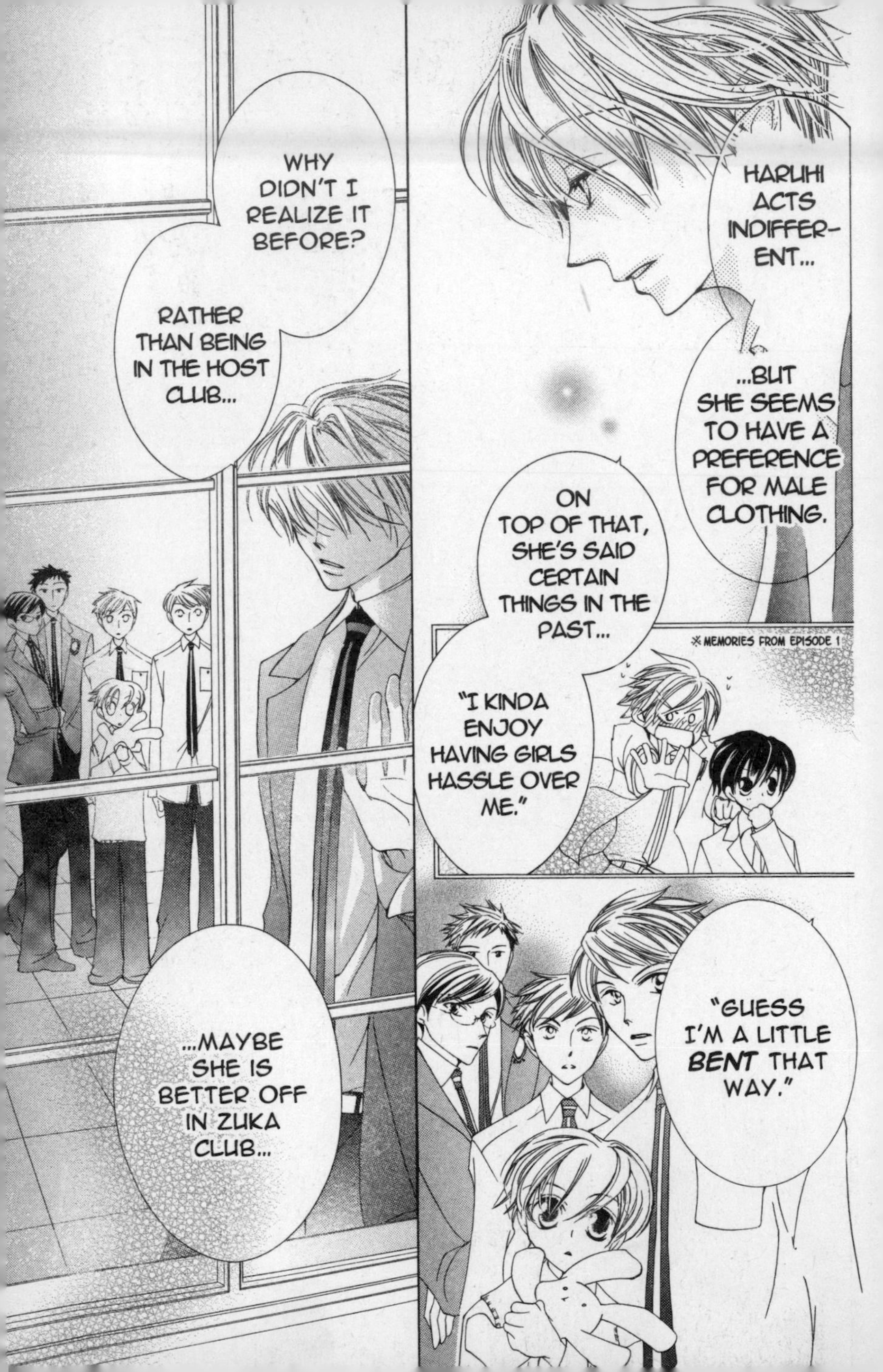
HARUHI ACTS INDIFFER-ENT...
...BUT SHE SEEMS TO HAVE A PREFERENCE FOR MALE CLOTHING.
ON TOP OF THAT, SHE'S SAID CERTAIN THINGS IN THE PAST...
※ MEMORIES FROM EPISODE 1
"I KINDA ENJOY HAVING GIRLS HASSLE OVER ME."
"GUESS I'M A LITTLE BENT THAT WAY."
WHY DIDN'T I REALIZE IT BEFORE?
RATHER THAN BEING IN THE HOST CLUB...
...MAYBE SHE IS BETTER OFF IN ZUKA CLUB...

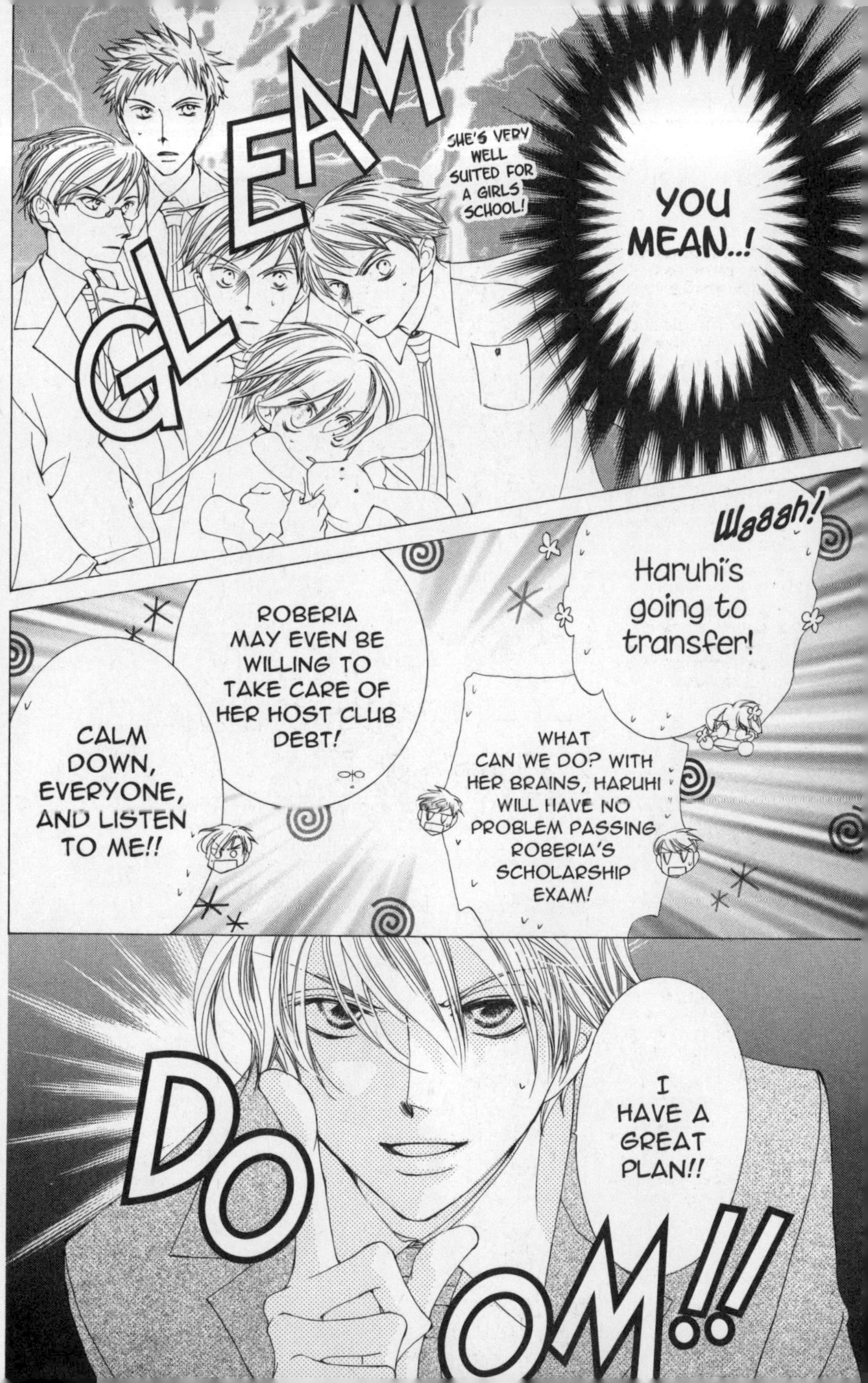
YOU MEAN..!
SHE'S VERY WELL SUITED FOR A GIRLS SCHOOL!
GLEAM
Waaah!
Haruhi's going to transfer!
WHAT CAN WE DO? WITH HER BRAINS, HARUHI WILL HAVE NO PROBLEM PASSING ROBERIA'S SCHOLARSHIP EXAM!
ROBERIA MAY EVEN BE WILLING TO TAKE CARE OF HER HOST CLUB DEBT!
CALM DOWN, EVERYONE, AND LISTEN TO ME!!
I HAVE A GREAT PLAN!!
DOOM!!

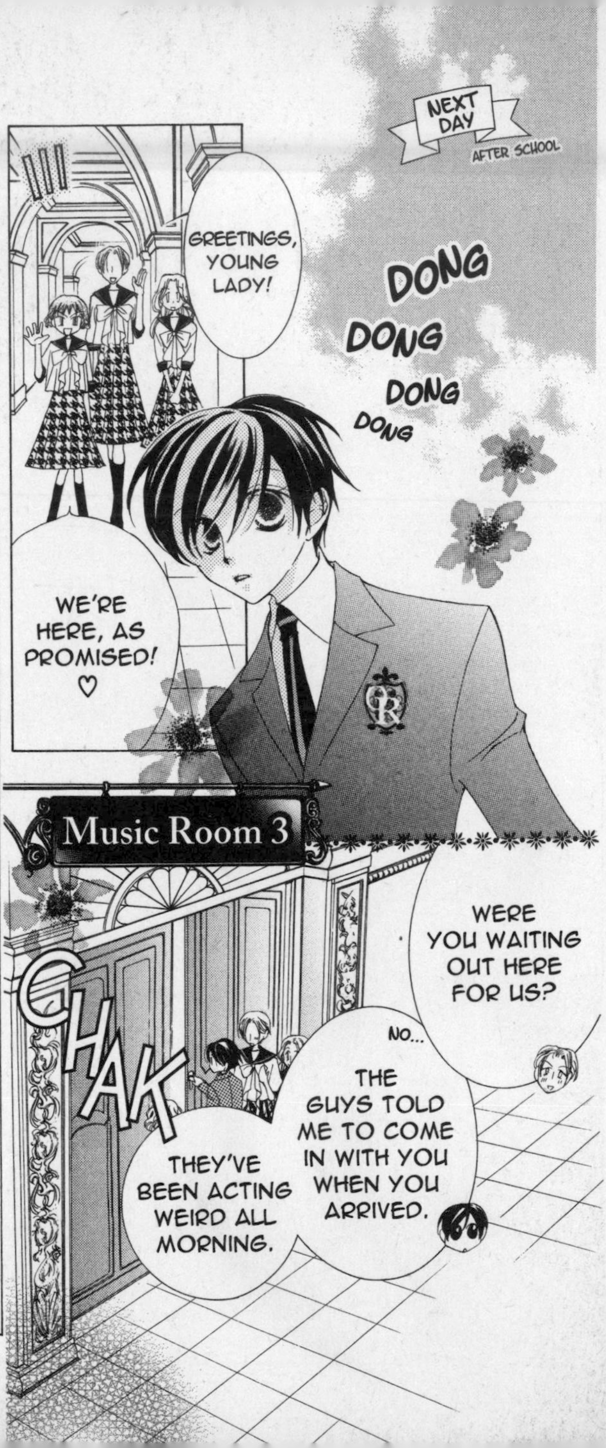
NEXT DAY
AFTER SCHOOL
DONG
DONG
DONG
DONG
GREETINGS, YOUNG LADY!
WE'RE HERE, AS PROMISED! ♡
Music Room 3
WERE YOU WAITING OUT HERE FOR US?
NO...
THE GUYS TOLD ME TO COME IN WITH YOU WHEN YOU ARRIVED.
THEY'VE BEEN ACTING WEIRD ALL MORNING.
CHAK

3

✿AH, THE DRAMA CD...I WAS CONVINCED THE COMPUTER WAS GODLIKE WHEN I WROTE KYOYA'S GOOD-NIGHT MESSAGE FOR THE CD. WHEN I WAS THINKING CONSCIOUSLY, ***NOTHING*** CAME TO MIND. BUT WHEN I WENT TO TYPE, "THIS IS KYOYA OHTORI," KYOYA'S MESSAGE FLOWED OUT, AS THOUGH KYOYA HIMSELF HAD POSSESSED ME. WHAT IS LIVING IN MY COMPUTER? (I HOPE IT'S NOT KYOYA...)

✿RETURNING TO THE MAIN TOPIC...THERE ARE TIMES WHEN I TYPE UP THE PLOT IN DETAIL ON THE COMPUTER.

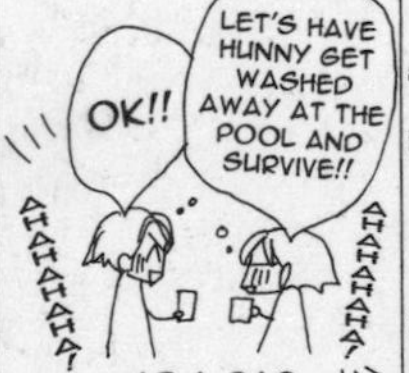
LET'S HAVE HUNNY GET WASHED AWAY AT THE POOL AND SURVIVE!!
OK!!
AHAHAHAHA!
AHAHAHAHA!
AT A BAR

THEN THERE ARE TIMES I COME UP WITH PLOTS LIKE THIS. (DANGEROUS.) SMALL JOKES AND BITS THAT MOVE THE PLOT ALONG SEEM TO WORK OUT BETTER THIS WAY, I THINK.

※THIS IS SPEAKING STRICTLY FOR MYSELF. THE COMPUTER WORKS FOR SOME PEOPLE AND NOT OTHERS.

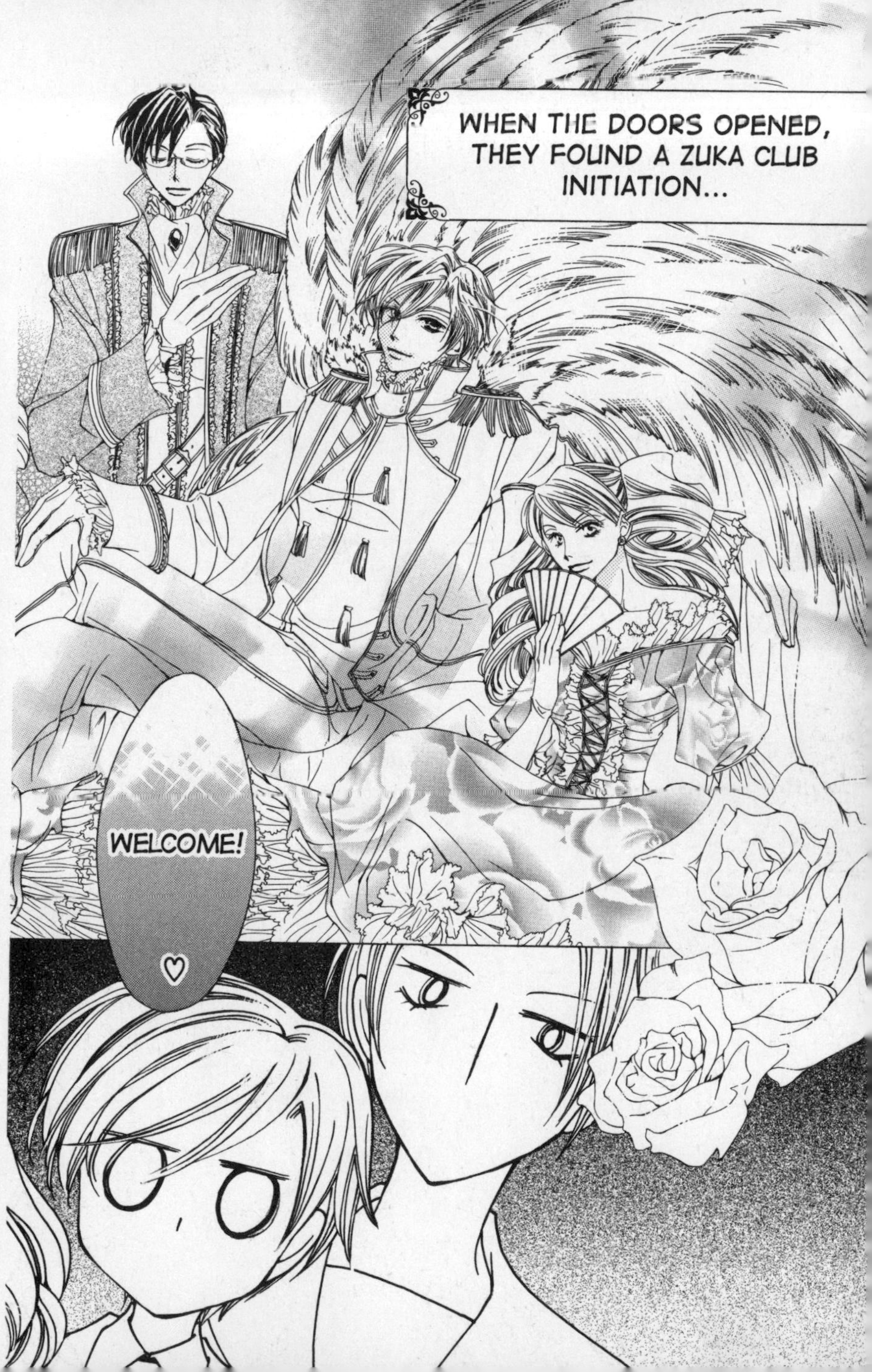
WHEN THE DOORS OPENED, THEY FOUND A ZUKA CLUB INITIATION...
WELCOME! ♡

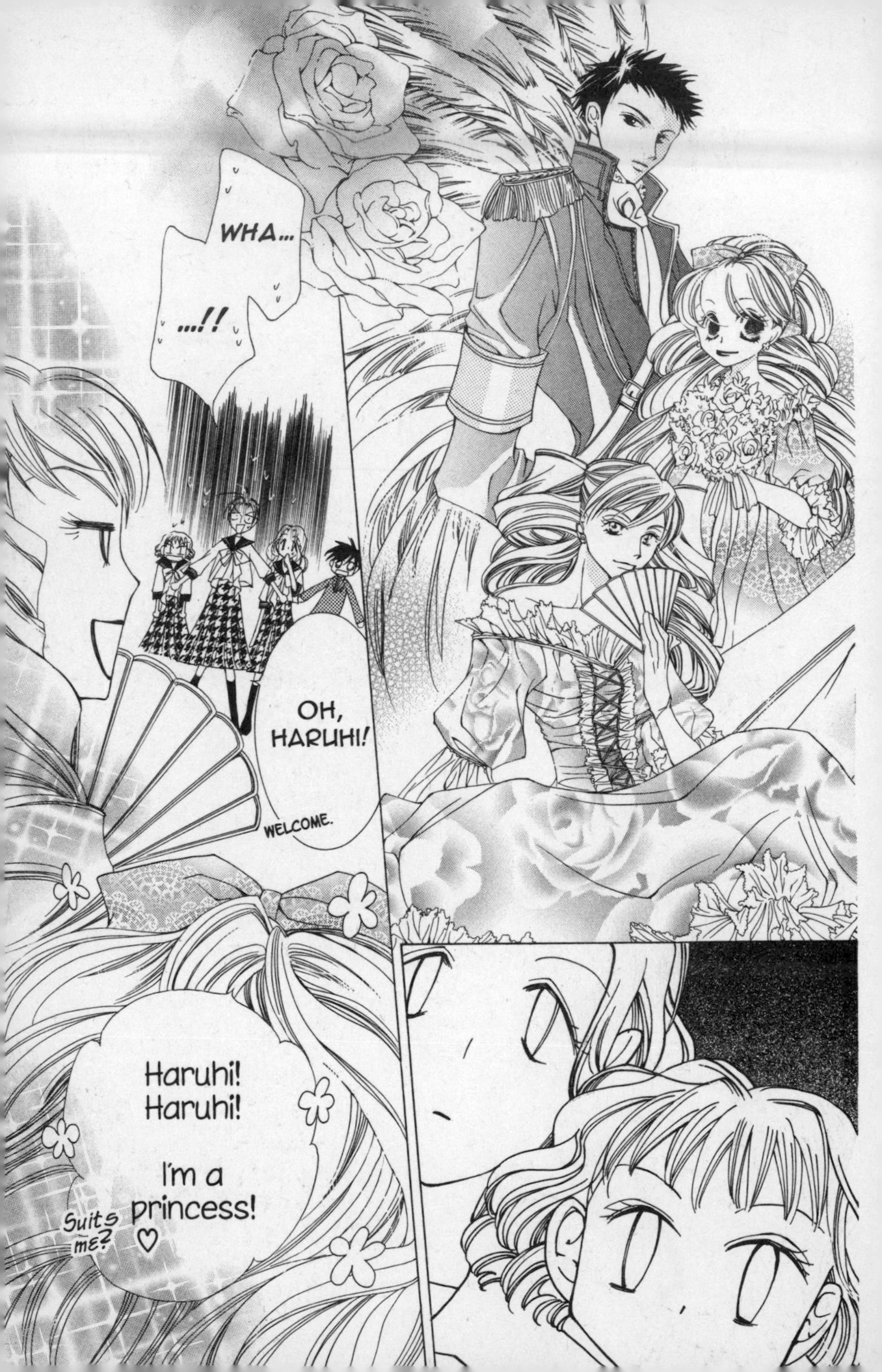
WHA...
...!!
OH, HARUHI!
WELCOME.
Haruhi! Haruhi!
I'm a princess! ♡
Suits me?

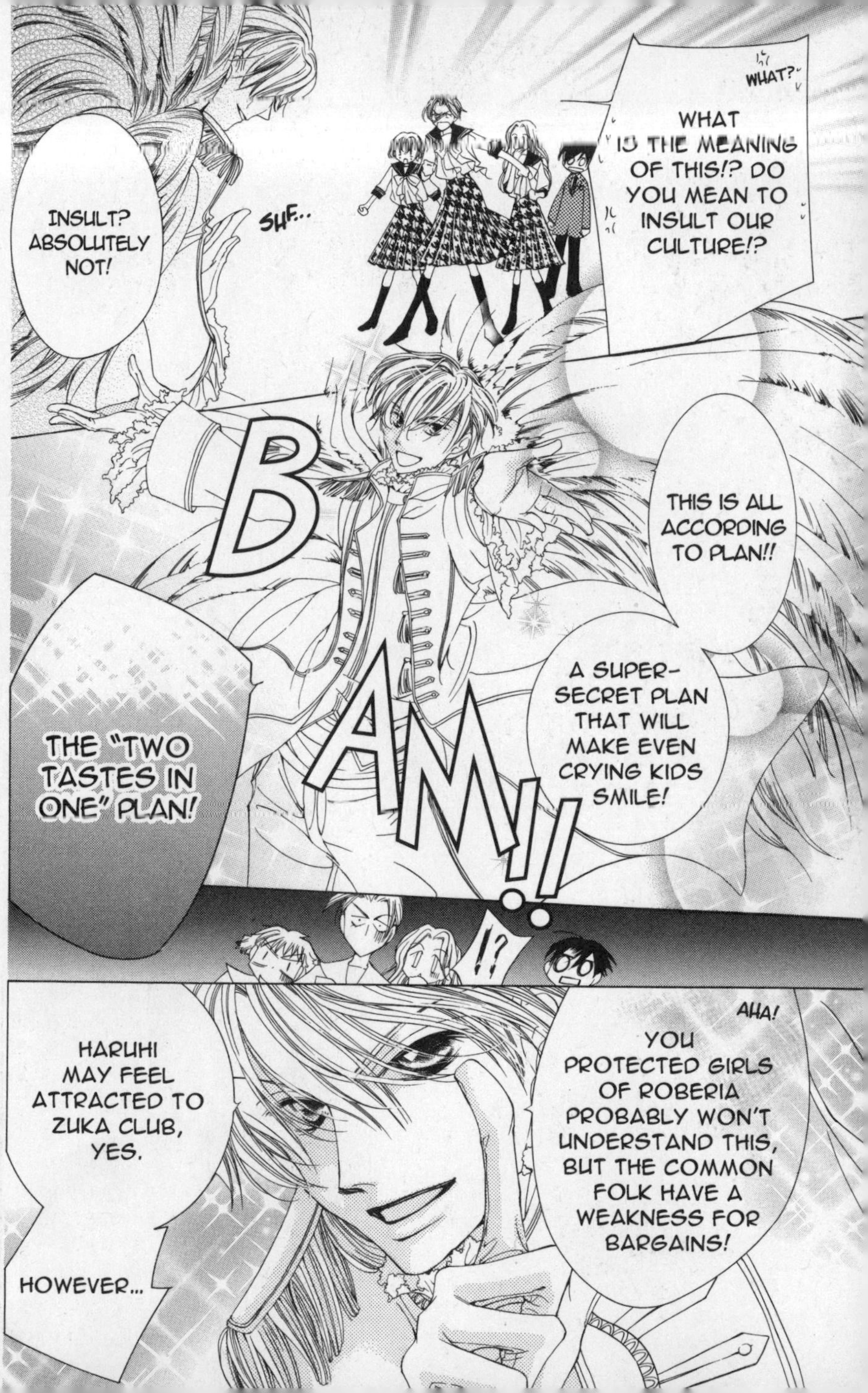
WHAT?
WHAT IS THE MEANING OF THIS!? DO YOU MEAN TO INSULT OUR CULTURE!?
SHF...
INSULT? ABSOLUTELY NOT!
THIS IS ALL ACCORDING TO PLAN!!
BAM!!
A SUPER-SECRET PLAN THAT WILL MAKE EVEN CRYING KIDS SMILE!
THE "TWO TASTES IN ONE" PLAN!
!?
AHA!
YOU PROTECTED GIRLS OF ROBERIA PROBABLY WON'T UNDERSTAND THIS, BUT THE COMMON FOLK HAVE A WEAKNESS FOR BARGAINS!
HARUHI MAY FEEL ATTRACTED TO ZUKA CLUB, YES.
HOWEVER...

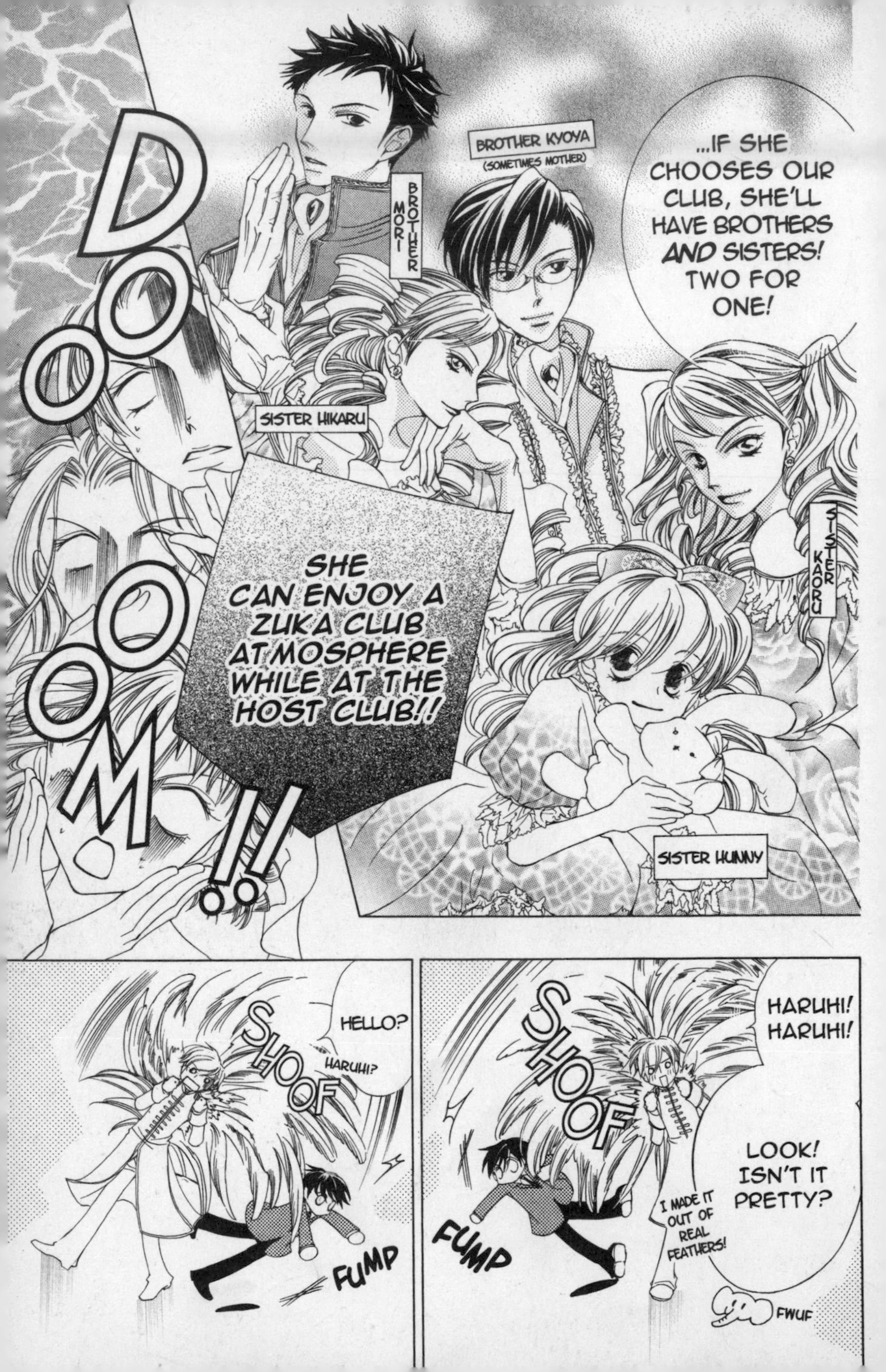
...IF SHE CHOOSES OUR CLUB, SHE'LL HAVE BROTHERS AND SISTERS! TWO FOR ONE!
BROTHER KYOYA
(SOMETIMES MOTHER)
BROTHER MORI
SISTER KAORU
SISTER HIKARU
SISTER HUNNY
SHE CAN ENJOY A ZUKA CLUB ATMOSPHERE WHILE AT THE HOST CLUB!!
DOOOOOM!!
HARUHI! HARUHI!
SHOOF
LOOK! ISN'T IT PRETTY?
I MADE IT OUT OF REAL FEATHERS!
FUMP
FWUF
HELLO?
HARUHI?
SHOOF
FUMP

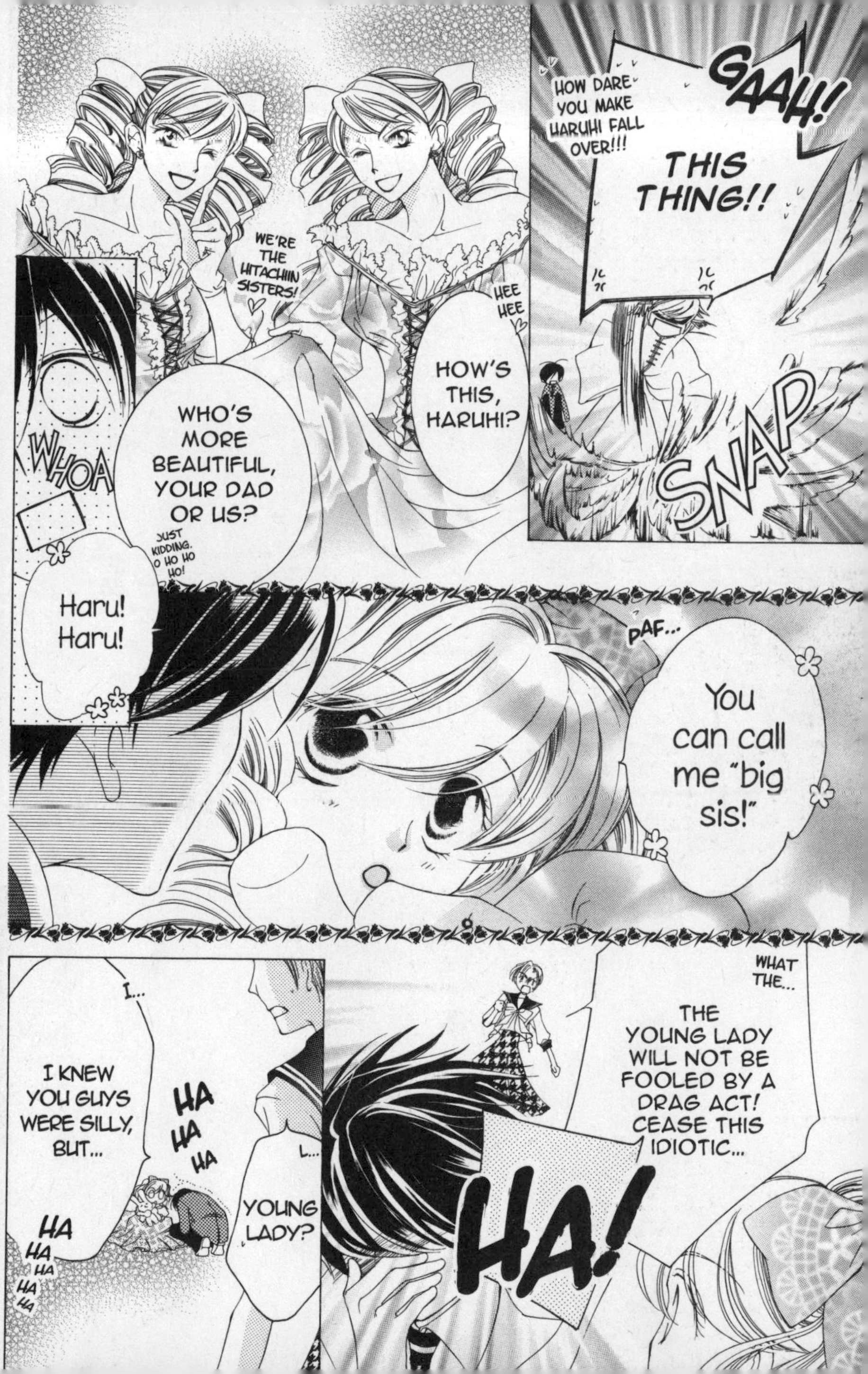
GAAH!
HOW DARE YOU MAKE HARUHI FALL OVER!!!
THIS THING!!
SNAP
WE'RE THE HITACHIIN SISTERS!
HEE HEE
HOW'S THIS, HARUHI?
WHO'S MORE BEAUTIFUL, YOUR DAD OR US?
JUST KIDDING. O HO HO HO!
WHOA
Haru! Haru!
PAF...
You can call me "big sis!"
WHAT THE...
THE YOUNG LADY WILL NOT BE FOOLED BY A DRAG ACT! CEASE THIS IDIOTIC...
HA!
I...
I KNEW YOU GUYS WERE SILLY, BUT...
HA HA HA
L...
YOUNG LADY?
HA HA HA HA HA

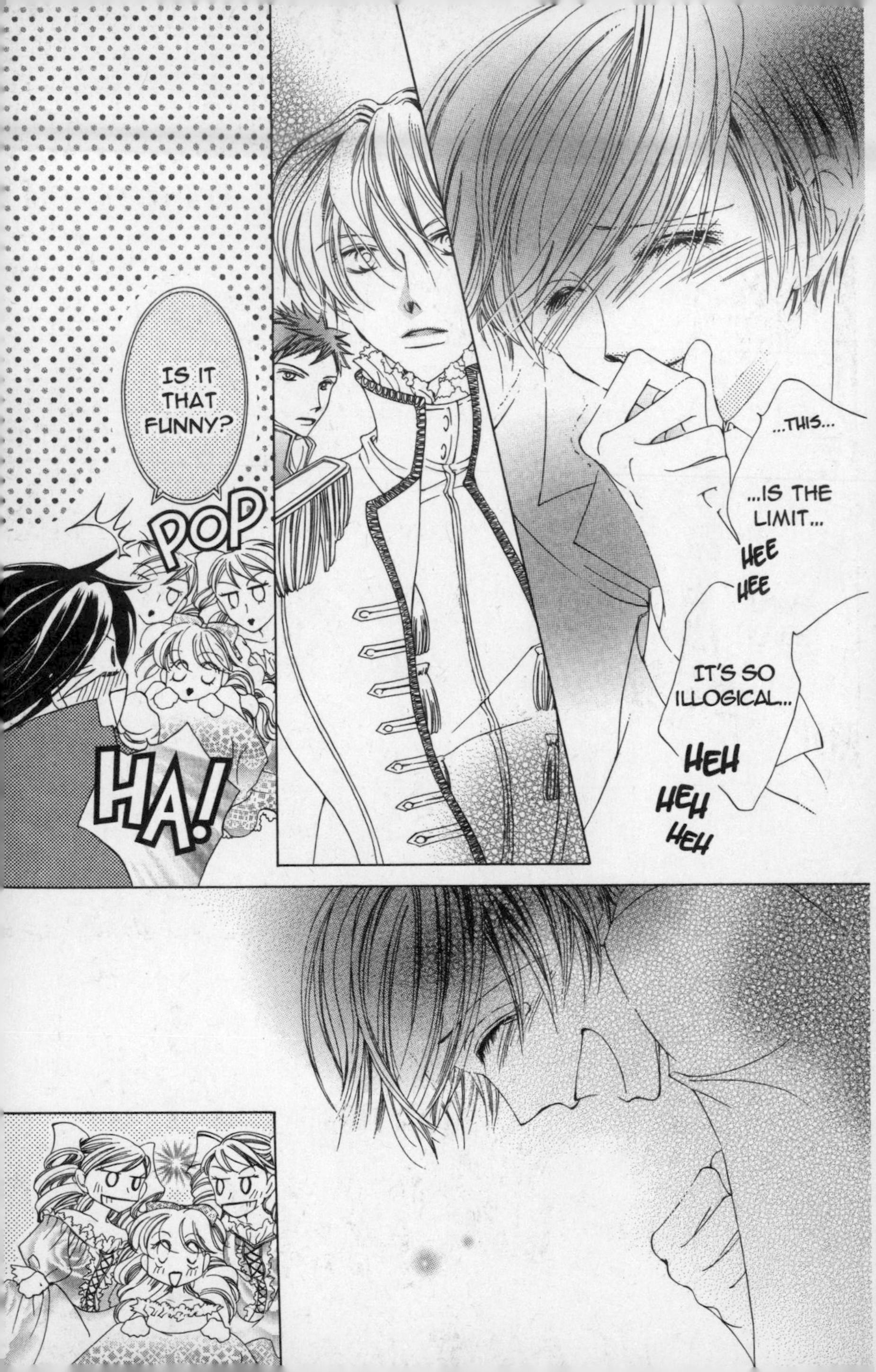
...THIS...
...IS THE LIMIT...
HEE HEE
IT'S SO ILLOGICAL...
HEH HEH HEH
IS IT THAT FUNNY?
POP
HA!

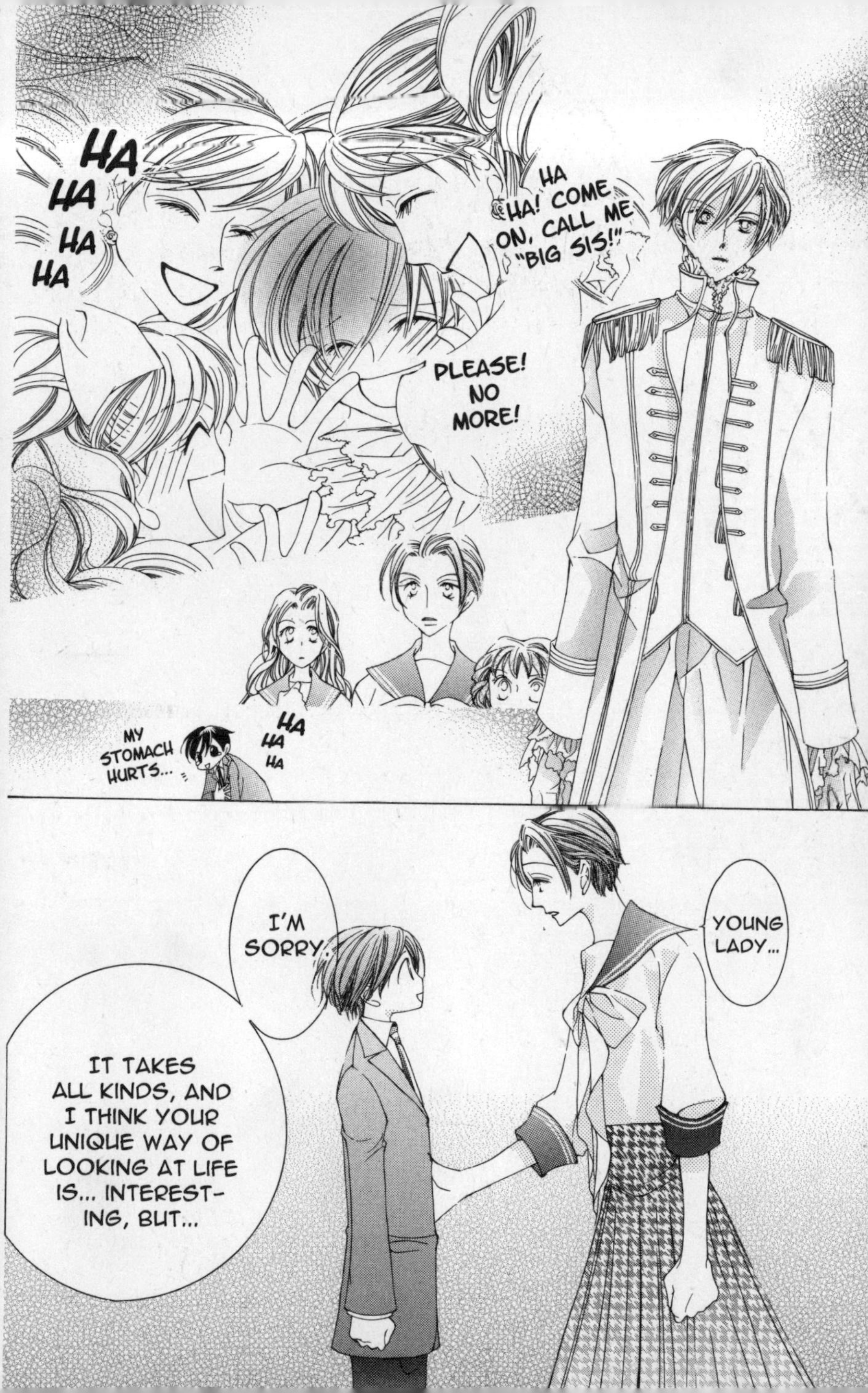
HA HA! COME ON, CALL ME "BIG SIS!"
PLEASE! NO MORE!
HA HA HA HA
HA HA HA
MY STOMACH HURTS...
YOUNG LADY...
I'M SORRY.
IT TAKES ALL KINDS, AND I THINK YOUR UNIQUE WAY OF LOOKING AT LIFE IS... INTEREST-ING, BUT...

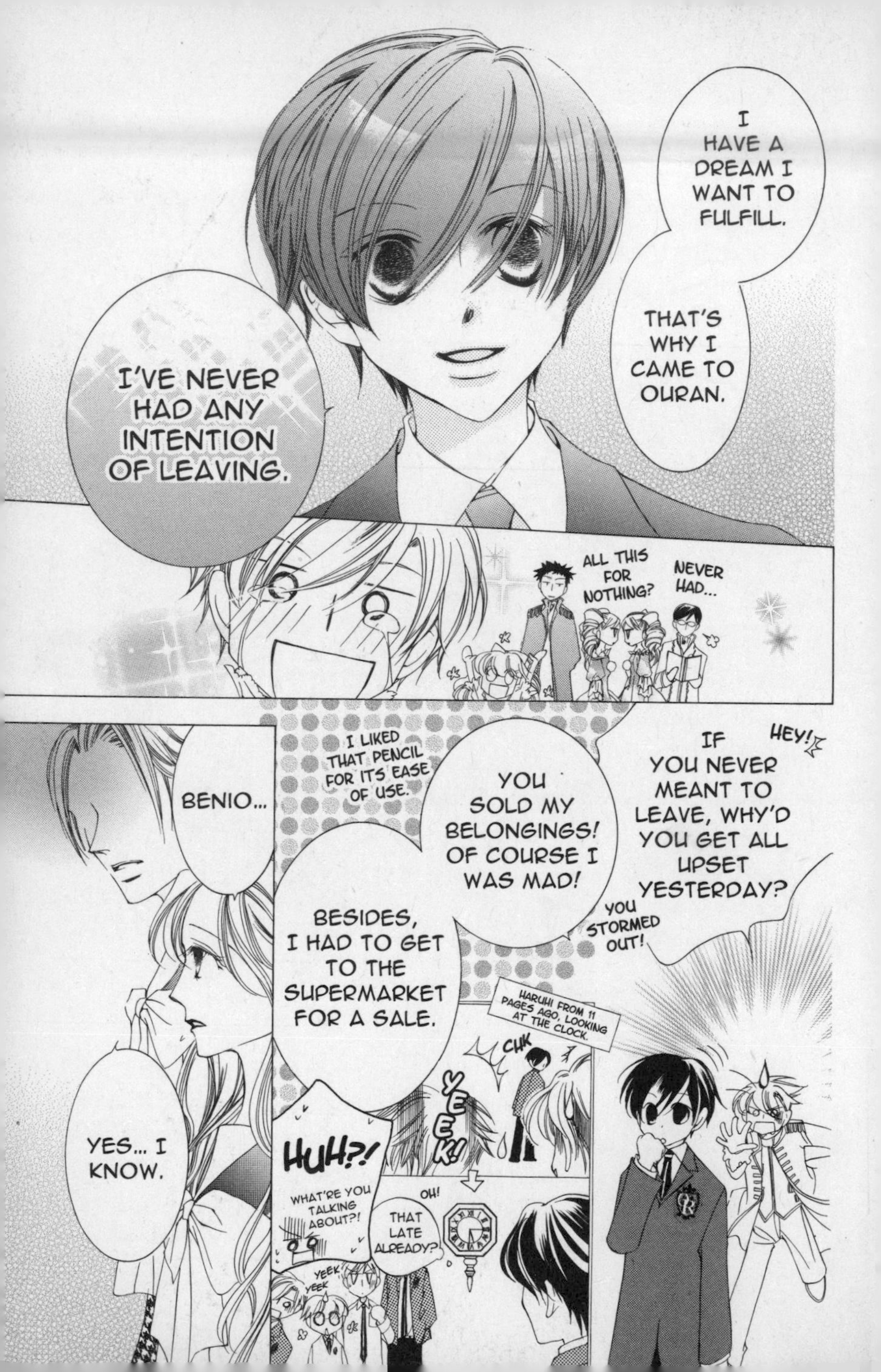
I HAVE A DREAM I WANT TO FULFILL.
THAT'S WHY I CAME TO OURAN.
I'VE NEVER HAD ANY INTENTION OF LEAVING.
NEVER HAD...
ALL THIS FOR NOTHING?
HEY!
IF YOU NEVER MEANT TO LEAVE, WHY'D YOU GET ALL UPSET YESTERDAY?
YOU STORMED OUT!
YOU SOLD MY BELONGINGS! OF COURSE I WAS MAD!
I LIKED THAT PENCIL FOR ITS EASE OF USE.
BESIDES, I HAD TO GET TO THE SUPERMARKET FOR A SALE.
HARUHI FROM 11 PAGES AGO, LOOKING AT THE CLOCK.
CHK
YEEK!
HUH?!
OH!
THAT LATE ALREADY?
WHAT'RE YOU TALKING ABOUT?!
YEEK YEEK
BENIO...
YES... I KNOW.

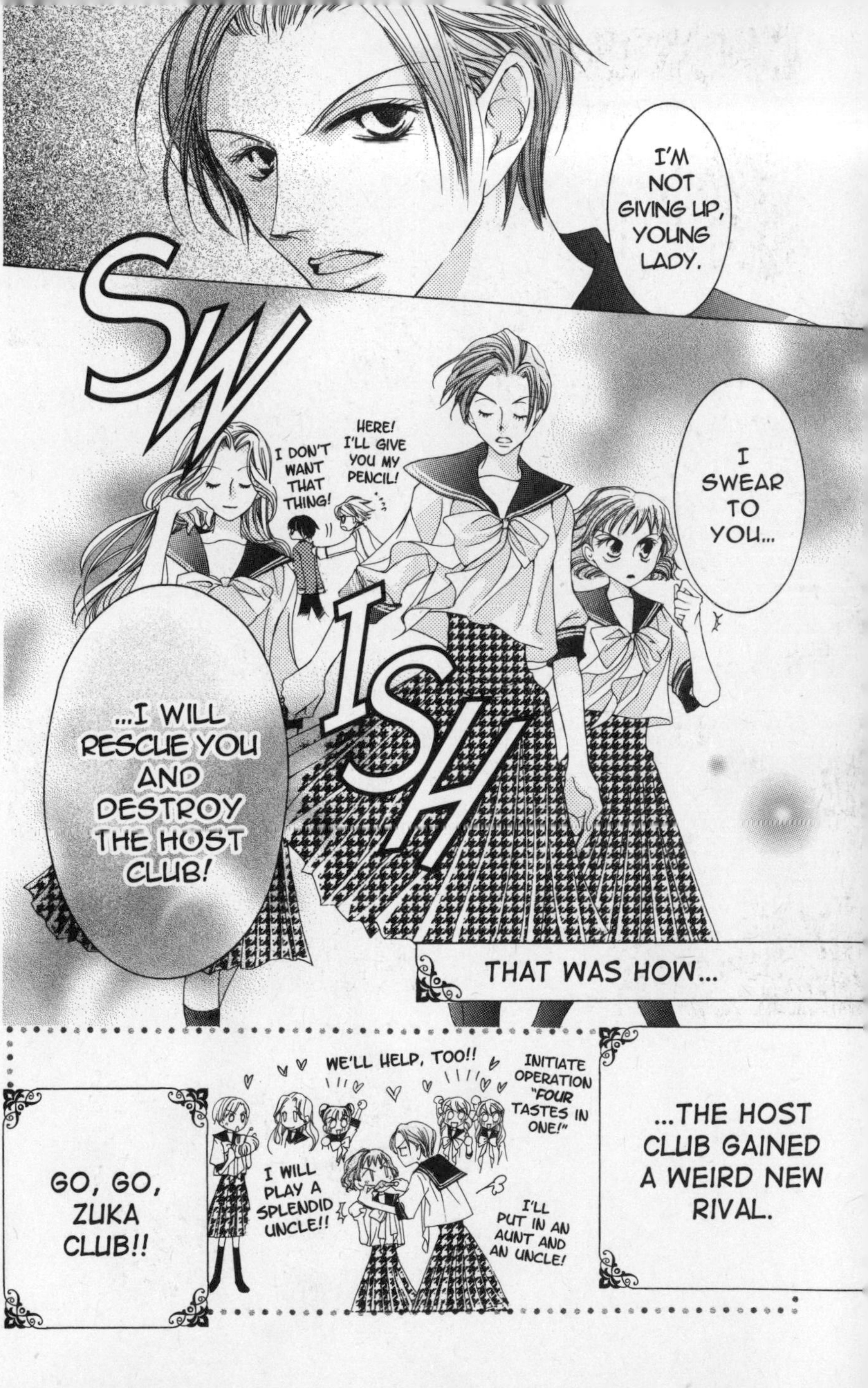
I'M NOT GIVING UP, YOUNG LADY.
SWISH
I SWEAR TO YOU...
HERE! I'LL GIVE YOU MY PENCIL!
I DON'T WANT THAT THING!
...I WILL RESCUE YOU AND DESTROY THE HOST CLUB!
THAT WAS HOW...
...THE HOST CLUB GAINED A WEIRD NEW RIVAL.
INITIATE OPERATION "FOUR TASTES IN ONE!"
WE'LL HELP, TOO!!
I'LL PUT IN AN AUNT AND AN UNCLE!
I WILL PLAY A SPLENDID UNCLE!!
GO, GO, ZUKA CLUB!!

Episode 11

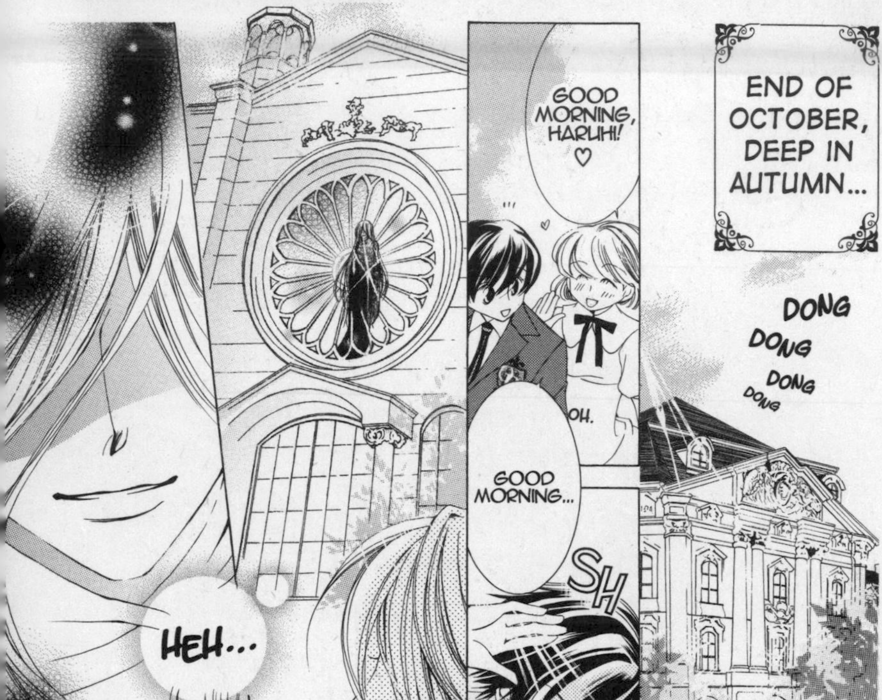
END OF OCTOBER, DEEP IN AUTUMN...
DONG
DONG
DONG
DONG
GOOD MORNING!
HIYA!
GOOD MORNING, HARUHI! ♡
OH.
GOOD MORNING...
SHING
HEH...

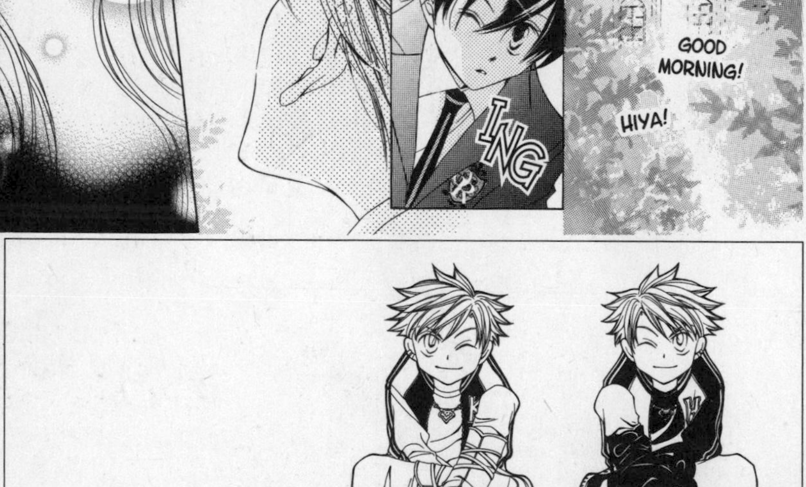

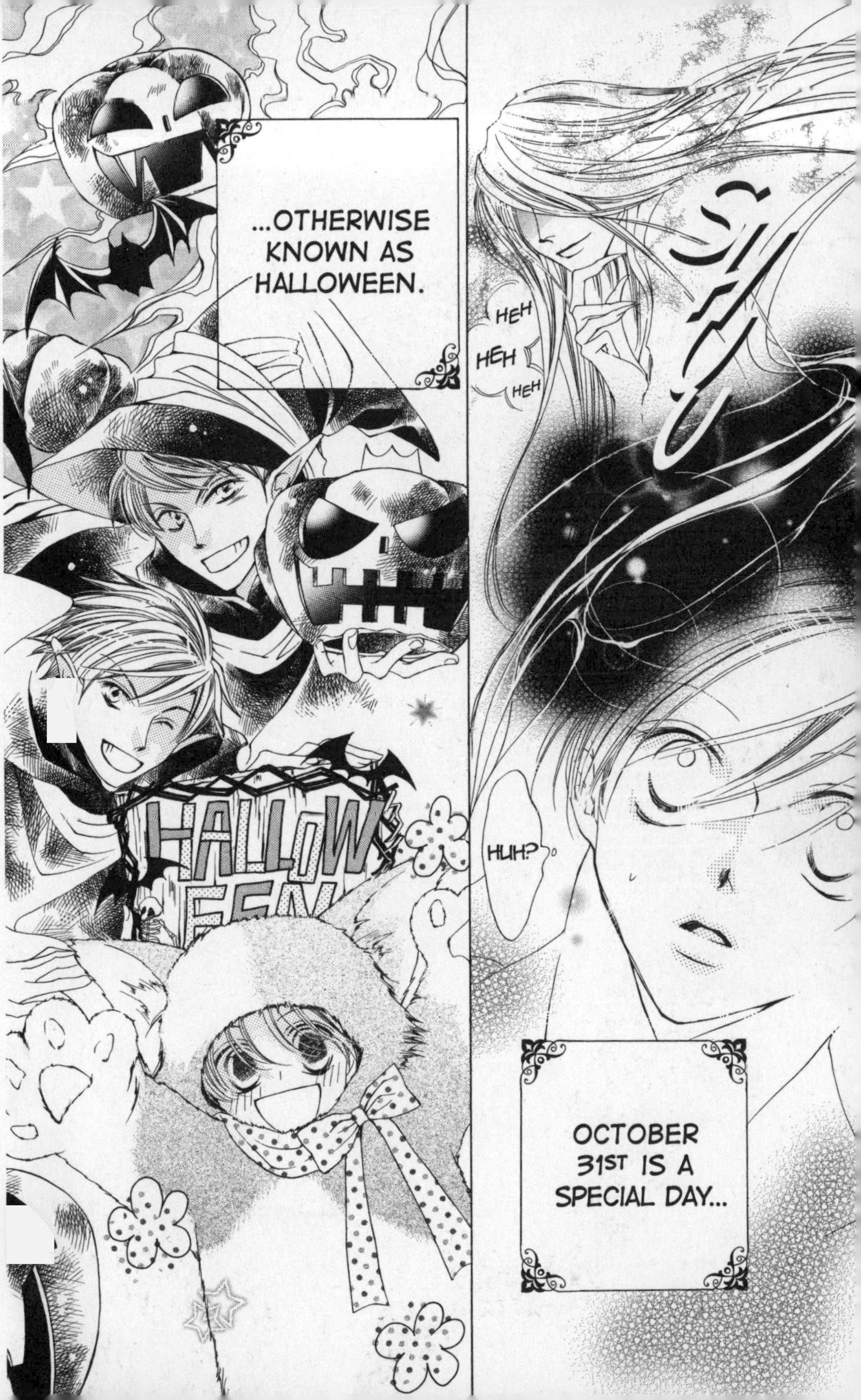
HEH HEH HEH
HUH?
OCTOBER 31ST IS A SPECIAL DAY...
...OTHERWISE KNOWN AS HALLOWEEN.
HALLOW

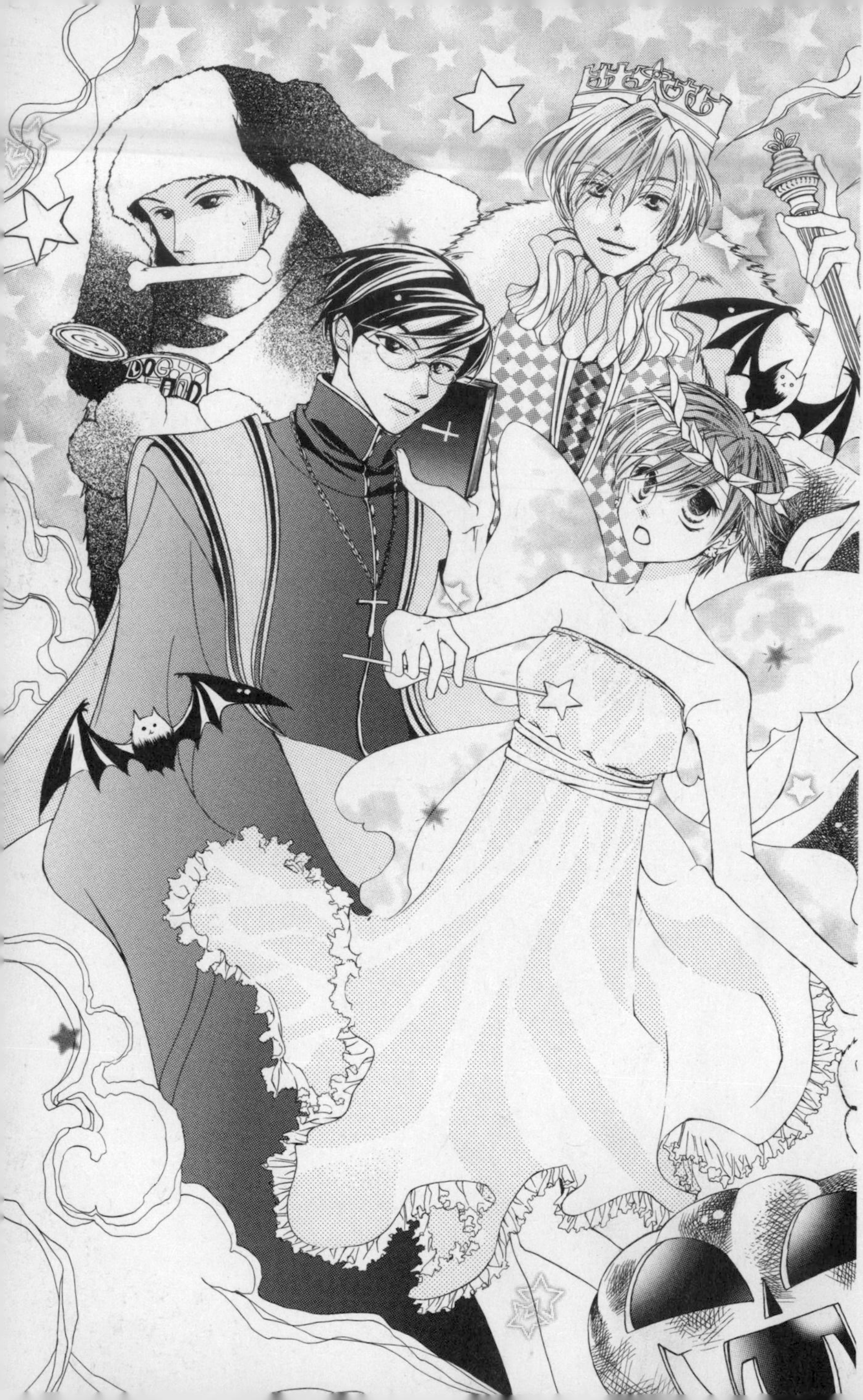

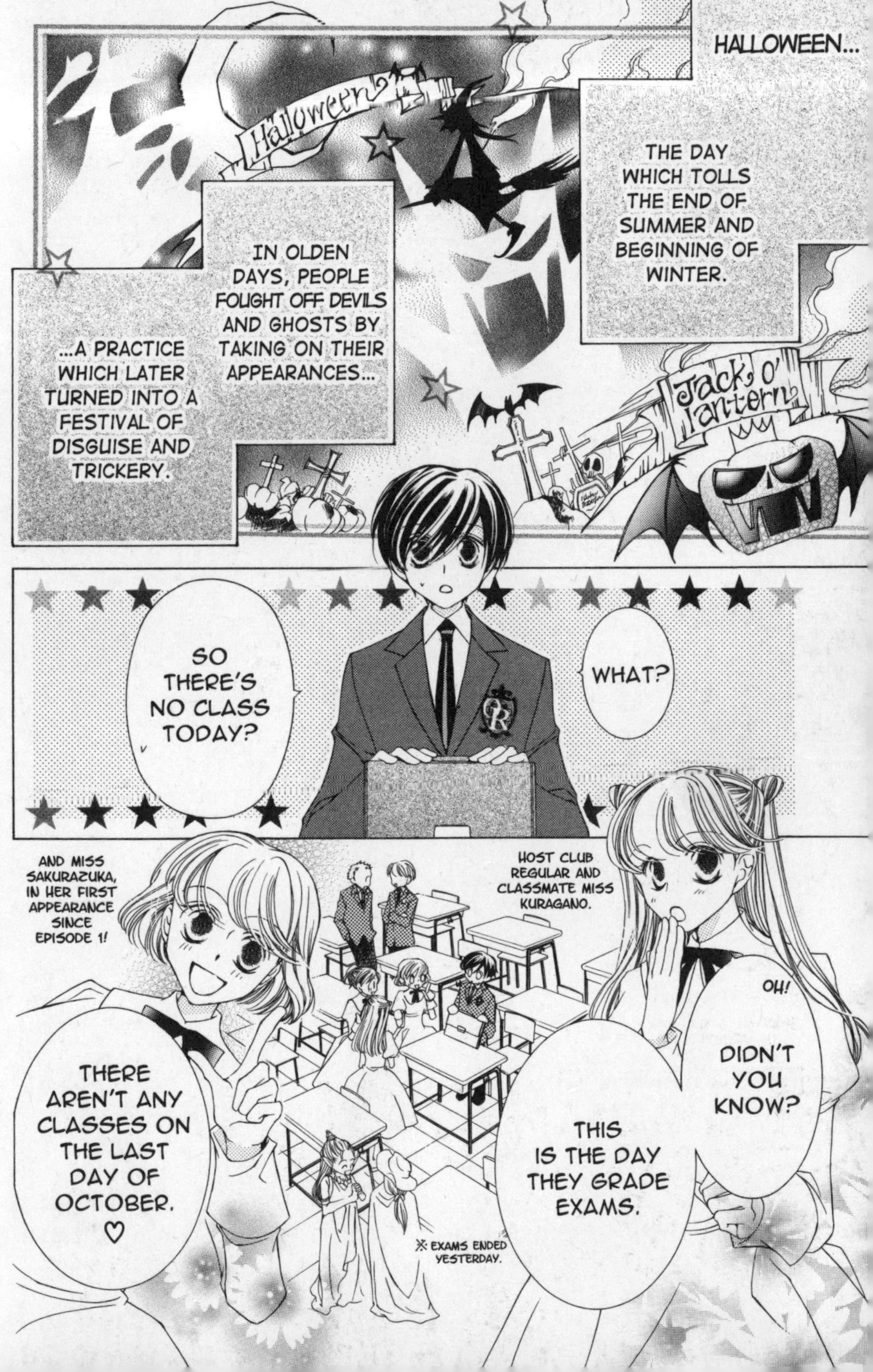
HALLOWEEN...
THE DAY WHICH TOLLS THE END OF SUMMER AND BEGINNING OF WINTER.
Halloween
Jack o' lantern
IN OLDEN DAYS, PEOPLE FOUGHT OFF DEVILS AND GHOSTS BY TAKING ON THEIR APPEARANCES...
...A PRACTICE WHICH LATER TURNED INTO A FESTIVAL OF DISGUISE AND TRICKERY.
WHAT?
SO THERE'S NO CLASS TODAY?
OH!
DIDN'T YOU KNOW?
HOST CLUB REGULAR AND CLASSMATE MISS KURAGANO.
THIS IS THE DAY THEY GRADE EXAMS.
※EXAMS ENDED YESTERDAY.
THERE AREN'T ANY CLASSES ON THE LAST DAY OF OCTOBER. ♡
AND MISS SAKURAZUKA, IN HER FIRST APPEARANCE SINCE EPISODE 1!

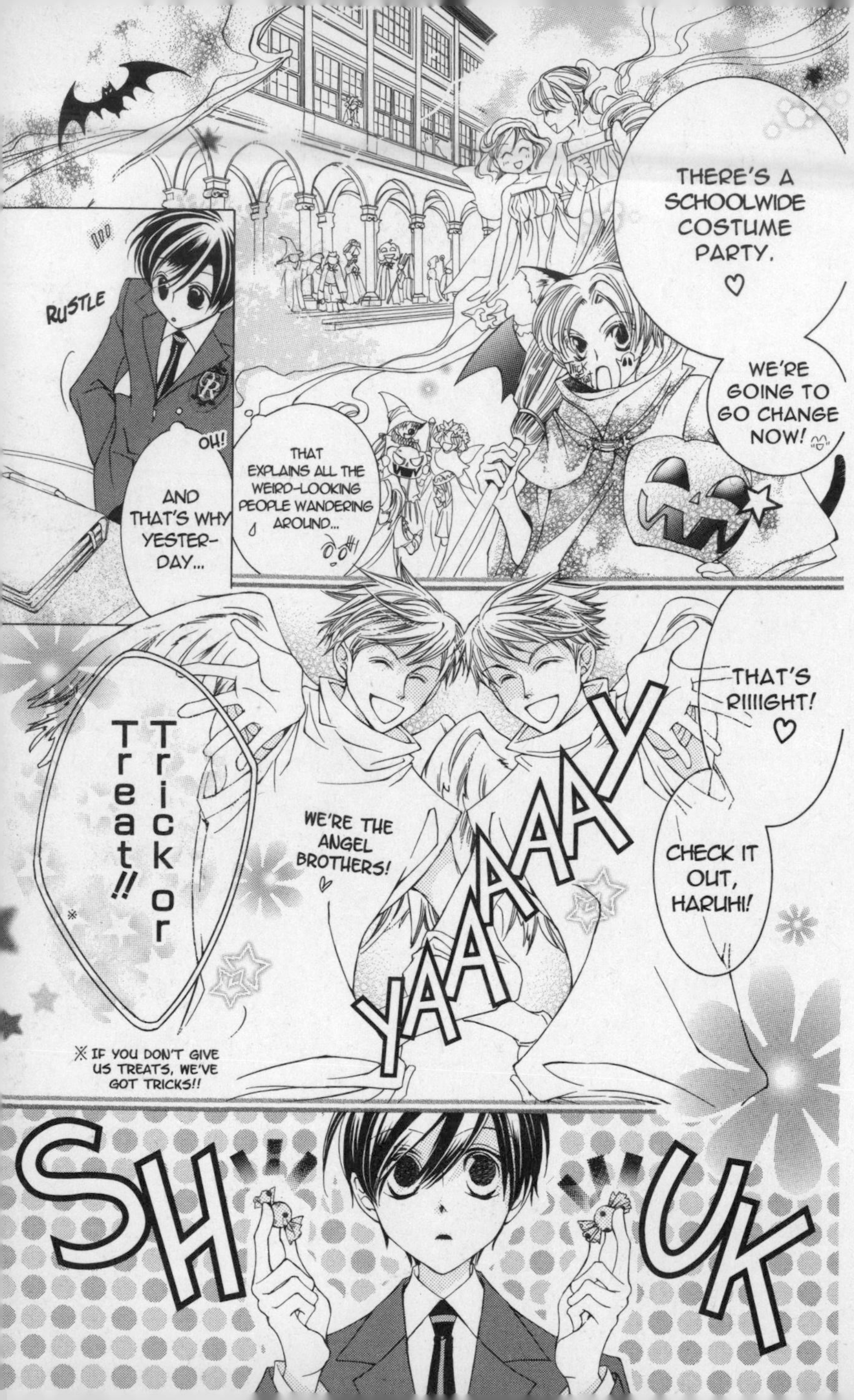
THERE'S A SCHOOLWIDE COSTUME PARTY. ♡
WE'RE GOING TO GO CHANGE NOW!
RUSTLE
OH!
AND THAT'S WHY YESTER-DAY...
THAT EXPLAINS ALL THE WEIRD-LOOKING PEOPLE WANDERING AROUND...
THAT'S RIIIIGHT! ♡
CHECK IT OUT, HARUHI!
YAAAAAAY
WE'RE THE ANGEL BROTHERS! ♡
Trick or Treat!! ※
※ IF YOU DON'T GIVE US TREATS, WE'VE GOT TRICKS!!
SH UK

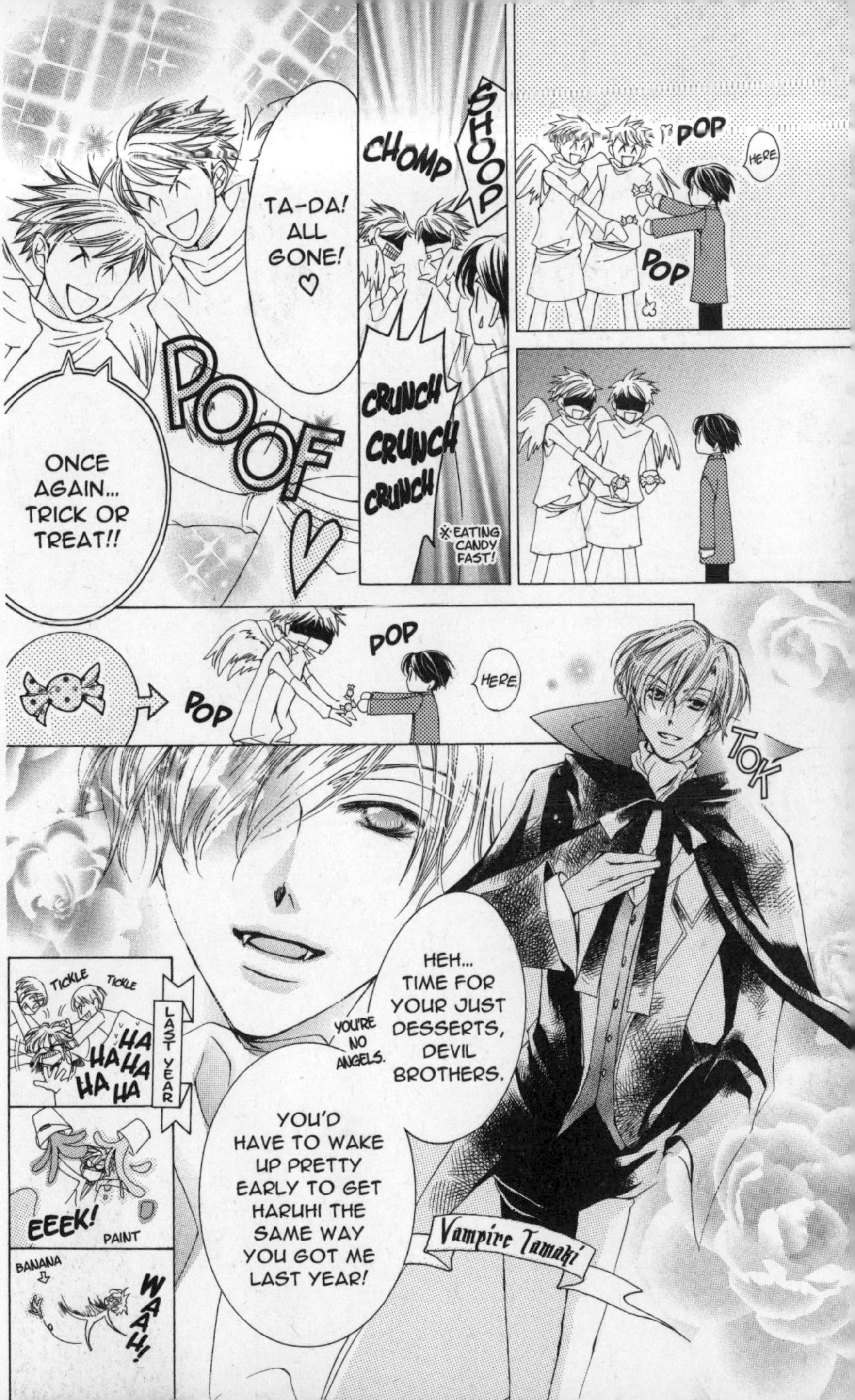
POP
HERE
POP
CHOMP
SHOOP
CRUNCH
CRUNCH
CRUNCH
※EATING CANDY FAST!
TA-DA! ALL GONE! ♥
POOF
ONCE AGAIN... TRICK OR TREAT!!
HERE.
POP
POP
TOK
HEH... TIME FOR YOUR JUST DESSERTS, DEVIL BROTHERS.
YOU'RE NO ANGELS.
YOU'D HAVE TO WAKE UP PRETTY EARLY TO GET HARUHI THE SAME WAY YOU GOT ME LAST YEAR!
Vampire Tamaki
LAST YEAR
TICKLE
TICKLE
HA HA HA HA HA HA
EEEK!
PAINT
BANANA
WAAAH!

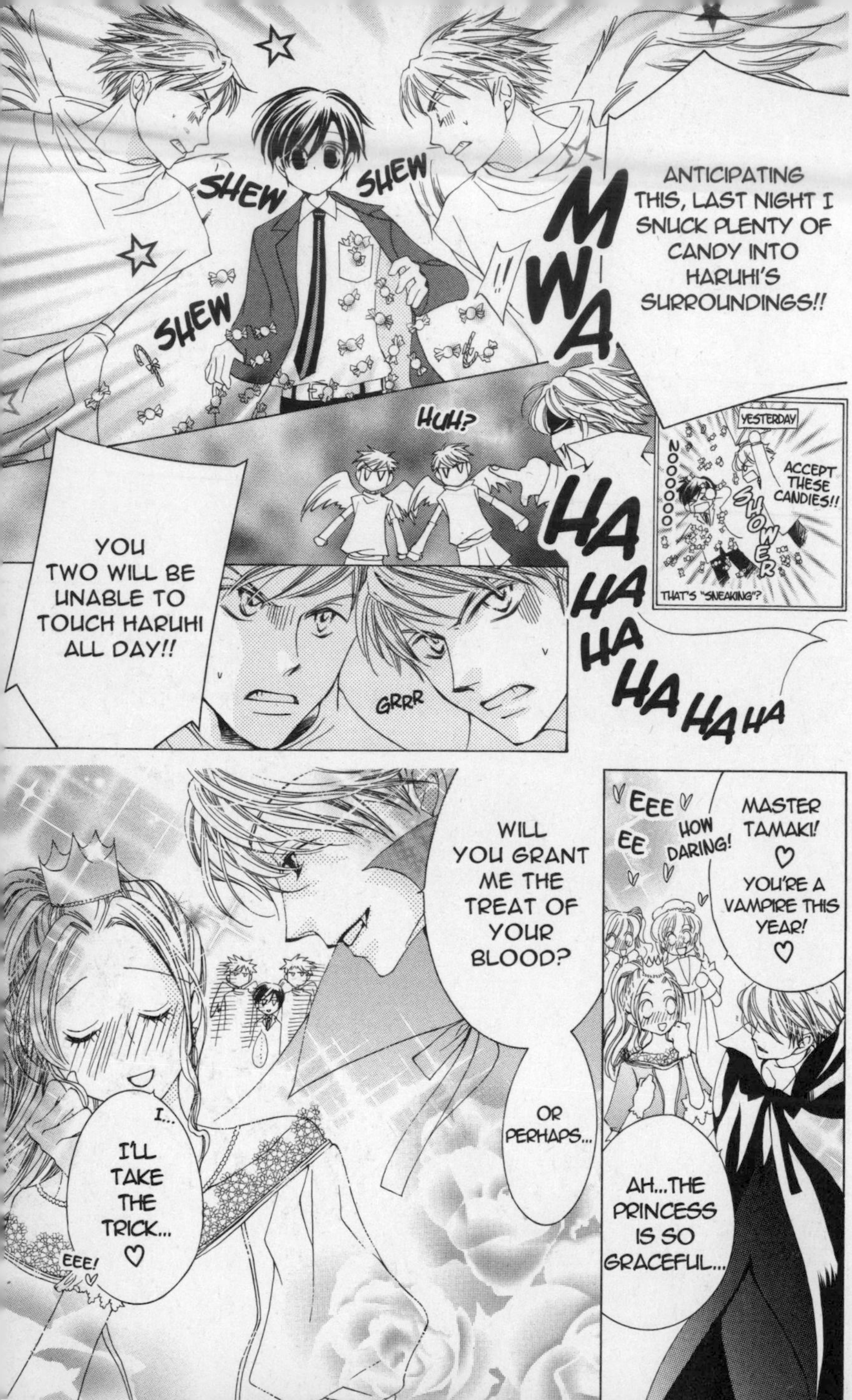
SHEW
SHEW
SHEW
!!
ANTICIPATING THIS, LAST NIGHT I SNUCK PLENTY OF CANDY INTO HARUHI'S SURROUNDINGS!!
MWA
HUH?
YESTERDAY
ACCEPT THESE CANDIES!!
SHOWER
NOOOOOOO
THAT'S "SNEAKING"?
HA HA HA HA HA HA HA
YOU TWO WILL BE UNABLE TO TOUCH HARUHI ALL DAY!!
GRRR
MASTER TAMAKI! ♡ YOU'RE A VAMPIRE THIS YEAR! ♡
HOW DARING!
EEE EE
AH...THE PRINCESS IS SO GRACEFUL...
WILL YOU GRANT ME THE TREAT OF YOUR BLOOD?
OR PERHAPS...
I...
I'LL TAKE THE TRICK... ♡
EEE!

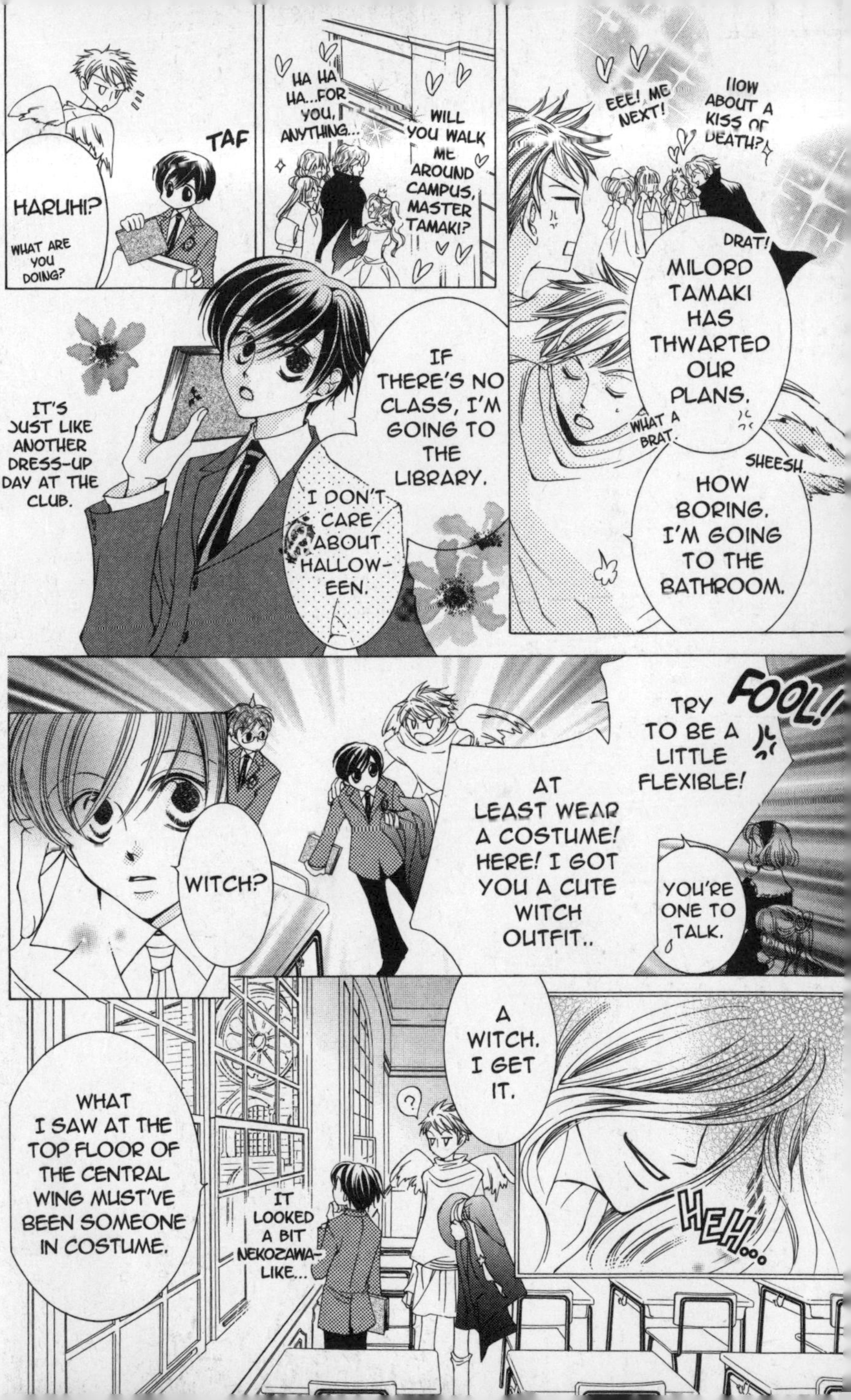
EEE! ME NEXT!
HOW ABOUT A KISS OF DEATH?
DRAT!
MILORD TAMAKI HAS THWARTED OUR PLANS.
WHAT A BRAT.
SHEESH.
HOW BORING. I'M GOING TO THE BATHROOM.
HA HA HA...FOR YOU, ANYTHING...
WILL YOU WALK ME AROUND CAMPUS, MASTER TAMAKI?
TAF
HARUHI?
WHAT ARE YOU DOING?
IF THERE'S NO CLASS, I'M GOING TO THE LIBRARY.
I DON'T CARE ABOUT HALLOW-EEN.
IT'S JUST LIKE ANOTHER DRESS-UP DAY AT THE CLUB.
FOOL!
TRY TO BE A LITTLE FLEXIBLE!
AT LEAST WEAR A COSTUME! HERE! I GOT YOU A CUTE WITCH OUTFIT..
YOU'RE ONE TO TALK.
WITCH?
A WITCH. I GET IT.
HEH...
?
WHAT I SAW AT THE TOP FLOOR OF THE CENTRAL WING MUST'VE BEEN SOMEONE IN COSTUME.
IT LOOKED A BIT NEKOZAWA-LIKE...

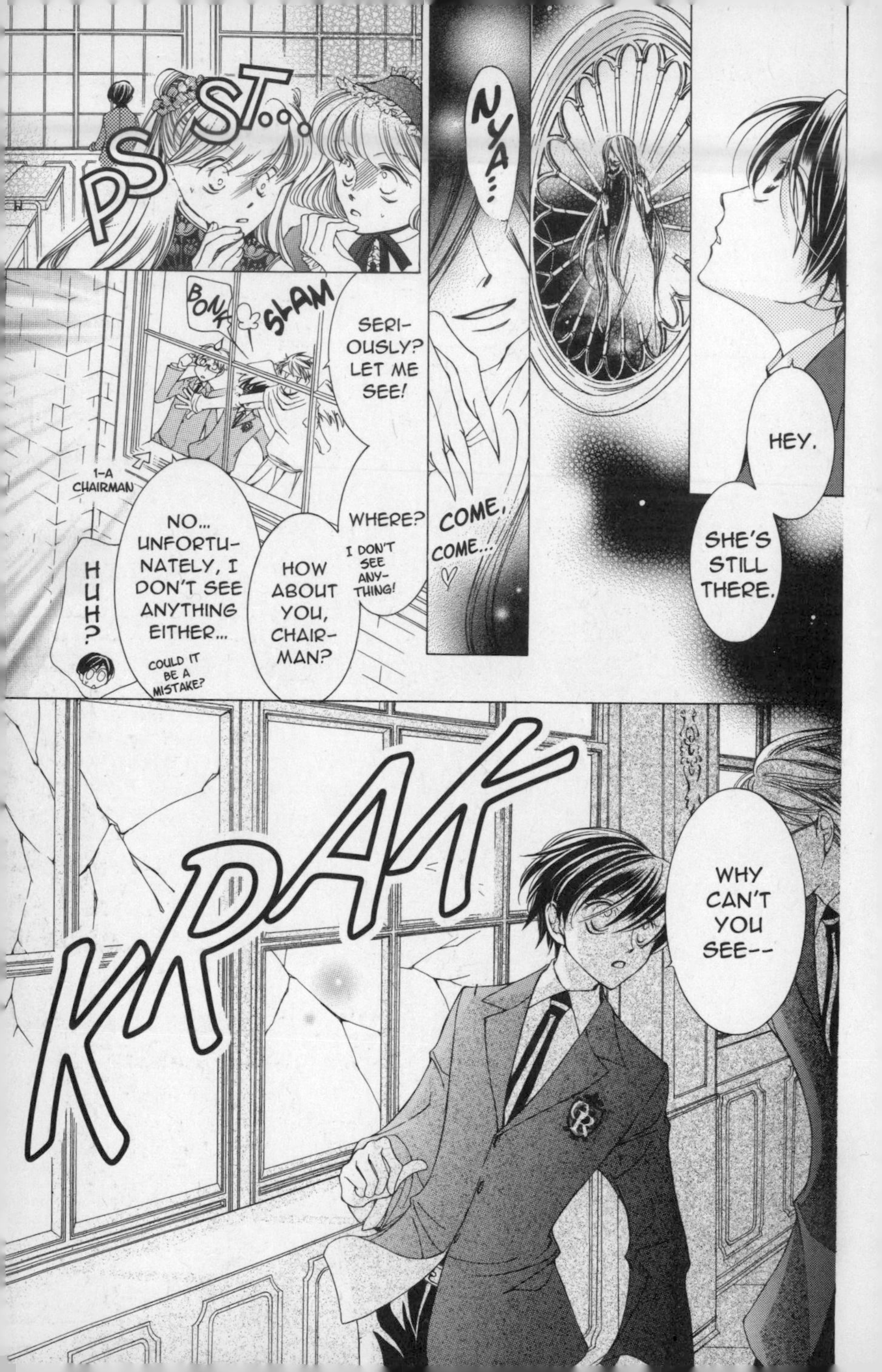
HEY.
SHE'S STILL THERE.
NYA...
COME, COME...
PSSST...
BONK
SLAM
SERIOUSLY? LET ME SEE!
WHERE?
I DON'T SEE ANYTHING!
HOW ABOUT YOU, CHAIRMAN?
NO... UNFORTUNATELY, I DON'T SEE ANYTHING EITHER...
COULD IT BE A MISTAKE?
HUH?
1-A CHAIRMAN
WHY CAN'T YOU SEE--
KPAY

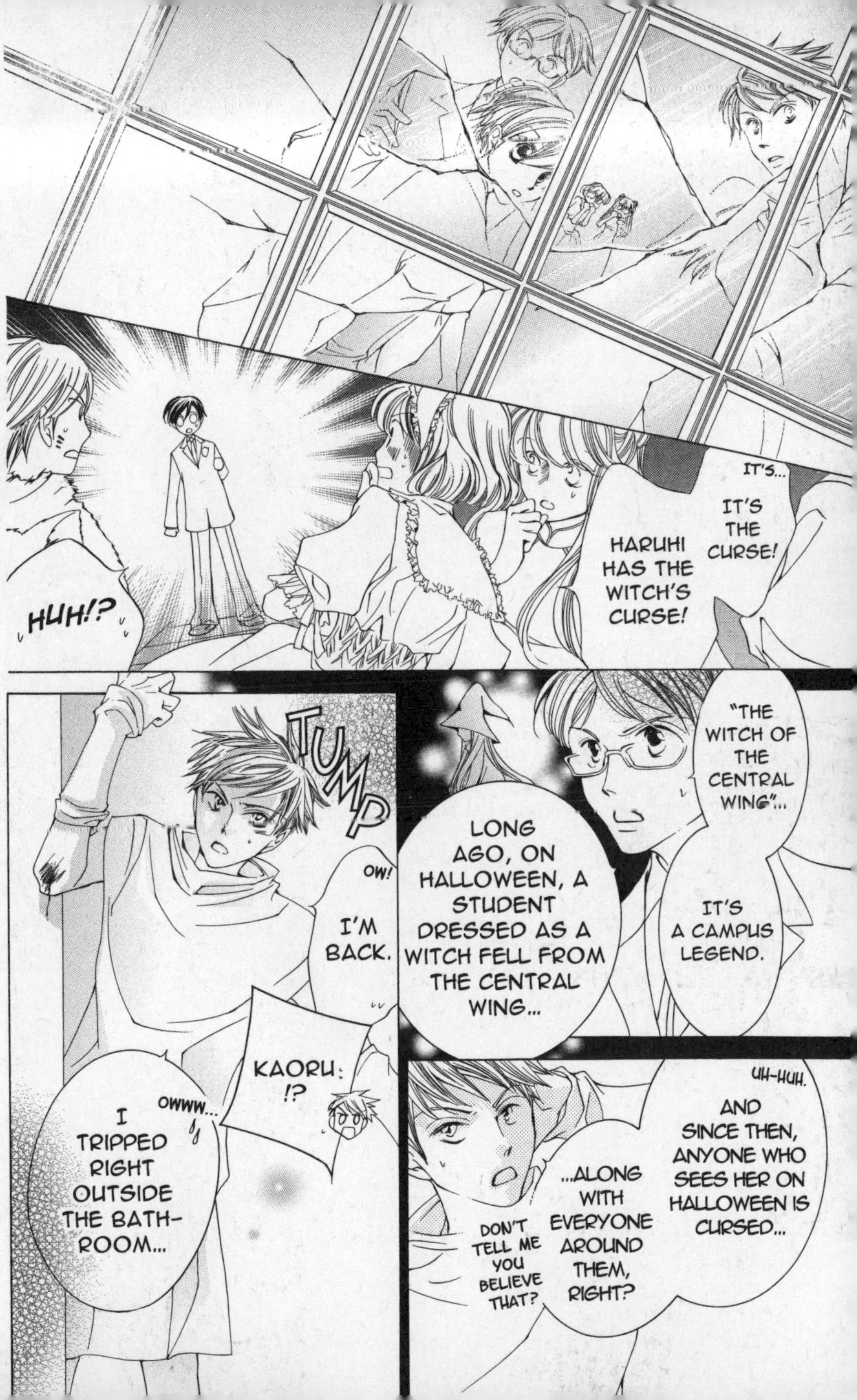
IT'S...
IT'S THE CURSE!
HARUHI HAS THE WITCH'S CURSE!
HUH!?
"THE WITCH OF THE CENTRAL WING"...
IT'S A CAMPUS LEGEND.
LONG AGO, ON HALLOWEEN, A STUDENT DRESSED AS A WITCH FELL FROM THE CENTRAL WING...
UH-HUH.
AND SINCE THEN, ANYONE WHO SEES HER ON HALLOWEEN IS CURSED...
...ALONG WITH EVERYONE AROUND THEM, RIGHT?
DON'T TELL ME YOU BELIEVE THAT?
TUMP
OW!
I'M BACK.
KAORU!?
OWWW...
I TRIPPED RIGHT OUTSIDE THE BATH-ROOM...

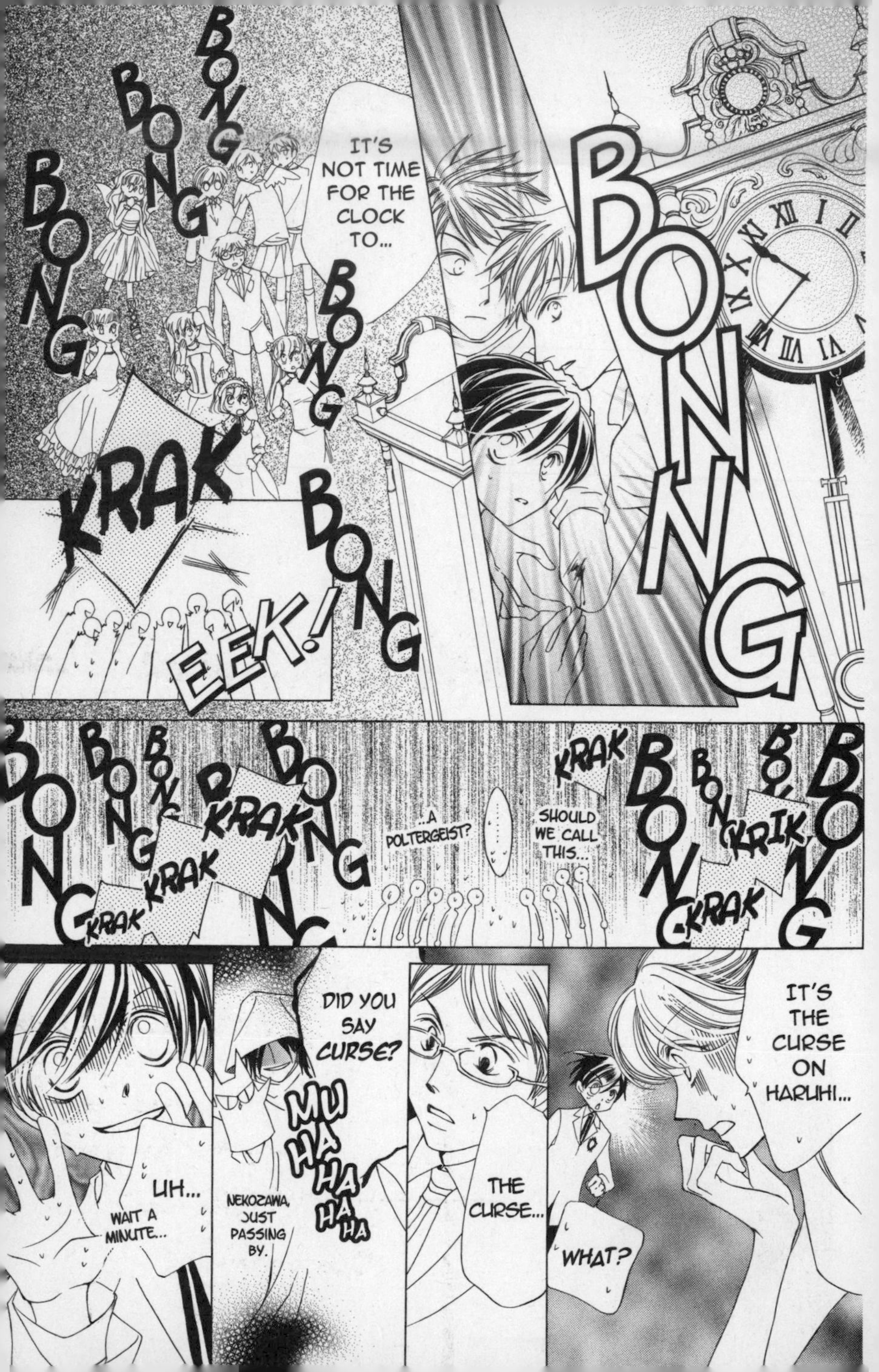
BONG
IT'S NOT TIME FOR THE CLOCK TO...
BONG
BONG
BONG
BONG
BONG
KRAK
EEK!
BONG
BONG
KRIK
BONG
KRAK
KRAK
SHOULD WE CALL THIS...
...A POLTERGEIST?
BONG
KRAK
KRAK
KRAK
BONG
BONG
BONG
IT'S THE CURSE ON HARUHI...
WHAT?
THE CURSE...
DID YOU SAY CURSE?
MU HA HA HA HA HA
NEKOZAWA, JUST PASSING BY.
UH...
WAIT A MINUTE...

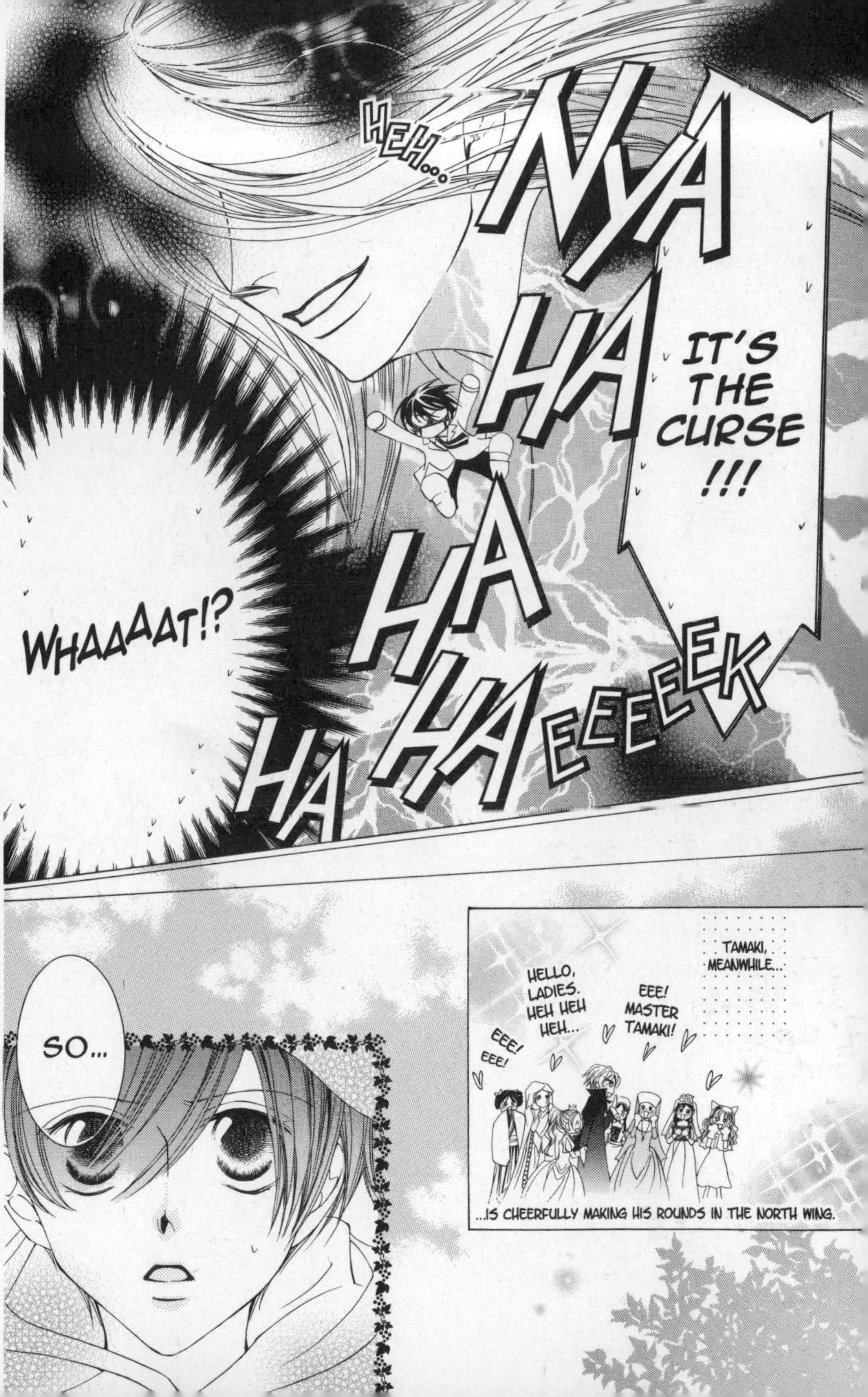
HEH...
NYA HA HA HA HA
IT'S THE CURSE!!!
EEEEEK
WHAAAAT!?
TAMAKI, MEANWHILE...
EEE! MASTER TAMAKI!
HELLO, LADIES. HEH HEH HEH...
EEE! EEE!
...IS CHEERFULLY MAKING HIS ROUNDS IN THE NORTH WING.
SO...

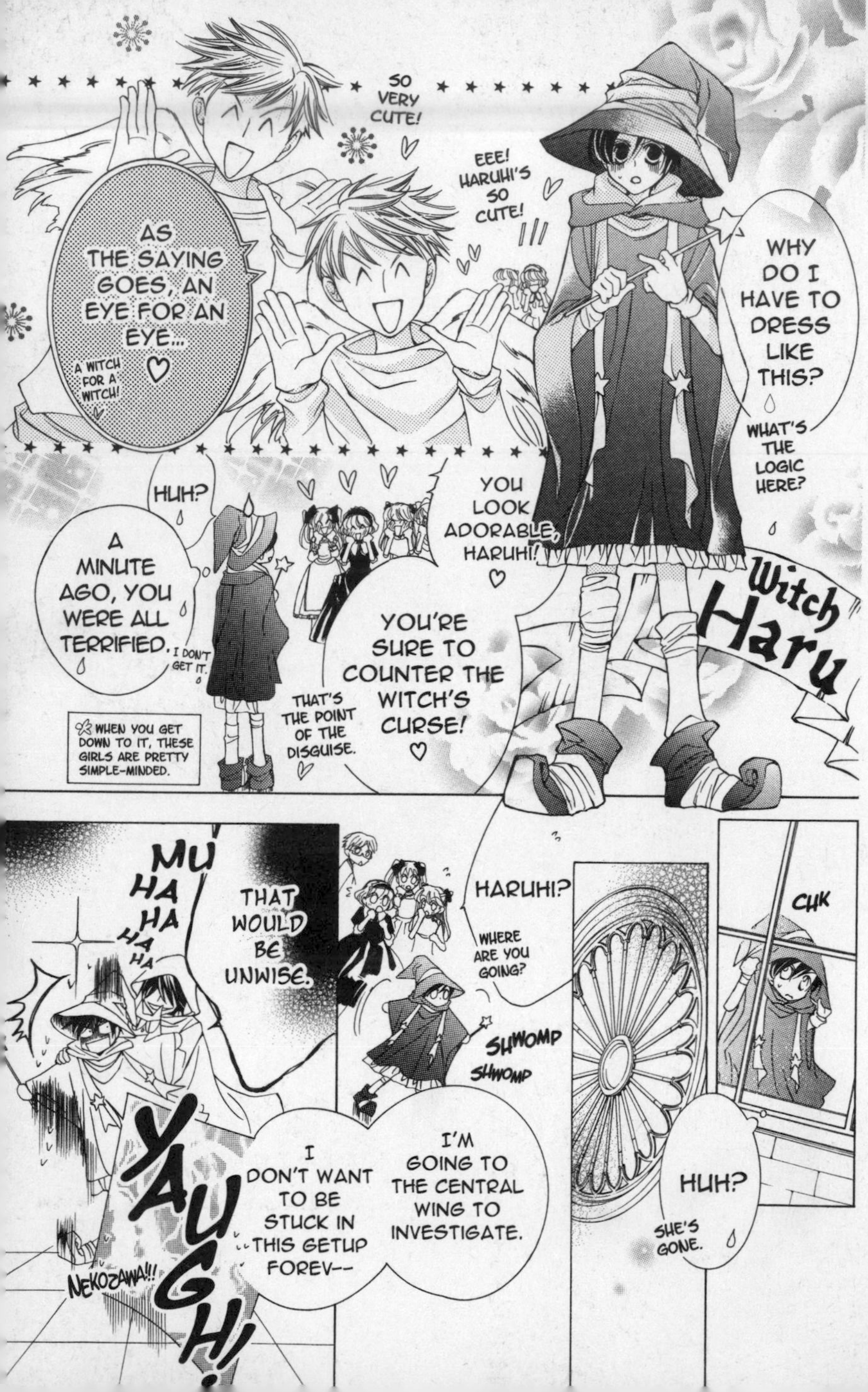
WHY DO I HAVE TO DRESS LIKE THIS?
WHAT'S THE LOGIC HERE?
Witch Haru
SO VERY CUTE!
EEE! HARUHI'S SO CUTE!
AS THE SAYING GOES, AN EYE FOR AN EYE...
A WITCH FOR A WITCH!
YOU LOOK ADORABLE, HARUHI!
YOU'RE SURE TO COUNTER THE WITCH'S CURSE!
THAT'S THE POINT OF THE DISGUISE.
HUH?
A MINUTE AGO, YOU WERE ALL TERRIFIED.
I DON'T GET IT.
WHEN YOU GET DOWN TO IT, THESE GIRLS ARE PRETTY SIMPLE-MINDED.
CHK
HUH?
SHE'S GONE.
HARUHI?
WHERE ARE YOU GOING?
I'M GOING TO THE CENTRAL WING TO INVESTIGATE.
SHWOMP
SHWOMP
I DON'T WANT TO BE STUCK IN THIS GETUP FOREV--
THAT WOULD BE UNWISE.
MU HA HA HA HA
YAUGH!
NEKOZAWA!!!

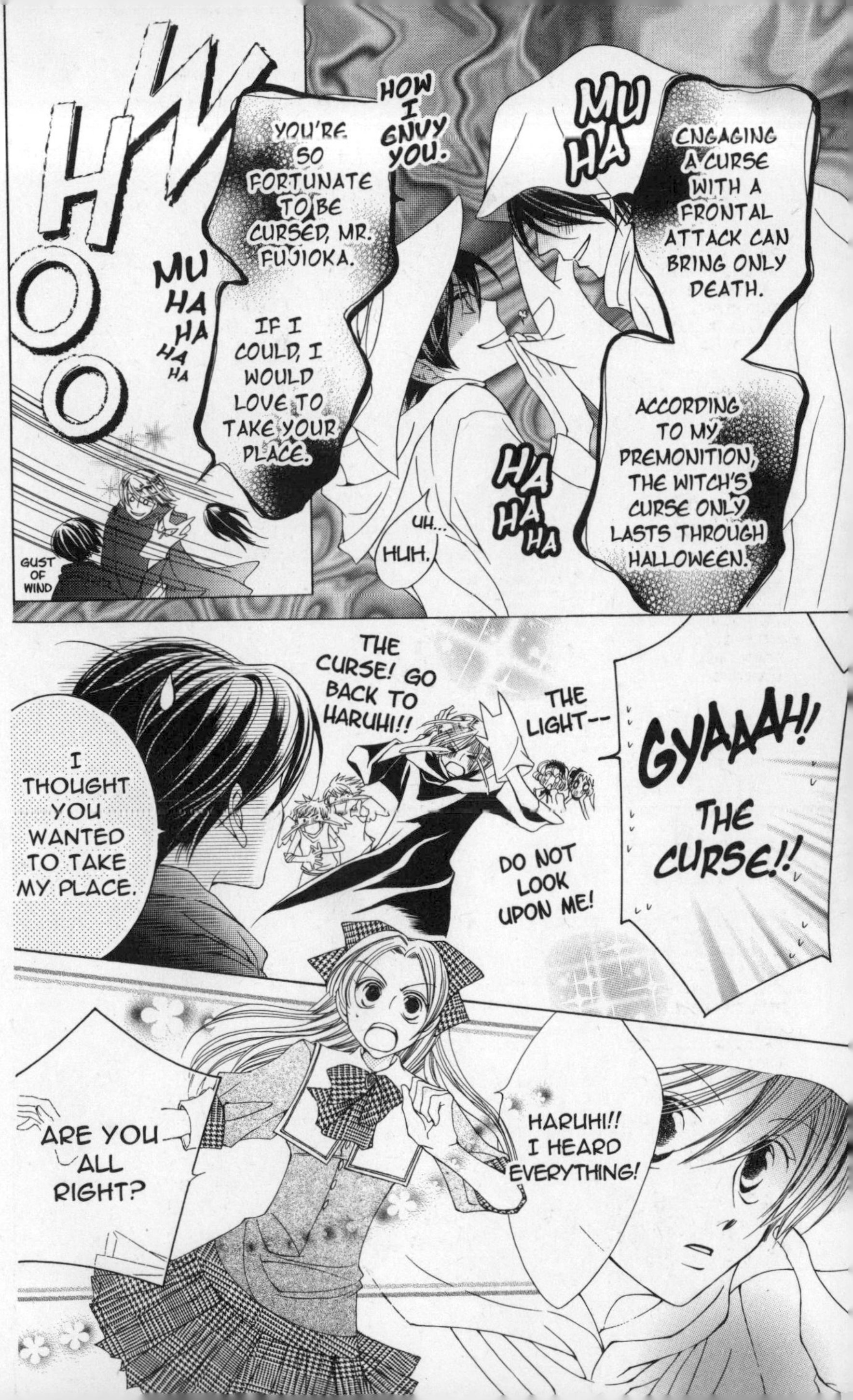
MU HA
ENGAGING A CURSE WITH A FRONTAL ATTACK CAN BRING ONLY DEATH.
HOW I ENVY YOU.
YOU'RE SO FORTUNATE TO BE CURSED, MR. FUJIOKA.
IF I COULD, I WOULD LOVE TO TAKE YOUR PLACE.
ACCORDING TO MY PREMONITION, THE WITCH'S CURSE ONLY LASTS THROUGH HALLOWEEN.
HA HA HA HA
UH... HUH.
MU HA HA HA HA
WHOOO
GUST OF WIND
GYAAAH! THE CURSE!!
THE LIGHT--
DO NOT LOOK UPON ME!
THE CURSE! GO BACK TO HARUHI!!
I THOUGHT YOU WANTED TO TAKE MY PLACE.
HARUHI!! I HEARD EVERYTHING!
ARE YOU ALL RIGHT?

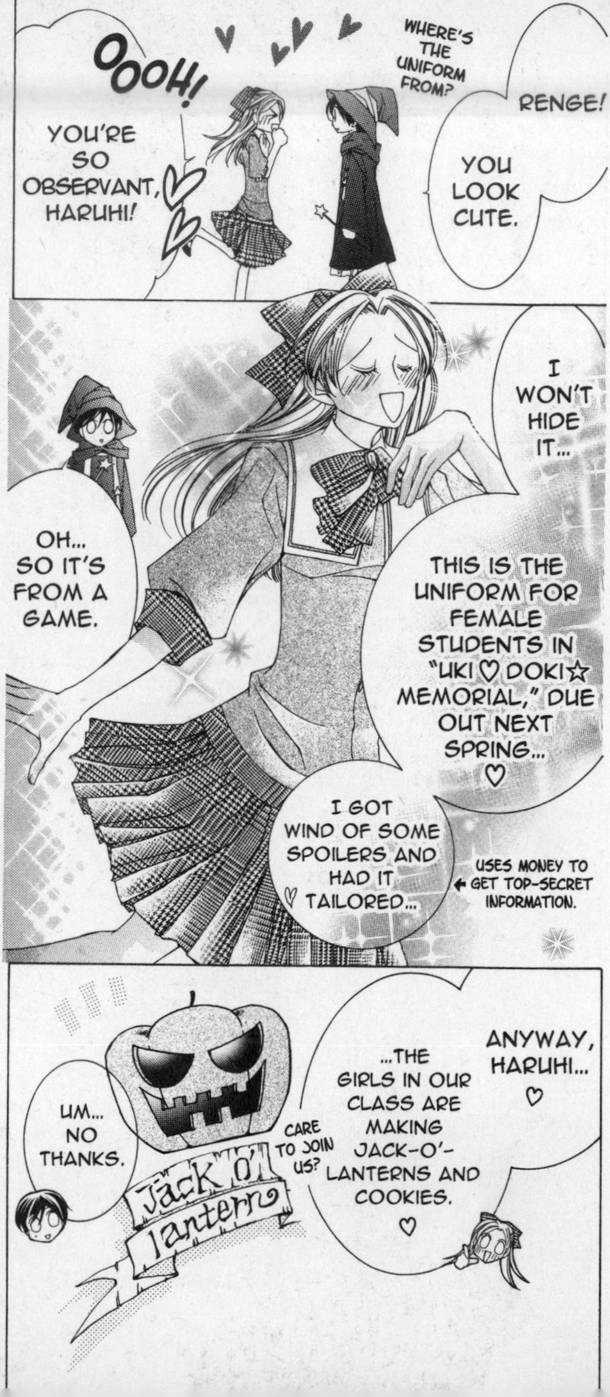
RENGE!
YOU LOOK CUTE.
WHERE'S THE UNIFORM FROM?
OOOH!
YOU'RE SO OBSERVANT, HARUHI!
I WON'T HIDE IT...
THIS IS THE UNIFORM FOR FEMALE STUDENTS IN "UKI♡DOKI☆ MEMORIAL," DUE OUT NEXT SPRING... ♡
I GOT WIND OF SOME SPOILERS AND HAD IT TAILORED... ♡
USES MONEY TO GET TOP-SECRET INFORMATION.
OH... SO IT'S FROM A GAME.
ANYWAY, HARUHI... ♡
...THE GIRLS IN OUR CLASS ARE MAKING JACK-O'-LANTERNS AND COOKIES. ♡
CARE TO JOIN US?
UM... NO THANKS.
Jack O' lantern

4

③NEXT WE GET INTO THE "NAME" [STORY LAYOUT]. THE MORE DIFFICULT THIS IS, THE LESS TIME I'LL HAVE FOR DRAWING IT OUT. THIS IS A SCARY PART.

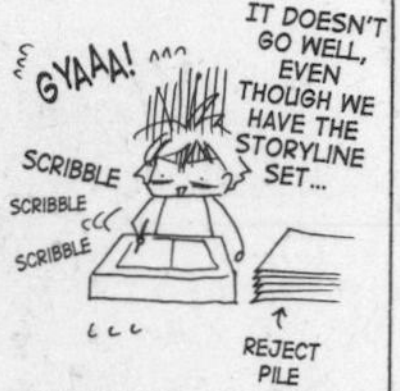
GYAAA!
SCRIBBLE
SCRIBBLE
SCRIBBLE
IT DOESN'T GO WELL, EVEN THOUGH WE HAVE THE STORYLINE SET...
REJECT PILE

BY THE WAY, THE WORST TIME I EVER HAD WITH LAYOUTS WAS EPISODE 1. I REWROTE OVER 300 PAGES. IT WAS A HORROR I WISH NEVER TO EXPERIENCE AGAIN.

OH, A "NAME" LOOKS...

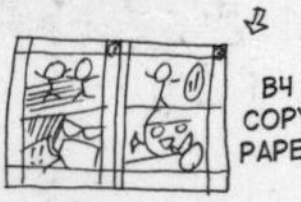
B4 COPY PAPER

...SOMETHING LIKE THIS. IT'S ROUGH DRAFT OF A ROUGH DRAFT, SORT OF.

I SOMETIMES TRY TO LISTEN TO UPBEAT SONGS ON MY WALKMAN TO RAISE MY ENERGY LEVEL. (IT DOESN'T SEEM TO HAVE MUCH EFFECT, THOUGH.) AND WHEN I DRAW LAYOUTS FOR A STORY AS HIGH-ENERGY AS HOST CLUB, I USUALLY GET SOMETHING ONLY I CAN DECIPHER, SO I HAVE TO REDRAW THEM.

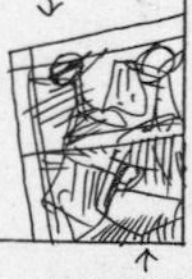
THIS IS WHAT I GET WHEN I DRAW AT THE MANGA'S PACE—A FULL SPRINT!
VERY ROUGH

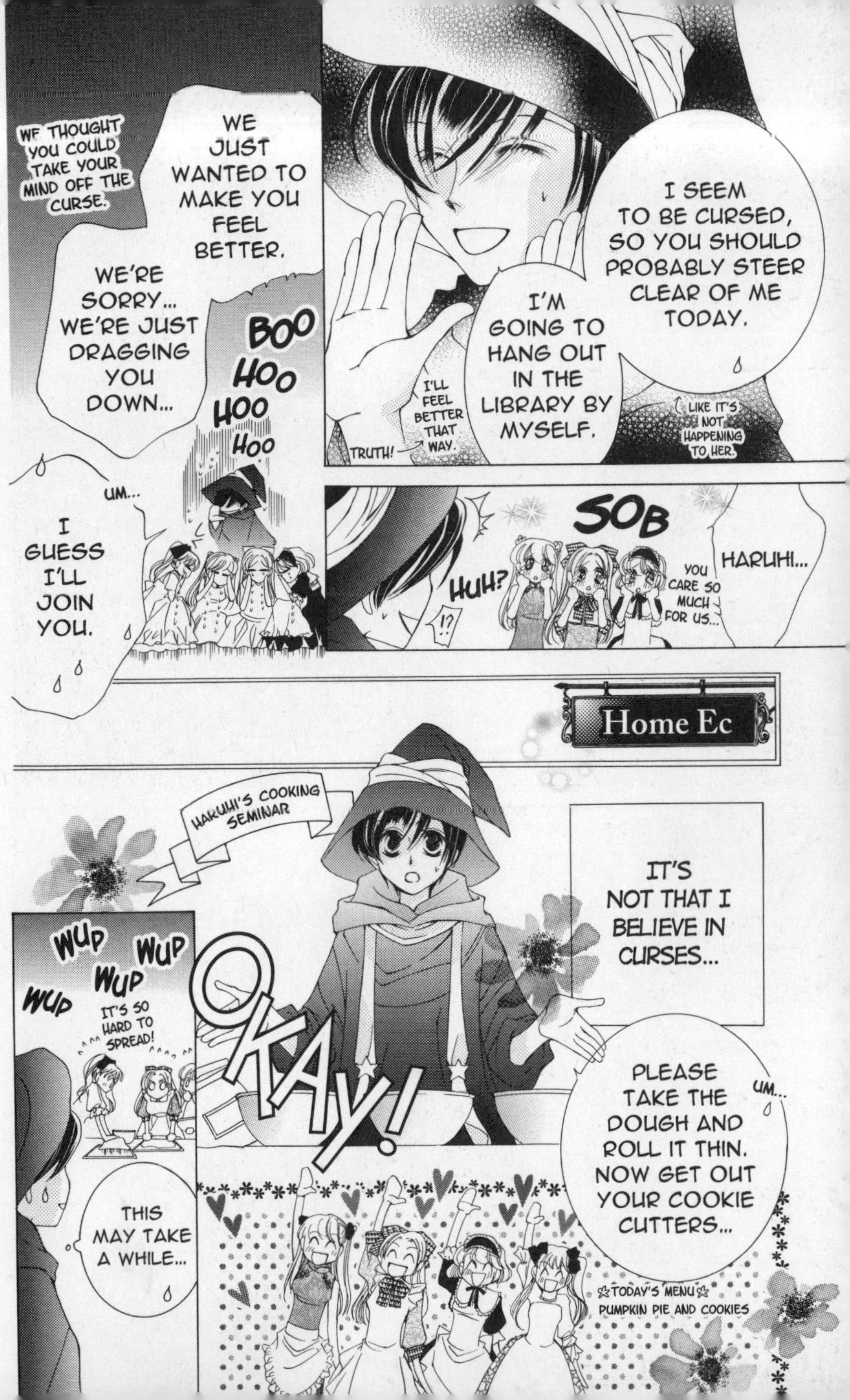
I SEEM TO BE CURSED, SO YOU SHOULD PROBABLY STEER CLEAR OF ME TODAY.
LIKE IT'S NOT HAPPENING TO HER.
I'M GOING TO HANG OUT IN THE LIBRARY BY MYSELF.
I'LL FEEL BETTER THAT WAY.
TRUTH!
WE JUST WANTED TO MAKE YOU FEEL BETTER.
WE THOUGHT YOU COULD TAKE YOUR MIND OFF THE CURSE.
WE'RE SORRY... WE'RE JUST DRAGGING YOU DOWN...
BOO HOO HOO HOO
HARUHI...
YOU CARE SO MUCH FOR US...
SOB
HUH?
!?
UM...
I GUESS I'LL JOIN YOU.
Home Ec
HARUHI'S COOKING SEMINAR
IT'S NOT THAT I BELIEVE IN CURSES...
OKAY!
PLEASE TAKE THE DOUGH AND ROLL IT THIN. NOW GET OUT YOUR COOKIE CUTTERS...
UM...
TODAY'S MENU
PUMPKIN PIE AND COOKIES
WUP WUP WUP WUP
IT'S SO HARD TO SPREAD!
THIS MAY TAKE A WHILE...

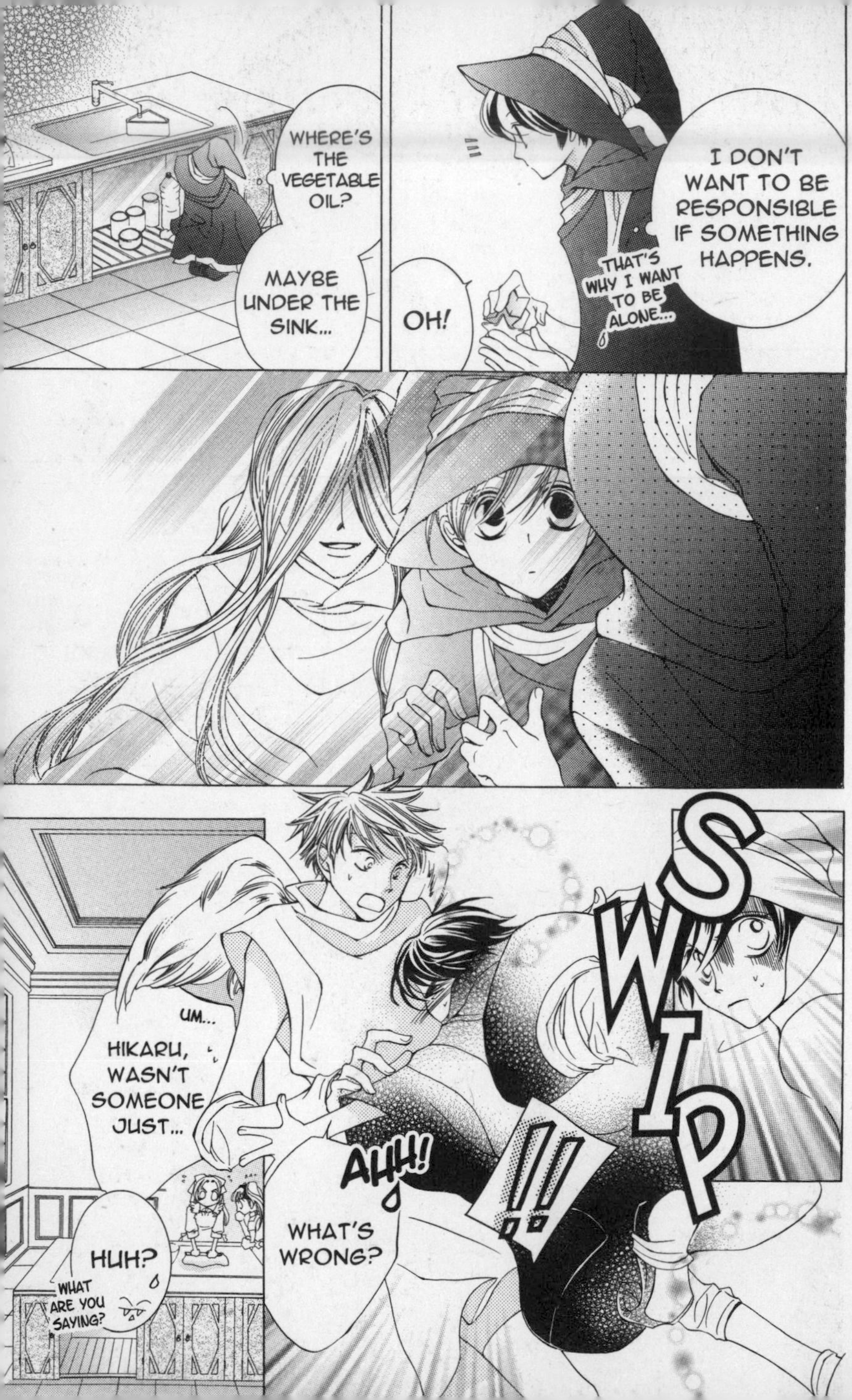
I DON'T WANT TO BE RESPONSIBLE IF SOMETHING HAPPENS.
THAT'S WHY I WANT TO BE ALONE...
OH!
WHERE'S THE VEGETABLE OIL?
MAYBE UNDER THE SINK...
SWIP
!!
AHH!
WHAT'S WRONG?
UM... HIKARU, WASN'T SOMEONE JUST...
HUH?
WHAT ARE YOU SAYING?

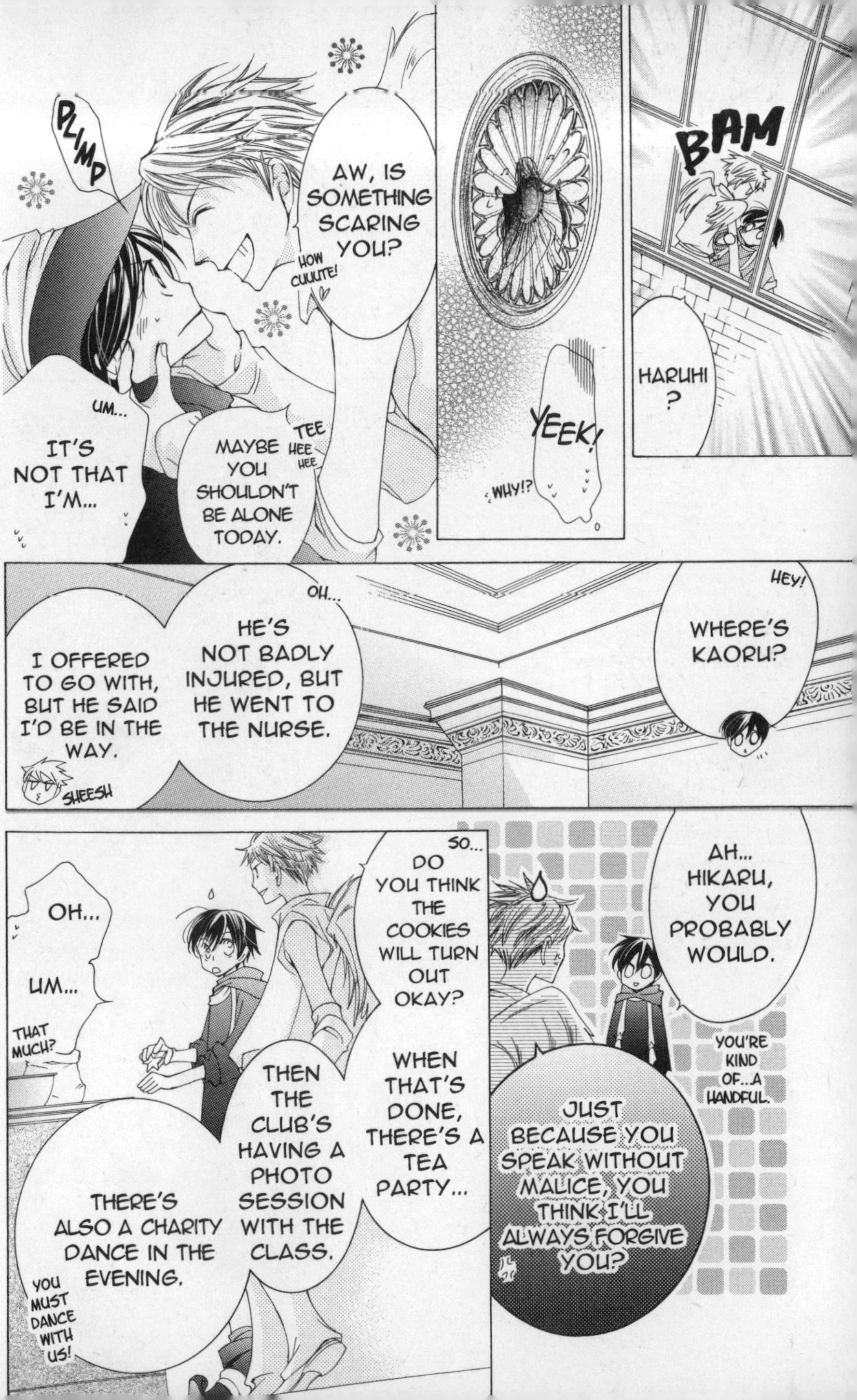
BAM
HARUHI?
YEEK!
WHY!?
AW, IS SOMETHING SCARING YOU?
HOW CUUUTE!
PLIMP
TEE HEE HEE
MAYBE YOU SHOULDN'T BE ALONE TODAY.
UM...
IT'S NOT THAT I'M...
HEY!
WHERE'S KAORU?
OH...
HE'S NOT BADLY INJURED, BUT HE WENT TO THE NURSE.
I OFFERED TO GO WITH, BUT HE SAID I'D BE IN THE WAY.
SHEESH
AH... HIKARU, YOU PROBABLY WOULD.
YOU'RE KIND OF...A HANDFUL.
JUST BECAUSE YOU SPEAK WITHOUT MALICE, YOU THINK I'LL ALWAYS FORGIVE YOU?
SO...
DO YOU THINK THE COOKIES WILL TURN OUT OKAY?
WHEN THAT'S DONE, THERE'S A TEA PARTY...
THEN THE CLUB'S HAVING A PHOTO SESSION WITH THE CLASS.
OH...
UM...
THAT MUCH?
THERE'S ALSO A CHARITY DANCE IN THE EVENING.
YOU MUST DANCE WITH US!

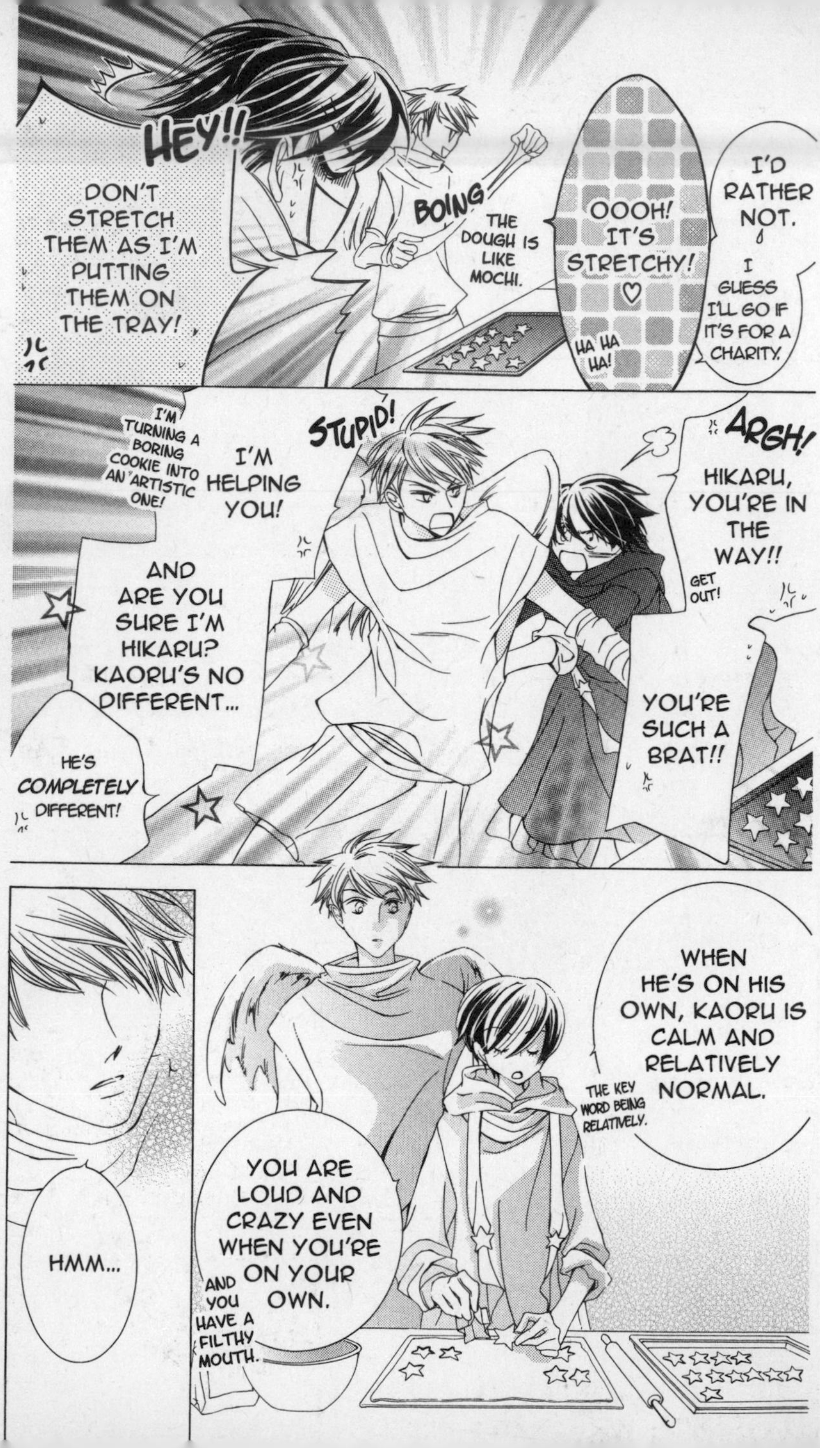

I'D RATHER NOT.
I GUESS I'LL GO IF IT'S FOR A CHARITY.
OOOH! IT'S STRETCHY! ♡
HA HA HA!
THE DOUGH IS LIKE MOCHI.
BOING
HEY!!
DON'T STRETCH THEM AS I'M PUTTING THEM ON THE TRAY!
ARGH!
HIKARU, YOU'RE IN THE WAY!!
GET OUT!
STUPID!
I'M HELPING YOU!
I'M TURNING A BORING COOKIE INTO AN "ARTISTIC" ONE!
YOU'RE SUCH A BRAT!!
AND ARE YOU SURE I'M HIKARU? KAORU'S NO DIFFERENT...
HE'S COMPLETELY DIFFERENT!
WHEN HE'S ON HIS OWN, KAORU IS CALM AND RELATIVELY NORMAL.
THE KEY WORD BEING RELATIVELY.
YOU ARE LOUD AND CRAZY EVEN WHEN YOU'RE ON YOUR OWN.
AND YOU HAVE A FILTHY MOUTH.
HMM...

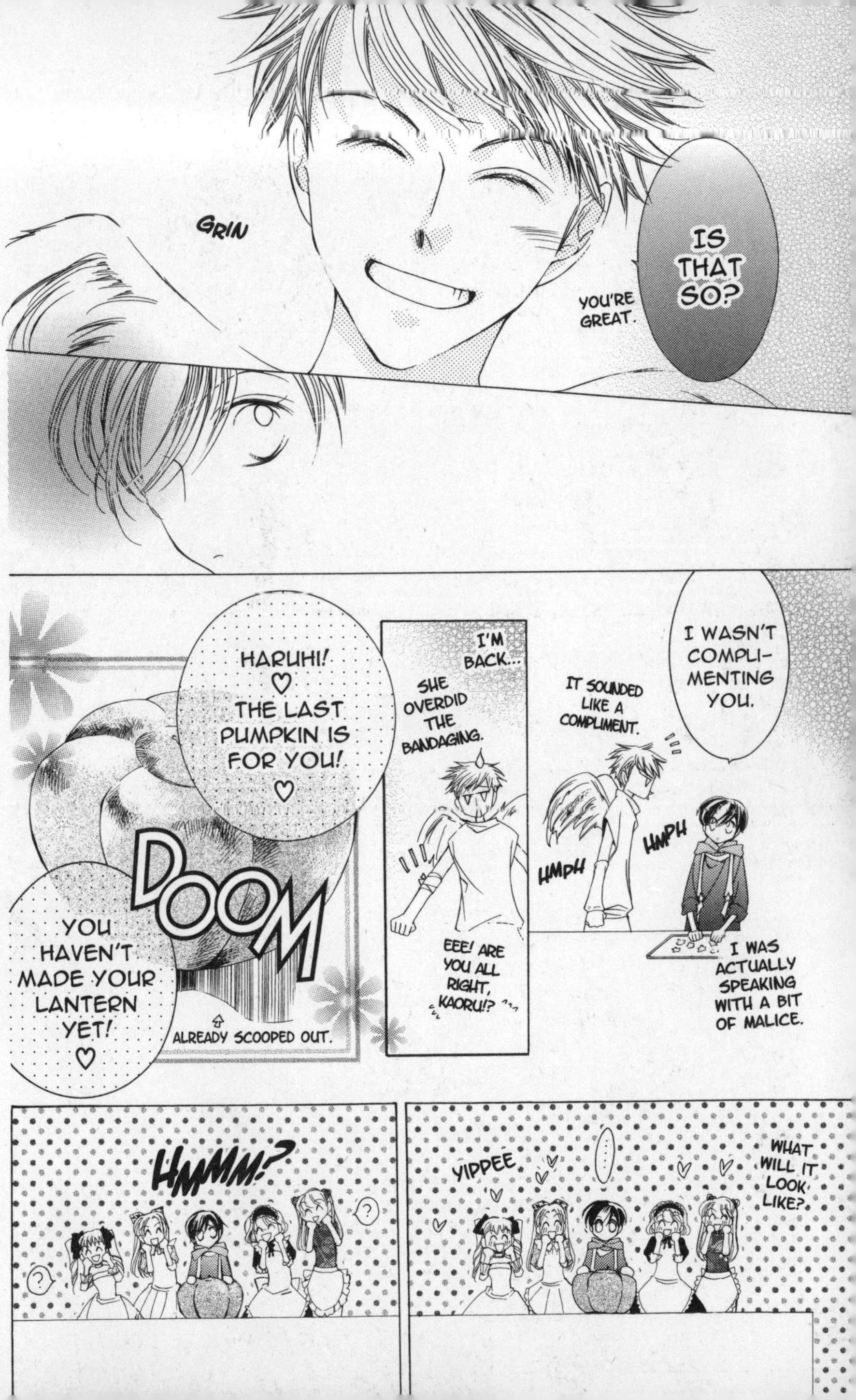
IS THAT SO?
YOU'RE GREAT.
GRIN
I WASN'T COMPLI-MENTING YOU.
IT SOUNDED LIKE A COMPLIMENT.
HMPH
HMPH
I WAS ACTUALLY SPEAKING WITH A BIT OF MALICE.
I'M BACK...
SHE OVERDID THE BANDAGING.
EEE! ARE YOU ALL RIGHT, KAORU!?
HARUHI! ♡ THE LAST PUMPKIN IS FOR YOU! ♡
DOOM
YOU HAVEN'T MADE YOUR LANTERN YET! ♡
ALREADY SCOOPED OUT.
WHAT WILL IT LOOK LIKE?
...
YIPPEE
HMMM?

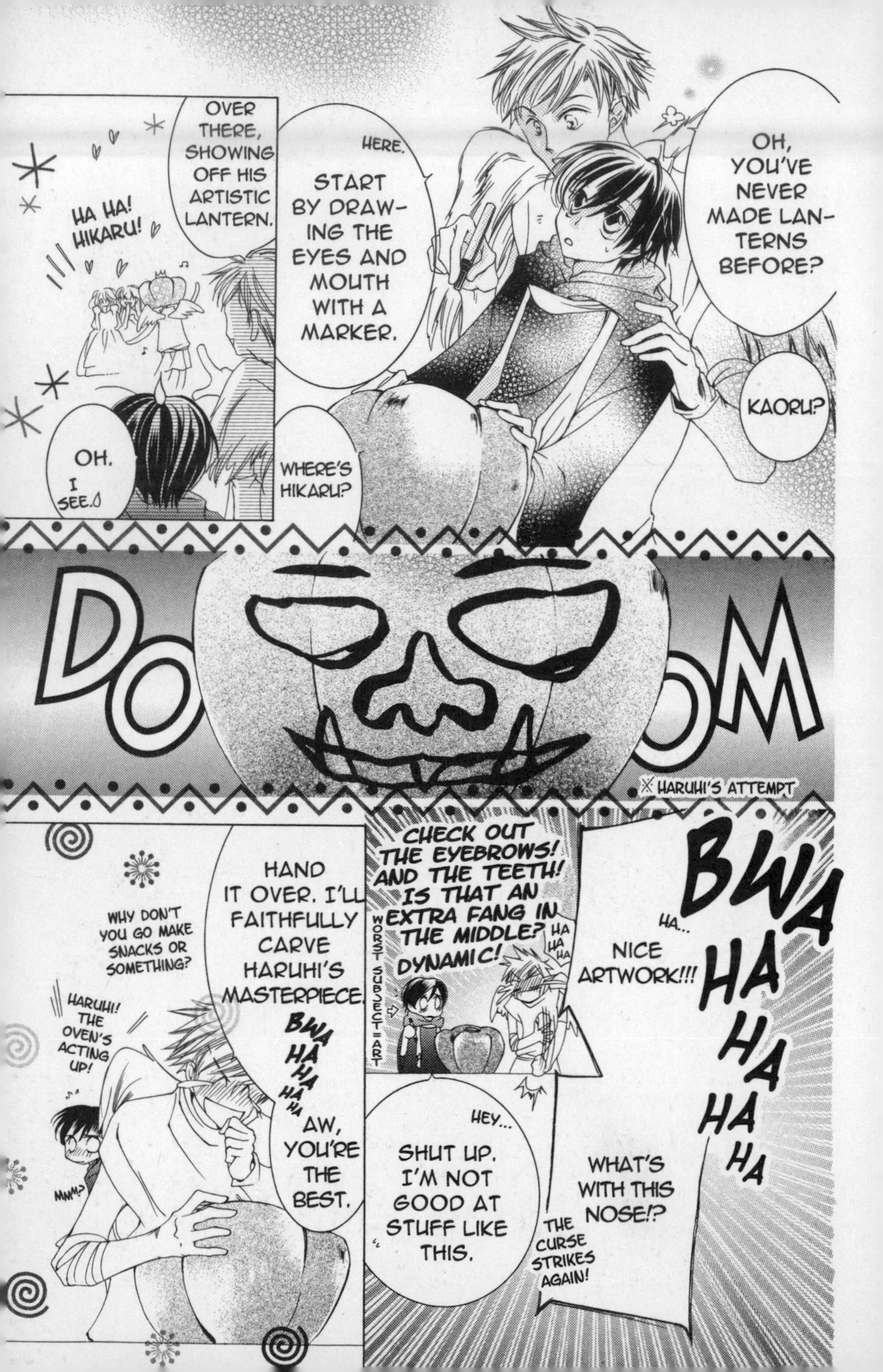
OH, YOU'VE NEVER MADE LANTERNS BEFORE?
HERE.
START BY DRAWING THE EYES AND MOUTH WITH A MARKER.
KAORU?
WHERE'S HIKARU?
OVER THERE, SHOWING OFF HIS ARTISTIC LANTERN.
HA HA! HIKARU!
OH.
I SEE.
DO
OM
※HARUHI'S ATTEMPT
BWA HA HA HA HA HA
HA...
NICE ARTWORK!!!
CHECK OUT THE EYEBROWS! AND THE TEETH! IS THAT AN EXTRA FANG IN THE MIDDLE? DYNAMIC!
HA HA HA
WORST SUBJECT=ART
WHAT'S WITH THIS NOSE!?
THE CURSE STRIKES AGAIN!
HEY...
SHUT UP. I'M NOT GOOD AT STUFF LIKE THIS.
HAND IT OVER. I'LL FAITHFULLY CARVE HARUHI'S MASTERPIECE.
WHY DON'T YOU GO MAKE SNACKS OR SOMETHING?
BWA HA HA HA HA
AW, YOU'RE THE BEST.
HARUHI! THE OVEN'S ACTING UP!
MMM?

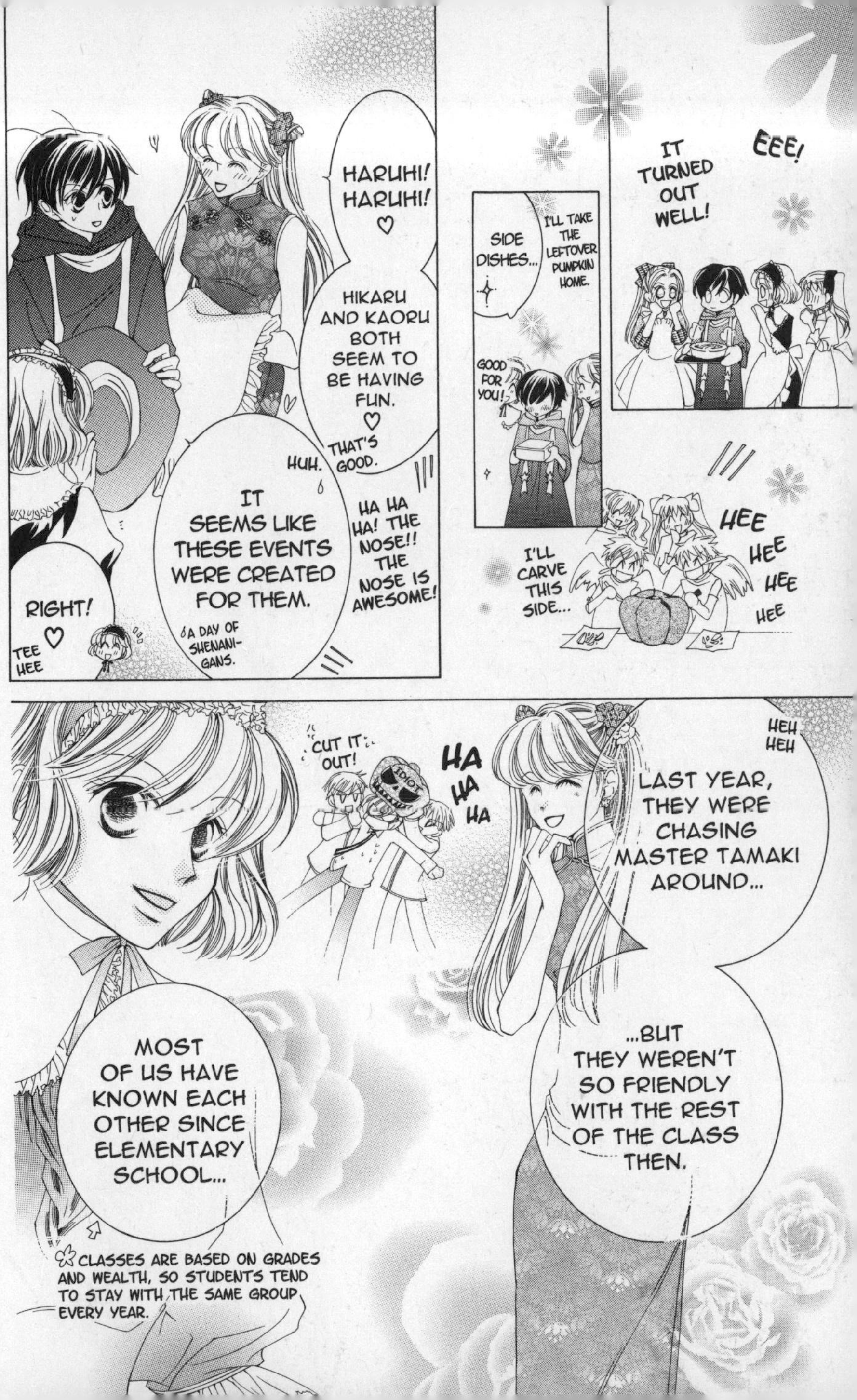
EEE!
IT TURNED OUT WELL!
SIDE DISHES...
I'LL TAKE THE LEFTOVER PUMPKIN HOME.
GOOD FOR YOU!
HEE HEE HEE HEE
I'LL CARVE THIS SIDE...
HARUHI! HARUHI! ♡
HIKARU AND KAORU BOTH SEEM TO BE HAVING FUN. ♡
THAT'S GOOD.
HA HA HA! THE NOSE!! THE NOSE IS AWESOME!
HUH.
IT SEEMS LIKE THESE EVENTS WERE CREATED FOR THEM.
A DAY OF SHENANIGANS.
RIGHT! ♡
TEE HEE
HEH HEH
LAST YEAR, THEY WERE CHASING MASTER TAMAKI AROUND...
...BUT THEY WEREN'T SO FRIENDLY WITH THE REST OF THE CLASS THEN.
HA HA HA
CUT IT OUT!
IDIOT
MOST OF US HAVE KNOWN EACH OTHER SINCE ELEMENTARY SCHOOL...
CLASSES ARE BASED ON GRADES AND WEALTH, SO STUDENTS TEND TO STAY WITH THE SAME GROUP EVERY YEAR.

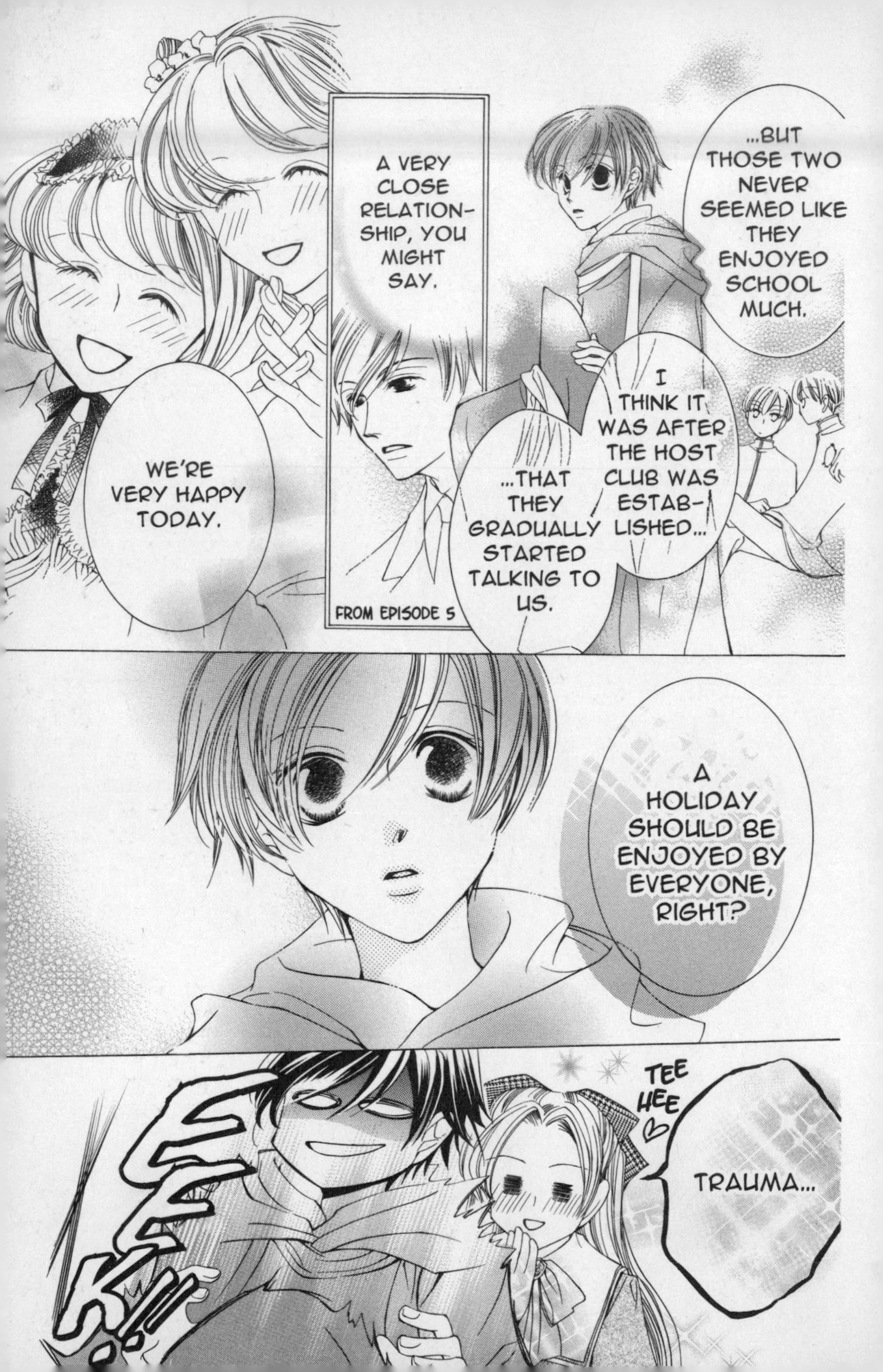
...BUT THOSE TWO NEVER SEEMED LIKE THEY ENJOYED SCHOOL MUCH.
I THINK IT WAS AFTER THE HOST CLUB WAS ESTAB-LISHED...
...THAT THEY GRADUALLY STARTED TALKING TO US.
A VERY CLOSE RELATION-SHIP, YOU MIGHT SAY.
FROM EPISODE 5
WE'RE VERY HAPPY TODAY.
A HOLIDAY SHOULD BE ENJOYED BY EVERYONE, RIGHT?
TEE HEE
TRAUMA...
EEK!!

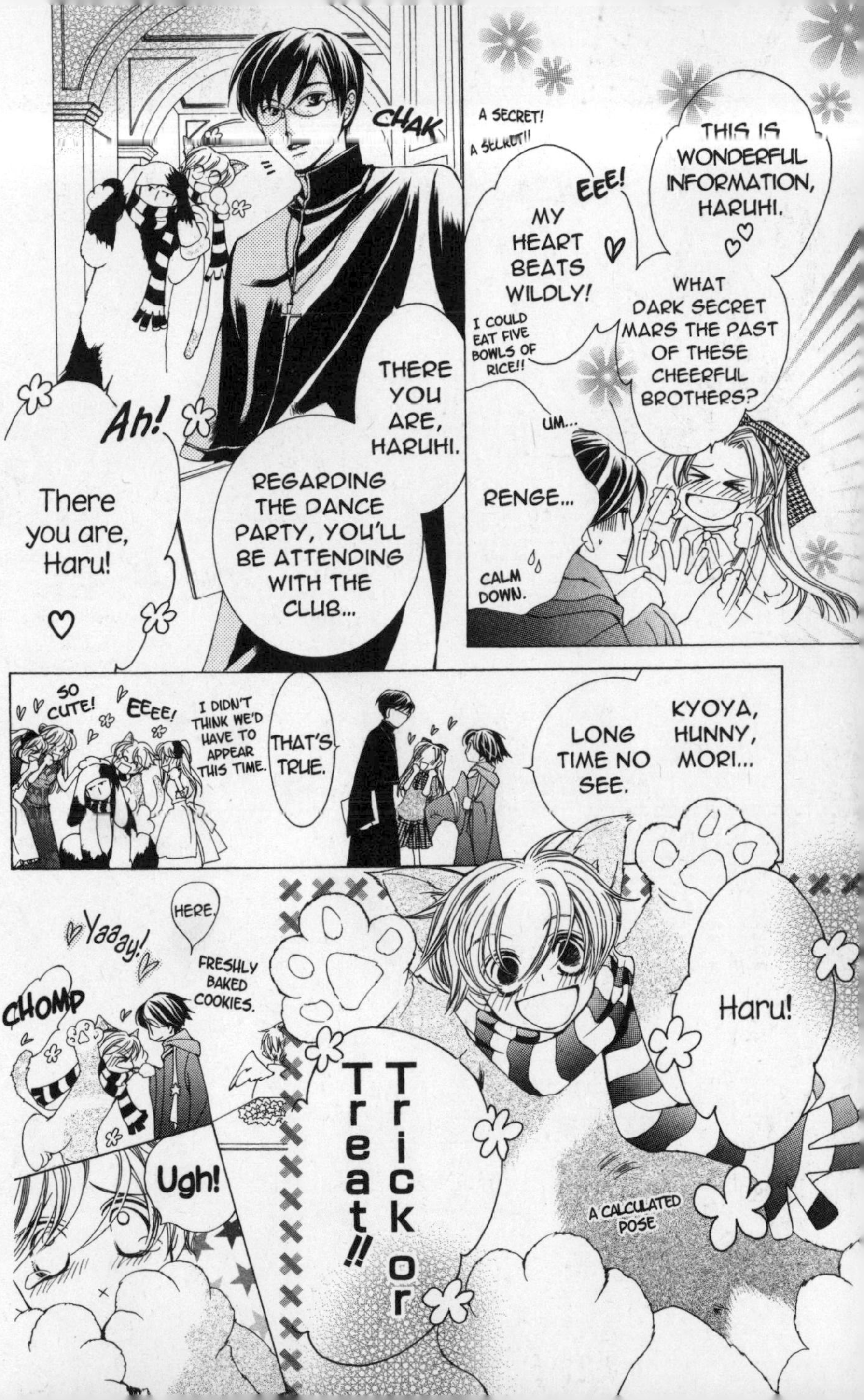
THIS IS WONDERFUL INFORMATION, HARUHI.
WHAT DARK SECRET MARS THE PAST OF THESE CHEERFUL BROTHERS?
A SECRET!
A SECRET!!
EEE!
MY HEART BEATS WILDLY!
I COULD EAT FIVE BOWLS OF RICE!!
UM...
RENGE...
CALM DOWN.
CHAK
THERE YOU ARE, HARUHI.
REGARDING THE DANCE PARTY, YOU'LL BE ATTENDING WITH THE CLUB...
Ah!
There you are, Haru!
KYOYA, HUNNY, MORI...
LONG TIME NO SEE.
THAT'S TRUE.
I DIDN'T THINK WE'D HAVE TO APPEAR THIS TIME.
EEEE!
SO CUTE!
Haru!
Trick or Treat!!
A CALCULATED POSE
HERE.
Yaaay!
FRESHLY BAKED COOKIES.
CHOMP
Ugh!

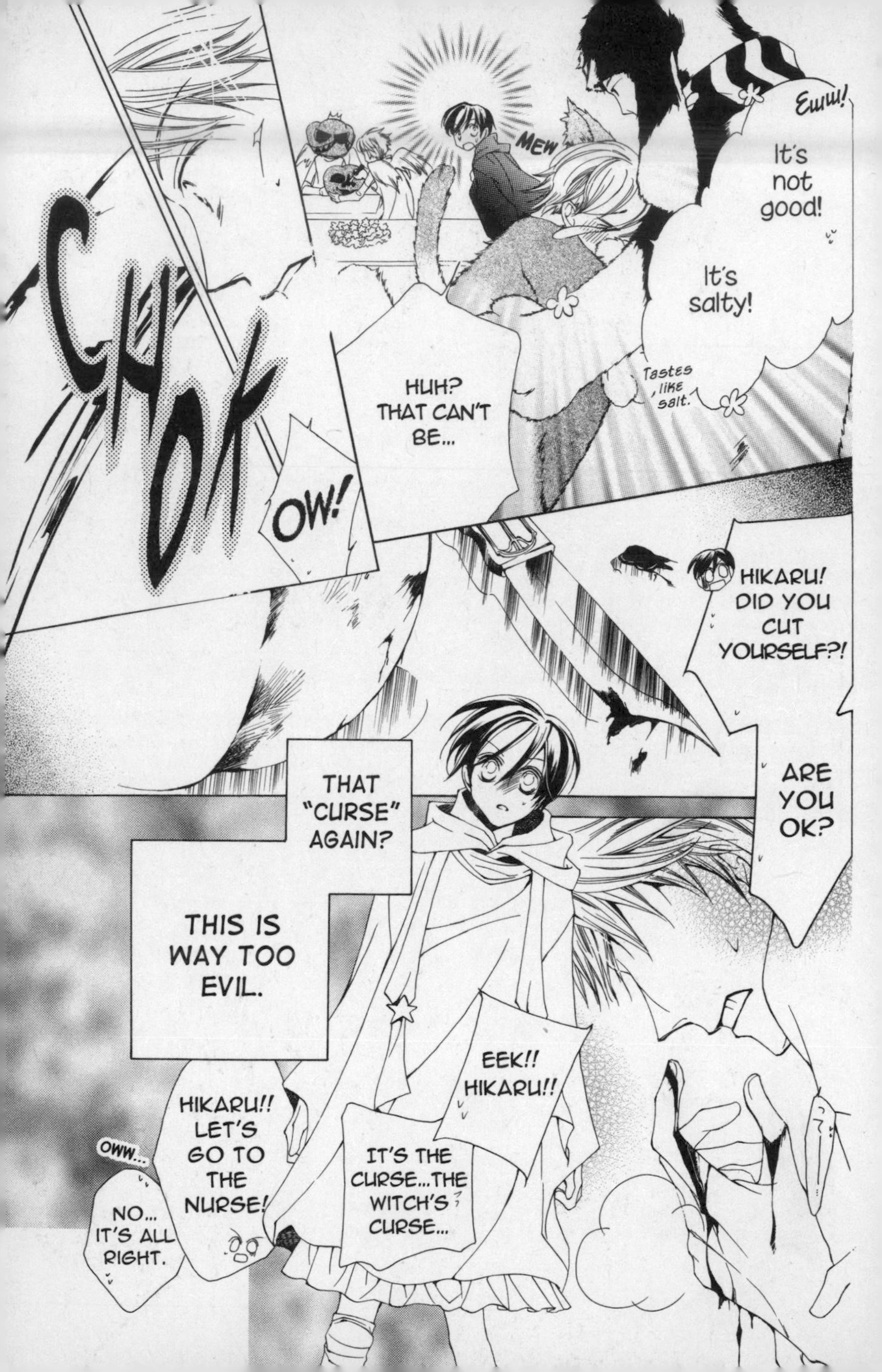
Ewww!
It's not good!
It's salty!
MEW
Tastes like salt.
HUH? THAT CAN'T BE...
CHOK
OW!
HIKARU! DID YOU CUT YOURSELF?!
ARE YOU OK?
THAT "CURSE" AGAIN?
THIS IS WAY TOO EVIL.
EEK!! HIKARU!!
IT'S THE CURSE...THE WITCH'S CURSE...
HIKARU!! LET'S GO TO THE NURSE!
OWW...
NO... IT'S ALL RIGHT.

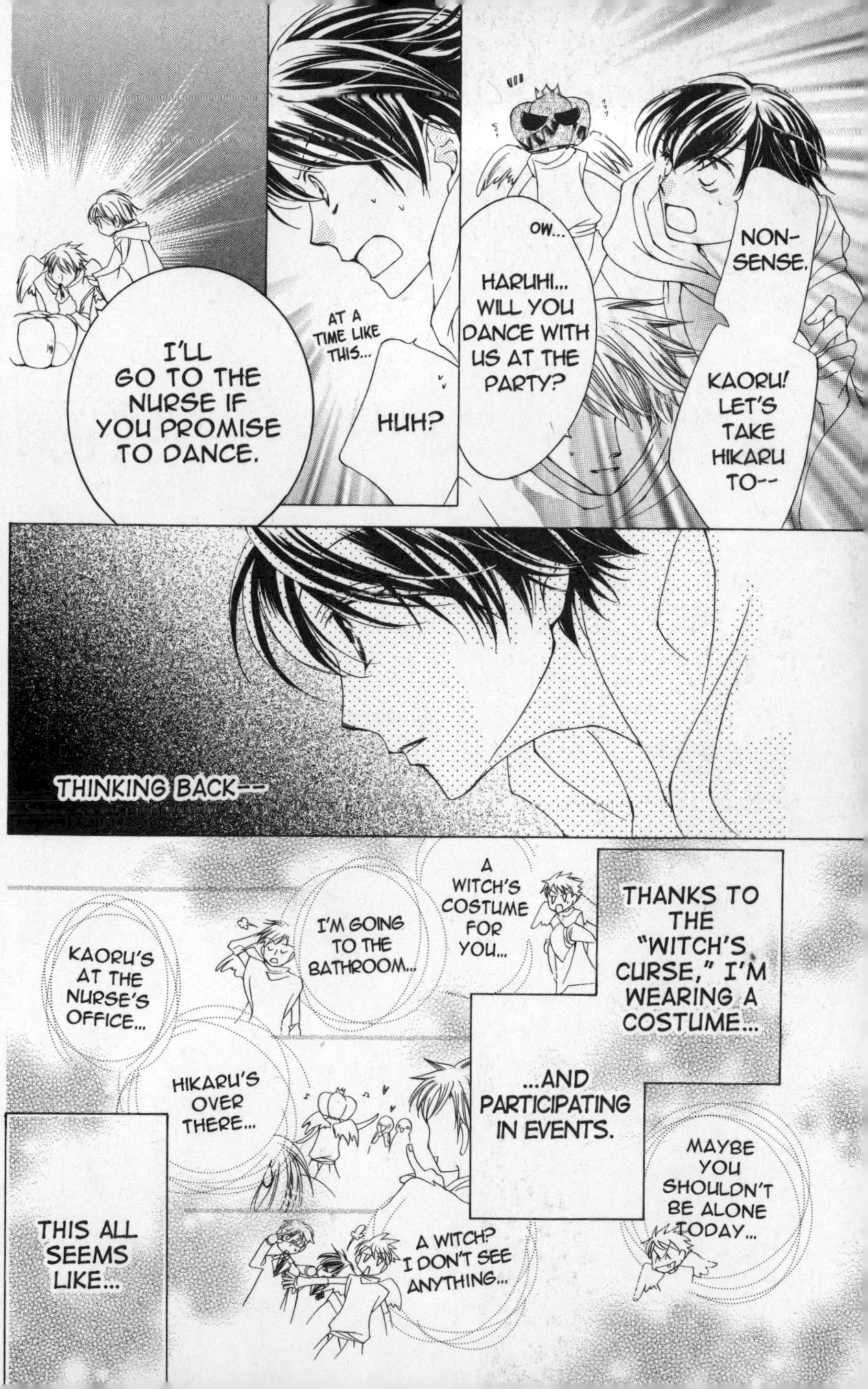
NON-SENSE.
KAORU! LET'S TAKE HIKARU TO--
OW...
HARUHI... WILL YOU DANCE WITH US AT THE PARTY?
AT A TIME LIKE THIS...
HUH?
I'LL GO TO THE NURSE IF YOU PROMISE TO DANCE.
THINKING BACK--
THANKS TO THE "WITCH'S CURSE," I'M WEARING A COSTUME...
A WITCH'S COSTUME FOR YOU...
I'M GOING TO THE BATHROOM...
KAORU'S AT THE NURSE'S OFFICE...
...AND PARTICIPATING IN EVENTS.
MAYBE YOU SHOULDN'T BE ALONE TODAY...
A WITCH? I DON'T SEE ANYTHING...
HIKARU'S OVER THERE...
THIS ALL SEEMS LIKE...

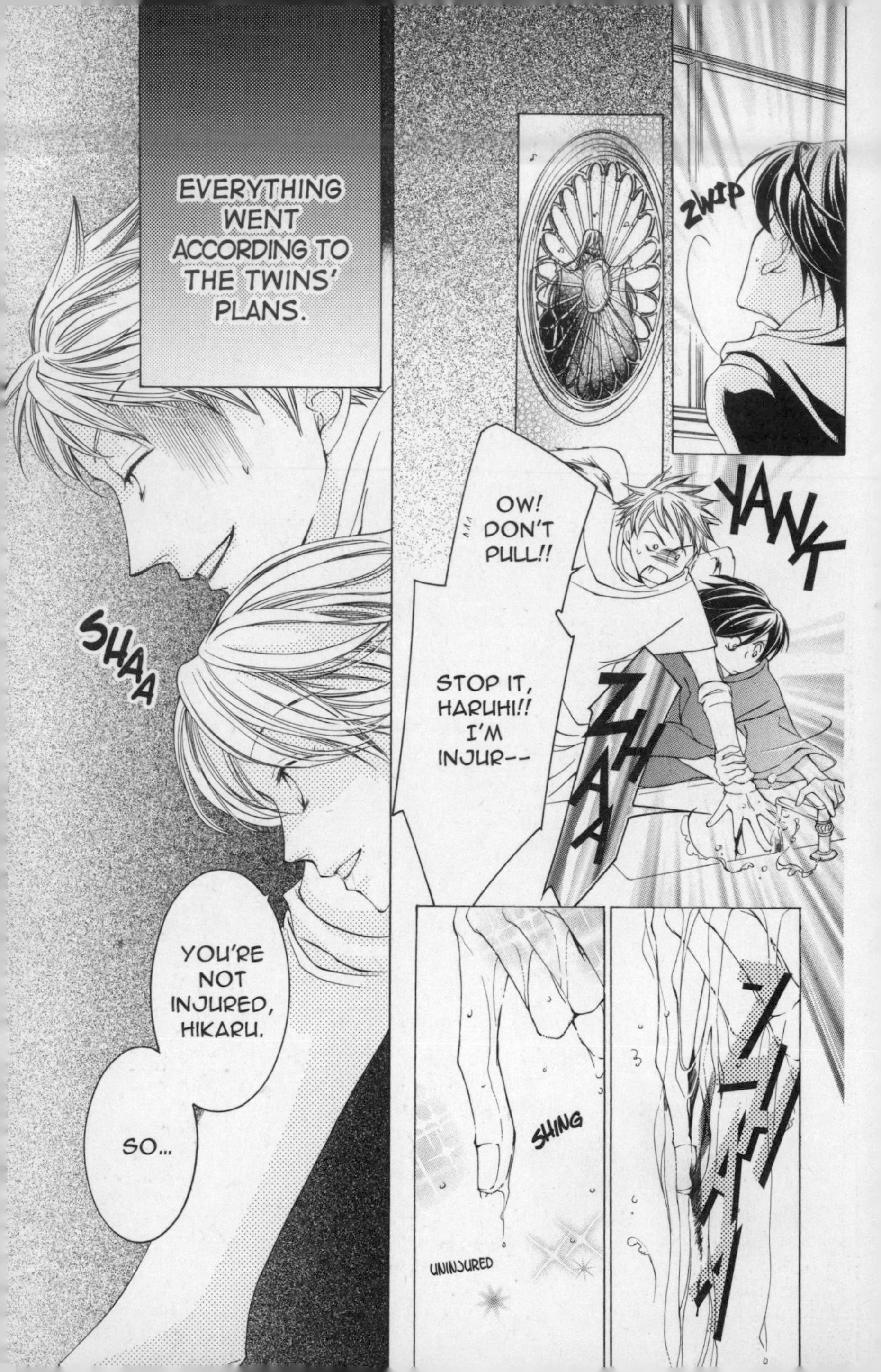
ZWIP
YANK
OW! DON'T PULL!!
STOP IT, HARUHI!! I'M INJUR--
ZHAA
SHING
UNINJURED
EVERYTHING WENT ACCORDING TO THE TWINS' PLANS.
SHAA
YOU'RE NOT INJURED, HIKARU.
SO...

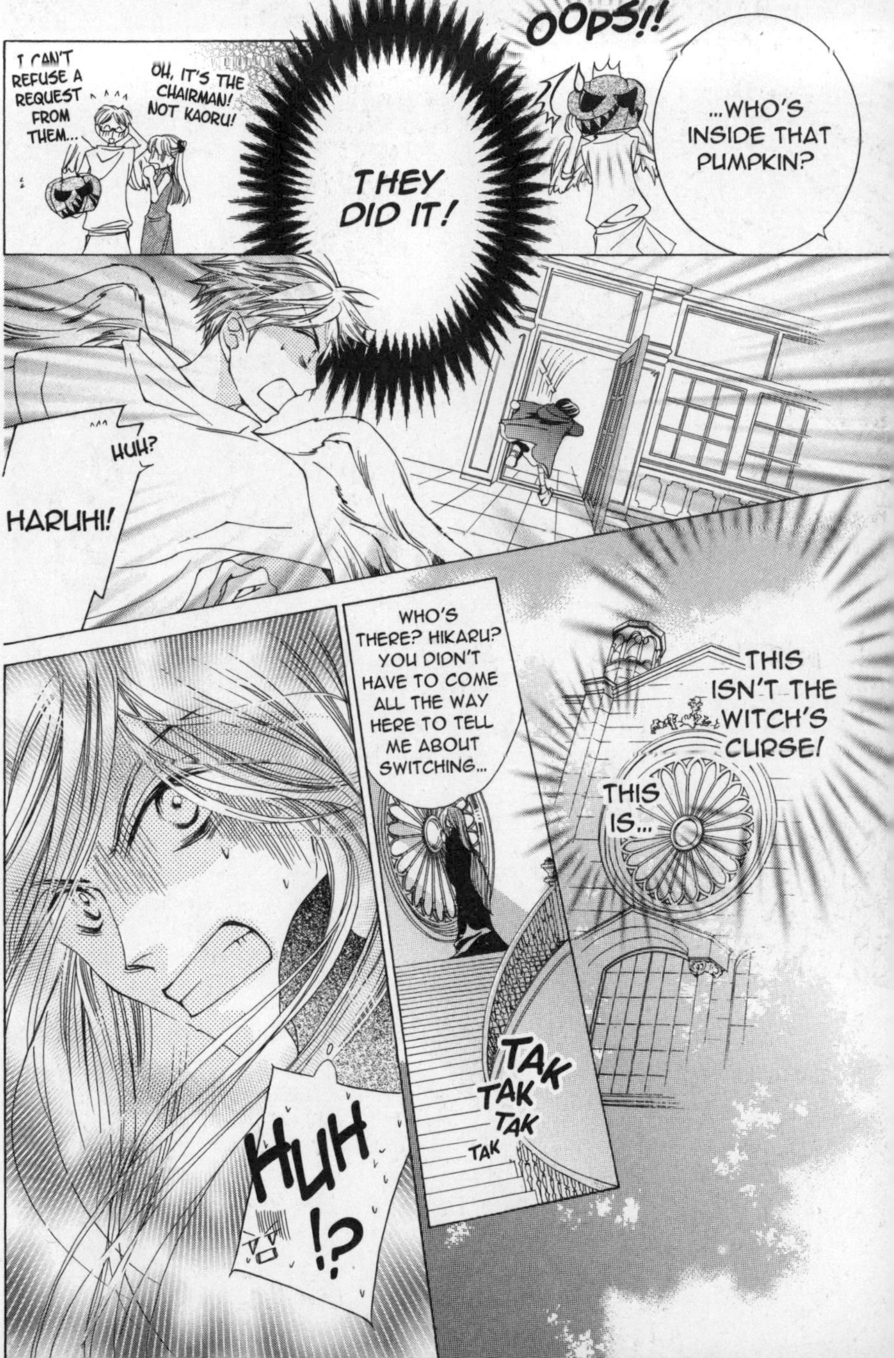
OOPS!!
...WHO'S INSIDE THAT PUMPKIN?
THEY DID IT!
OH, IT'S THE CHAIRMAN! NOT KAORU!
I CAN'T REFUSE A REQUEST FROM THEM...
HUH?
HARUHI!
THIS ISN'T THE WITCH'S CURSE!
THIS IS...
TAK TAK TAK TAK
WHO'S THERE? HIKARU? YOU DIDN'T HAVE TO COME ALL THE WAY HERE TO TELL ME ABOUT SWITCHING...
HUH !?

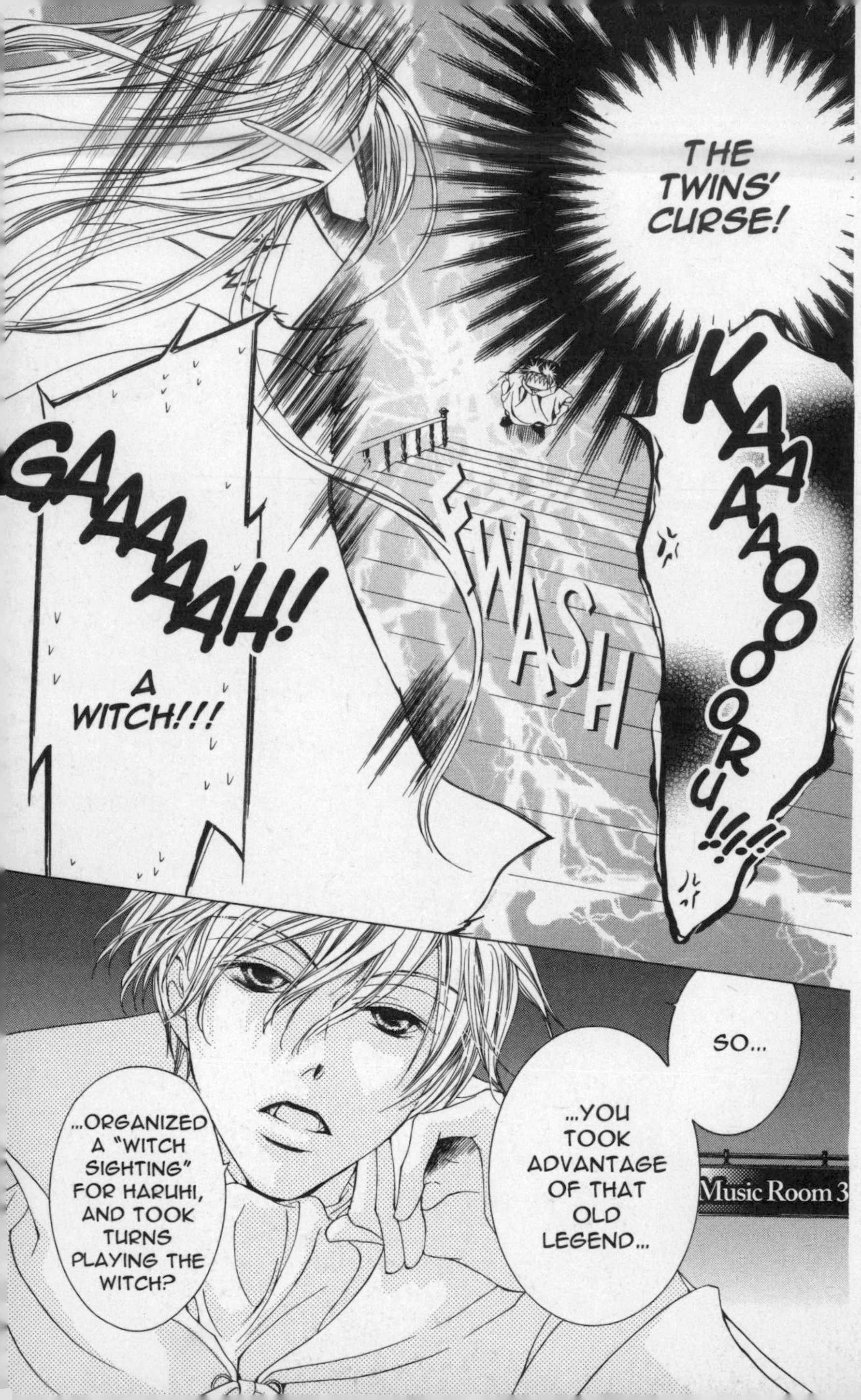
THE TWINS' CURSE!
KAAAAOOOORU!!!!
FWASH
GAAAAAH!
A WITCH!!!
Music Room 3
SO...
...YOU TOOK ADVANTAGE OF THAT OLD LEGEND...
...ORGANIZED A "WITCH SIGHTING" FOR HARUHI, AND TOOK TURNS PLAYING THE WITCH?

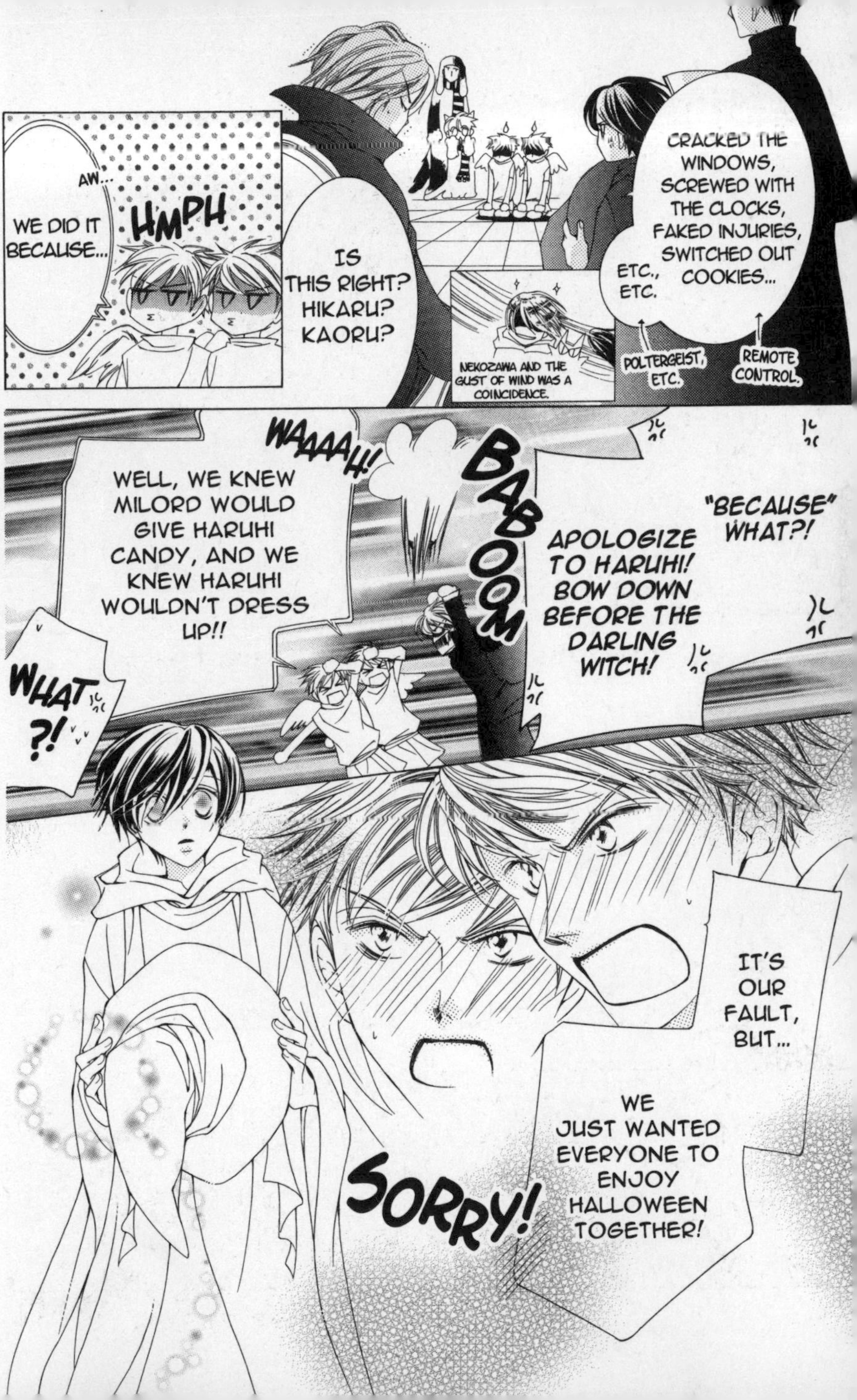
CRACKED THE WINDOWS, SCREWED WITH THE CLOCKS, FAKED INJURIES, SWITCHED OUT COOKIES...
ETC., ETC.
REMOTE CONTROL.
POLTERGEIST, ETC.
NEKOZAWA AND THE GUST OF WIND WAS A COINCIDENCE.
IS THIS RIGHT? HIKARU? KAORU?
HMPH
WE DID IT BECAUSE...
AW...
"BECAUSE" WHAT?!
APOLOGIZE TO HARUHI! BOW DOWN BEFORE THE DARLING WITCH!
BABOOM
WAAAAH!
WELL, WE KNEW MILORD WOULD GIVE HARUHI CANDY, AND WE KNEW HARUHI WOULDN'T DRESS UP!!
WHAT ?!
IT'S OUR FAULT, BUT...
WE JUST WANTED EVERYONE TO ENJOY HALLOWEEN TOGETHER!
SORRY!

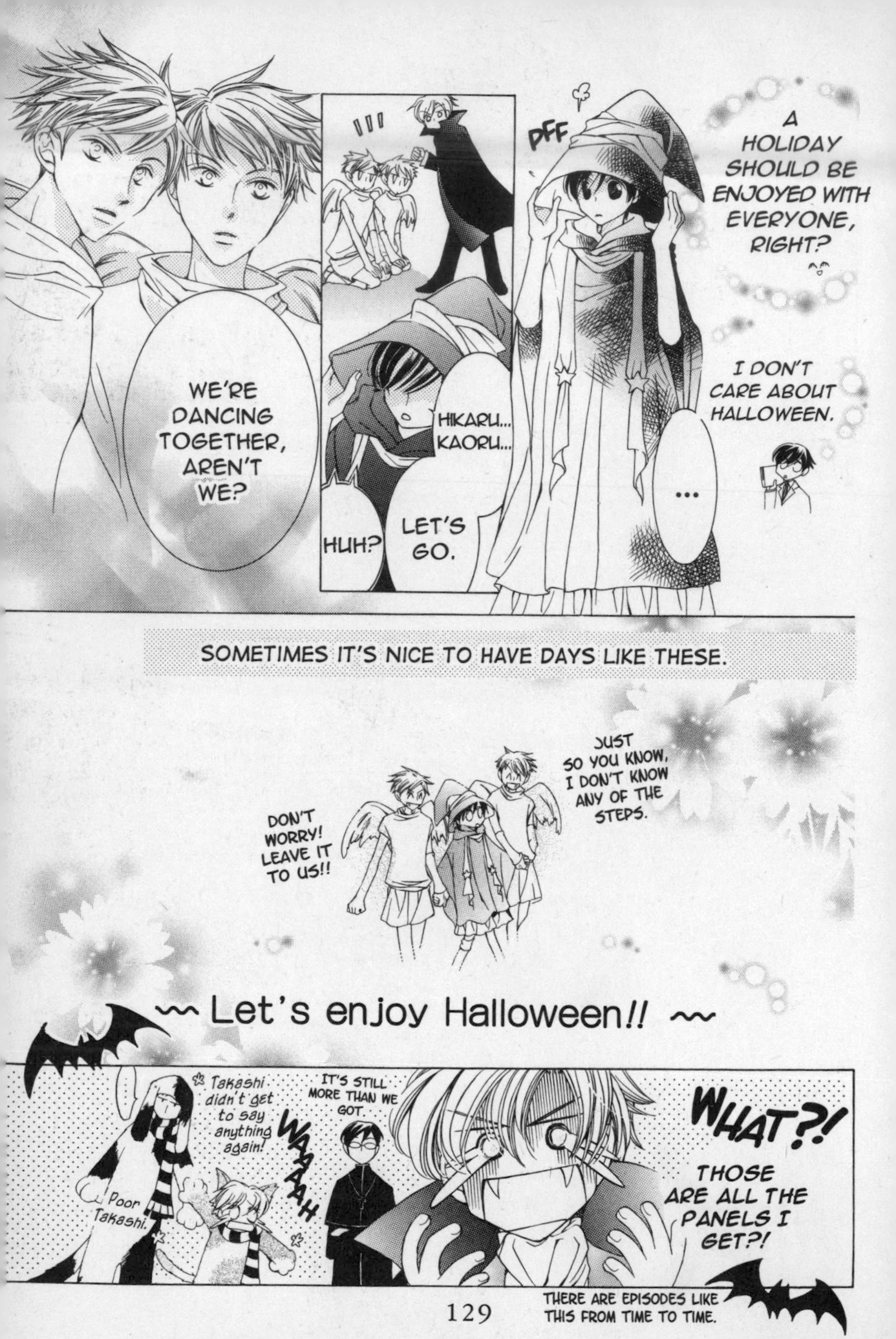
A HOLIDAY SHOULD BE ENJOYED WITH EVERYONE, RIGHT?
I DON'T CARE ABOUT HALLOWEEN.
...
PFF
!!!
HIKARU... KAORU...
LET'S GO.
HUH?
WE'RE DANCING TOGETHER, AREN'T WE?
SOMETIMES IT'S NICE TO HAVE DAYS LIKE THESE.
JUST SO YOU KNOW, I DON'T KNOW ANY OF THE STEPS.
DON'T WORRY! LEAVE IT TO US!!
~Let's enjoy Halloween!! ~
WHAT?!
THOSE ARE ALL THE PANELS I GET?!
IT'S STILL MORE THAN WE GOT.
WAAAAH
Takashi didn't get to say anything again!
Poor Takashi.
THERE ARE EPISODES LIKE THIS FROM TIME TO TIME.

EPISODE 12

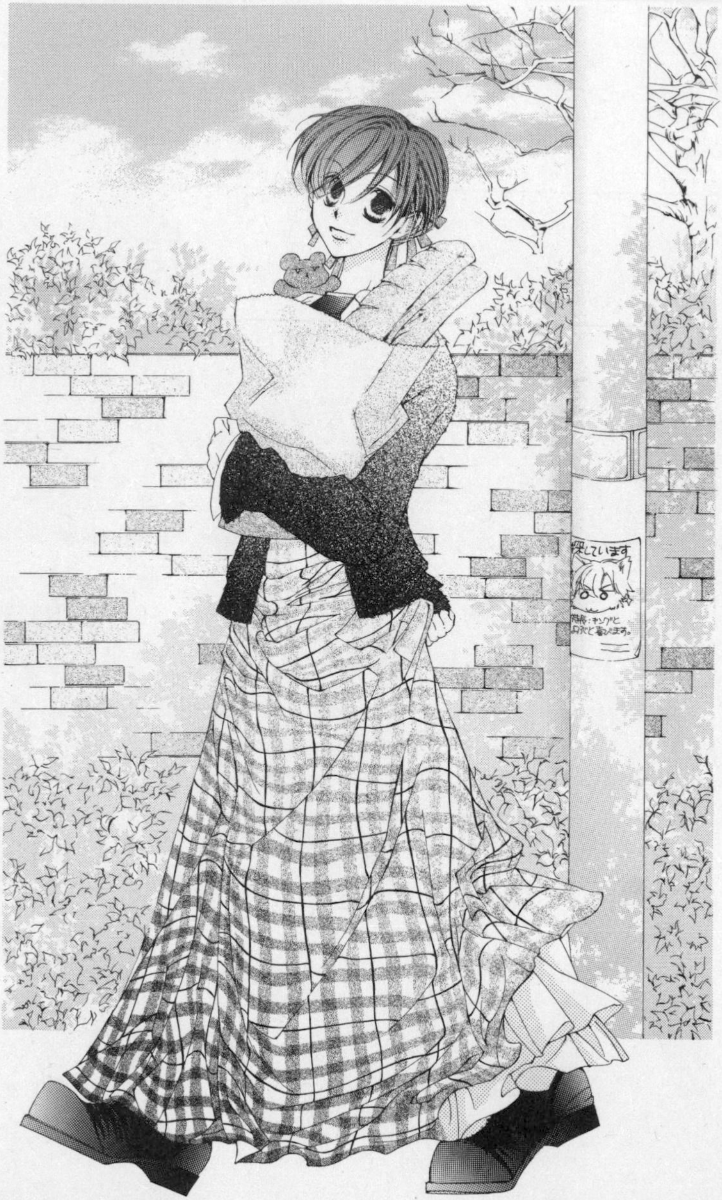
探していま す
特長：キングと
呼ぶと喜びます。

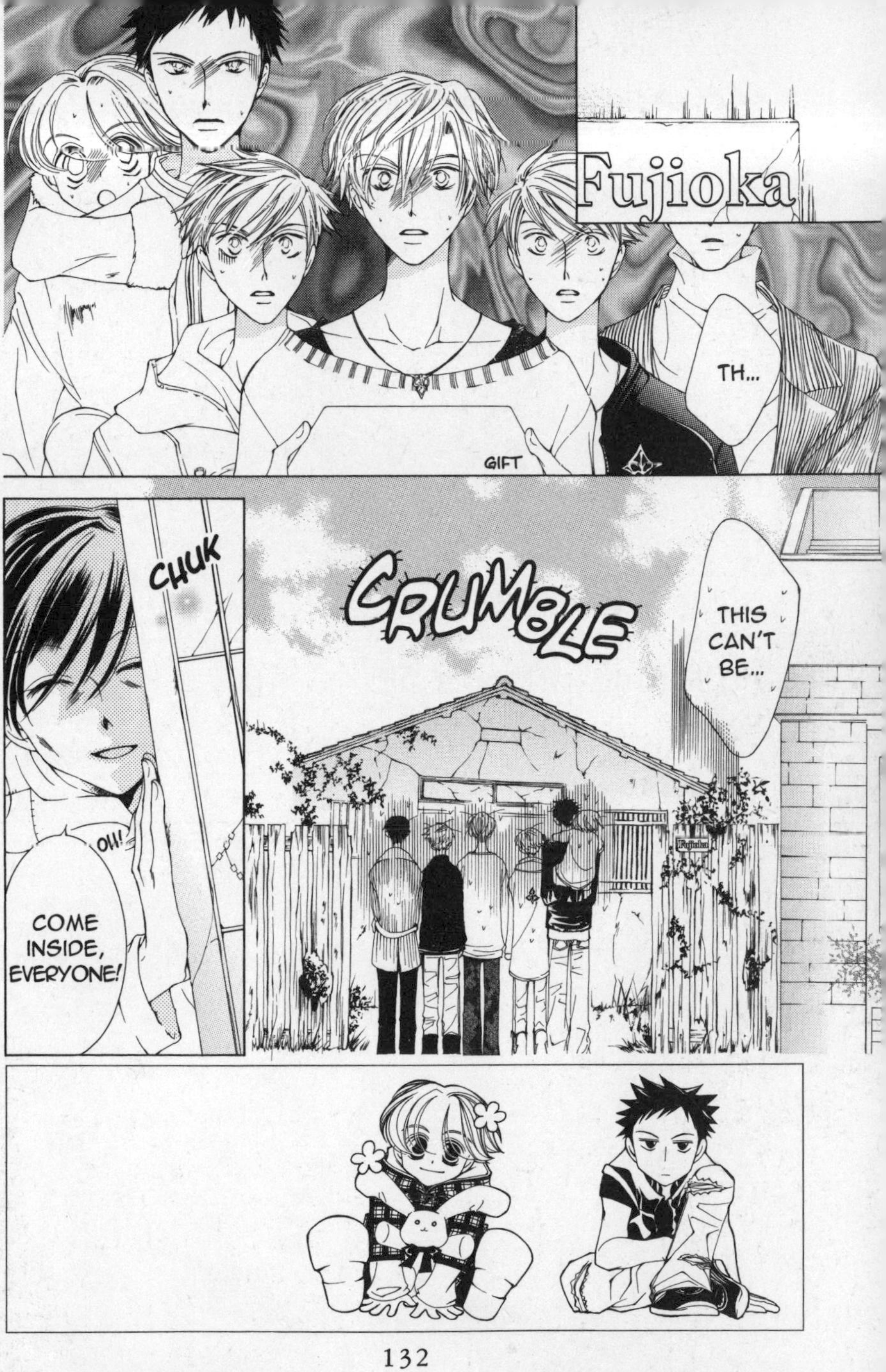
Fujioka
TH...
GIFT
THIS CAN'T BE...
CRUMBLE
CHUK
OH!
COME INSIDE, EVERYONE!

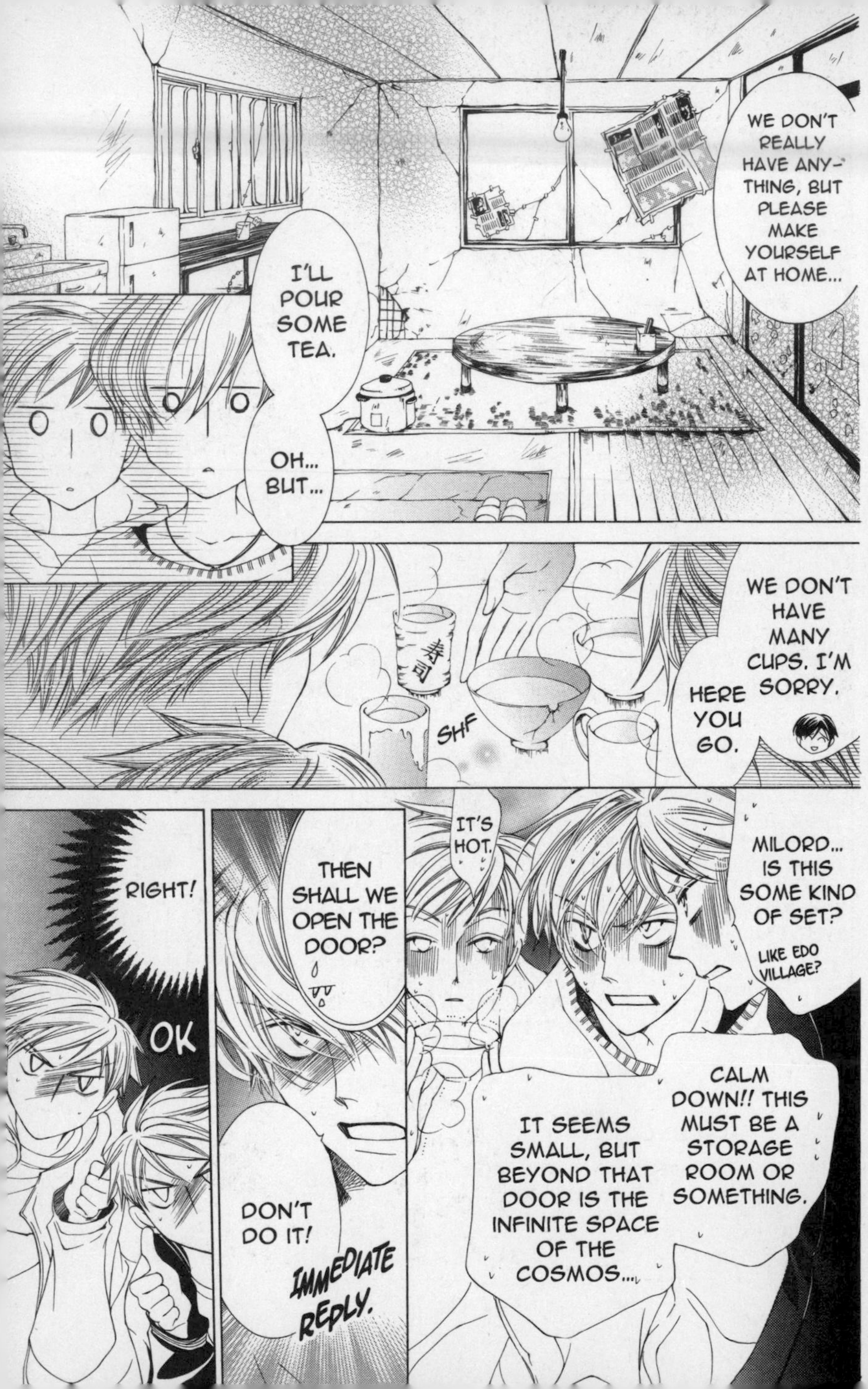
WE DON'T REALLY HAVE ANY-THING, BUT PLEASE MAKE YOURSELF AT HOME...
I'LL POUR SOME TEA.
OH... BUT...
WE DON'T HAVE MANY CUPS. I'M SORRY.
HERE YOU GO.
SHF
MILORD... IS THIS SOME KIND OF SET?
LIKE EDO VILLAGE?
IT'S HOT.
CALM DOWN!! THIS MUST BE A STORAGE ROOM OR SOMETHING.
IT SEEMS SMALL, BUT BEYOND THAT DOOR IS THE INFINITE SPACE OF THE COSMOS...
THEN SHALL WE OPEN THE DOOR?
DON'T DO IT!
IMMEDIATE REPLY.
RIGHT!
OK

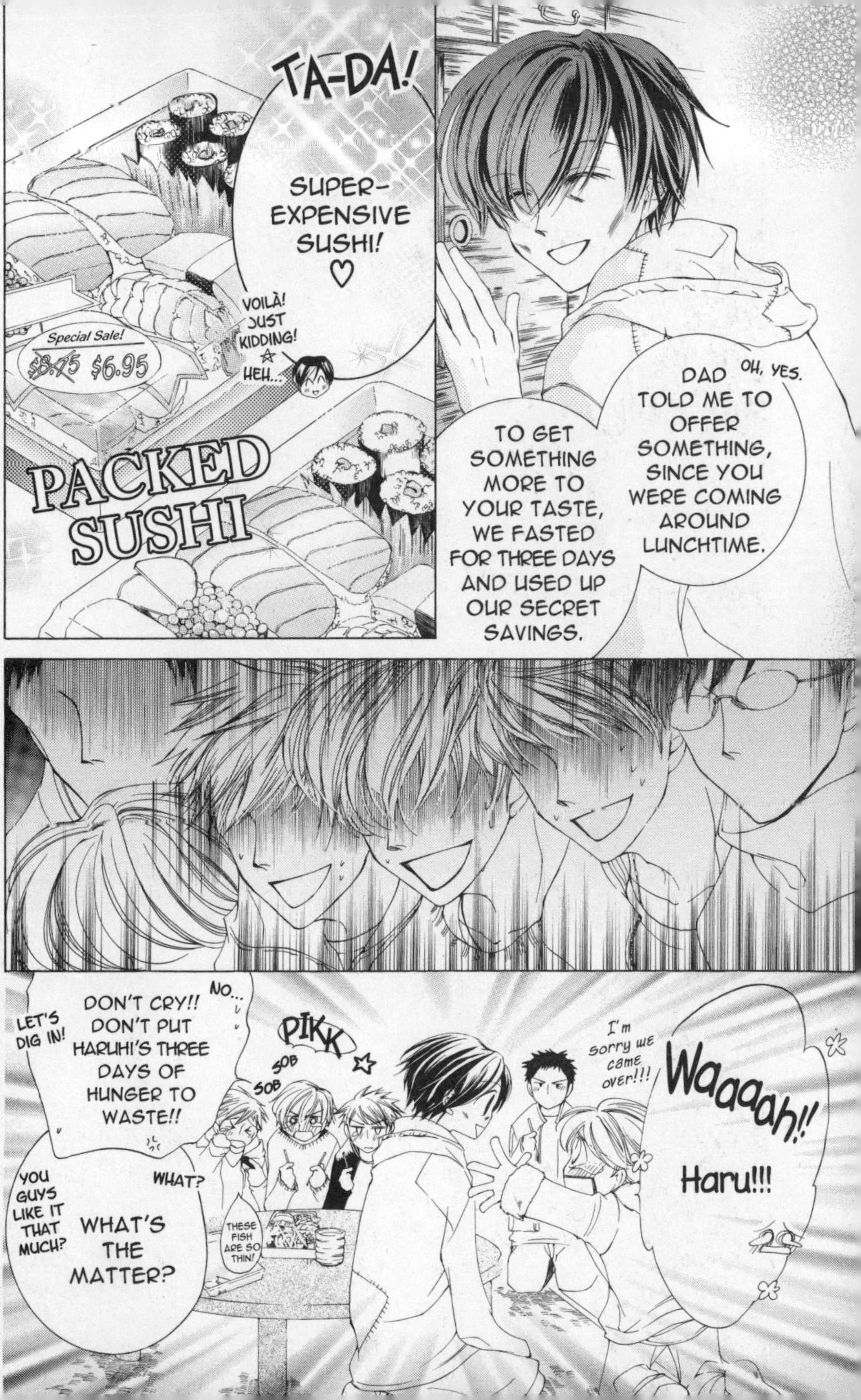
OH, YES.
DAD TOLD ME TO OFFER SOMETHING, SINCE YOU WERE COMING AROUND LUNCHTIME.
TO GET SOMETHING MORE TO YOUR TASTE, WE FASTED FOR THREE DAYS AND USED UP OUR SECRET SAVINGS.
TA-DA!
SUPER-EXPENSIVE SUSHI! ♡
VOILÀ! JUST KIDDING! ☆
HEH...
Special Sale!
$8.75 $6.95
PACKED SUSHI
Waaaah!!
Haru!!!
I'm sorry we came over!!!
PIKK
SOB
SOB
NO...
DON'T CRY!! DON'T PUT HARUHI'S THREE DAYS OF HUNGER TO WASTE!!
LET'S DIG IN!
THESE FISH ARE SO THIN!
WHAT?
YOU GUYS LIKE IT THAT MUCH?
WHAT'S THE MATTER?

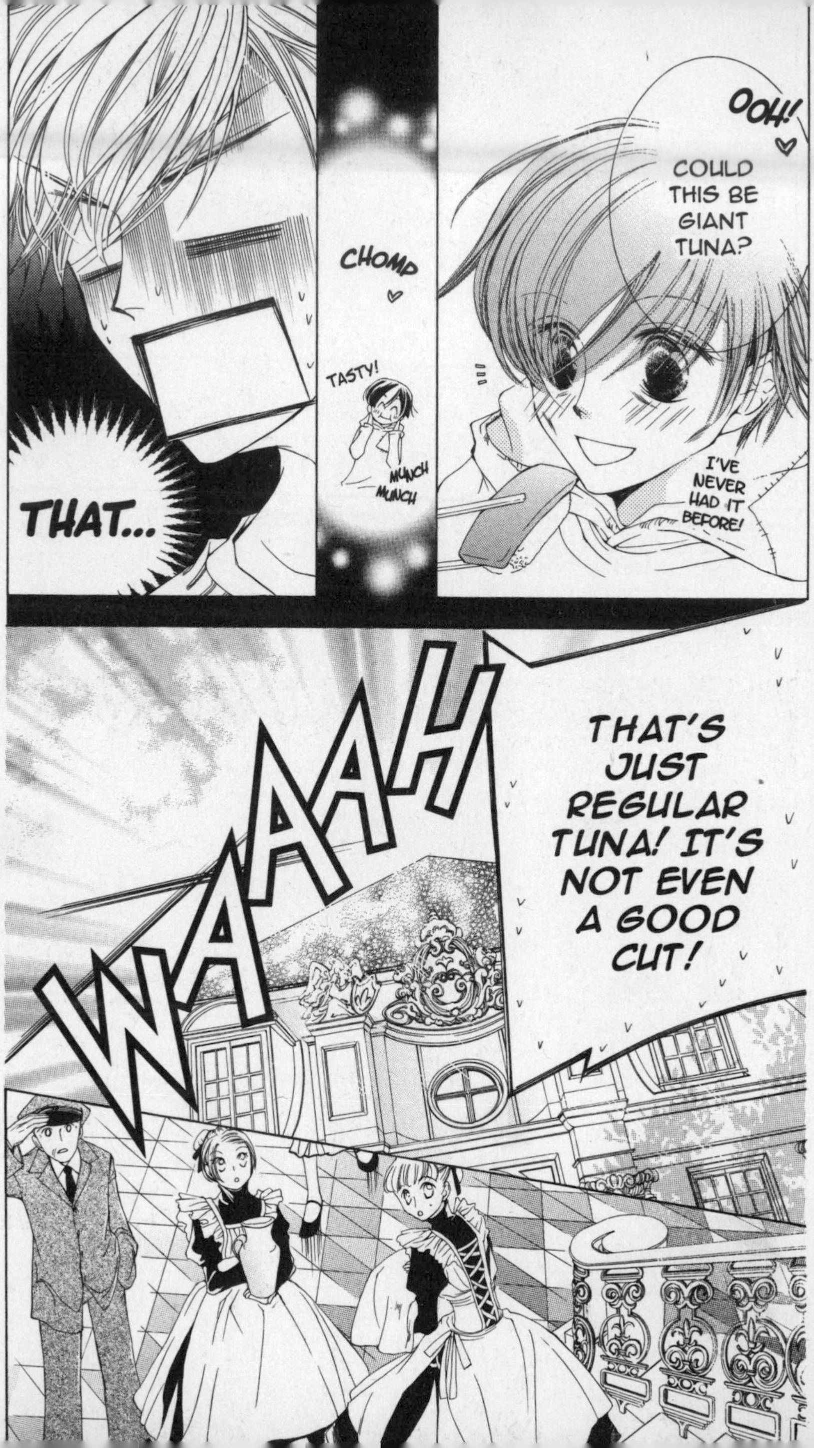
OOH!
COULD THIS BE GIANT TUNA?
I'VE NEVER HAD IT BEFORE!
CHOMP
TASTY!
MUNCH MUNCH
THAT...
THAT'S JUST REGULAR TUNA! IT'S NOT EVEN A GOOD CUT!
WAAAH

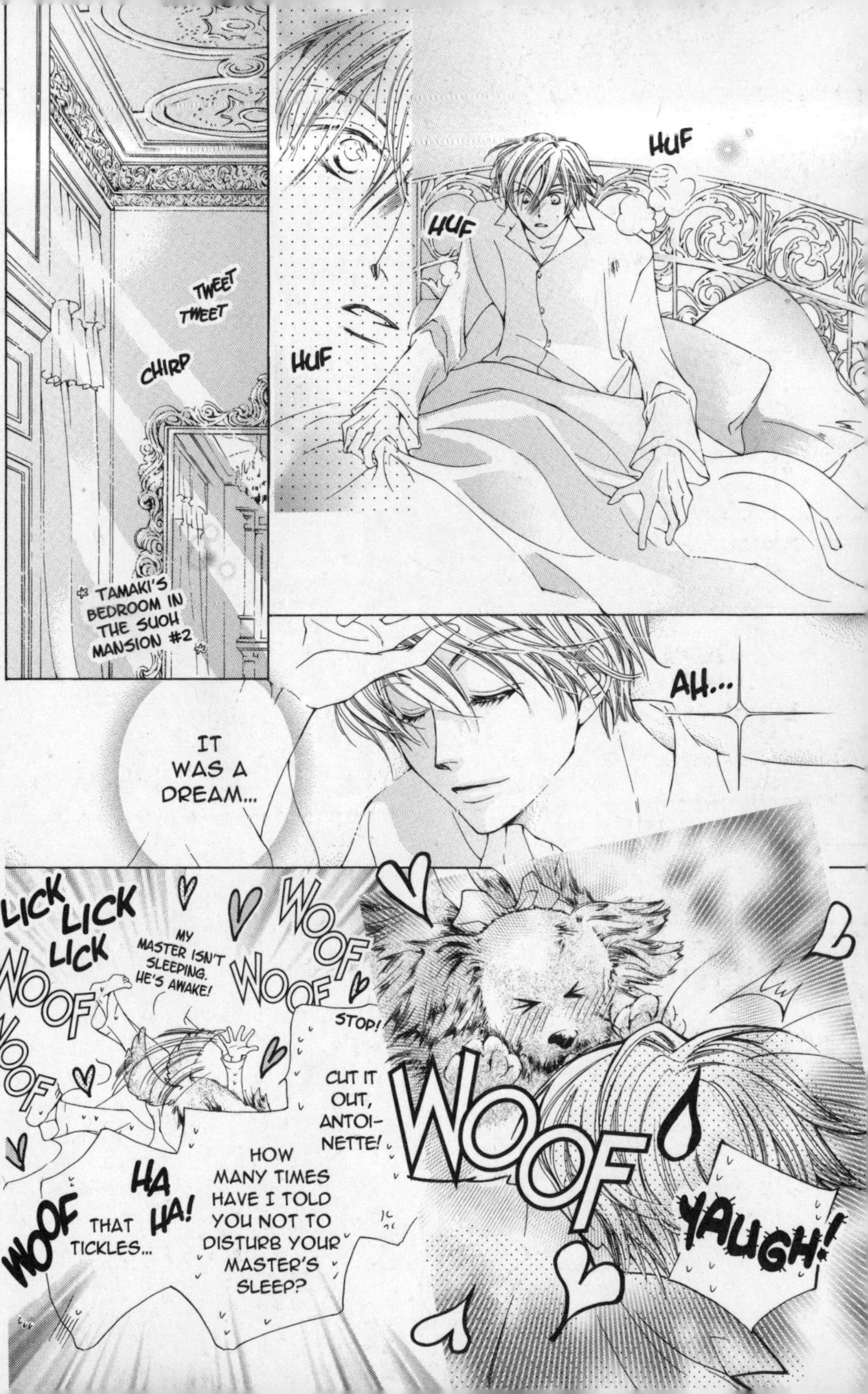
HUF
HUF
HUF
AH...
IT WAS A DREAM...
TWEET TWEET
CHIRP
TAMAKI'S BEDROOM IN THE SUOH MANSION #2
YAUGH!
WOOF
STOP!
CUT IT OUT, ANTOINETTE!
HOW MANY TIMES HAVE I TOLD YOU NOT TO DISTURB YOUR MASTER'S SLEEP?
WOOF WOOF
MY MASTER ISN'T SLEEPING. HE'S AWAKE!
LICK LICK LICK
WOOF WOOF
HA HA!
THAT TICKLES...
WOOF

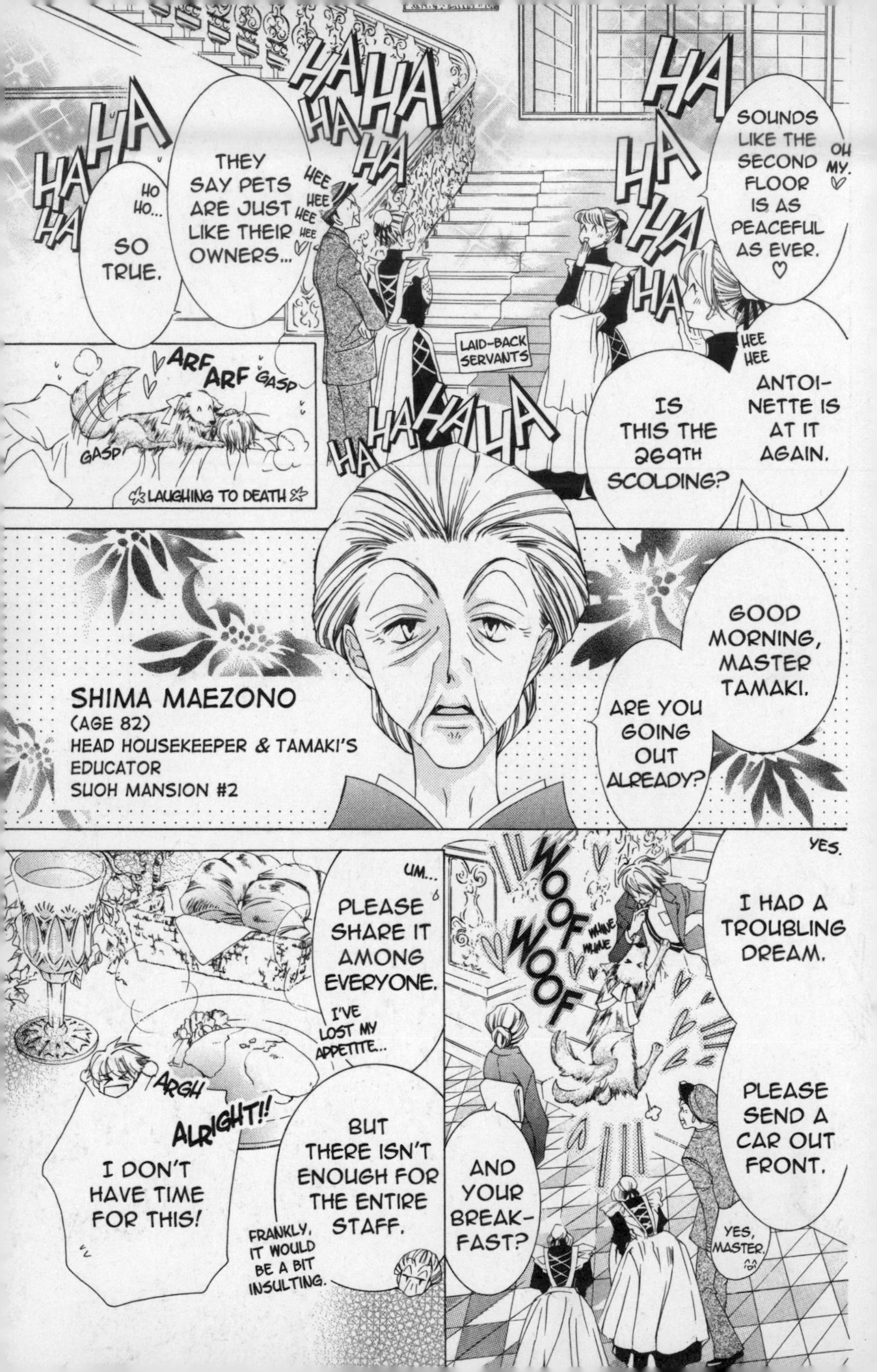
HA HA HA HA HA HA
SOUNDS LIKE THE SECOND FLOOR IS AS PEACEFUL AS EVER. ♡
OH MY. ♡
HEE HEE
ANTOINETTE IS AT IT AGAIN.
IS THIS THE 269TH SCOLDING?
HA HA HA HA
LAID-BACK SERVANTS
HA HA HA HA HA
HEE HEE HEE HEE
THEY SAY PETS ARE JUST LIKE THEIR OWNERS...
HO HO...
SO TRUE.
HA HA HA
ARF ARF
GASP
GASP
LAUGHING TO DEATH
GOOD MORNING, MASTER TAMAKI.
ARE YOU GOING OUT ALREADY?
SHIMA MAEZONO
(AGE 82)
HEAD HOUSEKEEPER & TAMAKI'S EDUCATOR
SUOH MANSION #2
YES.
I HAD A TROUBLING DREAM.
PLEASE SEND A CAR OUT FRONT.
YES, MASTER.
WOOF WOOF WOOF
WHINE WHINE
AND YOUR BREAKFAST?
UM...
PLEASE SHARE IT AMONG EVERYONE.
I'VE LOST MY APPETITE...
BUT THERE ISN'T ENOUGH FOR THE ENTIRE STAFF.
FRANKLY, IT WOULD BE A BIT INSULTING.
ALRIGHT!!
ARGH
I DON'T HAVE TIME FOR THIS!

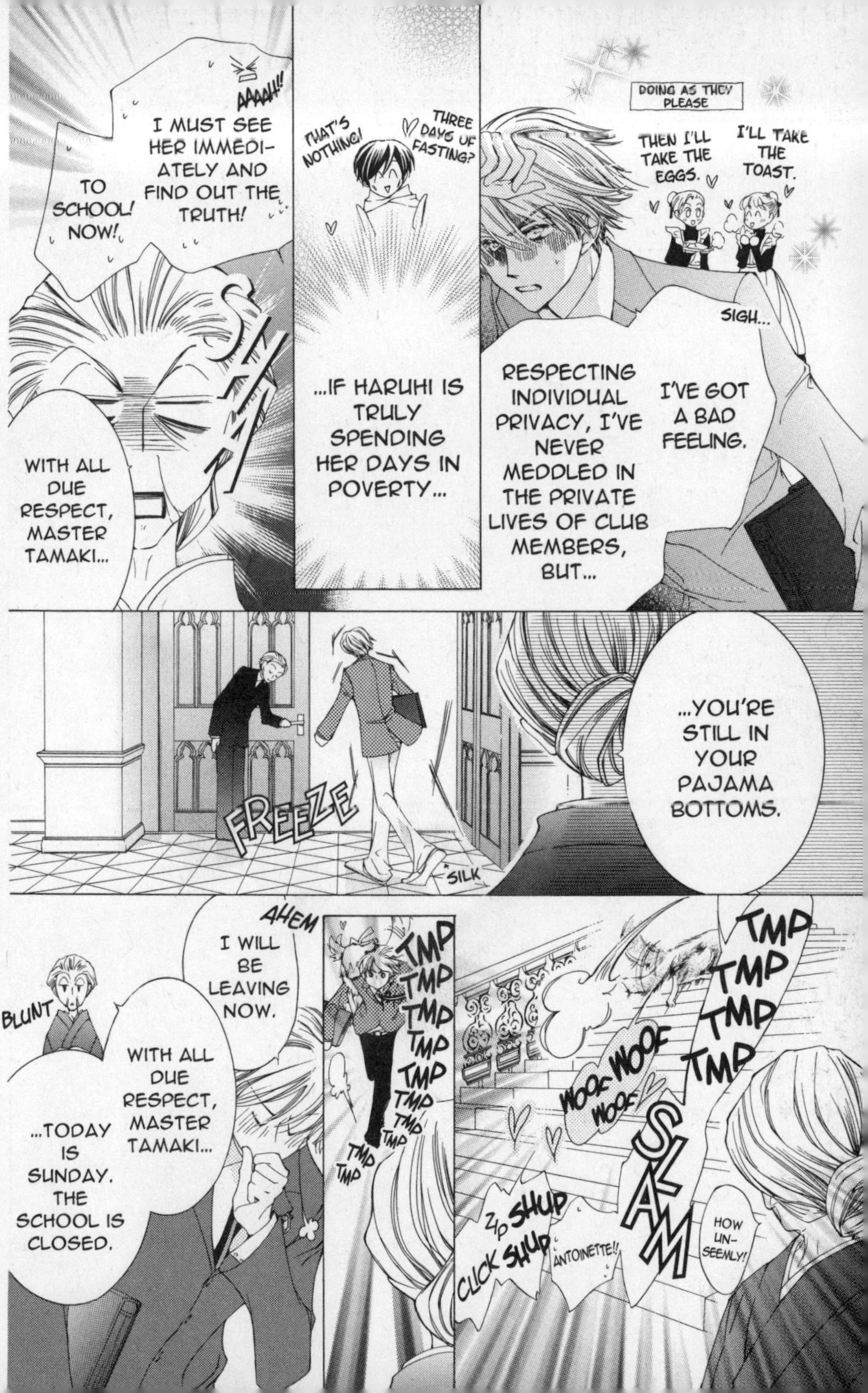
DOING AS THEY PLEASE
I'LL TAKE THE TOAST.
THEN I'LL TAKE THE EGGS.
SIGH...
I'VE GOT A BAD FEELING.
RESPECTING INDIVIDUAL PRIVACY, I'VE NEVER MEDDLED IN THE PRIVATE LIVES OF CLUB MEMBERS, BUT...
THREE DAYS OF FASTING?
THAT'S NOTHING!
...IF HARUHI IS TRULY SPENDING HER DAYS IN POVERTY...
AAAAH!!
I MUST SEE HER IMMEDIATELY AND FIND OUT THE TRUTH!
TO SCHOOL! NOW!
WITH ALL DUE RESPECT, MASTER TAMAKI...
...YOU'RE STILL IN YOUR PAJAMA BOTTOMS.
FREEZE
SILK
TMP TMP TMP TMP TMP
HOW UN-SEEMLY!
SLAM
WOOF WOOF WOOF
ANTOINETTE!!
ZIP SHUP
CLICK SHUP
TMP TMP TMP TMP TMP TMP TMP TMP TMP TMP
AHEM
I WILL BE LEAVING NOW.
BLUNT
WITH ALL DUE RESPECT, MASTER TAMAKI...
...TODAY IS SUNDAY. THE SCHOOL IS CLOSED.

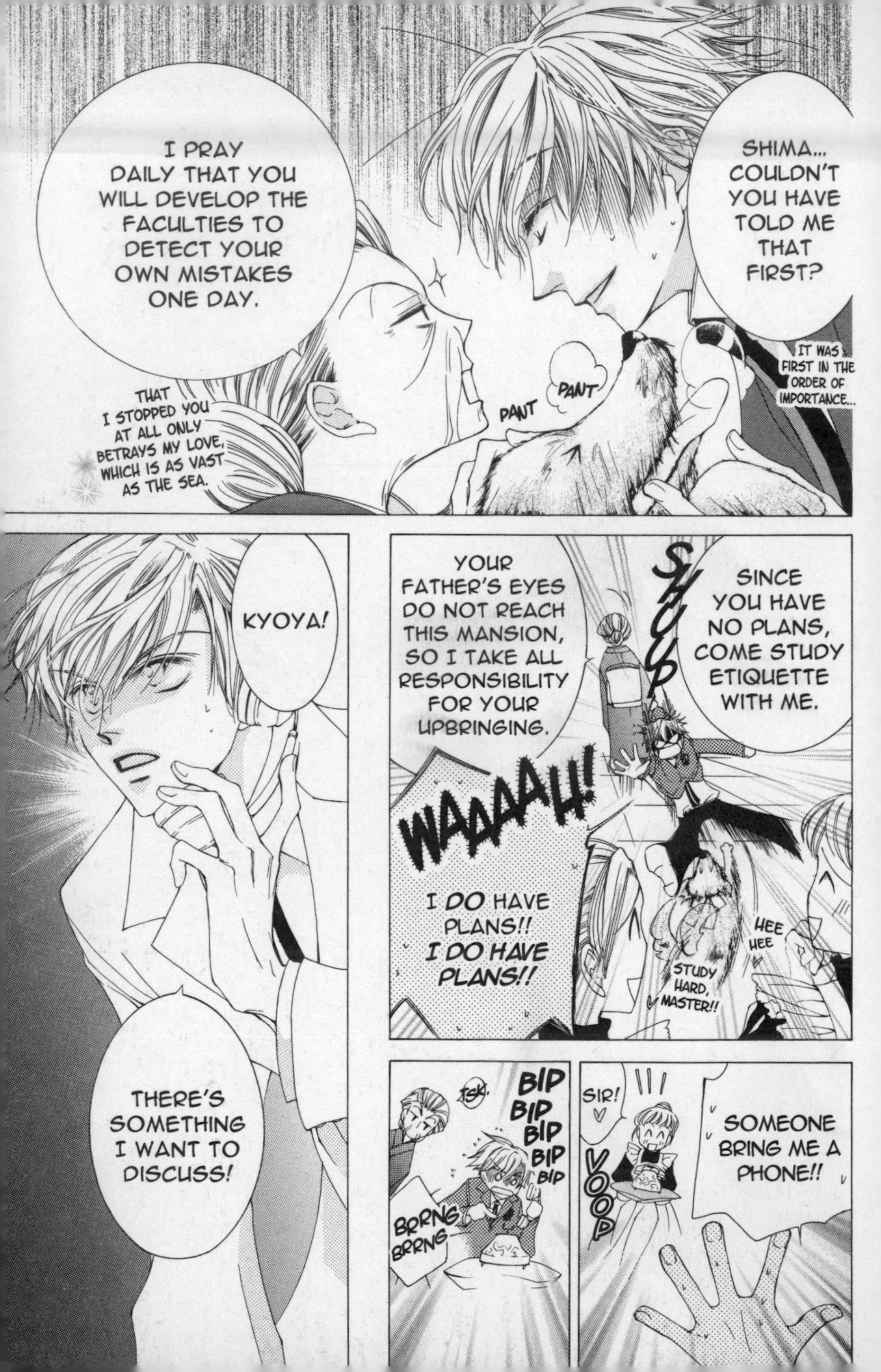
SHIMA... COULDN'T YOU HAVE TOLD ME THAT FIRST?
IT WAS FIRST IN THE ORDER OF IMPORTANCE...
PANT
PANT
I PRAY DAILY THAT YOU WILL DEVELOP THE FACULTIES TO DETECT YOUR OWN MISTAKES ONE DAY.
THAT I STOPPED YOU AT ALL ONLY BETRAYS MY LOVE, WHICH IS AS VAST AS THE SEA.
SINCE YOU HAVE NO PLANS, COME STUDY ETIQUETTE WITH ME.
YOUR FATHER'S EYES DO NOT REACH THIS MANSION, SO I TAKE ALL RESPONSIBILITY FOR YOUR UPBRINGING.
SHOOP
WAAAAH!
I *DO* HAVE PLANS!! I DO HAVE PLANS!!
HEE HEE
STUDY HARD, MASTER!!
SOMEONE BRING ME A PHONE!!
SIR!
VOOP
BIP BIP BIP BIP BIP
TSK.
BRRNG BRRNG
KYOYA!
THERE'S SOMETHING I WANT TO DISCUSS!

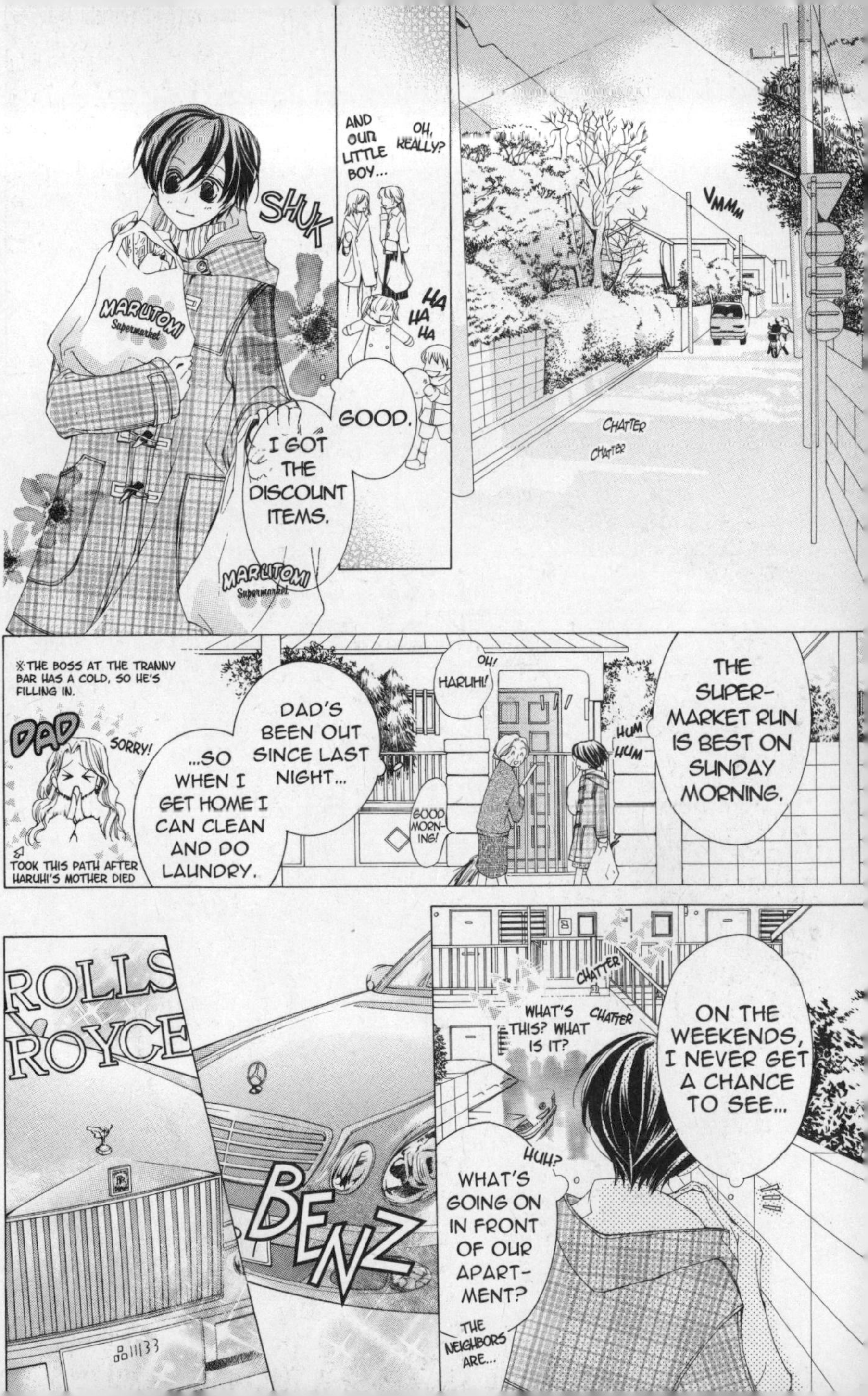
VMMM
CHATTER
CHATTER
OH, REALLY?
AND OUR LITTLE BOY...
HA HA HA
SHUK
MARUTOMI Supermarket
GOOD.
I GOT THE DISCOUNT ITEMS.
MARUTOMI Supermarket
THE SUPER-MARKET RUN IS BEST ON SUNDAY MORNING.
HUM HUM
OH! HARUHI!
GOOD MORNING!
DAD'S BEEN OUT SINCE LAST NIGHT...
...SO WHEN I GET HOME I CAN CLEAN AND DO LAUNDRY.
※THE BOSS AT THE TRANNY BAR HAS A COLD, SO HE'S FILLING IN.
DAD
SORRY!
TOOK THIS PATH AFTER HARUHI'S MOTHER DIED
ON THE WEEKENDS, I NEVER GET A CHANCE TO SEE...
CHATTER
WHAT'S THIS? WHAT IS IT?
CHATTER
HUH?
WHAT'S GOING ON IN FRONT OF OUR APART-MENT?
THE NEIGHBORS ARE...
ROLLS ROYCE
BENZ

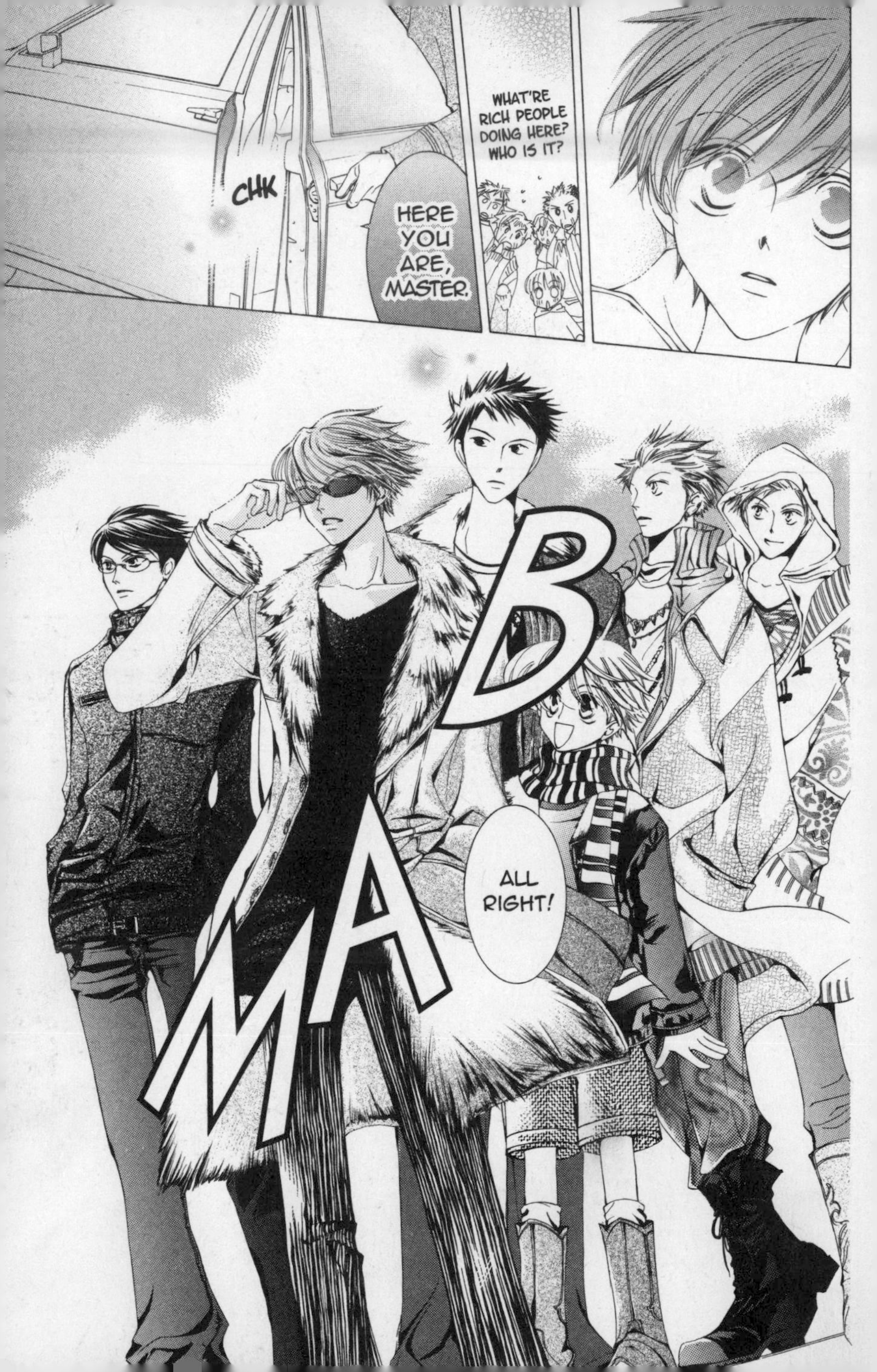
WHAT'RE RICH PEOPLE DOING HERE? WHO IS IT?
HERE YOU ARE, MASTER.
CHK
BAM
ALL RIGHT!

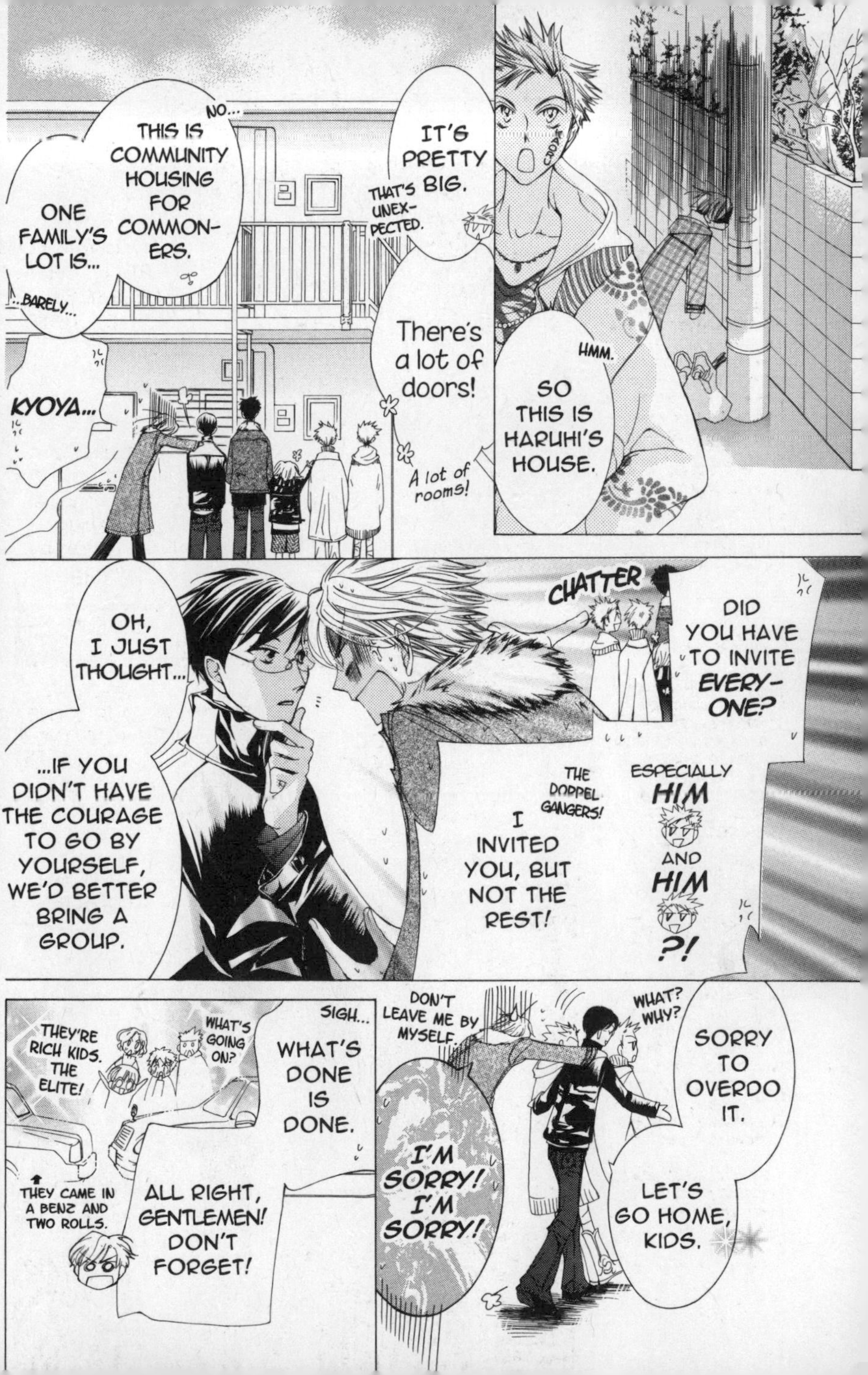
HMM.
SO THIS IS HARUHI'S HOUSE.
IT'S PRETTY BIG.
THAT'S UNEXPECTED.
There's a lot of doors!
A lot of rooms!
NO... THIS IS COMMUNITY HOUSING FOR COMMONERS.
ONE FAMILY'S LOT IS...
...BARELY...
KYOYA...
DID YOU HAVE TO INVITE EVERYONE?
CHATTER
ESPECIALLY HIM AND HIM?!
I INVITED YOU, BUT NOT THE REST!
THE DOPPEL GANGERS!
OH, I JUST THOUGHT...
...IF YOU DIDN'T HAVE THE COURAGE TO GO BY YOURSELF, WE'D BETTER BRING A GROUP.
SORRY TO OVERDO IT.
WHAT? WHY?
LET'S GO HOME, KIDS.
DON'T LEAVE ME BY MYSELF.
I'M SORRY! I'M SORRY!
SIGH...
WHAT'S DONE IS DONE.
WHAT'S GOING ON?
THEY'RE RICH KIDS. THE ELITE!
ALL RIGHT, GENTLEMEN! DON'T FORGET!
THEY CAME IN A BENZ AND TWO ROLLS.

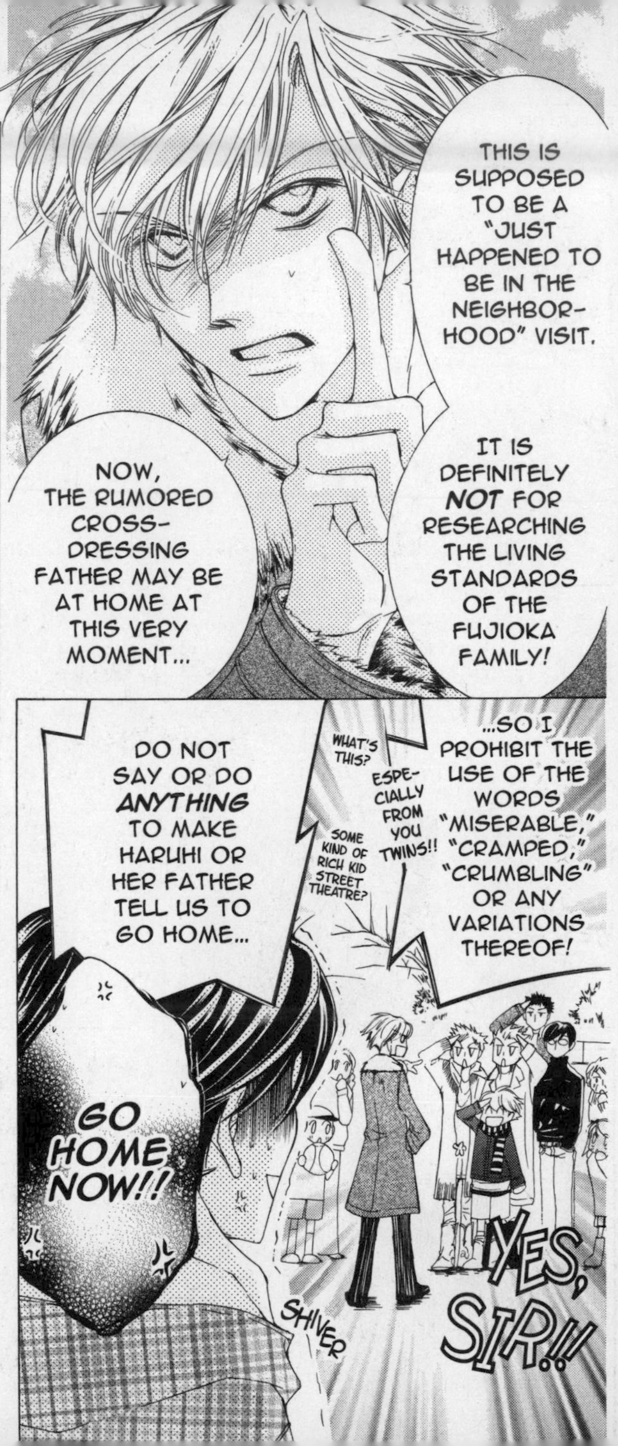
THIS IS SUPPOSED TO BE A "JUST HAPPENED TO BE IN THE NEIGHBOR-HOOD" VISIT.
IT IS DEFINITELY NOT FOR RESEARCHING THE LIVING STANDARDS OF THE FUJIOKA FAMILY!
NOW, THE RUMORED CROSS-DRESSING FATHER MAY BE AT HOME AT THIS VERY MOMENT...
...SO I PROHIBIT THE USE OF THE WORDS "MISERABLE," "CRAMPED," "CRUMBLING" OR ANY VARIATIONS THEREOF!
ESPE-CIALLY FROM YOU TWINS!!
WHAT'S THIS?
SOME KIND OF RICH KID STREET THEATRE?
DO NOT SAY OR DO ANYTHING TO MAKE HARUHI OR HER FATHER TELL US TO GO HOME...
YES, SIR!!
GO HOME NOW!!
SHIVER

5

THERE'S A STOCK OF RUNNING GAGS IN HOST CLUB, BUT I THINK OF MOST OF THE JOKES AS I GO ALONG. TAMAKI WILL JUST KEEP TALKING ON HIS OWN, TAKING THE STORY OFF ON A TANGENT, SO HE'S A LITTLE ANNOYING.←THIS IS A LIE. ACTUALLY, HE PROVIDES A UNIQUE TENSION.

I SOMETIMES THINK OF GAGS WHILE TRYING TO SLEEP...

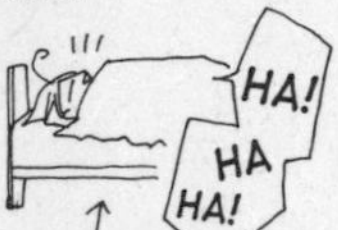
HA!
HA HA!

HATORI, THINKING UP A JOKE. DANGEROUS!!

THIS "VISITING HARUHI'S HOME" STORYLINE IS ONE OF THE RARE "STOCK GAGS UNLEASHED" EPISODES. I PLANNED MANY MORE, BUT I DIDN'T HAVE ENOUGH SPACE TO USE THEM ALL. I GUESS IT'S EASY TO THINK OF JOKES ABOUT PUBLIC HOUSING SINCE THAT'S WHERE I LIVE.

④DRAWING IT OUT
MY PEN IS VERY SLOW, SO I ALWAYS HAVE TO USE A LOT OF HELP. IT'S LIKE BEING AT SUMMER CAMP. MY ASSISTANTS AND I ARE ALL GOOD FRIENDS, SO, WHEN WE GET TIRED, EVERY LITTLE THING BECOMES HILARIOUS. IT'S A VERY ENJOYABLE WORKPLACE (THOUGH IT CAN BE VERY HECTIC).

AND THAT'S HOW HOST CLUB HAPPENS! THANK YOU, EVERYONE!

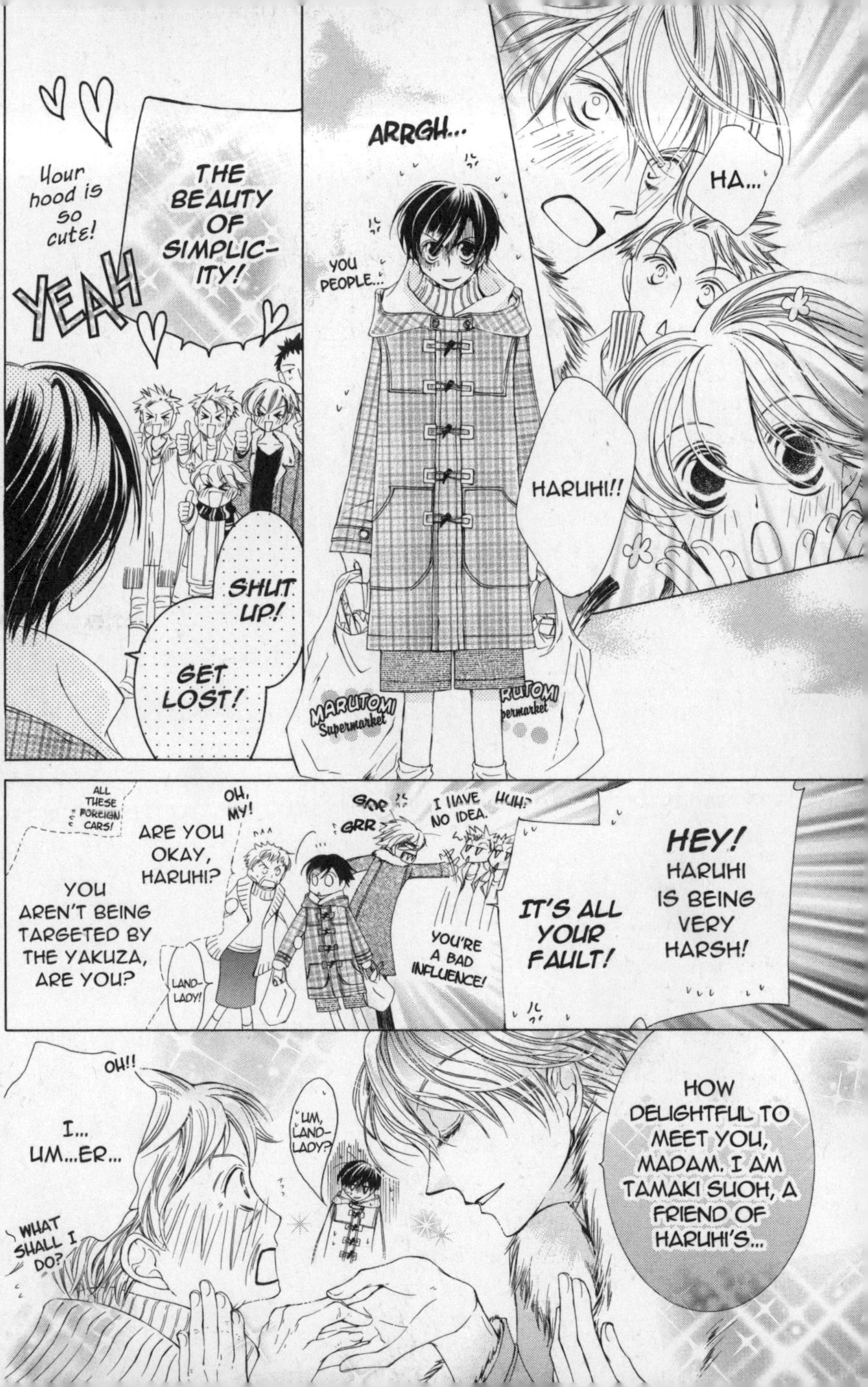
HA...
HARUHI!!
ARRGH...
YOU PEOPLE...
THE BEAUTY OF SIMPLICITY!
Your hood is so cute!
YEAH
SHUT UP!
GET LOST!
HEY! HARUHI IS BEING VERY HARSH!
IT'S ALL YOUR FAULT!
HUH?
I HAVE NO IDEA.
GRR GRR
YOU'RE A BAD INFLUENCE!
OH, MY!
ARE YOU OKAY, HARUHI?
ALL THESE FOREIGN CARS!
YOU AREN'T BEING TARGETED BY THE YAKUZA, ARE YOU?
LAND-LADY!
HOW DELIGHTFUL TO MEET YOU, MADAM. I AM TAMAKI SUOH, A FRIEND OF HARUHI'S...
UM, LAND-LADY?
OH!!
I... UM...ER...
WHAT SHALL I DO?

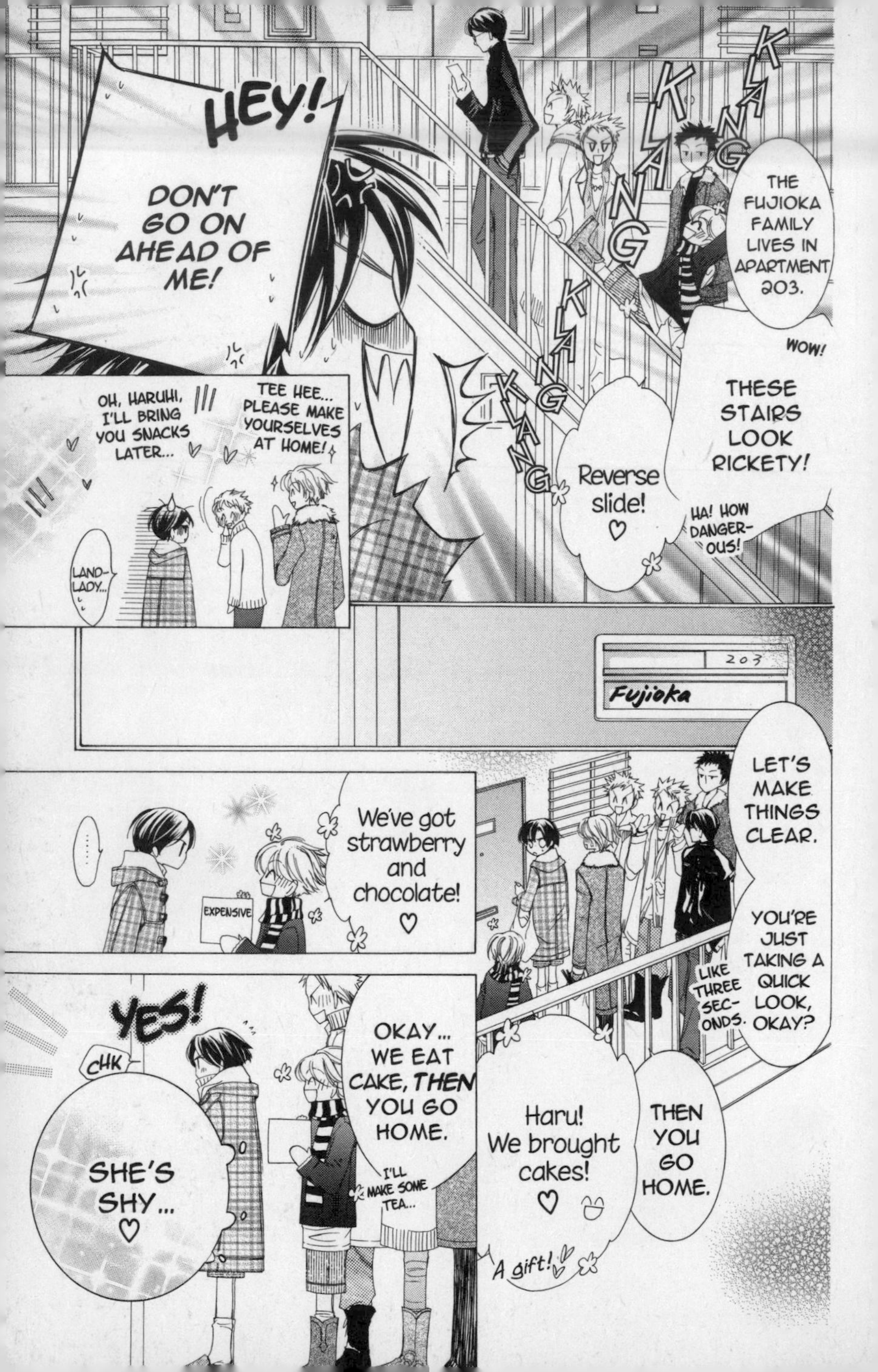
THE FUJIOKA FAMILY LIVES IN APARTMENT 203.
KLANG KLANG
WOW!
THESE STAIRS LOOK RICKETY!
HA! HOW DANGER-OUS!
KLANG KLANG
Reverse slide! ♡
HEY!
DON'T GO ON AHEAD OF ME!
TEE HEE... PLEASE MAKE YOURSELVES AT HOME!
OH, HARUHI, I'LL BRING YOU SNACKS LATER...
LAND-LADY...
203
Fujioka
LET'S MAKE THINGS CLEAR.
YOU'RE JUST TAKING A QUICK LOOK, OKAY?
LIKE THREE SEC-ONDS.
We've got strawberry and chocolate! ♡
EXPENSIVE
......
THEN YOU GO HOME.
Haru! We brought cakes! ♡
A gift!
OKAY... WE EAT CAKE, THEN YOU GO HOME.
I'LL MAKE SOME TEA...
YES!
CHK
SHE'S SHY... ♡

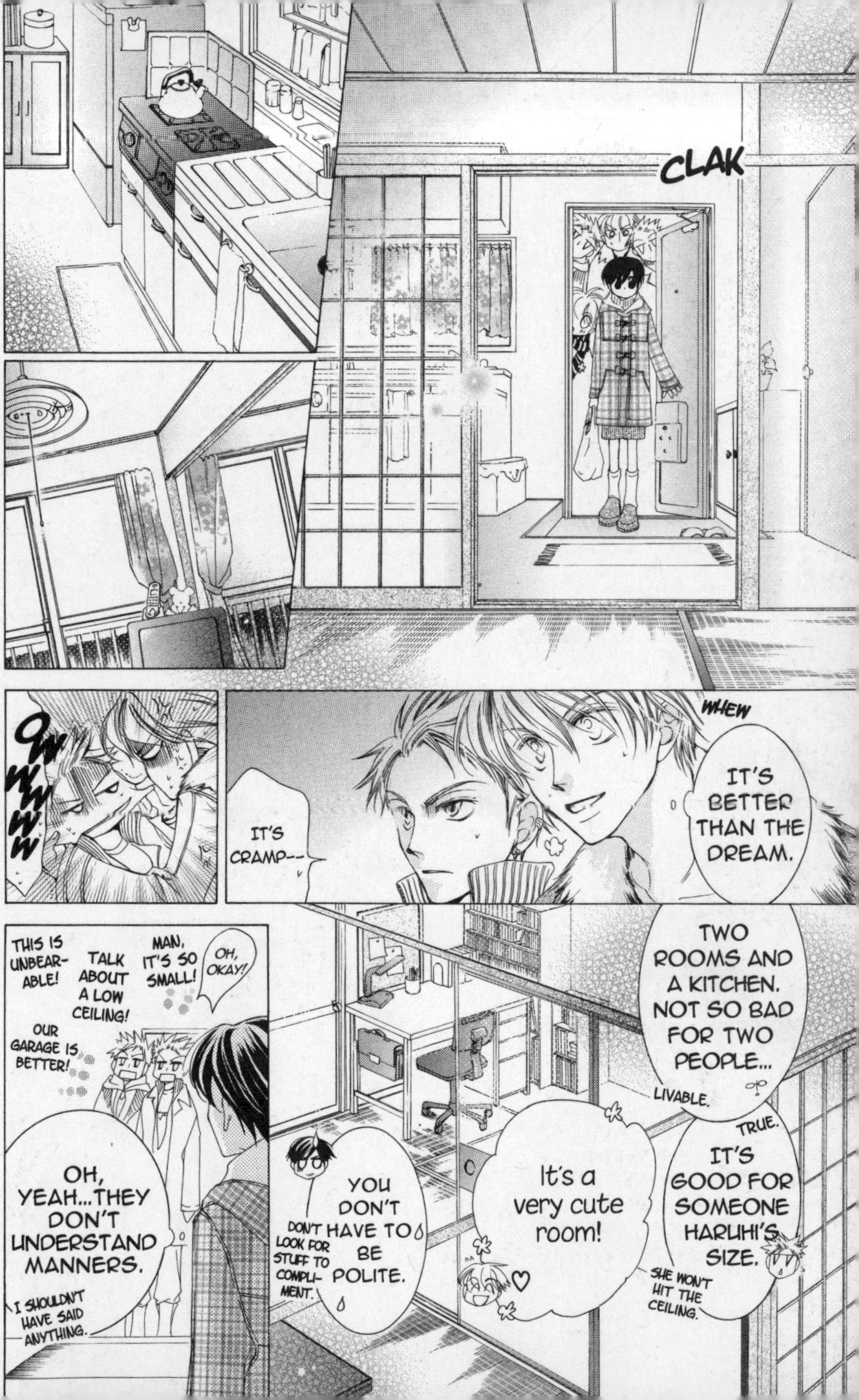
CLAK
WHEW
IT'S BETTER THAN THE DREAM.
IT'S CRAMP--
OWWWWWW
TWO ROOMS AND A KITCHEN. NOT SO BAD FOR TWO PEOPLE...
LIVABLE.
TRUE.
IT'S GOOD FOR SOMEONE HARUHI'S SIZE.
SHE WON'T HIT THE CEILING.
It's a very cute room!
YOU DON'T HAVE TO BE POLITE.
DON'T LOOK FOR STUFF TO COMPLI-MENT.
OH, OKAY!
MAN, IT'S SO SMALL!
TALK ABOUT A LOW CEILING!
THIS IS UNBEAR-ABLE!
OUR GARAGE IS BETTER!
OH, YEAH...THEY DON'T UNDERSTAND MANNERS.
I SHOULDN'T HAVE SAID ANYTHING.

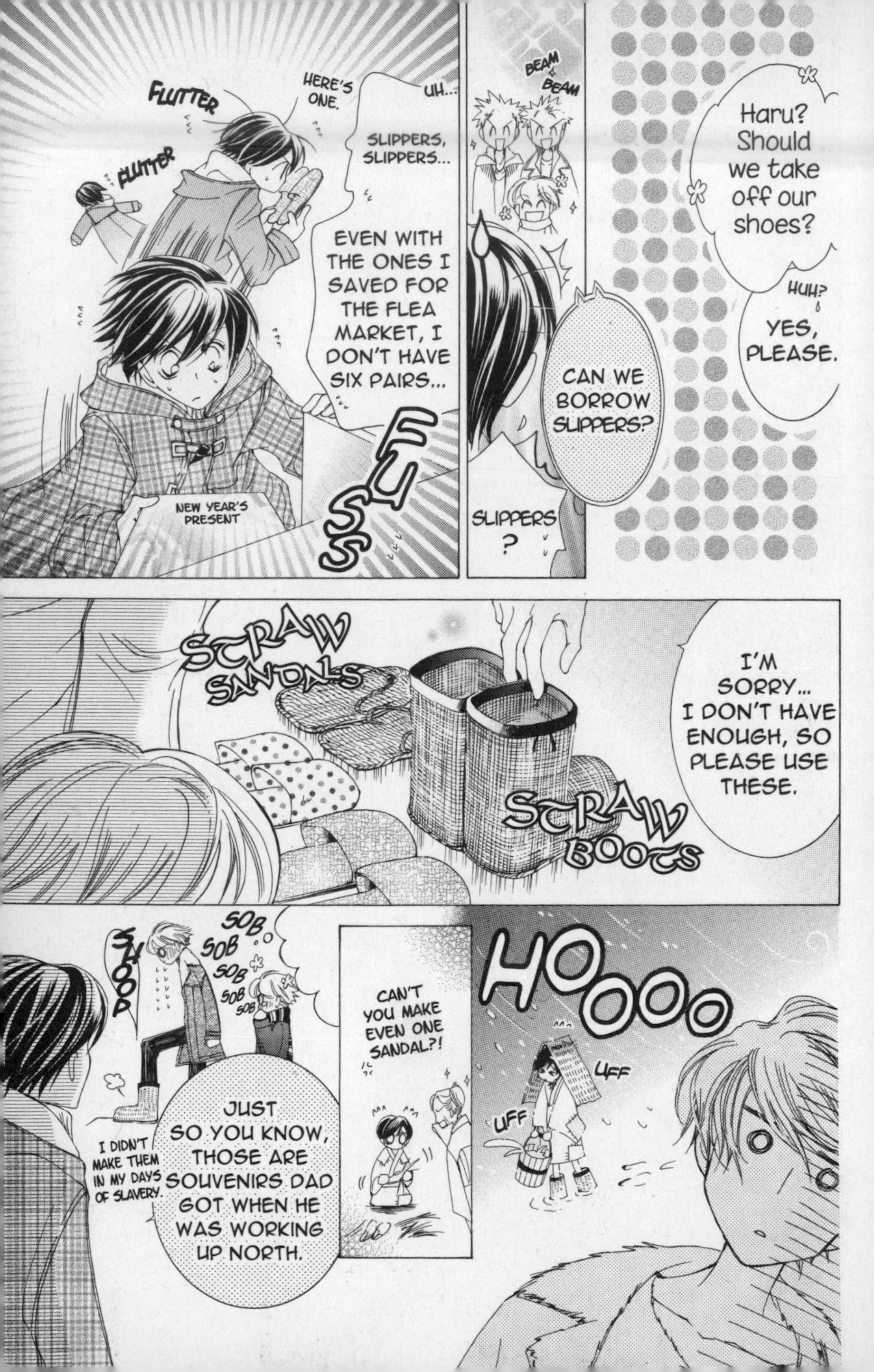
Haru? Should we take off our shoes?
HUH?
YES, PLEASE.
BEAM
BEAM
CAN WE BORROW SLIPPERS?
SLIPPERS?
UH...
SLIPPERS, SLIPPERS...
HERE'S ONE.
FLUTTER
FLUTTER
EVEN WITH THE ONES I SAVED FOR THE FLEA MARKET, I DON'T HAVE SIX PAIRS...
NEW YEAR'S PRESENT
FUSS
I'M SORRY... I DON'T HAVE ENOUGH, SO PLEASE USE THESE.
STRAW BOOTS
STRAW SANDALS
HOOOO
UFF
UFF
CAN'T YOU MAKE EVEN ONE SANDAL?!
SOB
SOB
SOB
SOB
SOB
SHOOP
JUST SO YOU KNOW, THOSE ARE SOUVENIRS DAD GOT WHEN HE WAS WORKING UP NORTH.
I DIDN'T MAKE THEM IN MY DAYS OF SLAVERY.

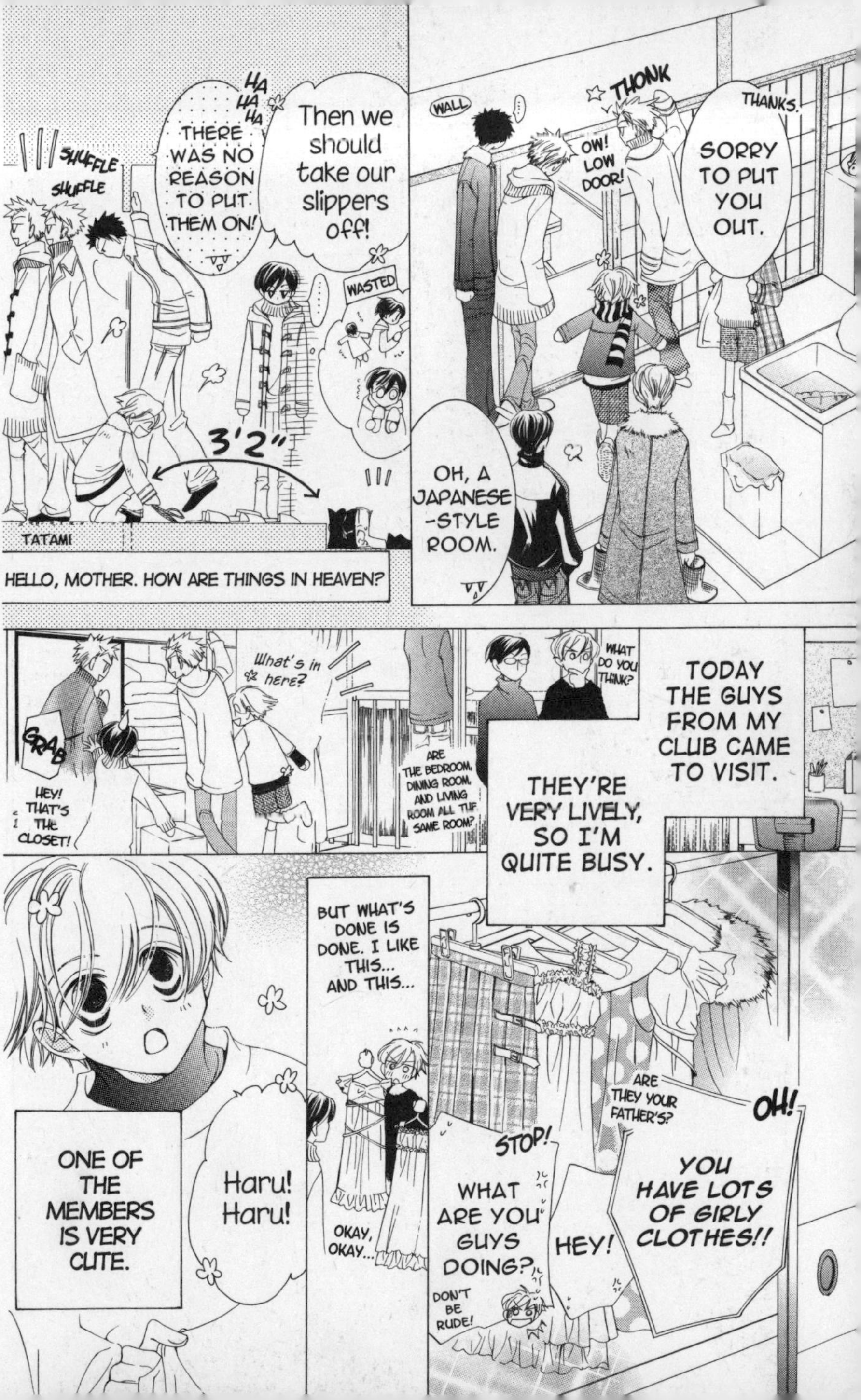
THONK
THANKS.
SORRY TO PUT YOU OUT.
OW! LOW DOOR!
WALL
OH, A JAPANESE -STYLE ROOM.
Then we should take our slippers off!
HA HA HA
THERE WAS NO REASON TO PUT THEM ON!
SHUFFLE
SHUFFLE
WASTED
3'2"
TATAMI
HELLO, MOTHER. HOW ARE THINGS IN HEAVEN?
TODAY THE GUYS FROM MY CLUB CAME TO VISIT.
WHAT DO YOU THINK?
ARE THE BEDROOM, DINING ROOM, AND LIVING ROOM ALL THE SAME ROOM?
THEY'RE VERY LIVELY, SO I'M QUITE BUSY.
What's in here?
GRAB
HEY! THAT'S THE CLOSET!
OH!
YOU HAVE LOTS OF GIRLY CLOTHES!!
ARE THEY YOUR FATHER'S?
HEY!
STOP!
WHAT ARE YOU GUYS DOING?
DON'T BE RUDE!
BUT WHAT'S DONE IS DONE. I LIKE THIS... AND THIS...
OKAY, OKAY...
Haru! Haru!
ONE OF THE MEMBERS IS VERY CUTE.

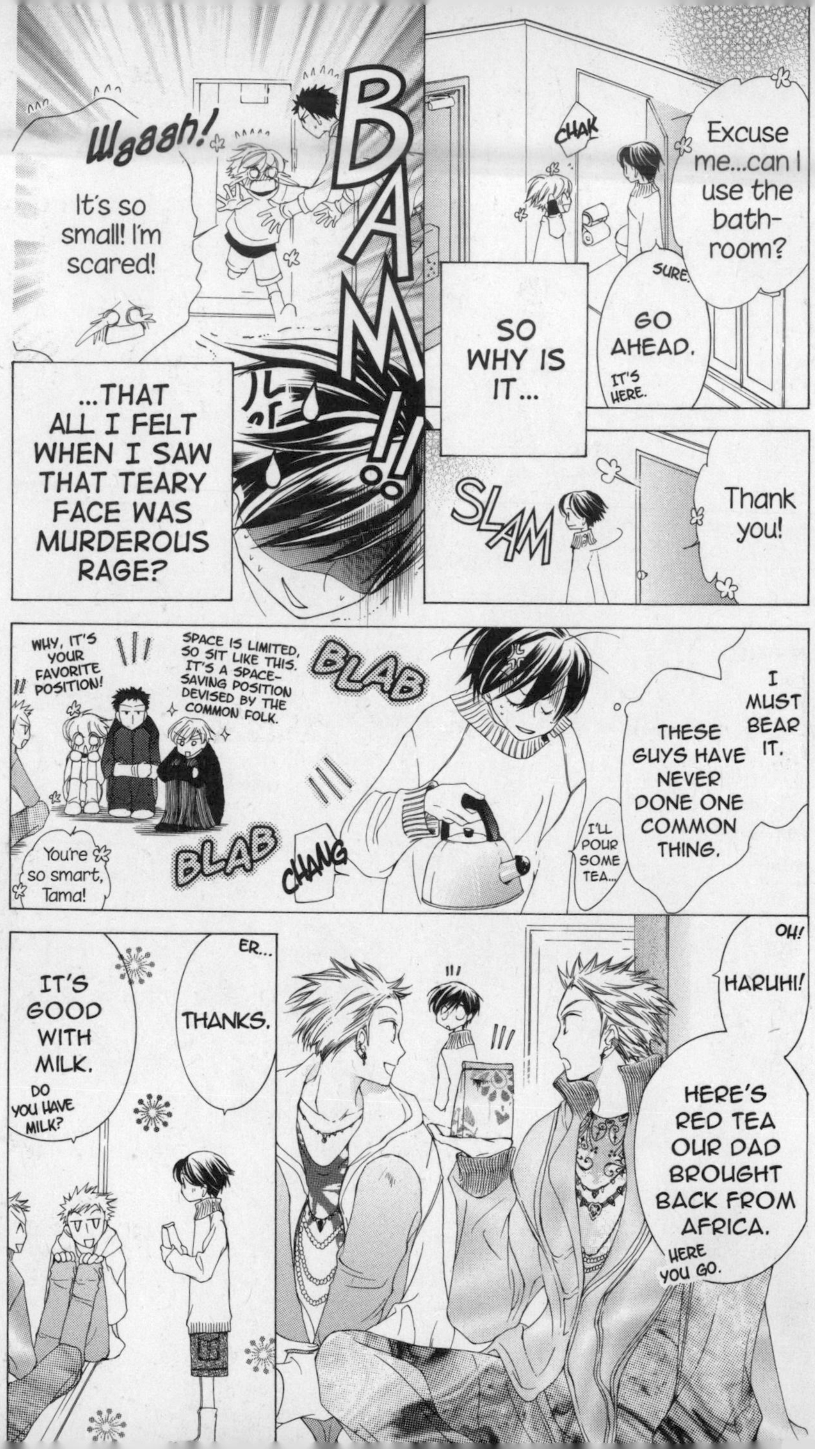

CHAK
Excuse me...can I use the bath-room?
SURE.
GO AHEAD.
IT'S HERE.
SO WHY IS IT...
SLAM
Thank you!
BAM!!
Waaah!
It's so small! I'm scared!
...THAT ALL I FELT WHEN I SAW THAT TEARY FACE WAS MURDEROUS RAGE?
I MUST BEAR IT.
THESE GUYS HAVE NEVER DONE ONE COMMON THING.
I'LL POUR SOME TEA...
CHANG
BLAB
SPACE IS LIMITED, SO SIT LIKE THIS. IT'S A SPACE-SAVING POSITION DEVISED BY THE COMMON FOLK.
WHY, IT'S YOUR FAVORITE POSITION!
BLAB
You're so smart, Tama!
OH!
HARUHI!
HERE'S RED TEA OUR DAD BROUGHT BACK FROM AFRICA.
HERE YOU GO.
ER...
THANKS.
IT'S GOOD WITH MILK.
DO YOU HAVE MILK?

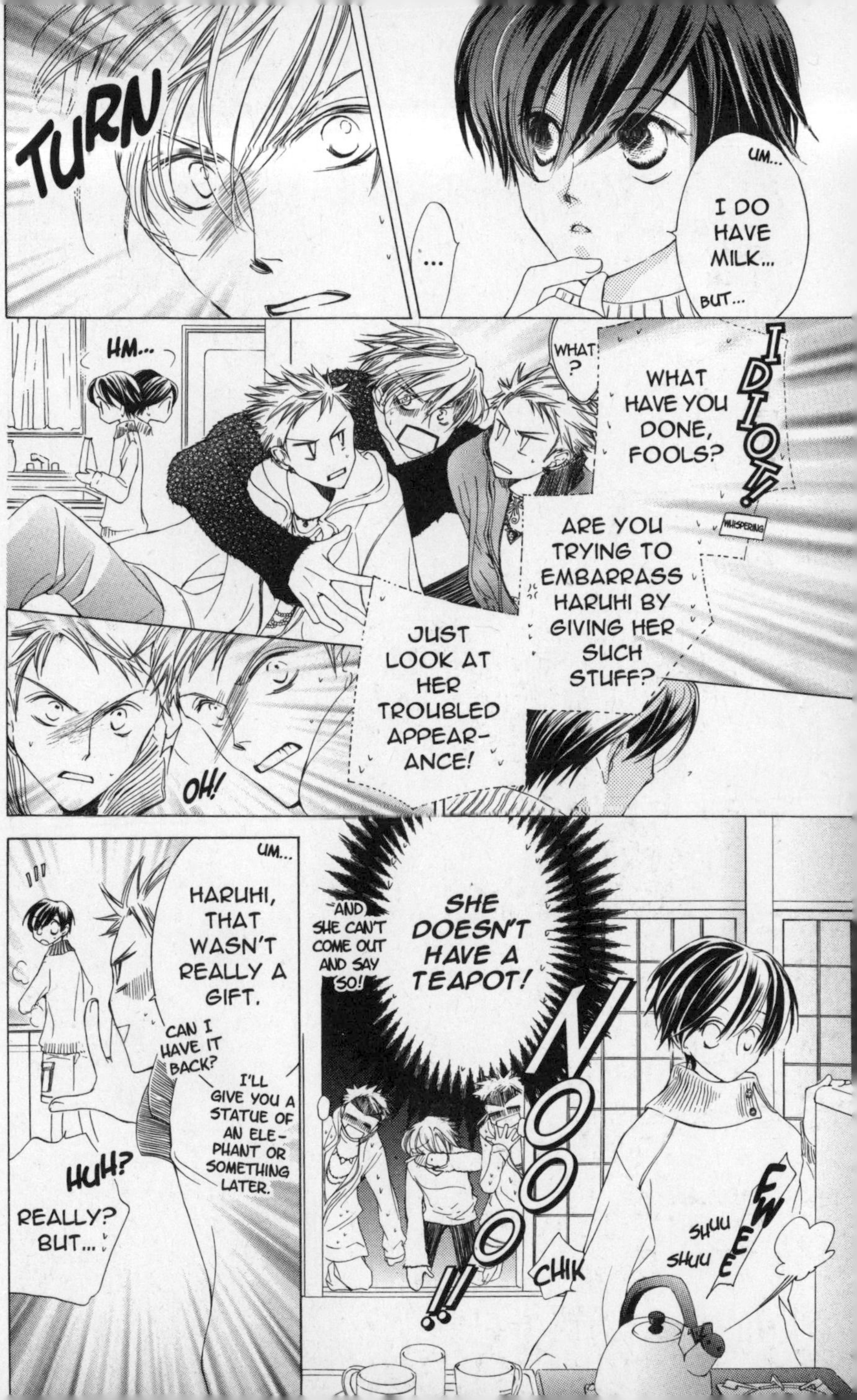
UM...
I DO HAVE MILK...
BUT...
...
TURN
IDIOT!
WHAT HAVE YOU DONE, FOOLS?
WHISPERING
ARE YOU TRYING TO EMBARRASS HARUHI BY GIVING HER SUCH STUFF?
WHAT?
HM...
JUST LOOK AT HER TROUBLED APPEARANCE!
OH!
SHE DOESN'T HAVE A TEAPOT!
AND SHE CAN'T COME OUT AND SAY SO!
NOOOO!!
SHUU SHUU
FWEE
CHIK
UM...
HARUHI, THAT WASN'T REALLY A GIFT.
CAN I HAVE IT BACK?
I'LL GIVE YOU A STATUE OF AN ELEPHANT OR SOMETHING LATER.
HUH?
REALLY? BUT...

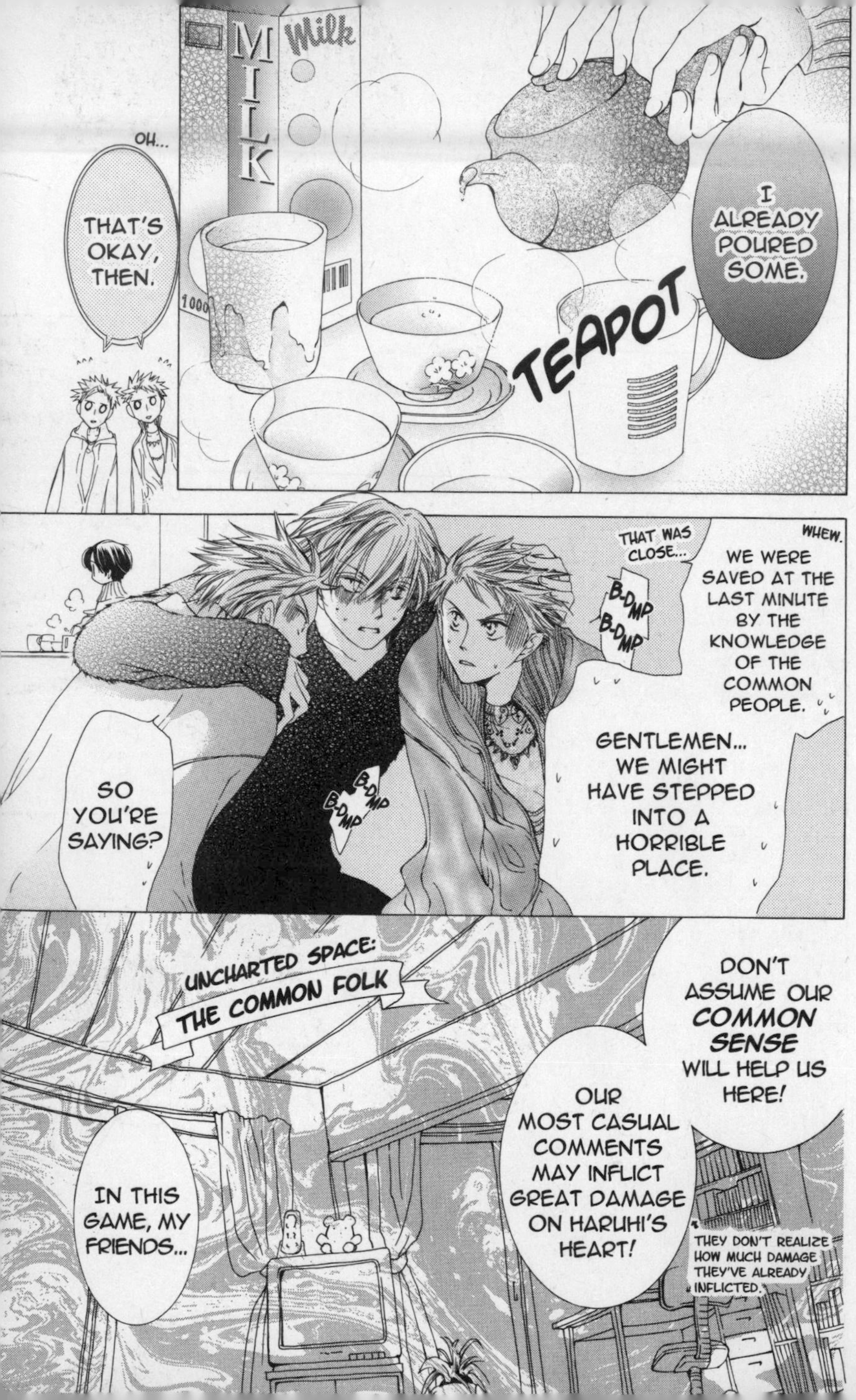
I ALREADY POURED SOME.
TEAPOT
OH...
THAT'S OKAY, THEN.
WHEW.
WE WERE SAVED AT THE LAST MINUTE BY THE KNOWLEDGE OF THE COMMON PEOPLE.
THAT WAS CLOSE...
B-DMP B-DMP
GENTLEMEN... WE MIGHT HAVE STEPPED INTO A HORRIBLE PLACE.
B-DMP B-DMP
SO YOU'RE SAYING?
DON'T ASSUME OUR COMMON SENSE WILL HELP US HERE!
UNCHARTED SPACE: THE COMMON FOLK
OUR MOST CASUAL COMMENTS MAY INFLICT GREAT DAMAGE ON HARUHI'S HEART!
THEY DON'T REALIZE HOW MUCH DAMAGE THEY'VE ALREADY INFLICTED.
IN THIS GAME, MY FRIENDS...

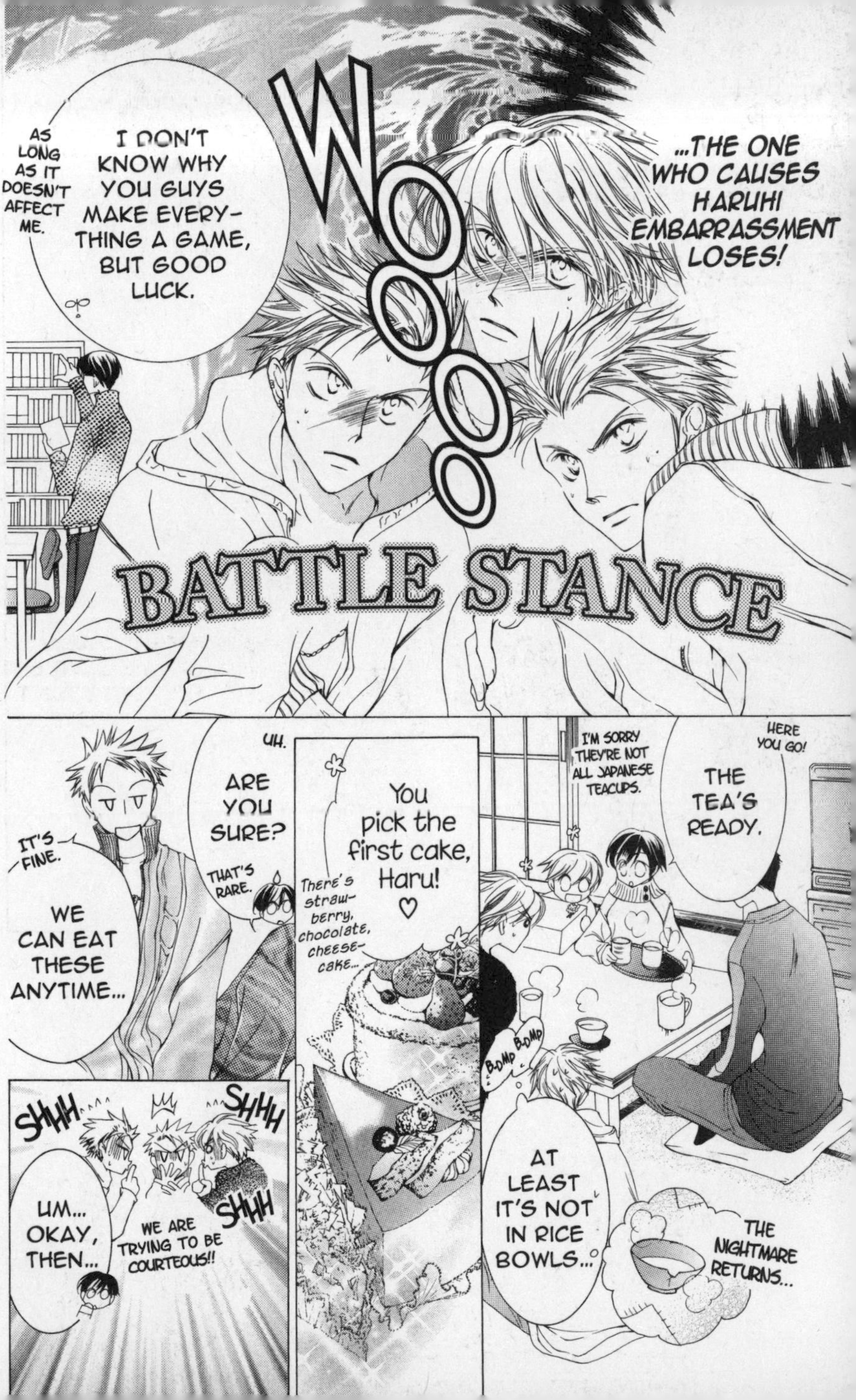
...THE ONE WHO CAUSES HARUHI EMBARRASSMENT LOSES!
WOOOOOO
I DON'T KNOW WHY YOU GUYS MAKE EVERY-THING A GAME, BUT GOOD LUCK.
AS LONG AS IT DOESN'T AFFECT ME.
BATTLE STANCE
HERE YOU GO!
THE TEA'S READY.
I'M SORRY THEY'RE NOT ALL JAPANESE TEACUPS.
B-DMP B-DMP
AT LEAST IT'S NOT IN RICE BOWLS...
THE NIGHTMARE RETURNS...
You pick the first cake, Haru! ♡
There's straw-berry, chocolate, cheese-cake...
UH.
ARE YOU SURE?
THAT'S RARE.
IT'S FINE.
WE CAN EAT THESE ANYTIME...
SHHH
SHHH
SHHH
UM... OKAY, THEN...
WE ARE TRYING TO BE COURTEOUS!!

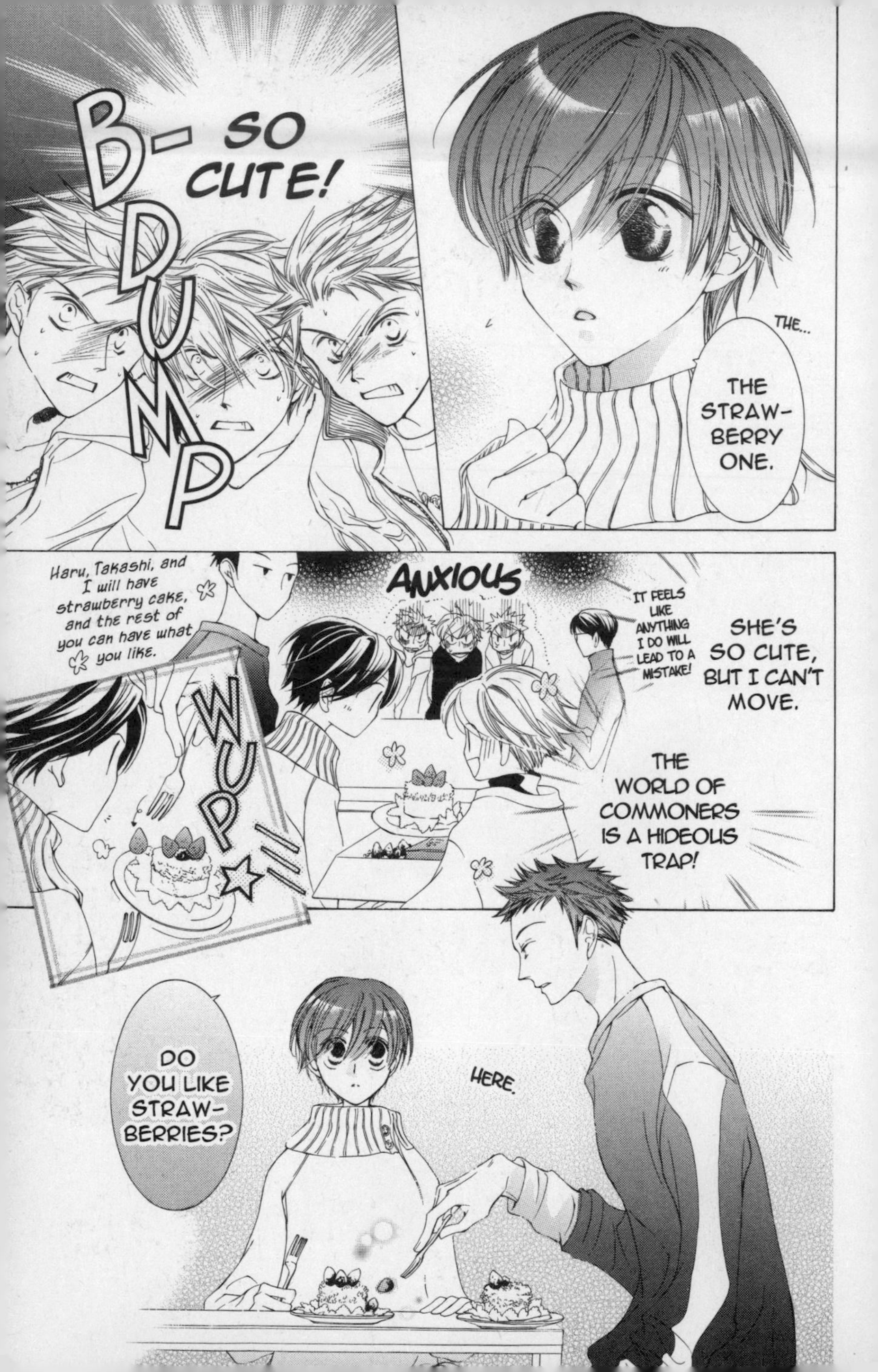
THE...
THE STRAW-BERRY ONE.
B-BDUMP
SO CUTE!
SHE'S SO CUTE, BUT I CAN'T MOVE.
IT FEELS LIKE ANYTHING I DO WILL LEAD TO A MISTAKE!
ANXIOUS
Haru, Takashi, and I will have strawberry cake, and the rest of you can have what you like.
THE WORLD OF COMMONERS IS A HIDEOUS TRAP!
WUP
HERE.
DO YOU LIKE STRAW-BERRIES?

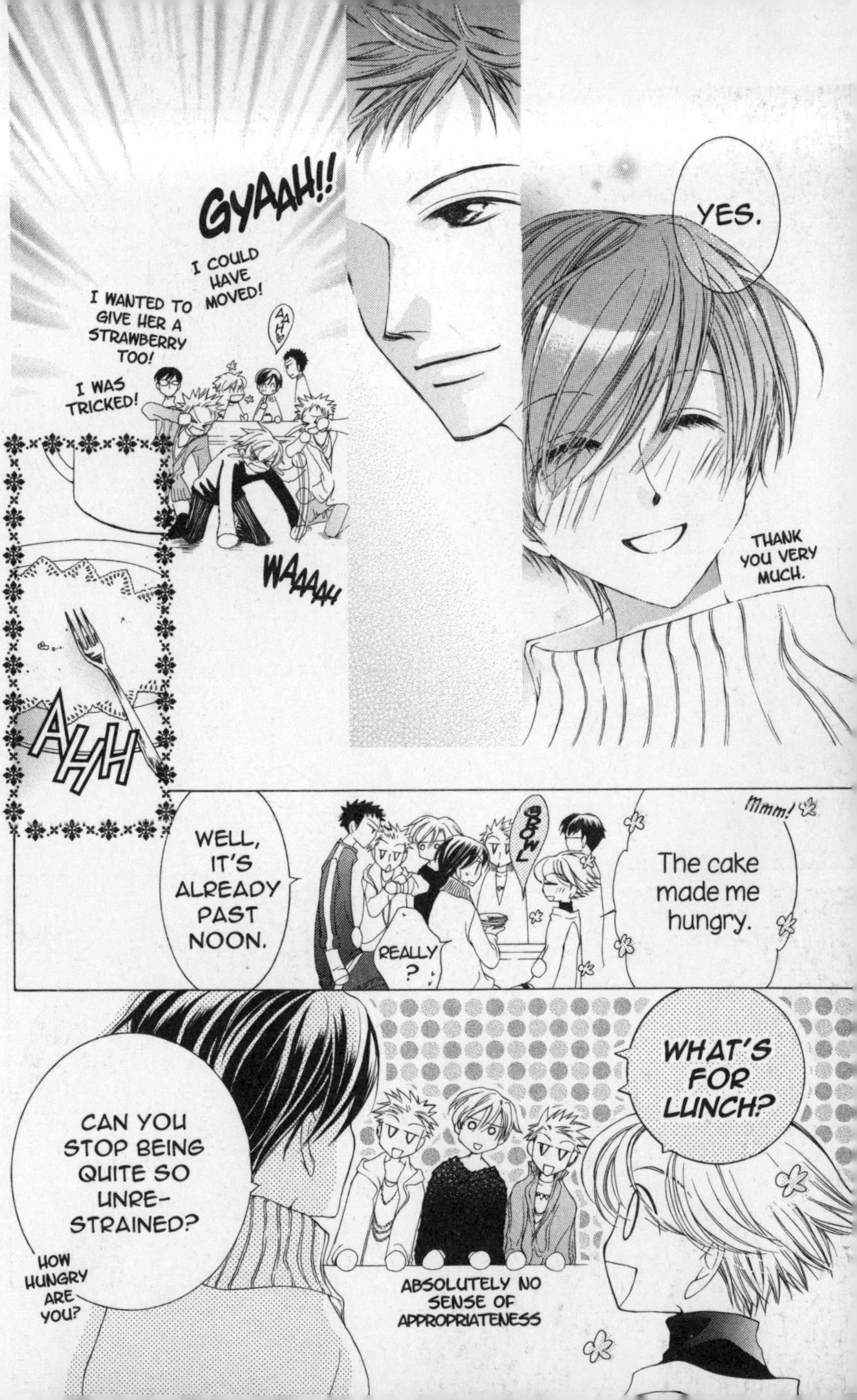
YES.
THANK YOU VERY MUCH.
GYAAH!!
I COULD HAVE MOVED!
I WANTED TO GIVE HER A STRAWBERRY TOO!
I WAS TRICKED!
WAAAAH
AHH
Mmm!
The cake made me hungry.
GROWL
REALLY?
WELL, IT'S ALREADY PAST NOON.
WHAT'S FOR LUNCH?
ABSOLUTELY NO SENSE OF APPROPRIATENESS
CAN YOU STOP BEING QUITE SO UNRE-STRAINED?
HOW HUNGRY ARE YOU?

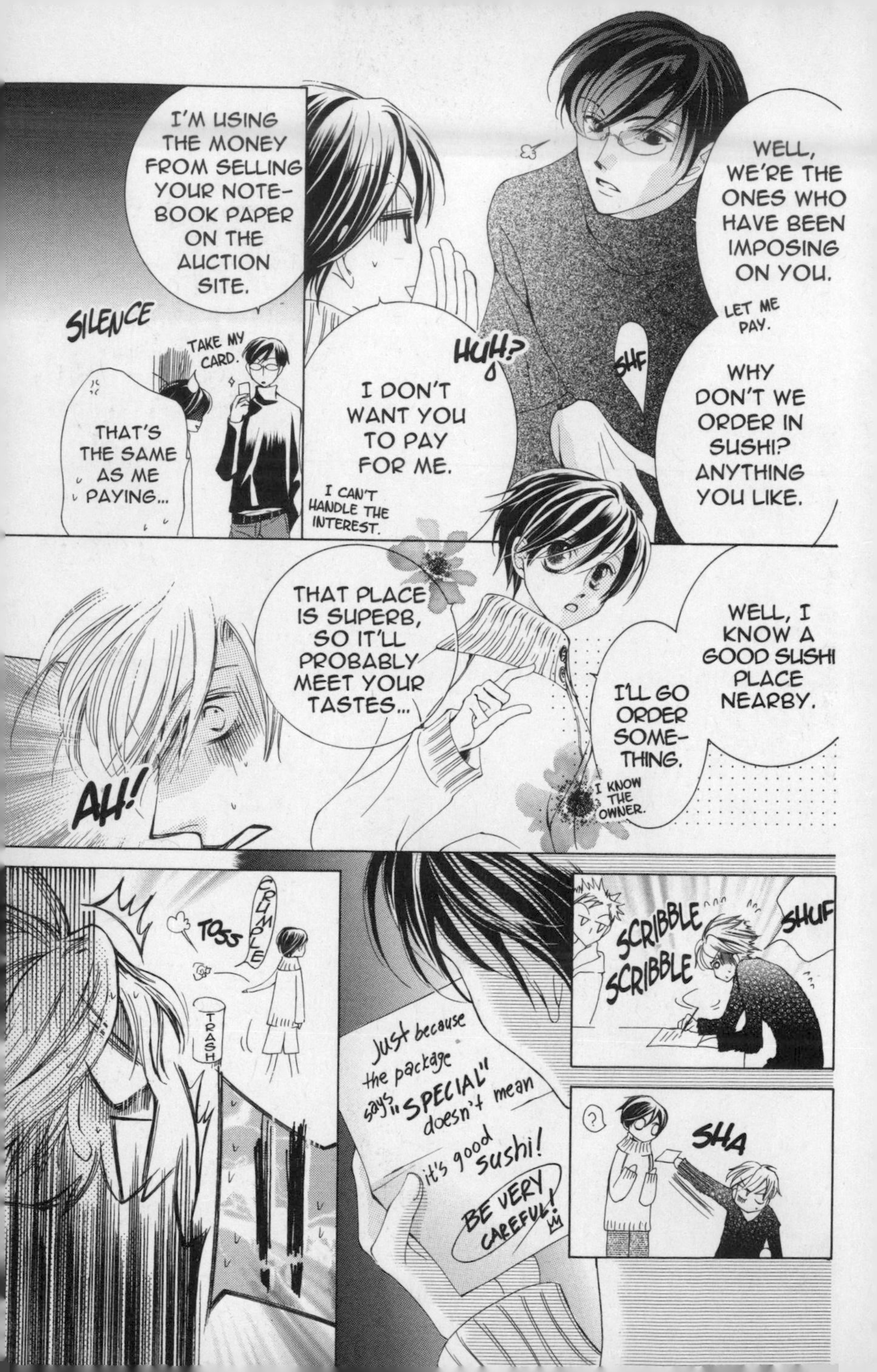
WELL, WE'RE THE ONES WHO HAVE BEEN IMPOSING ON YOU.
LET ME PAY.
SHF
WHY DON'T WE ORDER IN SUSHI? ANYTHING YOU LIKE.
HUH?
I DON'T WANT YOU TO PAY FOR ME.
I CAN'T HANDLE THE INTEREST.
I'M USING THE MONEY FROM SELLING YOUR NOTE-BOOK PAPER ON THE AUCTION SITE.
SILENCE
TAKE MY CARD.
THAT'S THE SAME AS ME PAYING...
WELL, I KNOW A GOOD SUSHI PLACE NEARBY.
I'LL GO ORDER SOME-THING.
I KNOW THE OWNER.
THAT PLACE IS SUPERB, SO IT'LL PROBABLY MEET YOUR TASTES...
AH!
SHUF
SCRIBBLE SCRIBBLE
SHA
Just because the package says "SPECIAL" doesn't mean it's good sushi!
BE VERY CAREFUL!
TOSS
CRUMPLE
TRASH

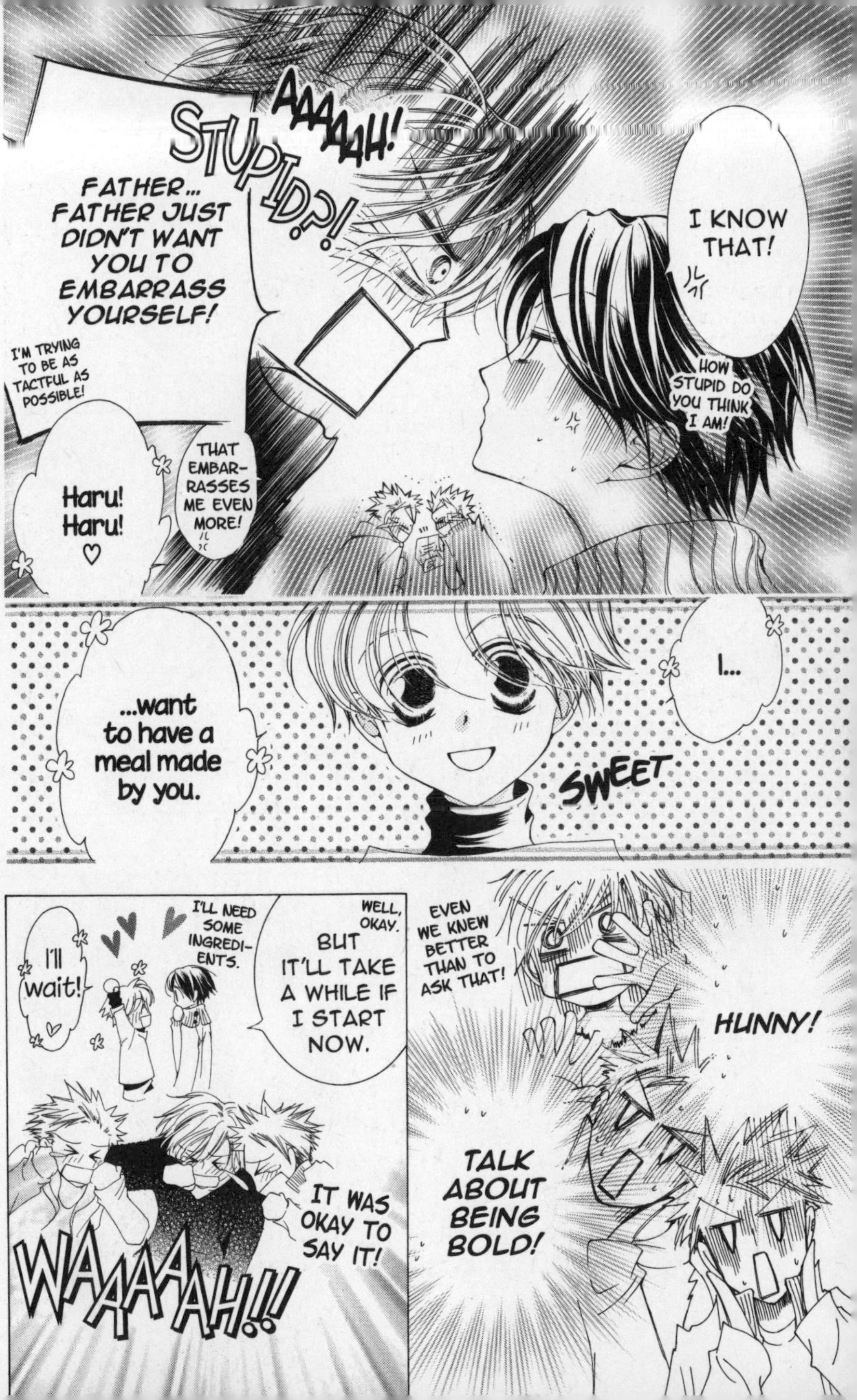
I KNOW THAT!
HOW STUPID DO YOU THINK I AM!
AAAAAAH!
STUPID?!
FATHER... FATHER JUST DIDN'T WANT YOU TO EMBARRASS YOURSELF!
I'M TRYING TO BE AS TACTFUL AS POSSIBLE!
THAT EMBARRASSES ME EVEN MORE!
Haru! Haru! ♡
I...
SWEET
...want to have a meal made by you.
HUNNY!
EVEN WE KNEW BETTER THAN TO ASK THAT!
TALK ABOUT BEING BOLD!
WELL, OKAY.
BUT IT'LL TAKE A WHILE IF I START NOW.
I'LL NEED SOME INGREDIENTS.
I'll wait!
IT WAS OKAY TO SAY IT!
WAAAAAH!!

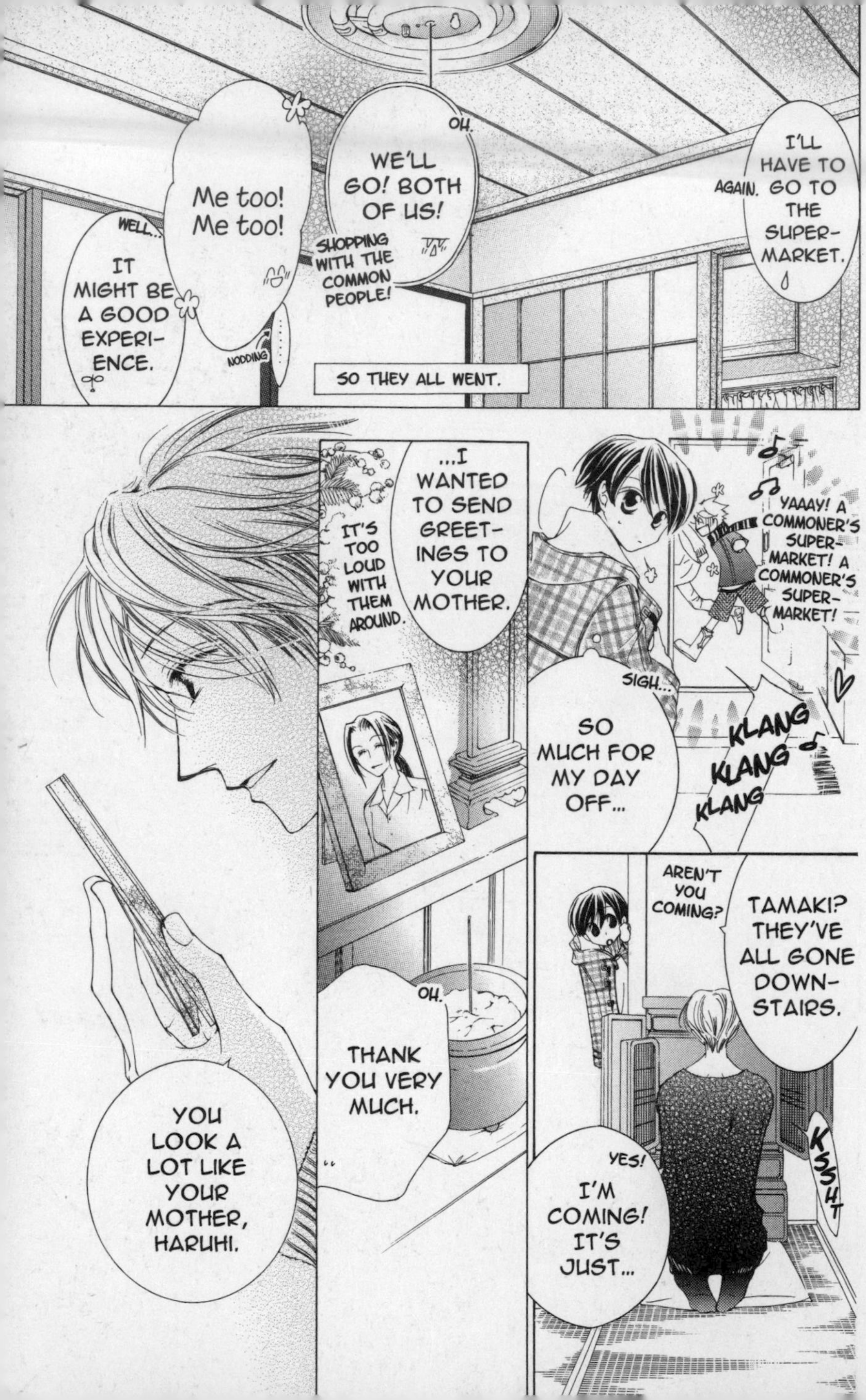
I'LL HAVE TO GO TO THE SUPER-MARKET.
AGAIN.
OH.
WE'LL GO! BOTH OF US!
SHOPPING WITH THE COMMON PEOPLE!
Me too! Me too!
NODDING
WELL...
IT MIGHT BE A GOOD EXPERI-ENCE.
SO THEY ALL WENT.
YAAAY! A COMMONER'S SUPER-MARKET! A COMMONER'S SUPER-MARKET!
SIGH...
SO MUCH FOR MY DAY OFF...
KLANG
KLANG
KLANG
TAMAKI? THEY'VE ALL GONE DOWN-STAIRS.
AREN'T YOU COMING?
KSSHT
YES!
I'M COMING! IT'S JUST...
...I WANTED TO SEND GREET-INGS TO YOUR MOTHER.
IT'S TOO LOUD WITH THEM AROUND.
OH.
THANK YOU VERY MUCH.
YOU LOOK A LOT LIKE YOUR MOTHER, HARUHI.

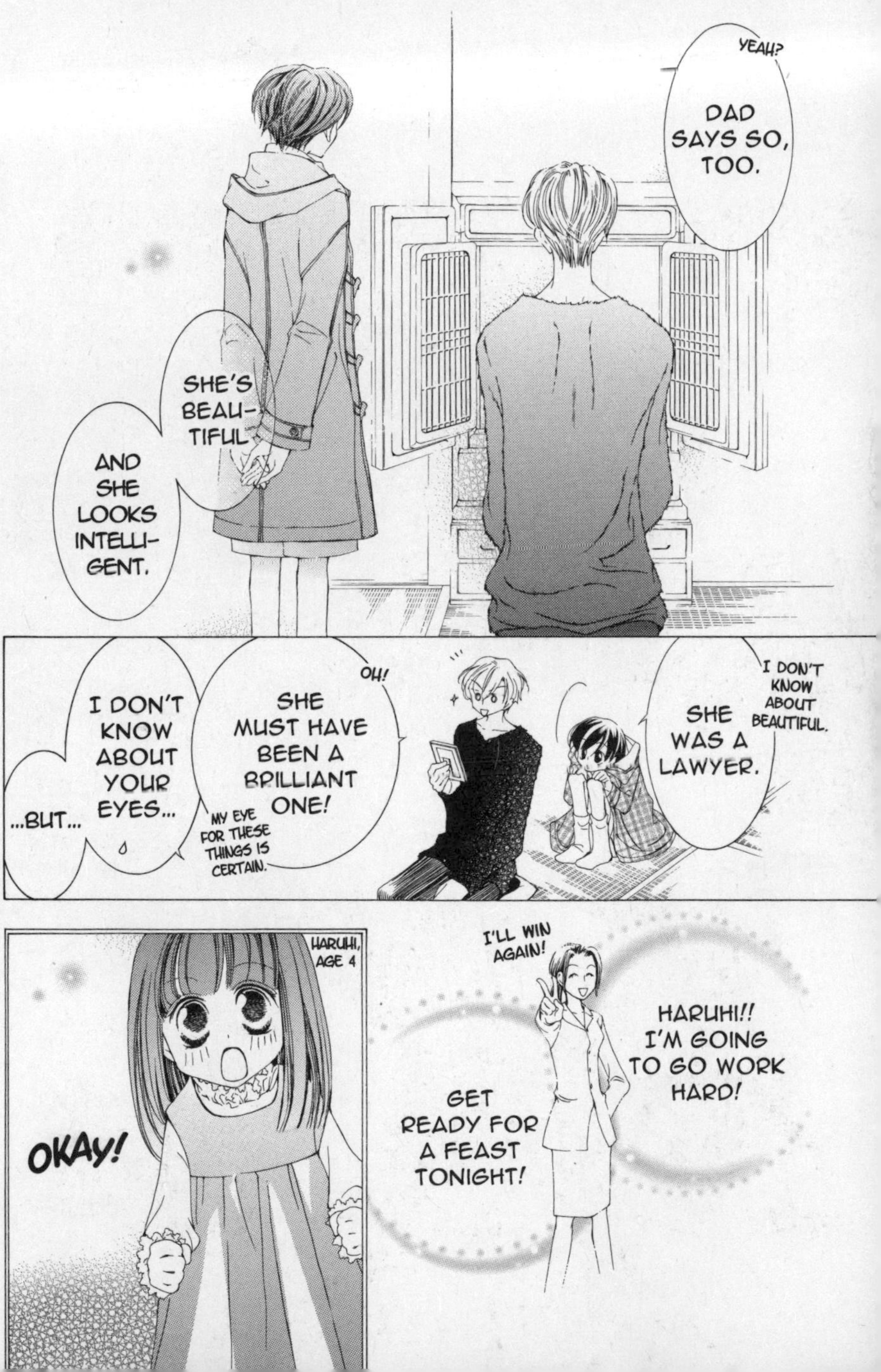
YEAH?
DAD SAYS SO, TOO.
SHE'S BEAU-TIFUL
AND SHE LOOKS INTELLI-GENT.
I DON'T KNOW ABOUT BEAUTIFUL.
SHE WAS A LAWYER.
OH!
SHE MUST HAVE BEEN A BRILLIANT ONE!
MY EYE FOR THESE THINGS IS CERTAIN.
I DON'T KNOW ABOUT YOUR EYES...
...BUT...
I'LL WIN AGAIN!
HARUHI!! I'M GOING TO GO WORK HARD!
GET READY FOR A FEAST TONIGHT!
HARUHI, AGE 4
OKAY!

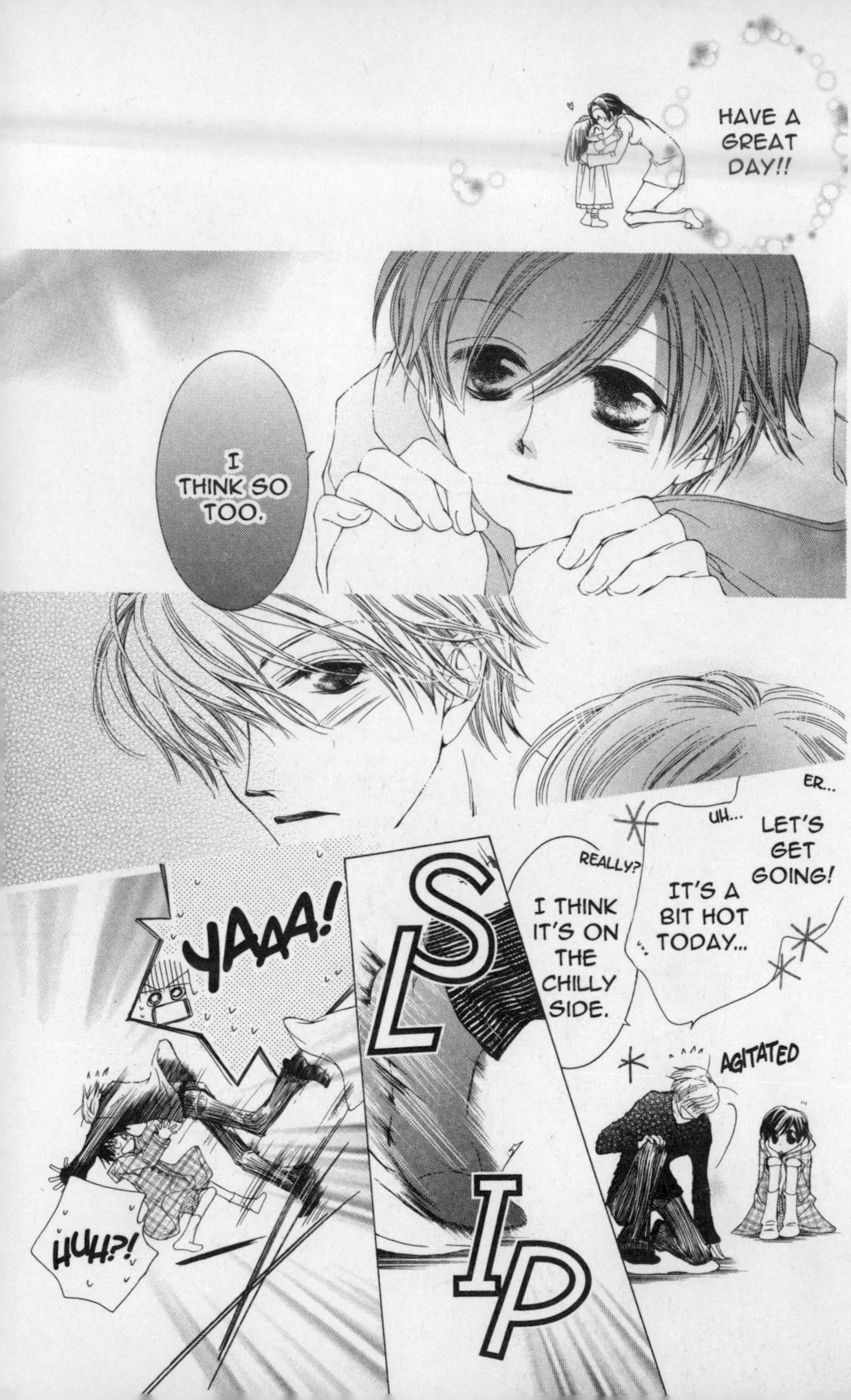
HAVE A GREAT DAY!!
I THINK SO TOO.
ER... LET'S GET GOING!
UH... IT'S A BIT HOT TODAY...
REALLY? I THINK IT'S ON THE CHILLY SIDE.
AGITATED
SLIP
YAAA!
HUH?!

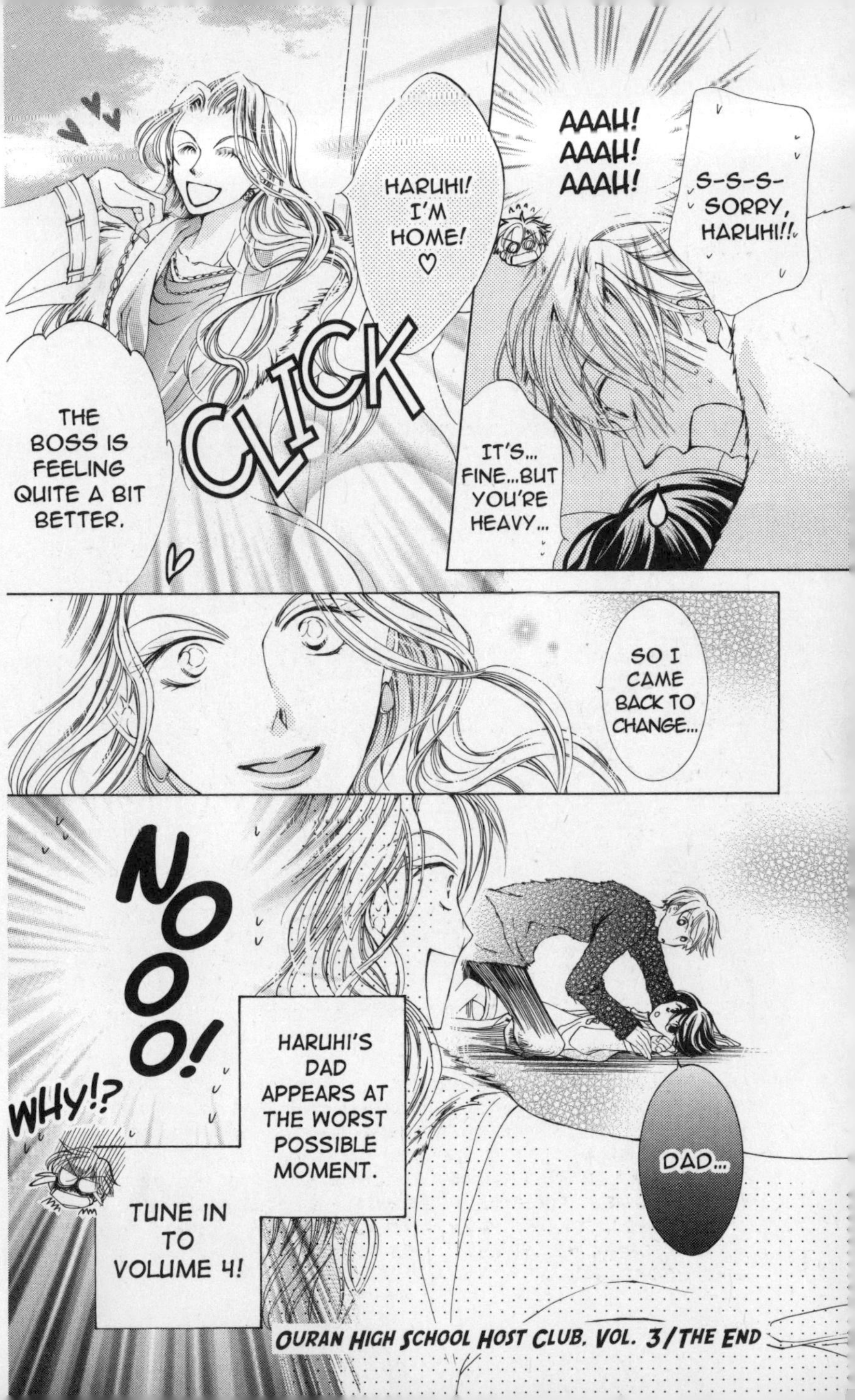
S-S-S-SORRY, HARUHI!!
AAAH! AAAH! AAAH!
IT'S... FINE...BUT YOU'RE HEAVY...
HARUHI! I'M HOME! ♡
CLICK
THE BOSS IS FEELING QUITE A BIT BETTER.
SO I CAME BACK TO CHANGE...
DAD...
NOOOO!
WHY!?
HARUHI'S DAD APPEARS AT THE WORST POSSIBLE MOMENT.
TUNE IN TO VOLUME 4!
OURAN HIGH SCHOOL HOST CLUB, VOL. 3/THE END

✿ AND NOW, A GUEST MANGA... FROM THE FAX MACHINE ✿

NATSUNA KAWASE

FROM 川瀬夏菜!!!

Thanks!!!

KYOYA HAS SOME "NEGOTIATION PHOTOS" UP HIS SLEEVE.

TH-THOSE ARE PHOTOS OF HARUHI'S FEMALE APPEARANCES SINCE JOINING THE CLUB!!
PHOTO
WHEN DID YOU?
THOSE AREN'T RARE AT ALL!
WE'VE EACH TAKEN SOME!
SEE?
WHAT DID YOU SAY!?
WHY DON'T YOU ASK HARUHI YOURSELF?
WSH
WSH
HARUHI!! LET'S MAKE AN ALBUM OF MEMORIES!
I'VE GOT AN APRON DRESS, TOO.
WHY WOULD I WANT THAT KIND OF ALBUM?
ABSOLUTELY NOT!
AN ALBUM OF MEMORIES... JUST ONE SHOT...
THEIR VALUE JUST SKYROCKETED.
FANGIRLS BUY THEM !!! TOO.
EEEEE!
FOR USE AGAINST TAMAKI!
HARUHI, CROSS-DRESSING? I MUST BUY!

PLEASE EXCUSE THIS IF RENGE ISN'T INTO CROSS-DRESSERS.

HATORI'S FAX CORNER:
HERE'S WHERE I SHOW OFF THE FAXES I'VE RECEIVED. NATSUNA KAWASE IS MY "TOP BATTER." THANK YOU SO MUCH! NATSUNA HAS A MANIA FOR MANY THINGS, SO I CONSIDER HER TO HAVE THE HEART OF A TEACHER. IF THERE'S SOMETHING I DON'T KNOW ABOUT ART SUPPLIES, I GO TO NATSUNA KAWASE! I TALK ABOUT HISTORY WITH NATSUNA KAWASE! ELECTRONICS? GO TO NATSUNA KAWASE! ← I FEEL LIKE I'VE BECOME A TERRIBLE PERSON.... NATSUNA, I LOOK FORWARD TO OUR LONG PHONE CONVERSATIONS! NEXT TIME I THINK I'LL SHOW OFF FAXES FROM MEKA TANAKA, NARI KUSAKAWA, AND AKANE OGURA. THEY'RE GREAT!!

THIS IS A
SHORT EXTRA EPISODE.
IN THE MAGAZINE, THIS FLASHBACK
TO THE EARLY LIFE OF HARUHI AND
HER DAD CAME AFTER THE END OF
THE ENTIRE "VISITING HARUHI'S
HOME" STORYLINE, BUT DUE TO
PAGE COUNT IT WILL APPEAR HERE IN
THE BOOK. I DON'T THINK IT'S TOO
MUCH OF AN INCONVENIENCE...
PLEASE READ IT. ♡

※ BEFORE HE BECAME A
CROSS-DRESSER.

EXTRA EPISODE: DAILY LIFE IN THE FUJIOKA FAMILY

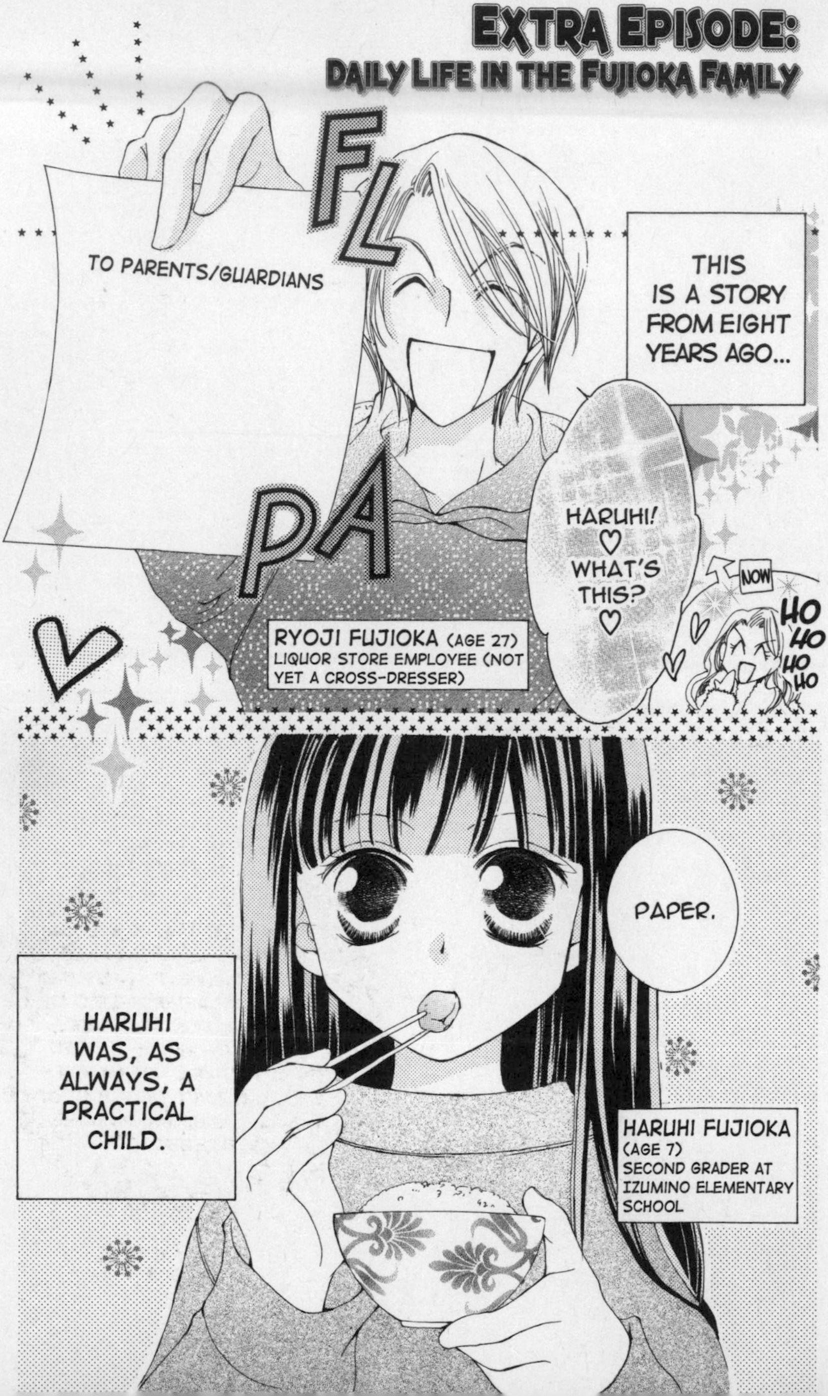
THIS IS A STORY FROM EIGHT YEARS AGO...
FLAPA
TO PARENTS/GUARDIANS
HARUHI! ♡ WHAT'S THIS? ♡
NOW
HO HO HO HO
RYOJI FUJIOKA (AGE 27) LIQUOR STORE EMPLOYEE (NOT YET A CROSS-DRESSER)
PAPER.
HARUHI FUJIOKA (AGE 7) SECOND GRADER AT IZUMINO ELEMENTARY SCHOOL
HARUHI WAS, AS ALWAYS, A PRACTICAL CHILD.

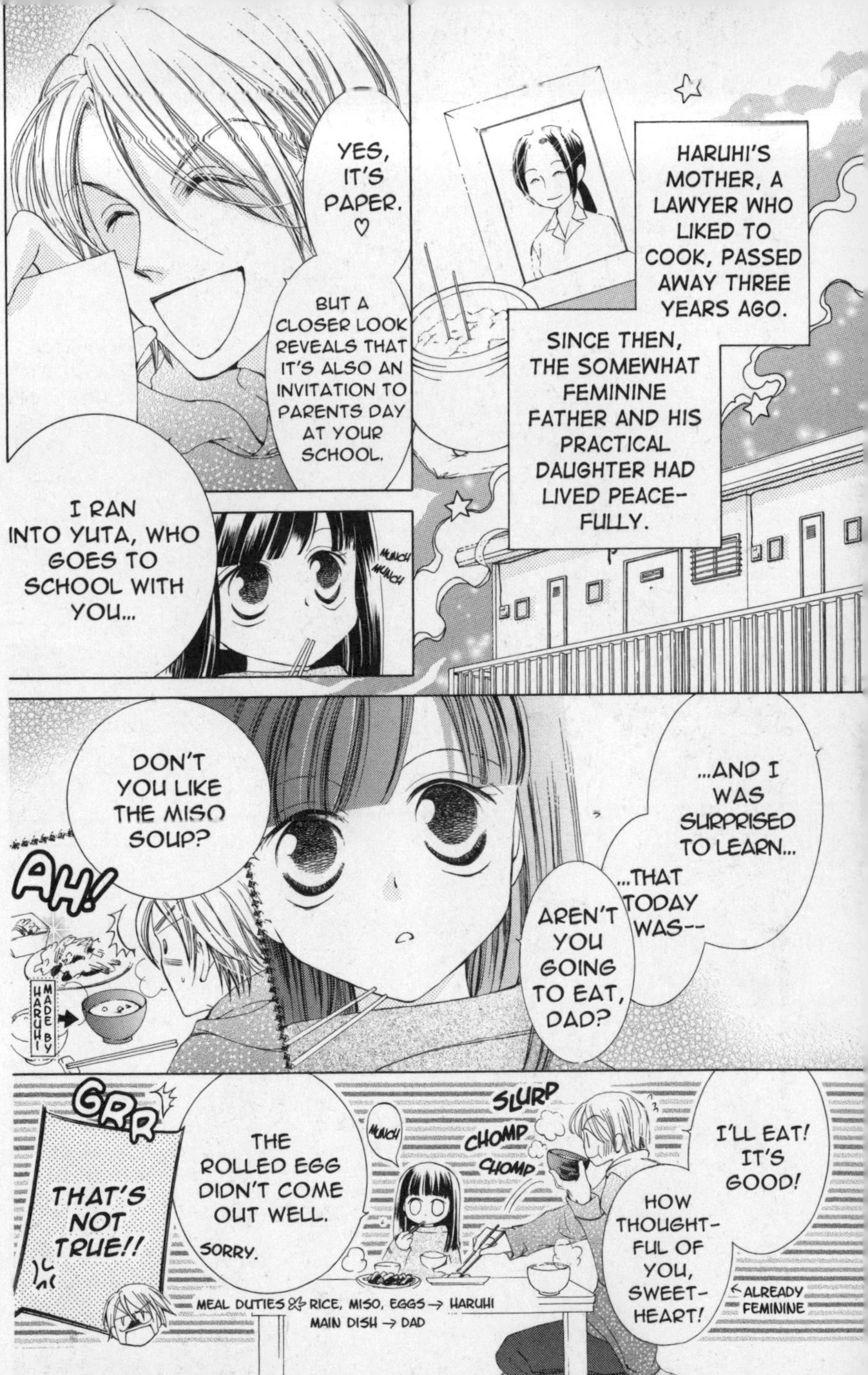
HARUHI'S MOTHER, A LAWYER WHO LIKED TO COOK, PASSED AWAY THREE YEARS AGO.
SINCE THEN, THE SOMEWHAT FEMININE FATHER AND HIS PRACTICAL DAUGHTER HAD LIVED PEACE-FULLY.
YES, IT'S PAPER. ♡
BUT A CLOSER LOOK REVEALS THAT IT'S ALSO AN INVITATION TO PARENTS DAY AT YOUR SCHOOL.
MUNCH MUNCH
I RAN INTO YUTA, WHO GOES TO SCHOOL WITH YOU...
...AND I WAS SURPRISED TO LEARN...
...THAT TODAY WAS--
AREN'T YOU GOING TO EAT, DAD?
DON'T YOU LIKE THE MISO SOUP?
AH!
MADE BY HARUHI
I'LL EAT! IT'S GOOD!
HOW THOUGHT-FUL OF YOU, SWEET-HEART!
← ALREADY FEMININE
SLURP
CHOMP CHOMP
MUNCH
THE ROLLED EGG DIDN'T COME OUT WELL.
SORRY.
GRR
THAT'S NOT TRUE!!
MEAL DUTIES ✿ RICE, MISO, EGGS → HARUHI
MAIN DISH → DAD

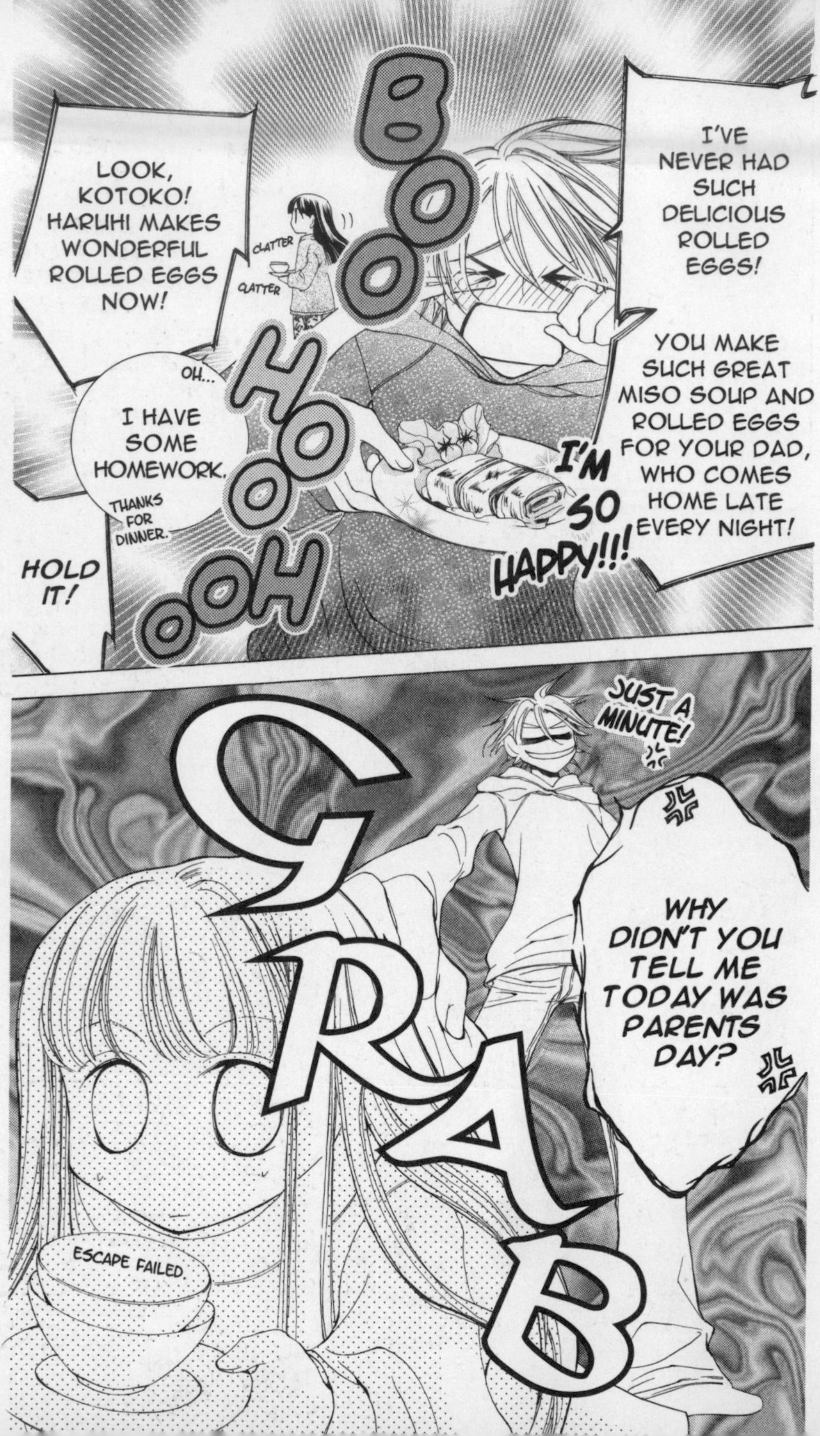
I'VE NEVER HAD SUCH DELICIOUS ROLLED EGGS!
YOU MAKE SUCH GREAT MISO SOUP AND ROLLED EGGS FOR YOUR DAD, WHO COMES HOME LATE EVERY NIGHT!
I'M SO HAPPY!!!
BOOOHOOOOH
LOOK, KOTOKO! HARUHI MAKES WONDERFUL ROLLED EGGS NOW!
CLATTER
CLATTER
OH...
I HAVE SOME HOMEWORK.
THANKS FOR DINNER.
HOLD IT!
JUST A MINUTE!
WHY DIDN'T YOU TELL ME TODAY WAS PARENTS DAY?
GRAB
ESCAPE FAILED.

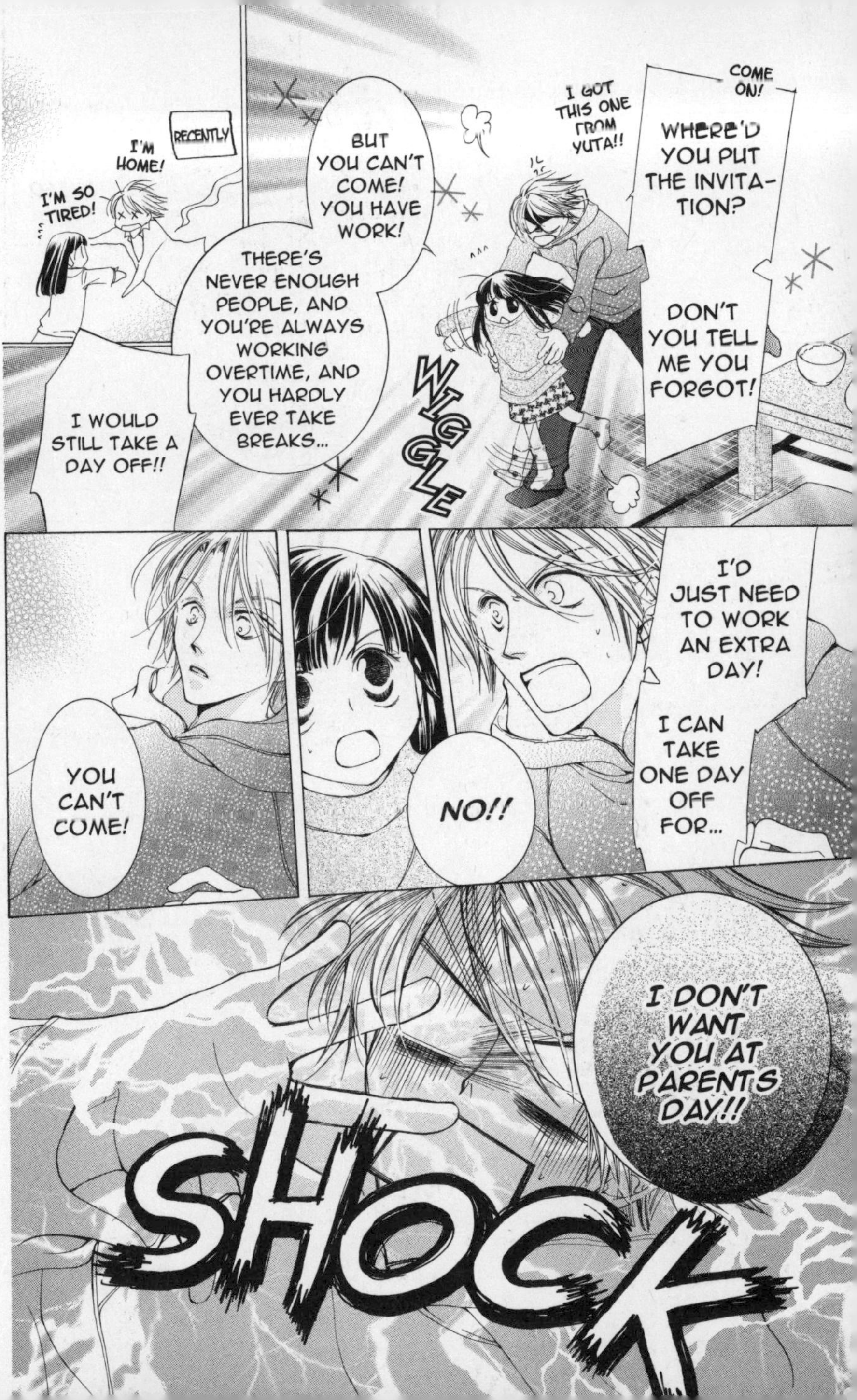
COME ON!
WHERE'D YOU PUT THE INVITATION?
I GOT THIS ONE FROM YUTA!!
DON'T YOU TELL ME YOU FORGOT!
BUT YOU CAN'T COME! YOU HAVE WORK!
RECENTLY
I'M HOME!
I'M SO TIRED!
THERE'S NEVER ENOUGH PEOPLE, AND YOU'RE ALWAYS WORKING OVERTIME, AND YOU HARDLY EVER TAKE BREAKS...
WIGGLE
I WOULD STILL TAKE A DAY OFF!!
I'D JUST NEED TO WORK AN EXTRA DAY!
I CAN TAKE ONE DAY OFF FOR...
NO!!
YOU CAN'T COME!
I DON'T WANT YOU AT PARENT'S DAY!!
SHOCK

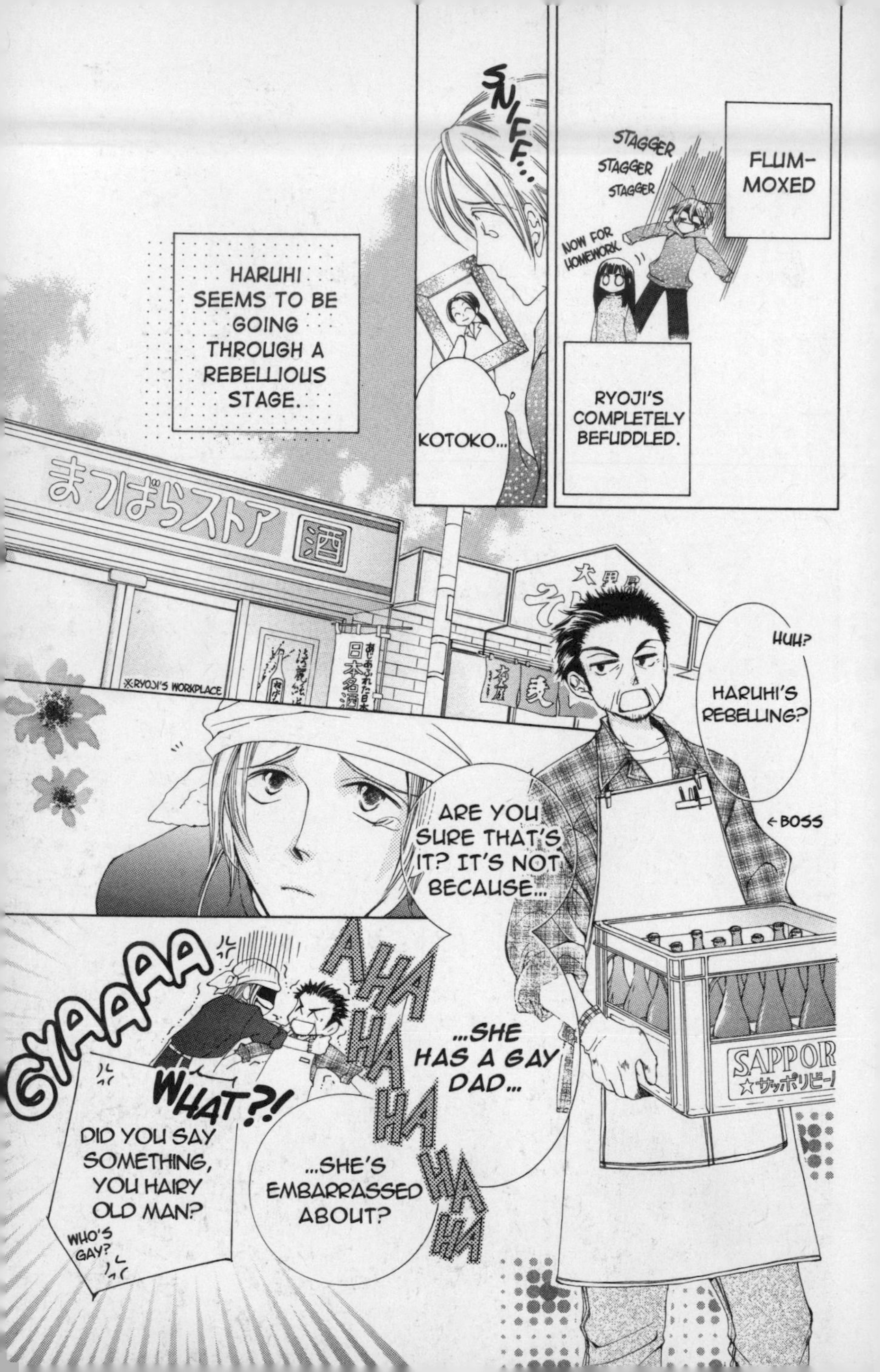
STAGGER
STAGGER
STAGGER
FLUM-MOXED
NOW FOR HOMEWORK.
RYOJI'S COMPLETELY BEFUDDLED.
SNIFF...
KOTOKO...
HARUHI SEEMS TO BE GOING THROUGH A REBELLIOUS STAGE.
まつばらストア
酒
※RYOJI'S WORKPLACE
HUH?
HARUHI'S REBELLING?
←BOSS
ARE YOU SURE THAT'S IT? IT'S NOT BECAUSE...
...SHE HAS A GAY DAD...
...SHE'S EMBARRASSED ABOUT?
AHAHAHAHAHA
WHAT?!
GYAAAA
DID YOU SAY SOMETHING, YOU HAIRY OLD MAN?
WHO'S GAY?

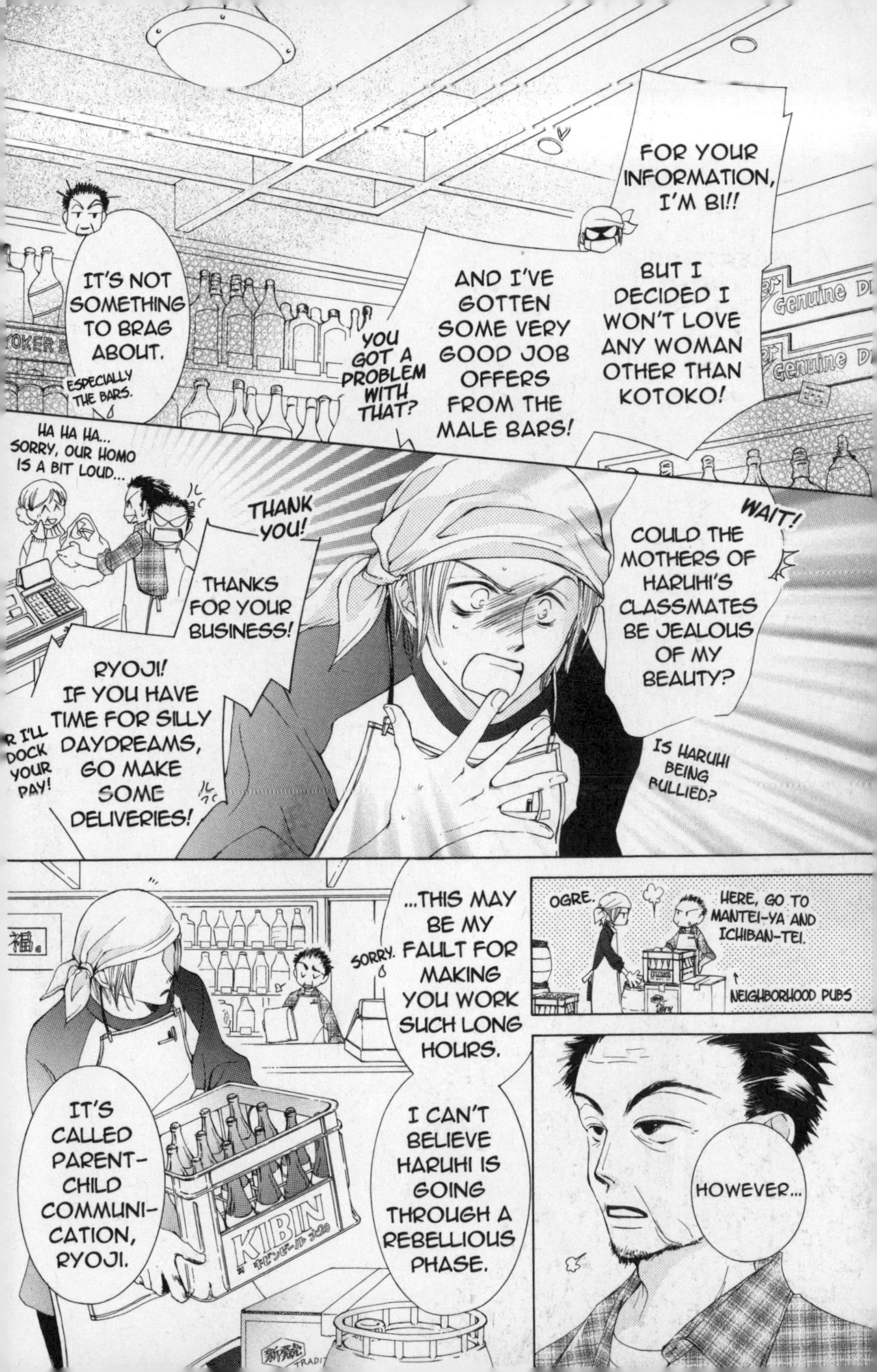
FOR YOUR INFORMATION, I'M BI!!
BUT I DECIDED I WON'T LOVE ANY WOMAN OTHER THAN KOTOKO!
AND I'VE GOTTEN SOME VERY GOOD JOB OFFERS FROM THE MALE BARS!
YOU GOT A PROBLEM WITH THAT?
IT'S NOT SOMETHING TO BRAG ABOUT.
ESPECIALLY THE BARS.
WAIT!
COULD THE MOTHERS OF HARUHI'S CLASSMATES BE JEALOUS OF MY BEAUTY?
IS HARUHI BEING BULLIED?
THANK YOU!
THANKS FOR YOUR BUSINESS!
HA HA HA... SORRY, OUR HOMO IS A BIT LOUD...
RYOJI! IF YOU HAVE TIME FOR SILLY DAYDREAMS, GO MAKE SOME DELIVERIES!
R I'LL DOCK YOUR PAY!
HERE, GO TO MANTEI-YA AND ICHIBAN-TEI.
OGRE.
NEIGHBORHOOD PUBS
HOWEVER...
...THIS MAY BE MY FAULT FOR MAKING YOU WORK SUCH LONG HOURS.
SORRY.
I CAN'T BELIEVE HARUHI IS GOING THROUGH A REBELLIOUS PHASE.
IT'S CALLED PARENT-CHILD COMMUNICATION, RYOJI.
KIBIN

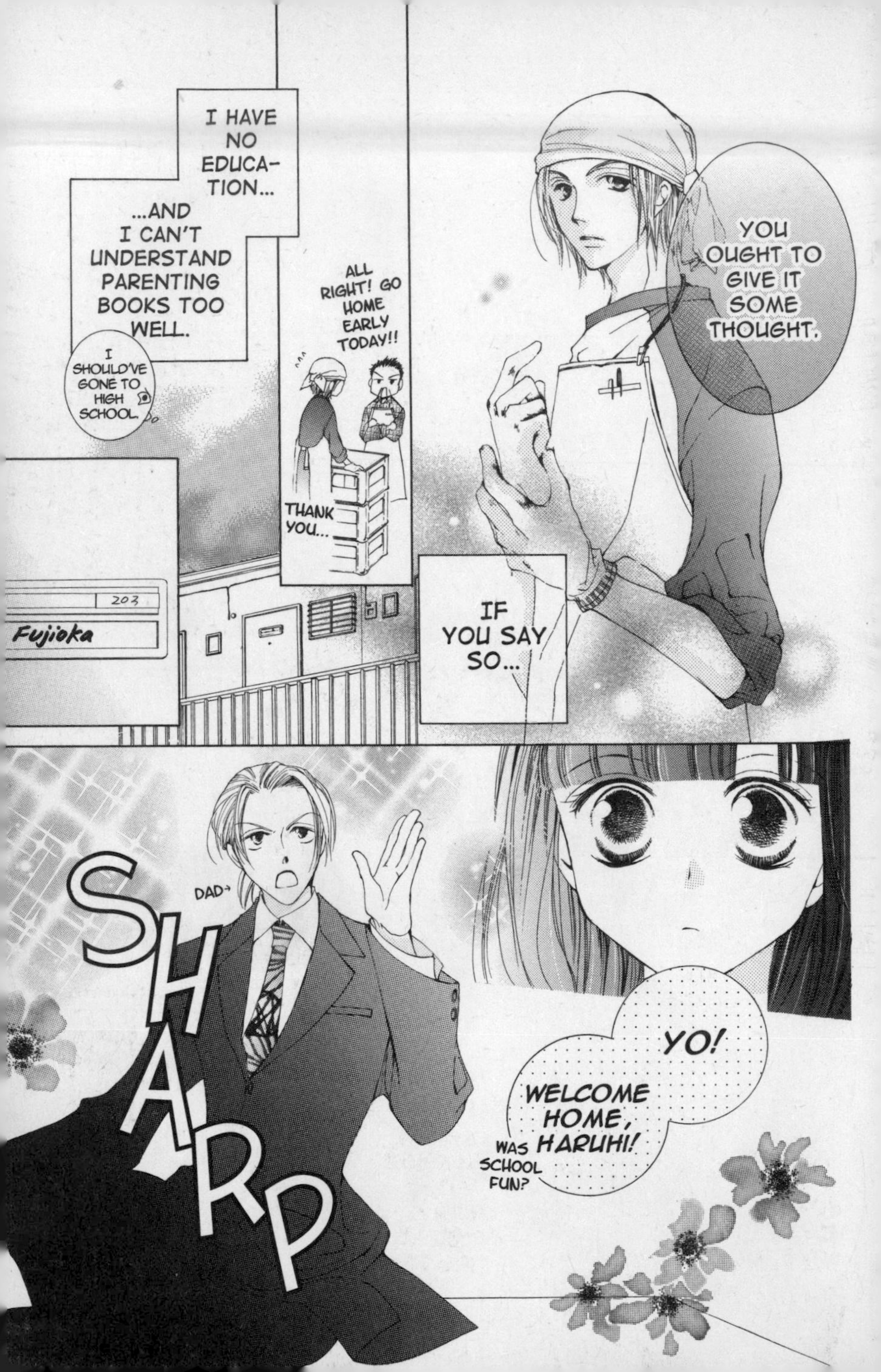
YOU OUGHT TO GIVE IT SOME THOUGHT.
IF YOU SAY SO...
ALL RIGHT! GO HOME EARLY TODAY!!
THANK YOU...
I HAVE NO EDUCATION...
...AND I CAN'T UNDERSTAND PARENTING BOOKS TOO WELL.
I SHOULD'VE GONE TO HIGH SCHOOL.
203
Fujioka
YO!
WELCOME HOME, HARUHI!
WAS SCHOOL FUN?
DAD→
SHARP

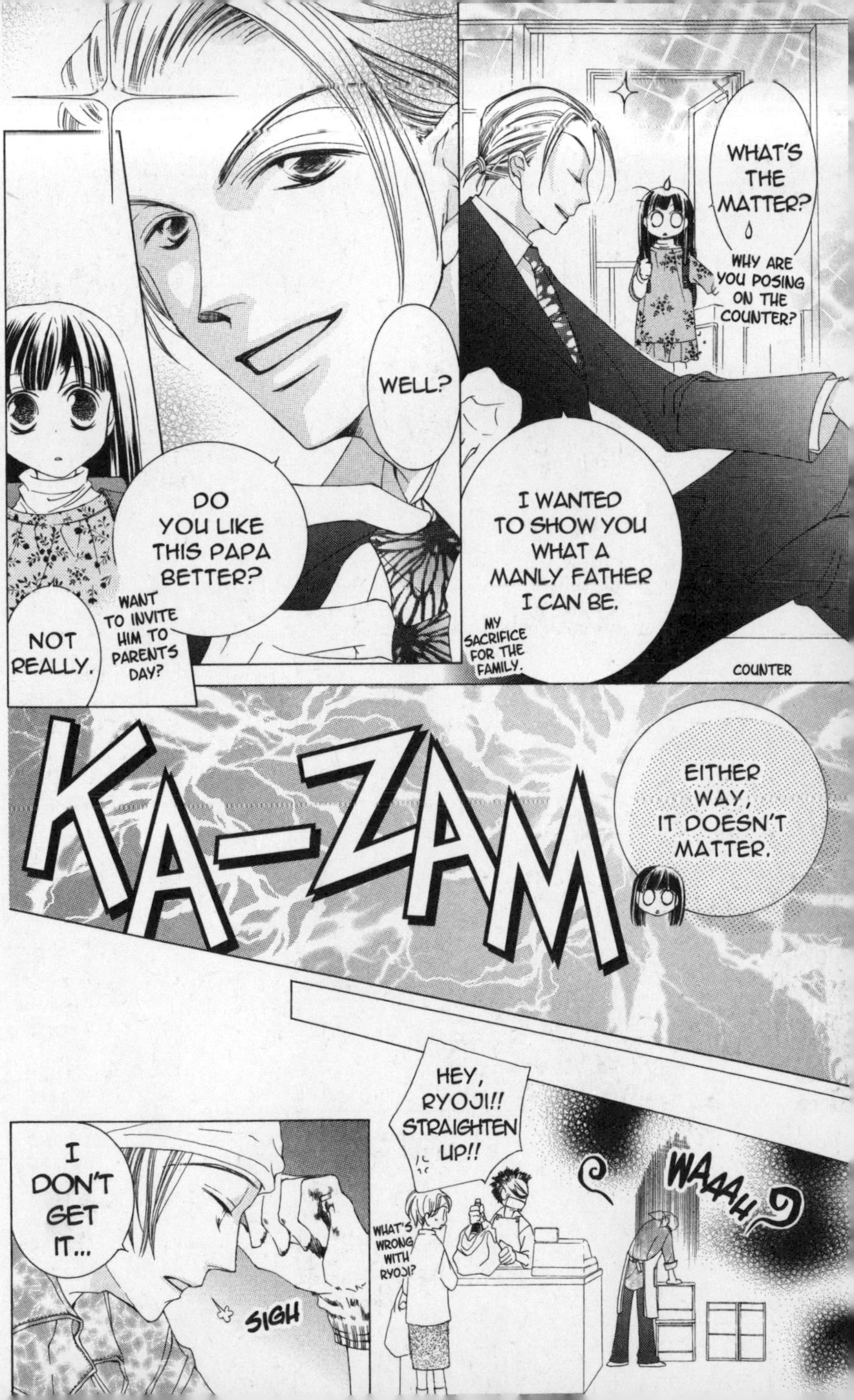
WHAT'S THE MATTER?
WHY ARE YOU POSING ON THE COUNTER?
I WANTED TO SHOW YOU WHAT A MANLY FATHER I CAN BE.
MY SACRIFICE FOR THE FAMILY.
COUNTER
WELL?
DO YOU LIKE THIS PAPA BETTER?
WANT TO INVITE HIM TO PARENTS DAY?
NOT REALLY.
EITHER WAY, IT DOESN'T MATTER.
KA-ZAM
HEY, RYOJI!! STRAIGHTEN UP!!
WAAAH
WHAT'S WRONG WITH RYOJI?
I DON'T GET IT...
SIGH

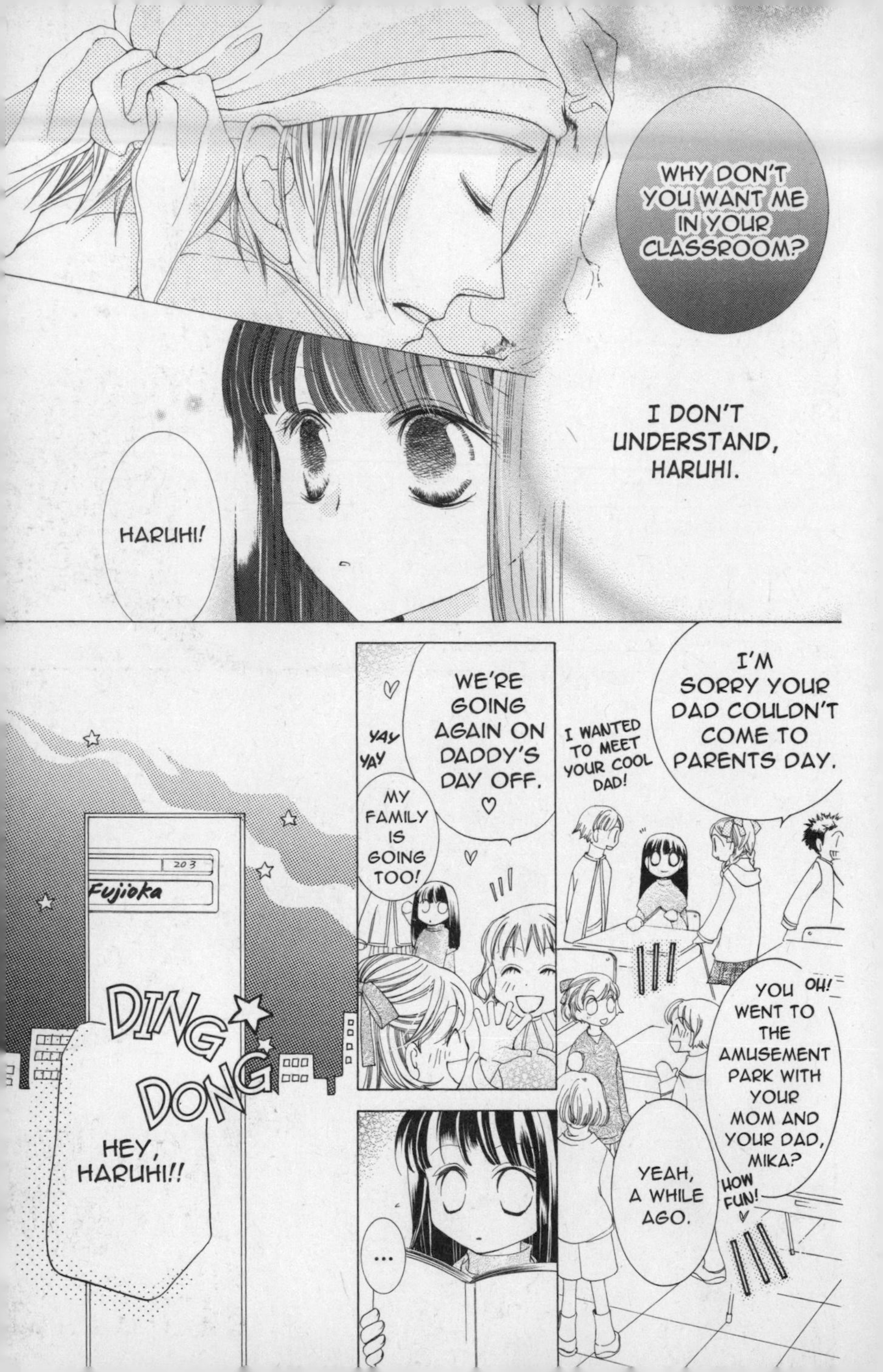
WHY DON'T YOU WANT ME IN YOUR CLASSROOM?
I DON'T UNDERSTAND, HARUHI.
HARUHI!
I'M SORRY YOUR DAD COULDN'T COME TO PARENTS DAY.
I WANTED TO MEET YOUR COOL DAD!
YOU WENT TO THE AMUSEMENT PARK WITH YOUR MOM AND YOUR DAD, MIKA?
OH!
YEAH, A WHILE AGO.
HOW FUN!
WE'RE GOING AGAIN ON DADDY'S DAY OFF.
YAY YAY
MY FAMILY IS GOING TOO!
...
203
Fujioka
DING DONG
HEY, HARUHI!!

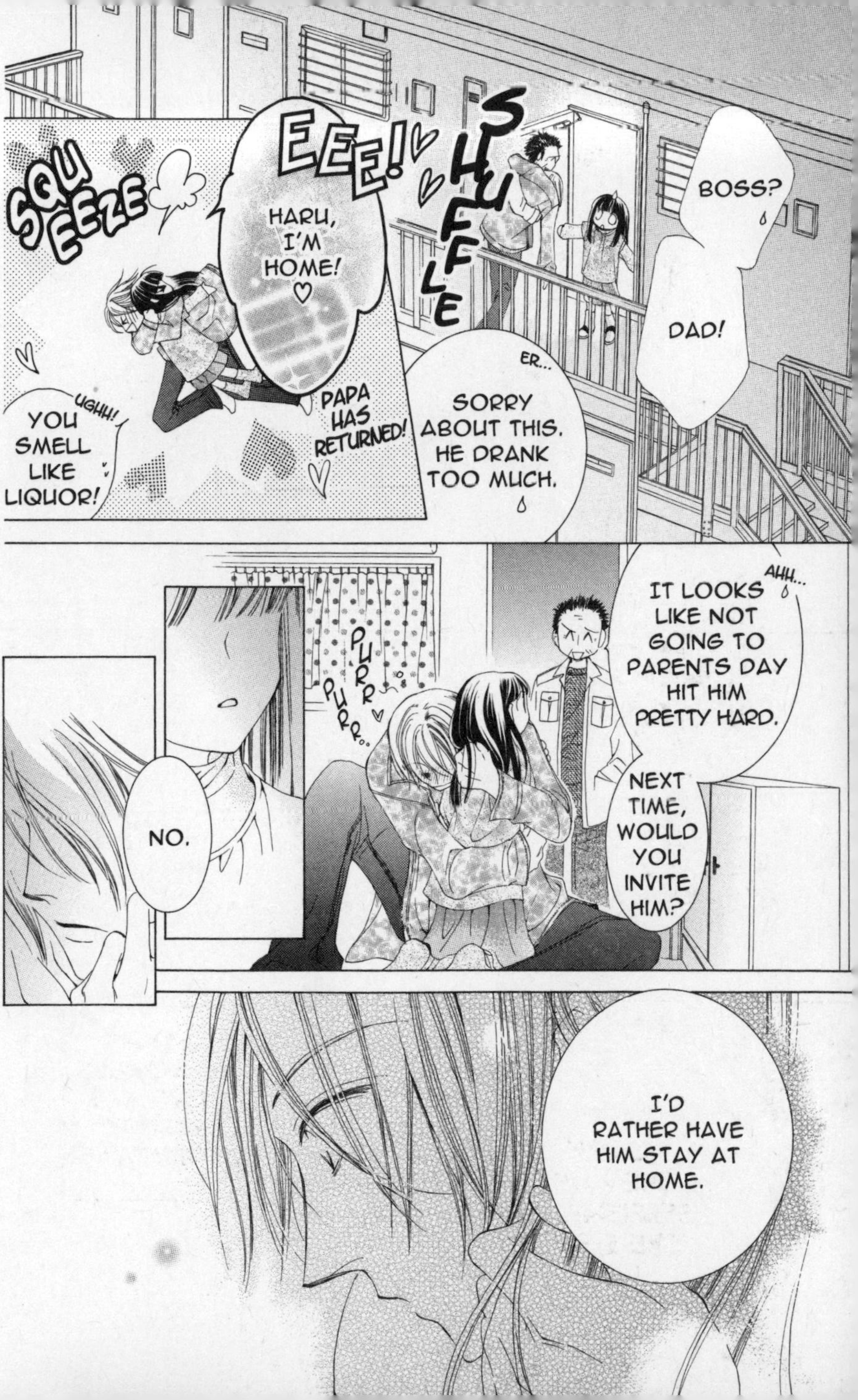
BOSS?
DAD!
SHUFFLE
EEE!
HARU, I'M HOME!
SQUEEZE
ER... SORRY ABOUT THIS. HE DRANK TOO MUCH.
PAPA HAS RETURNED!
UGHH! YOU SMELL LIKE LIQUOR!
AHH... IT LOOKS LIKE NOT GOING TO PARENTS DAY HIT HIM PRETTY HARD.
NEXT TIME, WOULD YOU INVITE HIM?
PURR PURR PURR...
NO.
I'D RATHER HAVE HIM STAY AT HOME.

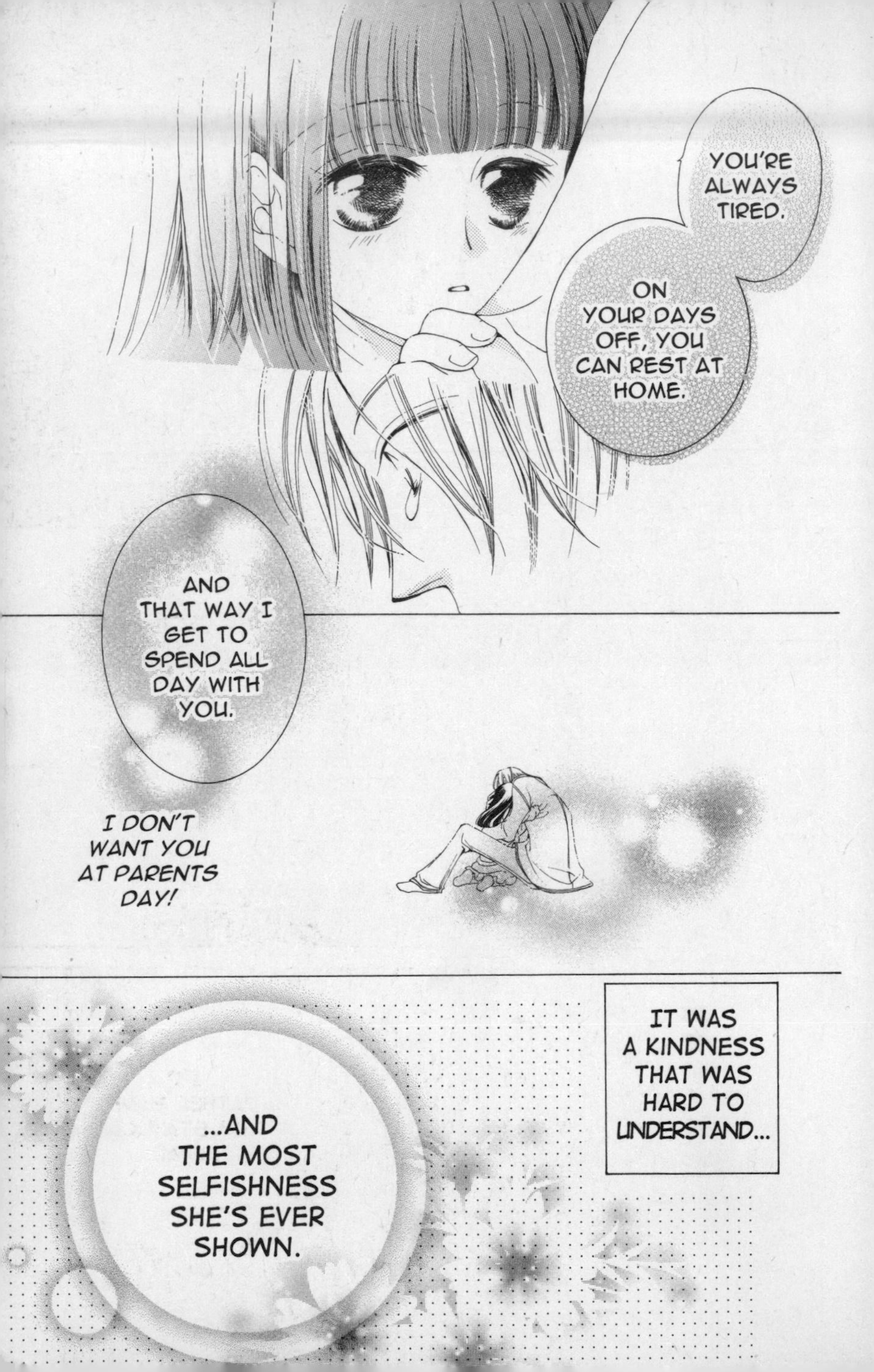
YOU'RE ALWAYS TIRED.
ON YOUR DAYS OFF, YOU CAN REST AT HOME.
AND THAT WAY I GET TO SPEND ALL DAY WITH YOU.
I DON'T WANT YOU AT PARENTS DAY!
IT WAS A KINDNESS THAT WAS HARD TO UNDERSTAND...
...AND THE MOST SELFISHNESS SHE'S EVER SHOWN.

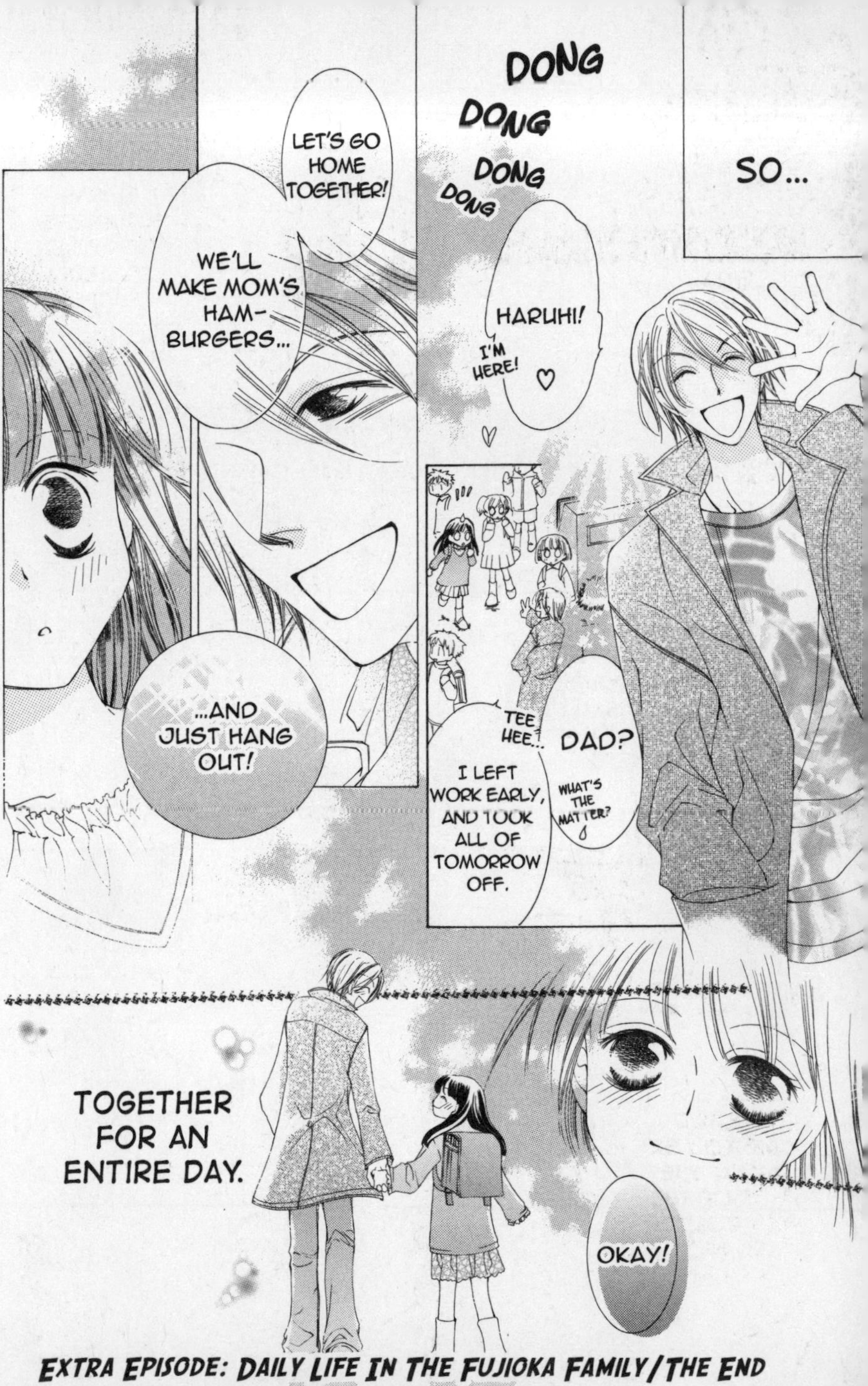
SO...
DONG DONG DONG DONG
HARUHI!
I'M HERE! ♡
DAD?
WHAT'S THE MATTER?
TEE HEE...
I LEFT WORK EARLY, AND TOOK ALL OF TOMORROW OFF.
LET'S GO HOME TOGETHER!
WE'LL MAKE MOM'S HAM-BURGERS...
...AND JUST HANG OUT!
OKAY!
TOGETHER FOR AN ENTIRE DAY.

EXTRA EPISODE: DAILY LIFE IN THE FUJIOKA FAMILY/THE END

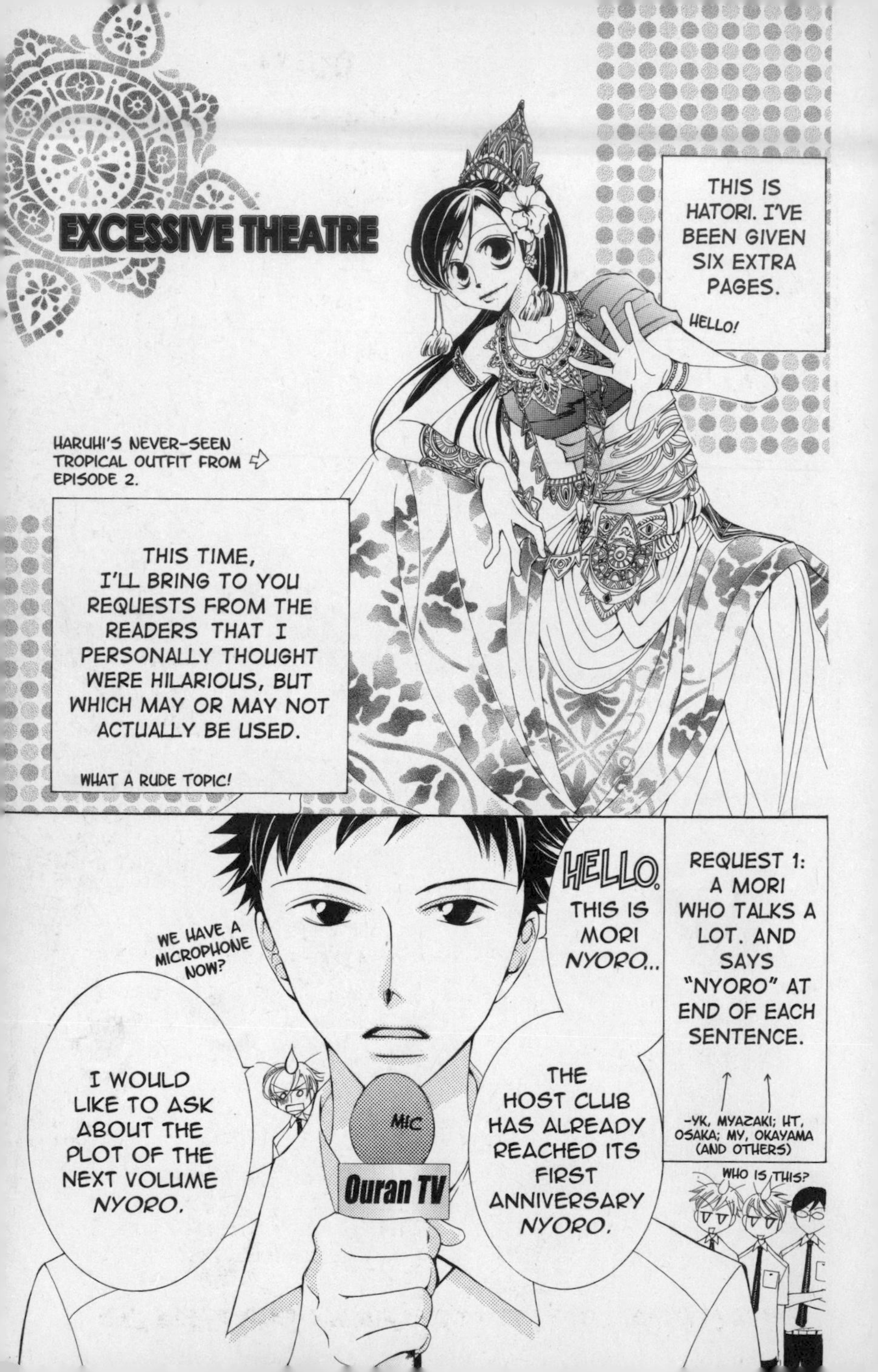
EXCESSIVE THEATRE
THIS IS HATORI. I'VE BEEN GIVEN SIX EXTRA PAGES.
HELLO!
HARUHI'S NEVER-SEEN TROPICAL OUTFIT FROM EPISODE 2.
THIS TIME, I'LL BRING TO YOU REQUESTS FROM THE READERS THAT I PERSONALLY THOUGHT WERE HILARIOUS, BUT WHICH MAY OR MAY NOT ACTUALLY BE USED.
WHAT A RUDE TOPIC!
REQUEST 1: A MORI WHO TALKS A LOT. AND SAYS "NYORO" AT END OF EACH SENTENCE.
-YK, MYAZAKI; HT, OSAKA; MY, OKAYAMA (AND OTHERS)
HELLO. THIS IS MORI *NYORO*...
WHO IS THIS?
THE HOST CLUB HAS ALREADY REACHED ITS FIRST ANNIVERSARY *NYORO*.
MIC
Ouran TV
WE HAVE A MICROPHONE NOW?
I WOULD LIKE TO ASK ABOUT THE PLOT OF THE NEXT VOLUME *NYORO*.

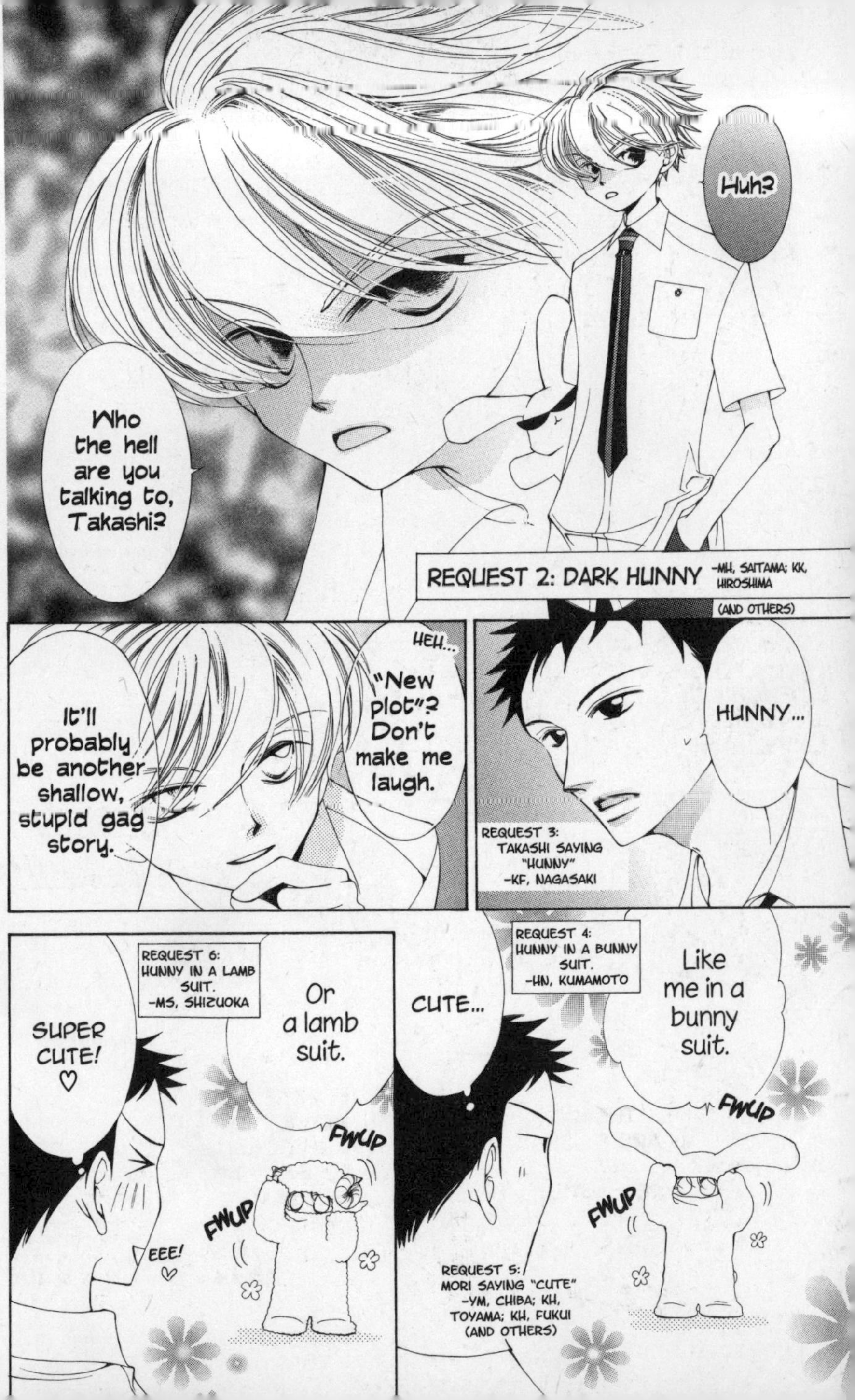
Huh?
Who the hell are you talking to, Takashi?
REQUEST 2: DARK HUNNY -MH, SAITAMA; KK, HIROSHIMA (AND OTHERS)
HUNNY...
REQUEST 3: TAKASHI SAYING "HUNNY" -KF, NAGASAKI
HEH...
"New plot"? Don't make me laugh.
It'll probably be another shallow, stupid gag story.
Like me in a bunny suit.
REQUEST 4: HUNNY IN A BUNNY SUIT. -HN, KUMAMOTO
CUTE...
FWUP
FWUP
REQUEST 5: MORI SAYING "CUTE" -YM, CHIBA; KH, TOYAMA; KH, FUKUI (AND OTHERS)
Or a lamb suit.
REQUEST 6: HUNNY IN A LAMB SUIT. -MS, SHIZUOKA
SUPER CUTE! ♡
FWUP
FWUP
EEE! ♡

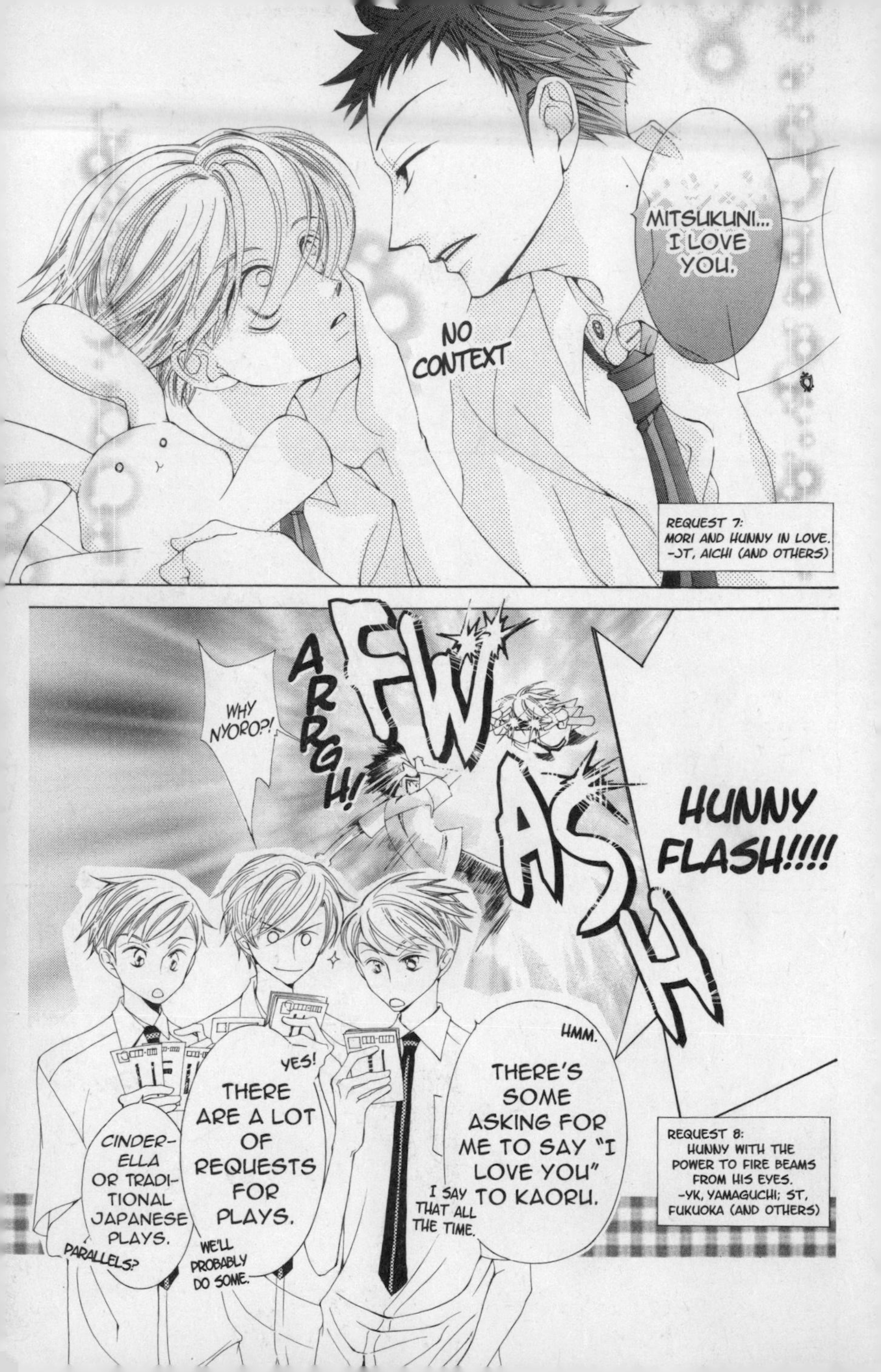
MITSUKUNI... I LOVE YOU.
NO CONTEXT
REQUEST 7: MORI AND HUNNY IN LOVE. -ST, AICHI (AND OTHERS)
HUNNY FLASH!!!!!
FWASH
ARRGH!
WHY NYORO?!
REQUEST 8: HUNNY WITH THE POWER TO FIRE BEAMS FROM HIS EYES. -YK, YAMAGUCHI; ST, FUKUOKA (AND OTHERS)
HMM.
THERE'S SOME ASKING FOR ME TO SAY "I LOVE YOU" TO KAORU.
I SAY THAT ALL THE TIME.
YES!
THERE ARE A LOT OF REQUESTS FOR PLAYS.
WE'LL PROBABLY DO SOME.
CINDERELLA OR TRADITIONAL JAPANESE PLAYS.
PARALLELS?

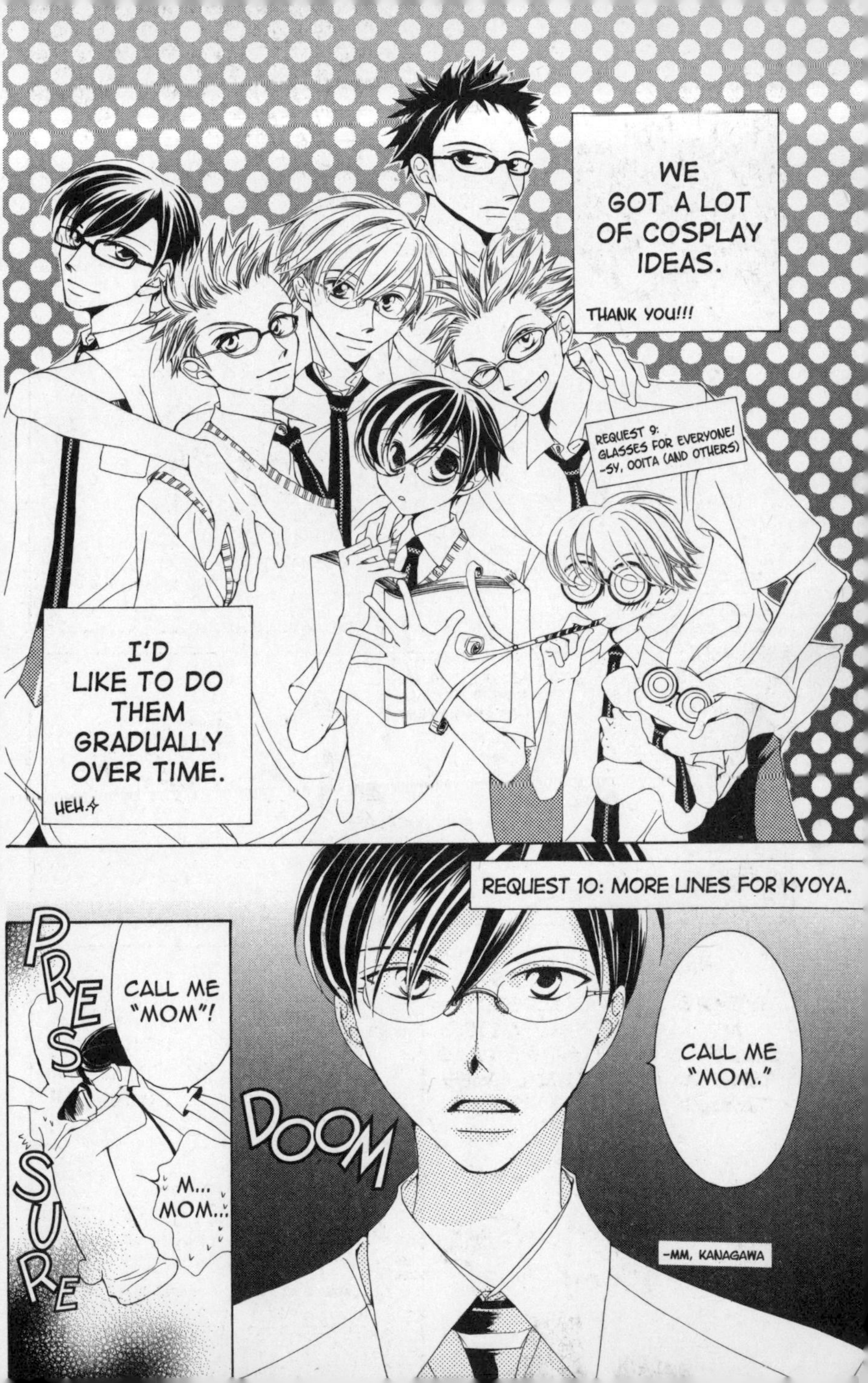
WE GOT A LOT OF COSPLAY IDEAS.
THANK YOU!!!
REQUEST 9: GLASSES FOR EVERYONE! -SY, OOITA (AND OTHERS)
I'D LIKE TO DO THEM GRADUALLY OVER TIME.
HEH.
REQUEST 10: MORE LINES FOR KYOYA.
CALL ME "MOM."
DOOM
-MM, KANAGAWA
CALL ME "MOM"!
PRESSURE
M... MOM...

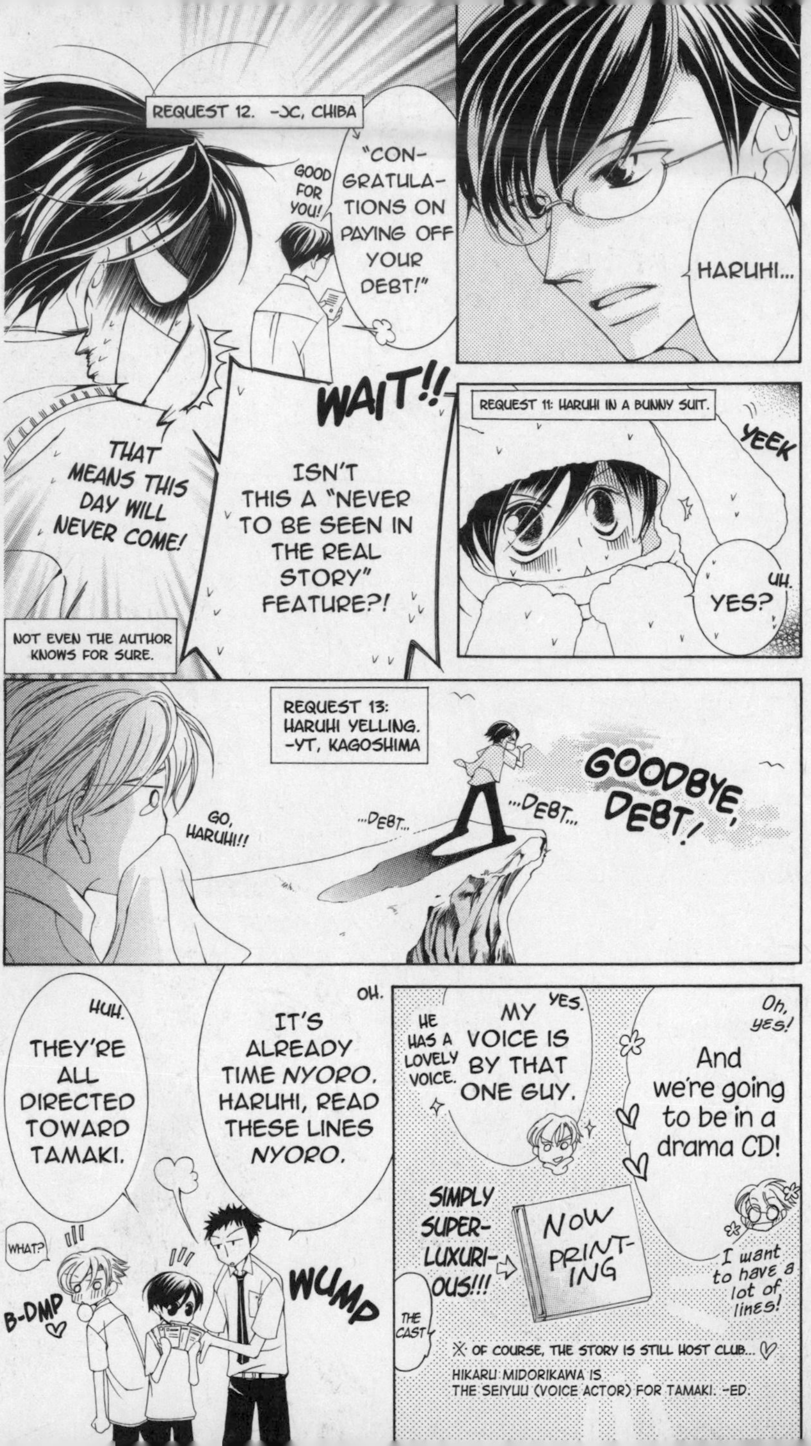
HARUHI...
REQUEST 12. -JC, CHIBA
"CONGRATULATIONS ON PAYING OFF YOUR DEBT!"
GOOD FOR YOU!
REQUEST 11: HARUHI IN A BUNNY SUIT.
YEEK
UH. YES?
WAIT!!
ISN'T THIS A "NEVER TO BE SEEN IN THE REAL STORY" FEATURE?!
THAT MEANS THIS DAY WILL NEVER COME!
NOT EVEN THE AUTHOR KNOWS FOR SURE.
REQUEST 13: HARUHI YELLING. -YT, KAGOSHIMA
GOODBYE, DEBT!
...DEBT...
...DEBT...
GO, HARUHI!!
Oh, yes!
And we're going to be in a drama CD!
YES.
MY VOICE IS BY THAT ONE GUY.
HE HAS A LOVELY VOICE.
I want to have a lot of lines!
NOW PRINTING
SIMPLY SUPER-LUXURIOUS!!!
THE CAST
※ OF COURSE, THE STORY IS STILL HOST CLUB...
HIKARU MIDORIKAWA IS THE SEIYUU (VOICE ACTOR) FOR TAMAKI. -ED.
OH.
IT'S ALREADY TIME NYORO. HARUHI, READ THESE LINES NYORO.
HUH.
THEY'RE ALL DIRECTED TOWARD TAMAKI.
WUMP
WHAT?
B-DMP

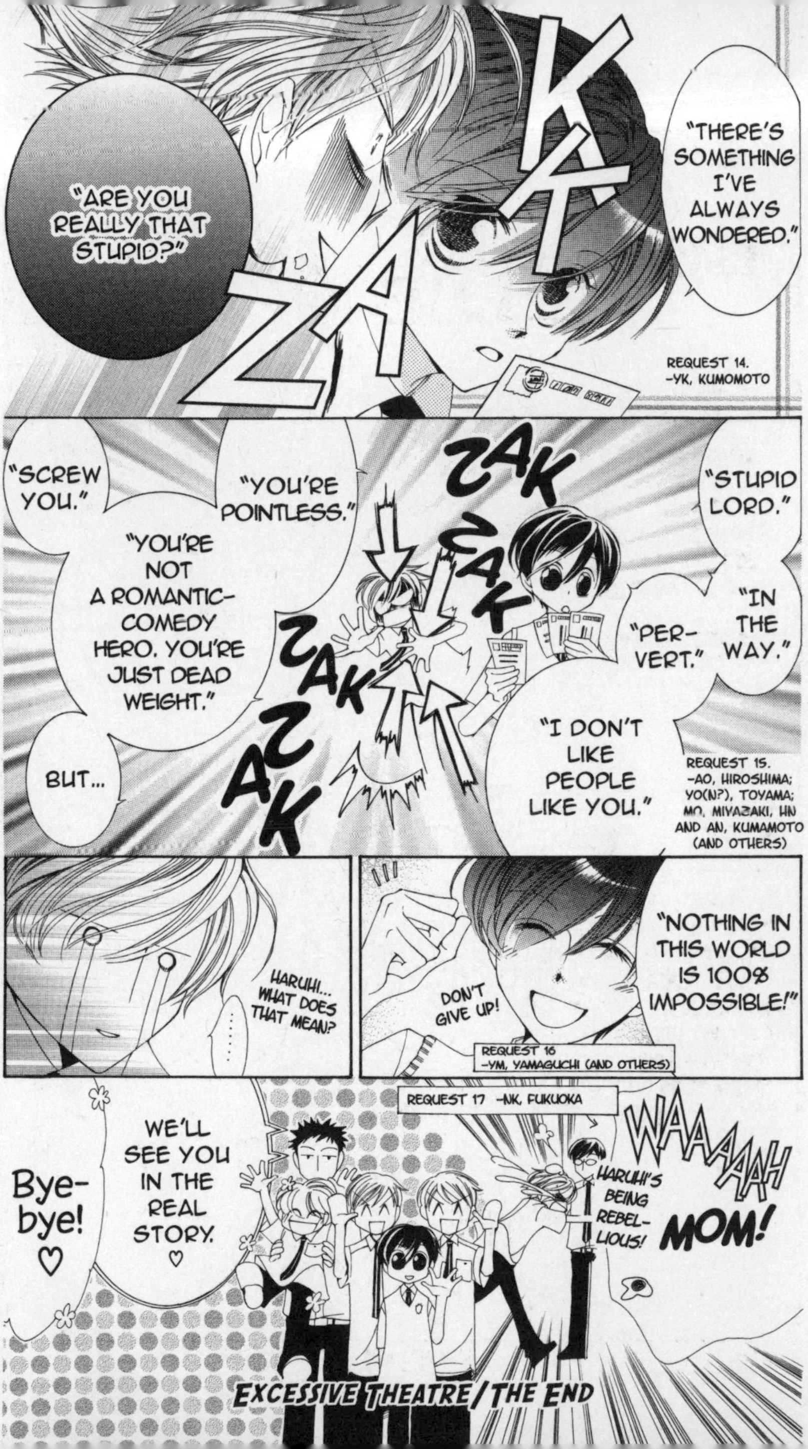
"THERE'S SOMETHING I'VE ALWAYS WONDERED."
ZAKK
"ARE YOU REALLY THAT STUPID?"
REQUEST 14. -YK, KUMOMOTO
"STUPID LORD."
"IN THE WAY."
"PER-VERT."
"I DON'T LIKE PEOPLE LIKE YOU."
ZAK
ZAK
ZAK
ZAK
"YOU'RE POINTLESS."
"SCREW YOU."
"YOU'RE NOT A ROMANTIC-COMEDY HERO. YOU'RE JUST DEAD WEIGHT."
BUT...
REQUEST 15. -AO, HIROSHIMA; YO(N?), TOYAMA; MO, MIYAZAKI, HN AND AN, KUMAMOTO (AND OTHERS)
"NOTHING IN THIS WORLD IS 100% IMPOSSIBLE!"
DON'T GIVE UP!
REQUEST 16 -YM, YAMAGUCHI (AND OTHERS)
HARUHI... WHAT DOES THAT MEAN?
......
REQUEST 17 -NK, FUKUOKA
WAAAAAH MOM!
HARUHI'S BEING REBEL-LIOUS!
WE'LL SEE YOU IN THE REAL STORY. ♡
Bye-bye! ♡
EXCESSIVE THEATRE / THE END

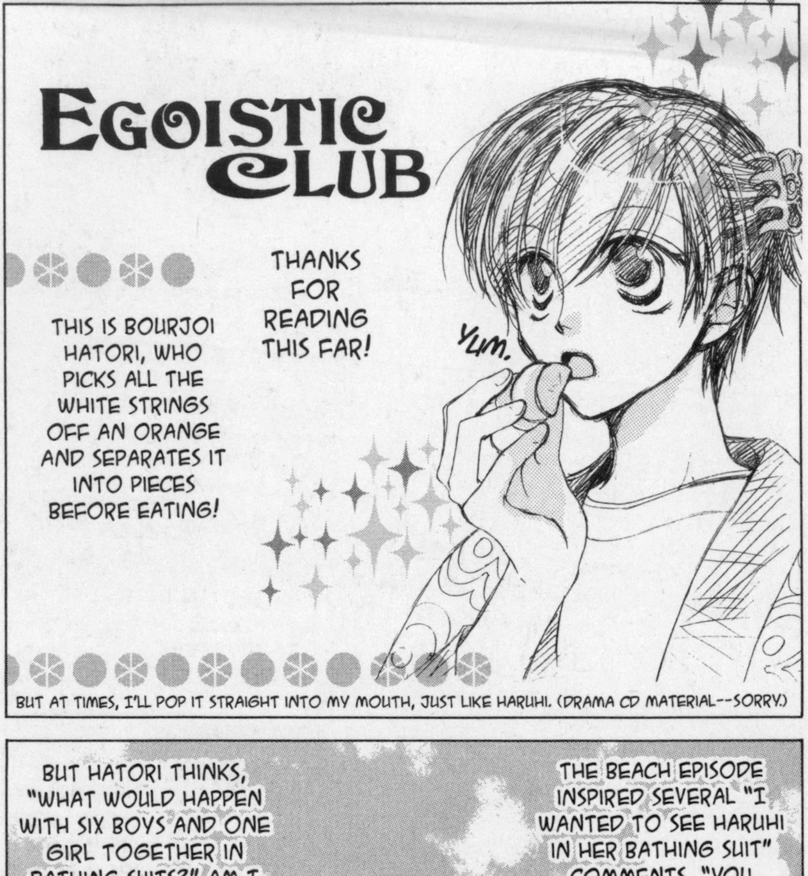
EGOISTIC CLUB
YUM.
THANKS FOR READING THIS FAR!
THIS IS BOURJOI HATORI, WHO PICKS ALL THE WHITE STRINGS OFF AN ORANGE AND SEPARATES IT INTO PIECES BEFORE EATING!
BUT AT TIMES, I'LL POP IT STRAIGHT INTO MY MOUTH, JUST LIKE HARUHI. (DRAMA CD MATERIAL--SORRY.)

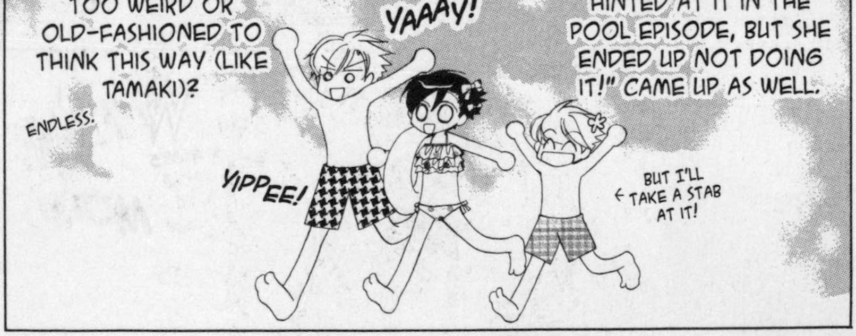
THE BEACH EPISODE INSPIRED SEVERAL "I WANTED TO SEE HARUHI IN HER BATHING SUIT" COMMENTS. "YOU HINTED AT IT IN THE POOL EPISODE, BUT SHE ENDED UP NOT DOING IT!" CAME UP AS WELL.
BUT HATORI THINKS, "WHAT WOULD HAPPEN WITH SIX BOYS AND ONE GIRL TOGETHER IN BATHING SUITS?" AM I TOO WEIRD OR OLD-FASHIONED TO THINK THIS WAY (LIKE TAMAKI)?
YAAAY!
ENDLESS.
BUT I'LL TAKE A STAB AT IT!
YIPPEE!
I KNOW. THIS IS NOT WHAT PEOPLE WANTED...

THIS IS A BIT SUDDEN, BUT MR. N FROM NAGOYA, WHO SENT ME A GREAT AMOUNT OF SUGAKIYA RAMEN, THANK YOU!!

IT JUST ARRIVED, SO HERE'S AN IMAGE OF HAPPINESS.

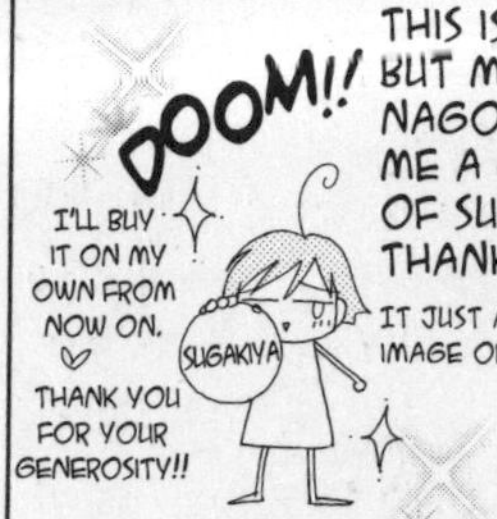
DOOM!!
I'LL BUY IT ON MY OWN FROM NOW ON. ♡
THANK YOU FOR YOUR GENEROSITY!!
SUGAKIYA

A KANTOU PERSON WHO LIKES SUGAKIYA.

("SUGAKIYA" IS AN ORIENTAL PORK RAMEN FRANCHISE IN NAGOYA.)

"THE TASTE AND PRICE THAT COMMONERS LIKE! PLEASE NEVER CHANGE!!" SAY MEMBERS OF THE SUGAKIYA FAN CLUB.
(MEMBERS ⇨ NARI KUSAKAWA, B-KO HATORI).
OKAY, **TWO** PEOPLE...

THIS IS OFF ON A TANGENT, BUT SUGAKIYA USED TO HAVE STORES IN THE KANTOU REGION. I WORKED AT ONE, AT JA●KO IN BOUFUNABASHI!!

※HATORI SAYS "FROM SAITAMA" IN HER PROFILE, BUT SHE WAS BORN IN AOMORI AND GREW UP IN SAITAMA, FUKUSHIMA, AND CHIBA.

MINI HATORI INFO

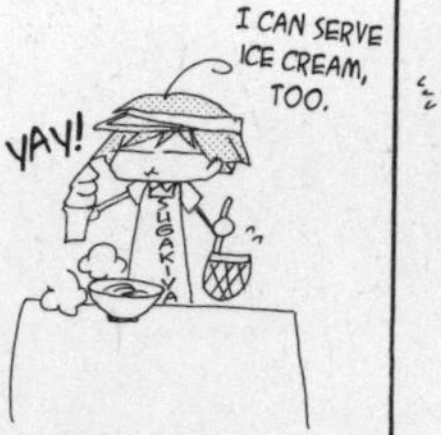
I CAN SERVE ICE CREAM, TOO.
YAY!
SUGAKIYA

I MOVED A LOT WHEN I WAS A KID, SO I DEBATED WHEN I WAS ASKED ABOUT MY ORIGIN. I WAS IN AOMORI UNTIL I WAS THREE YEARS OLD. THEN I WENT FROM AOMORI → SAITAMA → FUKUSHIMA → SAITAMA → CHIBA → SAITAMA (LOTS OF SAITAMA...)

THANK YOU FOR ALL THE LETTERS AND PRESENTS!! THANK YOU FOR THE MINIDISCS, TOO!! I'M SORRY I CAN'T REPLY TO ALL MY LETTERS! PLEASE BE PATIENT AND WAIT.

I'VE WRITTEN LETTERS ON PAPER BEFORE, BUT I'M USING POSTCARDS FROM NOW ON.

SO HERE IS A REQUEST FROM HATORI!

BY THE WAY, BESIDES ALL THE MUSIC CDS, I'VE RECEIVED TWO HOMEMADE DRAMA CDS BASED ON EPISODE 1 OF HOST CLUB. (LAUGH) THIS IS GREAT!! HOW DO YOU GUYS MAKE THESE?

THERE'S EVEN BACKGROUND MUSIC. THE TENSION IN TAMAKI'S VOICE IS GREAT! (LAUGH)

TO THOSE GENEROUS ENOUGH TO WRITE TO ME:

1. SELF-ADDRESSED, STAMPED ENVELOPES ARE NOT NECESSARY. (THANK YOU FOR BEING GENEROUS ENOUGH TO INCLUDE THESE, THOUGH!)

2. I CANNOT FULFILL REQUESTS TO SIGN ART BOARDS, DRAWING PADS, ETC. (I'M SORRY!)

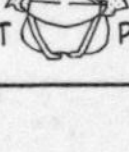

I'M SORRY ABOUT ALL THIS, BUT PLEASE KEEP SUPPORTING ME!

THOSE OF YOU WHO HAVE A PROBLEM WITH HAVING A POSTCARD WITH MANGA ART SENT TO YOUR HOME, PLEASE LET ME KNOW. ♡ (I'LL PUT IT IN AN ENVELOPE.)

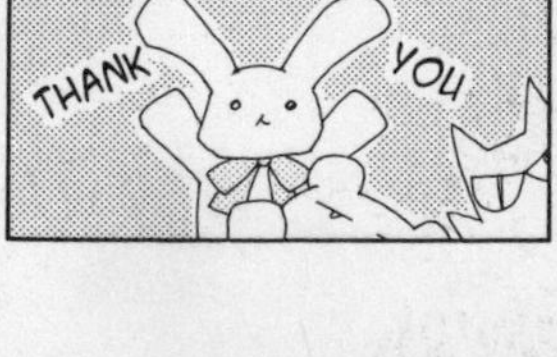
THANK YOU

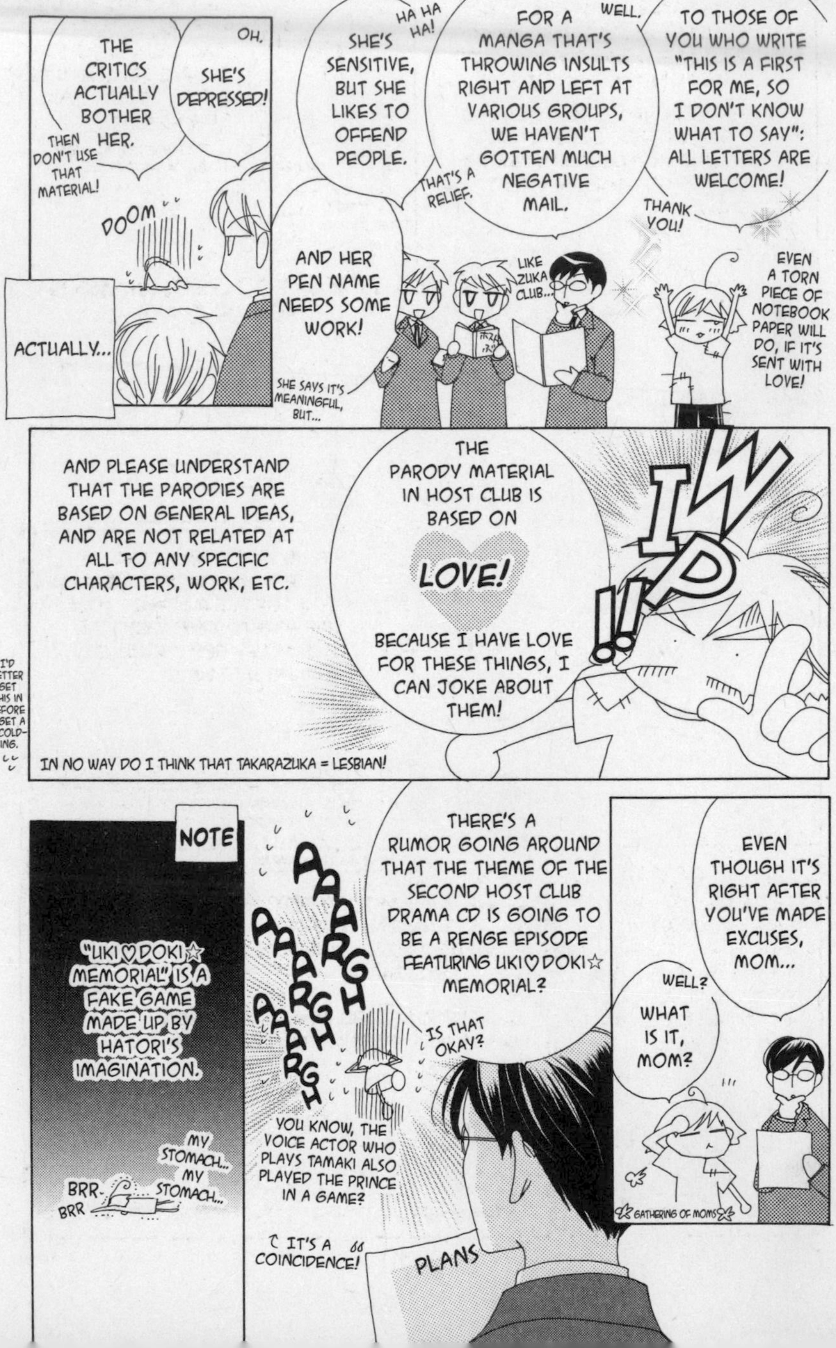
TO THOSE OF YOU WHO WRITE "THIS IS A FIRST FOR ME, SO I DON'T KNOW WHAT TO SAY": ALL LETTERS ARE WELCOME!
WELL.
FOR A MANGA THAT'S THROWING INSULTS RIGHT AND LEFT AT VARIOUS GROUPS, WE HAVEN'T GOTTEN MUCH NEGATIVE MAIL.
HA HA HA!
SHE'S SENSITIVE, BUT SHE LIKES TO OFFEND PEOPLE.
THAT'S A RELIEF.
THANK YOU!
EVEN A TORN PIECE OF NOTEBOOK PAPER WILL DO, IF IT'S SENT WITH LOVE!
LIKE ZUKA CLUB...
AND HER PEN NAME NEEDS SOME WORK!
SHE SAYS IT'S MEANINGFUL, BUT...
OH.
SHE'S DEPRESSED!
THE CRITICS ACTUALLY BOTHER HER.
THEN DON'T USE THAT MATERIAL!
DOOM
ACTUALLY...
THE PARODY MATERIAL IN HOST CLUB IS BASED ON
LOVE!
BECAUSE I HAVE LOVE FOR THESE THINGS, I CAN JOKE ABOUT THEM!
AND PLEASE UNDERSTAND THAT THE PARODIES ARE BASED ON GENERAL IDEAS, AND ARE NOT RELATED AT ALL TO ANY SPECIFIC CHARACTERS, WORK, ETC.
IN NO WAY DO I THINK THAT TAKARAZUKA = LESBIAN!
I'D BETTER GET THIS IN BEFORE I GET A SCOLDING.
EVEN THOUGH IT'S RIGHT AFTER YOU'VE MADE EXCUSES, MOM...
WELL?
WHAT IS IT, MOM?
GATHERING OF MOMS
THERE'S A RUMOR GOING AROUND THAT THE THEME OF THE SECOND HOST CLUB DRAMA CD IS GOING TO BE A RENGE EPISODE FEATURING UKI♡DOKI☆ MEMORIAL?
IS THAT OKAY?
AAAARGH
AAAARGH
AAAARGH
YOU KNOW, THE VOICE ACTOR WHO PLAYS TAMAKI ALSO PLAYED THE PRINCE IN A GAME?
IT'S A COINCIDENCE!
PLANS
NOTE
"UKI♡DOKI☆ MEMORIAL" IS A FAKE GAME MADE UP BY HATORI'S IMAGINATION.
MY STOMACH... MY STOMACH...
BRR-BRR

← THAT MEANS YOU CAN'T BUY IT IN STORES.

✿ THE ZEN-IN DRAMA CD WILL NOT BE SOLD IN STORES. PLEASE CHECK OUT THE MAGAZINE *LALA* FOR DETAILS! THERE SEEMS TO BE A LOT MORE IN THE WORKS! A VOICE-ACTOR SEARCH FOR THE READERS, AND CHOOSING BIRTHDATES FOR THE CHARACTERS! THINGS LIKE THAT! (NO, I HAVEN'T DECIDED YET...) PLEASE KEEP SUPPORTING HOST CLUB!

※ NEWS FROM SPRING 2004

TEASER PIC

THIS TIME IT'S KYOYA WITHOUT HIS GLASSES AND A LONG-HAIRED HARUHI. IT LOOKS LIKE FORBIDDEN LOVE BETWEEN A BROTHER AND SISTER. (MORE SO DUE TO THEIR UNIFORMS...)

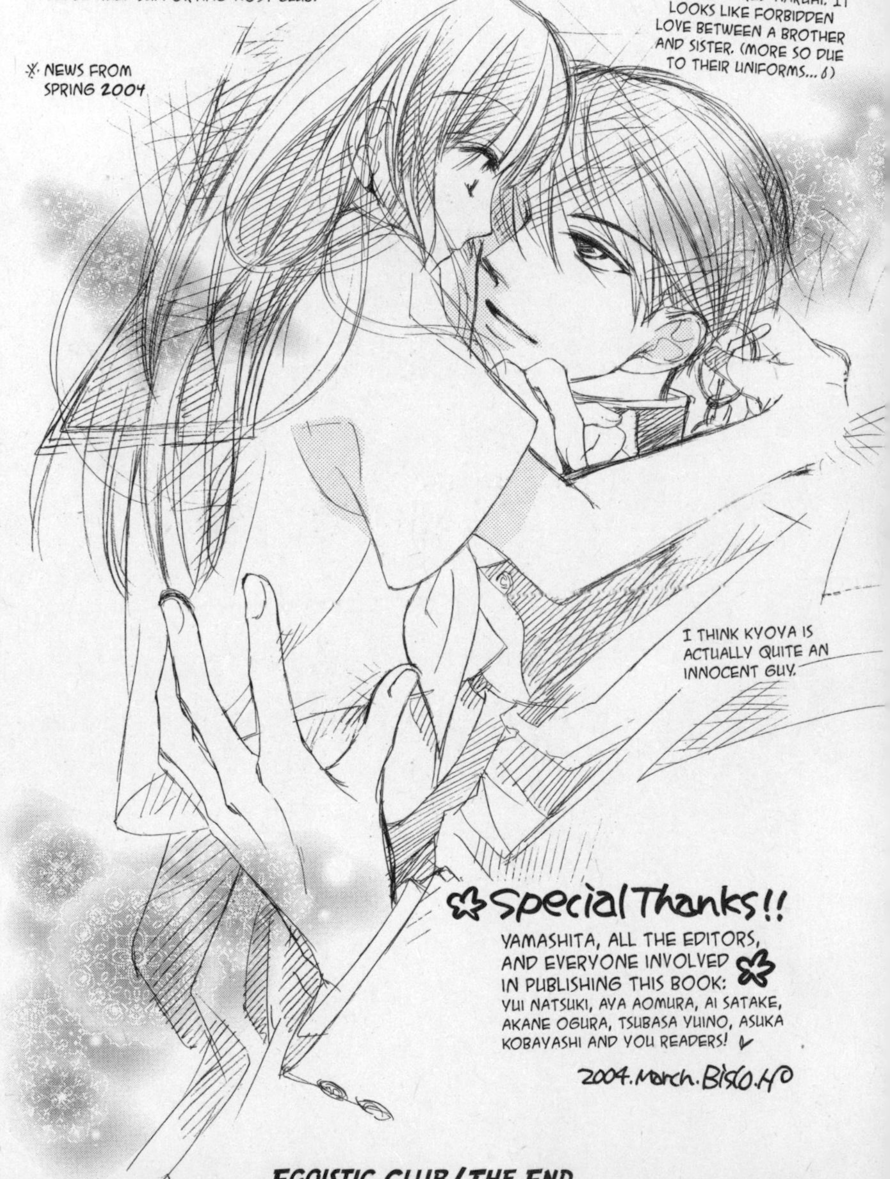

I THINK KYOYA IS ACTUALLY QUITE AN INNOCENT GUY.

✿ Special Thanks!!

YAMASHITA, ALL THE EDITORS, AND EVERYONE INVOLVED IN PUBLISHING THIS BOOK: ✿
YUI NATSUKI, AYA AOMURA, AI SATAKE, AKANE OGURA, TSUBASA YUINO, ASUKA KOBAYASHI AND YOU READERS!

2004. March. BISCO.H

EGOISTIC CLUB / THE END

LETTERS INTRO♪

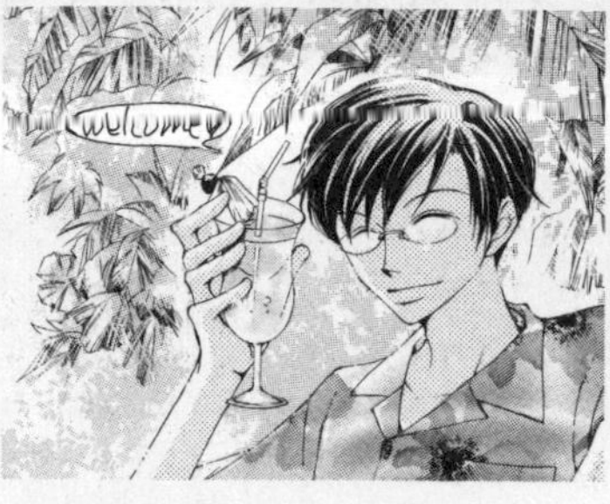
welcome

Letters sent to *LaLa* magazine revealed for the first time!
Here were ideas for "Ohtori Aqua Garden" in volume 2...

I enjoy reading every episode, but I'd like to get right to the point. Here's my idea for Ohtori Aqua Garden. At first, it looks like a normal public shower. But as you enter, horrors ensue. The changing room is actually a personality-exchanging machine. Hikaru and Kaoru find the changing room first, but they push Haruhi in ahead of them. Then Tamaki, Mitsukuni, and Mori all go in. Hikaru and Kaoru decide to wait for them at the exit, and Kyoya agrees. When they get there, they see...well, read and find out! How's that for a storyline?

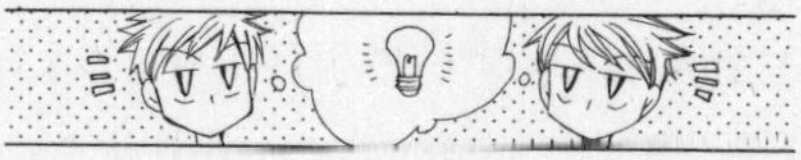

(S, Miyazaki)

1. It suddenly turns dark and the employees are scaring the customers.
   ※Haruhi ends up hanging onto Tamaki (← the objective).
2. The Host Club customers enter a monthly contest to choose the best couple. Each couple cooperates to get through a set of obstacles. There will probably be a fight for Haruhi.
   Go, go, Hatori Bisco!

(M, Ibaraki)

Deep-sea exploration in a submarine! It'd be interesting to have the characters explore an artificial deep-sea trench with a marine environment and dangers. It might be fun to have deep-sea creatures and sand to make it more real.

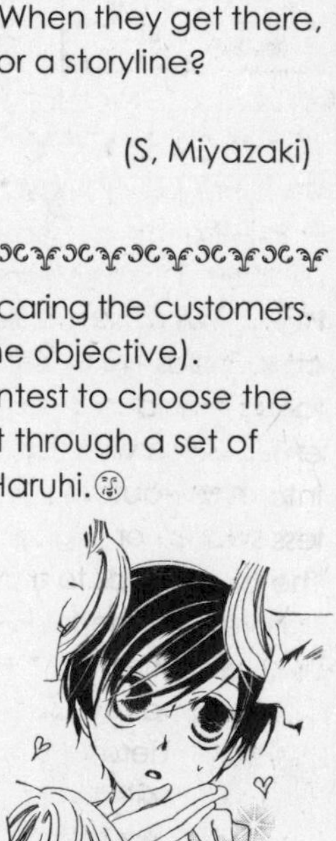

(Y, Tochigi)

The Commoners' Entertainment Center:

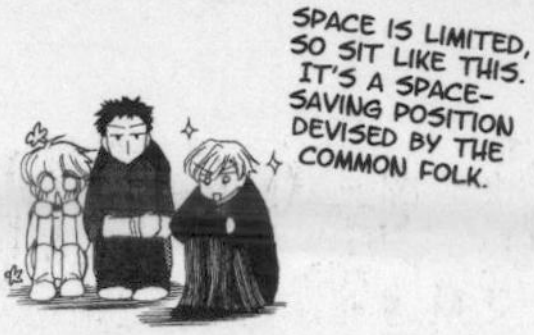
SPACE IS LIMITED, SO SIT LIKE THIS. IT'S A SPACE-SAVING POSITION DEVISED BY THE COMMON FOLK.

It would have a sand bath, ping-pong table, bottles of milk, easy chairs, and other ordinary rec-room stuff, just like Haruhi might have in her home...all thought up by the guys. "Get in Touch with Nature" Corner: In a jungle that one cannot get out of once inside, they will meet mysterious creatures born from gene-splicing experiments.

(N, Chiba)

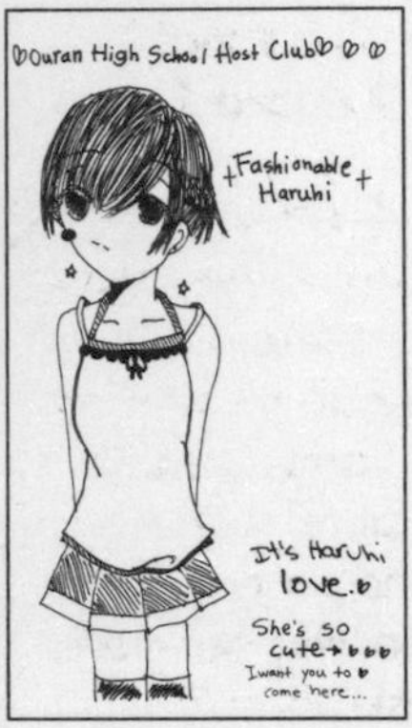
Ouran High School Host Club
+Fashionable Haruhi+
It's Haruhi love.
She's so cute
I want you to come here...
▲ (Yuzuringo, Niigata)

A Huge Aquarium & Desert Island:
It's okay to feed the fish you like! Glass walls will make you feel like you're swimming with the fish. Ohtori Aqua Garden is the size of three Tokyo Domes. The island should be huge too. They find treasures on the island!

→The treasures are...

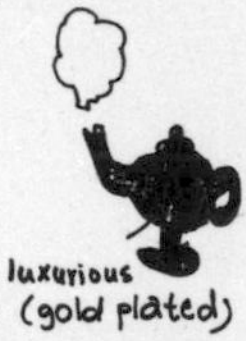
luxurious
(gold plated)

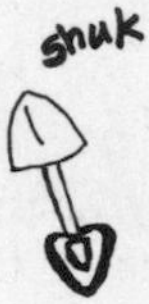
shuk

A magic lamp...

Kyoya's secret...and other things...

(T, Mie)

The Hero Experience Zone:
The entrance is a cave at the edge of the tropical zone in Ohtori Aqua Garden. This mysterious skull-shaped cavern is called the "Ohtori Black Hole." Will a hero arise who is able to get out alive?! Once entered, the cave leads uphill, with various traps along the way! There are the usual rolling boulders and flying arrows, testing the athleticism of those who enter. Those who fail are taken back to the entrance. Next, the road splits into three routes to test one's luck. Without luck, one reaches a bottomless swamp or a giant ant trap, where a near-death experience awaits. The other leads to a puzzle. The hero must use his brain to open the door before him. The fools who fail will be dropped into a hippo pond. At the end, a battle with "Houryu" tests one's courage. Those who lose will be stripped naked and returned to the park via a water slide. The true hero who wins will be rewarded!! The reward is a photo session with Kyoya! Will men undertake this dangerous journey for a prize like this? Or will only women step forward? Nobody knows..."

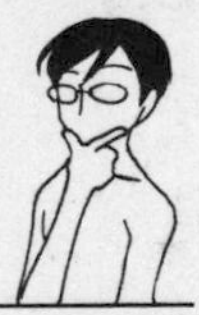

(S, Nagasaki)

HOURYU IS A DRAGONLIKE CREATURE. KYOYA'S LAST NAME SHARES THE SAME KANJI AS *HOU*. -ED.

THANK YOU FOR YOUR MANY ENTRIES. ♡

Author Bio

Bisco Hatori made her manga debut with **Isshun kan no Romance (A Moment of Romance)** in **LaLa DX** magazine. The comedy **Ouran High School Host Club** is her breakout hit. When she's stuck thinking up characters' names, she gets inspired by loud, upbeat music (her radio is set to NACK5 FM). She enjoys reading all kinds of manga, but she's especially fond of the sci-fi drama **Please Save My Earth** and **Slam Dunk**, a basketball classic.

OURAN HIGH SCHOOL HOST CLUB
Vol. 3

Shojo Beat Edition

STORY AND ART BY BISCO HATORI

English Adaptation/Shaenon K. Garrity
Translation/Kenichiro Yagi
Touch-up Art & Lettering/George Caltsoudas
Graphic Design/Izumi Evers
Editor/Nancy Thistlethwaite

Printed in Canada

Published by VIZ Media, LLC
P.O. Box 77010
San Francisco, CA 94107

15
First printing, October 2005
Fifteenth printing, August 2016

www.viz.com   www.shojobeat.com

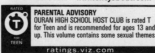

SURPRISE!

You may be reading the wrong way!

It's true: In keeping with the original Japanese comic format, this book reads from right to left—so action, sound effects, and word balloons are completely reversed. This preserves the orientation of the original artwork—plus, it's fun! Check out the diagram shown here to get the hang of things, and then turn to the other side of the book to get started!

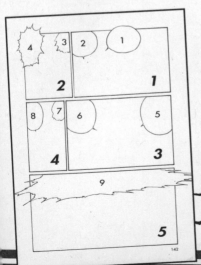